# BLESS YOU BOYS

*For my father*

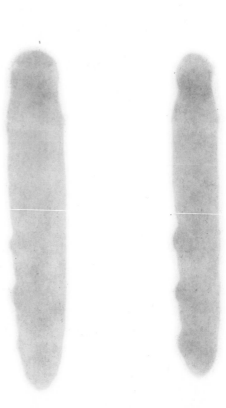

# BLESS YOU BOYS

## DIARY OF THE DETROIT TIGERS' 1984 SEASON

### BY SPARKY ANDERSON

WITH DAN EWALD

CONTEMPORARY
BOOKS, INC.
CHICAGO

Photos by Doc Holcomb are used courtesy of
*The Detroit News.*

The phrase "Bless You Boys" copyright © 1984
by Post-Newsweek Stations, Inc.

Published by Contemporary Books, Inc.
180 North Michigan Avenue, Chicago, Illinois 60601
Manufactured in the United States of America
International Standard Book Number: 0-8092-5307-0

Published simultaneously in Canada by Beaverbooks, Ltd.
195 Allstate Parkway, Valleywood Business Park
Markham, Ontario L3R 4T8 Canada

# CONTENTS

# FOREWORD

The New York Stock Exchange seemed even more hectic than usual. A slightly-built white-haired man of 50 was on the floor, surrounded by brokers with pencil and paper. The world economy wasn't exactly in upheaval, but Sparky Anderson was attracting more attention—at least at that moment—than IBM. Everybody wanted his autograph.

"Go get 'em, Sparky."

"How are you and Yogi?"

"Watch those Yankees, Sparky."

The cries were directed at the Tiger manager as he toured the Stock Exchange with Tiger President Jim Campbell, George Kell, Al Kaline, and me.

The brokers paid no attention to us—not even the Hall of Fame Tiger greats, Kaline and Kell. Sparky was their man.

Last May Sparky, Pitching Coach Roger Craig, and I were on our morning walk when we passed a group of telephone workers on strike.

"Nice going, Sparky," one of them yelled. Several stepped out of the picket line to get his autograph.

Later in Cleveland a stenographer interrupted our walk past an office building to tell Sparky how much she loved him and the Tigers.

Indeed, George (Sparky) Anderson is an American landmark. Almost as recognizable as the Statue of Liberty.

He is truly America's moveable feast.

Why this love affair between America and Anderson?

I think I know some of the reasons.

Sparky loves people and he loves his work. He is always available. He is personable and polite. He relates to the everyday person, and yet he is at home with captains of industry and government.

He has a great insight into people. I think that is his strength as a manager. He knows when to stroke a player and when to come down hard on him. The record books attest to his managerial ability. I'm more impressed by Sparky as a human being.

In 37 years of big league baseball announcing, I've known many managers. Sparky is the best both as a manager and as a human being.

In this book he reflects both sides. As you travel through the Tigers' 1984 season, I'm sure you will join me in my convictions about George (Sparky) Anderson.

*Ernie Harwell*
*Tiger Legend*

# BLESS YOU BOYS:
## A MAGIC SEASON

It was more than a regular baseball season for the Tigers and their fans of 1984. It was more like a six-month celebration. A carnival packed with magic, that went on . . . and on . . . and on.

No other season has matched it. No other season ever came close.

How do you explain the 1984 Year of the Tiger? Psychologists, sociologists, economists, and even the crafty baseball writer will spend their winter analyzing and re-analyzing the phenomenon that struck Detroit: record attendance both home and on the road; the Wave, the celebrations, the dancing in the streets; more major league records set in one season than were even approached in the combined several previous campaigns.

Part of the excitement had to be the long drought. The Tigers had not won the Eastern Division title since an aging band of 1968 heroes enjoyed their last hurrah in 1972. Part of the excitement undoubtedly was the result of an economically depressed city which starved for something around which to rally. And perhaps the biggest part was the fans themselves. No team in any professional sport enjoys the loyalty and love demonstrated by that phenomenon known as the ultimate Tiger fan.

That unique product of passion and tradition not only lives in the city of Detroit, but all across the United States. Wherever the Tigers play, it's not unusual for them to receive as much support from the hosting fans as the home team does.

No doubt this helped the Tigers to lead the major leagues in road attendance, as well as setting a club record for attendance on the road.

Of all the records the Tigers set in 1984, the most impressive had to be their stay in first place. From Opening Day through the end of the season, the Tigers entrenched themselves in first place and simply refused to budge.

Not since 1927 when the awesome New York Yankees led by the immortal Babe Ruth and the classic Lou Gehrig, had a team led the race wire-to-wire. That's 57 years ago and baseball has undergone a drastic facelift since.

1

Back then there were no night games—a bonanza for baseball business, but the bane of ideal playing conditions. Road trips never wandered west of the Mississippi. Coast-to-coast travel has taxed players perhaps more than any single factor in baseball. And relief pitching was not the specialty it now has become.

Besides the 1984 Tigers, only six other teams have led the league wire-to-wire. Besides the 1927 Yankees, the 1913 Philadelphia Athletics turned the trick in the American League. In the National League, the 1902 Pittsburgh Pirates, the 1905 New York Giants, and the 1923 New York Giants also reached this lofty level. Interestingly, the first club to lead wire-to-wire was the 1887 Detroit team playing in the National League under a 124-game schedule.

But since the expansion and stretching of the season to 162 games, the Tigers have become the first team to reach this mark of distinction.

Enroute to the division title, the Tigers also added a whole new page to the record book. The 1984 Tigers hold the American League mark for most days in first place alone—177. They were tied for first place with the Cleveland Indians for five days.

The Tigers charged from the gate like a herd of Secretariats, indiscriminately running over any and all foes in sight. The baseball world got the hint before the season was two weeks old. The Tigers didn't whisper that winning was on their mind. They shouted it to everyone and then dared all to try to make them stop.

They had five straight wins on the road before the Tigers returned home from spring training. In all, the Tigers were involved in four season openers. And except for the Tigers' own home opening victory over Texas, all of the opening day hometown fans went home crying after their team tangled with the surging Tigers. Minnesota, Chicago, and Boston endured their home season opener losses to the mean cats from Detroit.

The Tigers set a team record of nine straight wins to start the season. An 18-2 mark for April had many experts around the country wondering whether the rest of the season in the American League East would become a mere formality. The 18-2 April tied the best major league start for the first 20 games.

But there was more to come. Lots more.

The Tigers established the best mark for 30 games (26-4), the best for 40 (35-5), and came within one game of winning 70 of their first 100 games.

During their initial siege of the American League, the Tigers were equally deadly at home and on the road. They set the American League

**Tiger Manager Sparky Anderson.** Photo courtesy of Detroit Tigers

record and tied the major league mark of 17 straight road victories established by the 1917 New York Giants.

Obviously, the city of Detroit was turned on. So was the nation. Sparky Anderson, the Tiger players, and new owner Tom Monaghan were besieged with requests for national television and radio appearances.

The fans became part of the action as they played and reveled in their heroes' triumphs. The Wave, which began spontaneously one wildly delirious Friday evening at Tiger Stadium, quickly became the rage in all major league parks. Beachballs in the bleachers and those magnificently mad bleacher bums celebrated throughout the year as if it was a season-long Woodstock.

The fans were good to the Tigers. And the Tigers were good to them. From May 17 through the end of the season, the Tigers cracked the 25,000 attendance mark for each home date. Tiger trinketry, from caps, shirts, jackets, socks, and underwear,to balloons and pennants, were sold on every street corner and worn proudly. The Tigers truly became America's Team. Tom Selleck wasn't the only one seen sporting a Tiger cap.

Individual heroics crammed the calendar as national reputations were finally built. Jack Morris struggled in mid-season and refused all media interviews, but not before he stunned a national TV audience on April 7 at Chicago by firing Detroit's first no-hitter since Jim Bunning turned the trick on July 20, 1958 at Boston.

Kirk Gibson became the first Tiger ever to hit more than 20 home runs and steal 20 bases in one season. Gibson made the switch to rightfield and responded to the challenge by posting his finest season ever. In the process, Kirk also became a man.

Lance Parrish already had established himself as baseball's best catcher, and it looks as though he will add to that reputation with his second 30-home-run season.

Alan Trammell and Lou Whitaker, always accorded the best short-stop-second base combination in baseball by Detroit fans, finally proved it to the nation.

And in centerfield, Chet Lemon not only enjoyed his finest offensive season but also established himself as the best with the glove.

The Tiger bullpen was sensational. In fact, it almost defies words. Willie Hernandez relieved from the left side and Aurelio Lopez from the right. If strength up the middle was the heart of this Tiger team, then the bullpen was the soul. Rarely did the bullpen fail. Never did it deliver anything but a gutty performance.

Topping it all, the Tigers are right on course to win 100 victories under Manager Sparky Anderson. By reaching this lofty level, Sparky will become the first manager in baseball history to pilot a 100-game winning season for two different teams.

It's difficult to explain the 1984 magical Tigers or to uncover the real reasons for their success and excitement. Most fans prefer merely to savor all these unforgettable moments and to reflect upon a real piece of honest-to-goodness magic that will never die.

**A very full Tiger Stadium.**    Photo courtesy of Detroit Tigers

# APRIL

"This is it: Opening Day. . . . If your stomach doesn't do jumping jacks on Opening Day, then you don't belong in the big leagues."

**April 3, 1984**

# TUESDAY, APRIL 3

## AT MINNESOTA

# GAME 1

## TIGERS 8, TWINS 1

### (1-0 TIED 1ST)

| DETROIT | ab | r | h | bi | MINNESOTA | ab | r | h | bi |
|---|---|---|---|---|---|---|---|---|---|
| Whitaker 2b | 4 | 3 | 2 | 0 | Eisenrech cf | 4 | 0 | 0 | 0 |
| Trammell ss | 4 | 2 | 2 | 1 | Teufel 2b | 4 | 0 | 1 | 0 |
| Evans dh | 3 | 2 | 1 | 3 | Hrbek 1b | 4 | 0 | 0 | 0 |
| Parrish c | 4 | 0 | 1 | 2 | Brunnsky rf | 4 | 0 | 0 | 0 |
| Lowry c | 0 | 0 | 0 | 0 | Bush dh | 3 | 0 | 0 | 0 |
| Gibson rf | 4 | 0 | 0 | 0 | Meier dh | 1 | 0 | 0 | 0 |
| Kuntz rf | 0 | 0 | 0 | 0 | Gaetti 3b | 3 | 0 | 1 | 0 |
| Herndon lf | 4 | 0 | 1 | 1 | Hatcher lf | 3 | 1 | 2 | 0 |
| Bergman 1b | 3 | 0 | 0 | 0 | Laudner c | 3 | 0 | 0 | 0 |
| Garbey 1b | 1 | 0 | 0 | 0 | Faedo ss | 3 | 0 | 1 | 1 |
| Lemon cf | 4 | 1 | 1 | 0 | | | | | |
| Johnson 3b | 3 | 0 | 2 | 1 | | | | | |
| Brookens 3b | 1 | 0 | 0 | 0 | | | | | |
| **Totals** | **35** | **8** | **10** | **8** | **Totals** | **32** | **1** | **5** | **1** |

Detroit       002 003 300— 8
Minnesota     001 000 000— 1

Game-winning RBI—Johnson (1). LOB—Detroit 3, Minnesota 4. 2B—Johnson, Hatcher, Gaetti, Trammell. 3B—Lemon. HR—Evans (1).

| | IP | H | R | ER | BB | SO |
|---|---|---|---|---|---|---|
| **Detroit** | | | | | | |
| Morris (W 1-0) | 7 | 5 | 1 | 1 | 0 | 8 |
| Lopez | 1 | 0 | 0 | 0 | 0 | 0 |
| Hernandez | 1 | 0 | 0 | 0 | 0 | 0 |
| **Minnesota** | | | | | | |
| Williams (L 0-1) | 6 1-3 | 8 | 6 | 6 | 2 | 2 |
| Comstock | 1 2-3 | 1 | 2 | 2 | 1 | 2 |
| Filson | 1 | 1 | 0 | 0 | 0 | 1 |

T—2:10. A—34,381.

This is it: Opening Day. I don't care how many years you've been in the game, I don't care how good you think your team is—Opening Day is nerve city. If your stomach doesn't do jumping jacks on Opening Day, then you don't belong in the big leagues.

For the last two years, we've been lucky to open in Minnesota. I don't like the Dome; baseball should be played outside. And the field is like playing on a pool table. But at least you know the opener will be played on schedule. That's a big relief.

I got up at seven and lay in bed for awhile. I thought about tonight's game. I thought about my family. I thought about how lucky all of us in baseball really are. We're going to play 162 games to see just who really is the best. And they're going to pay us to do it. I hope every player in the game realizes how fortunate we are. This is legalized stealing.

I had a light breakfast in the coffee shop before joining pitching coach Roger Craig and radio broadcaster Ernie Harwell for an hour-and-fifteen-minute walk. It was sunny and cool. We walked the whole downtown. Everyone knew it was Opening Day. We covered about five miles . . . and I must have talked ten.

I was jabbering, but my mind was rolling all the time. I'm really high on this club. Really high. But we still have a few moves to make. If we could replace three men with three better, we would be closer to perfection. Within four to six weeks we could make those changes. If we just get off decently and stay close to the top for the first two months, this club will make a strong run.

You just don't know how much I care about making the Tigers the finest club in baseball. Jim Campbell, Bill Lajoie, and everyone in the organization has worked so hard that right there, I promised myself to make it all happen in 1984. Not in 1985 or in '86. Right now! If we can do that, I'll be the happiest person in the world.

I've burned inside ever since I was fired at Cincinnati. I hold no grudges—that's part of the game. But I still feel that firing me was the biggest mistake the Reds ever made. I won't stop driving until I prove I'm right.

The greatest accomplishment I could ever achieve would be to win more games in Detroit than I did in Cincinnati. I would love to manage longer in Detroit than I did in Cincinnati. And I would like to see Detroit on top again like it was before, when people had so much pride in the city.

Detroit is a great city. It's a hard one. But the people are real. The city has had so many things go wrong the last few years. The auto industry flopped. Shops folded. But the people fought on. Their hearts are bigger than any of the cars they make. They haven't given up.

I don't have the power to save the city. But I want so badly to help bring good times back. Come October third, this will be a great year for the Detroit Tigers.

\* \* \* \*

We went to the park early. Everyone does on Opening Day. You fool around with the players and writers. You act like it's just another game. But you can't fool your stomach.

The game is televised back in Detroit so it's time to put up or shut up. Everyone will be watching. And you cannot fool Detroit baseball fans.

Fortunately, Jack Morris pitched. No one beats Jack Morris when he wants to pitch. Jack went seven innings and struck out eight. He allowed only one run. Jack had exceptionally good stuff. I think he's going to have his best year. He could have finished, but I wanted to work in a lot of people. Aurelio Lopez and Willie Hernandez each worked one perfect inning. This is going to be a great bullpen.

We couldn't have planned the game any better than if we had written the script. I knew we had a great spring, but this team came to play. We were very alert. We didn't make an error. Just about everyone chipped in: Lou Whitaker and Alan Trammell each got two hits; Chet Lemon started the season with a triple; we were able to get Barbaro Garbey and Dwight Lowry into their first big league game.

Two big things were Howard Johnson and Darrell Evans. Johnson got two hits. I hope this relaxes him. I was hoping he could get rid of that tension. Evans hit a three-run homer. That's why he got the big bucks—to hit homers and drive in runs. A homer in his first game will help.

What a night! I ate pizza after the game. It was Domino's, of course.

**Opening Day—and nerves—for Sparky.**  Photo by Doc Holcomb, courtesy of *The Detroit News*

# WEDNESDAY, APRIL 4

## AT MINNESOTA

## (1-0 TIED 1ST)

A day off after an Opening Day victory. Don't you think life is great? We were busy, though. We played a simulated game so none of the players get rusty.

I've been walking 1½ hours each morning now. It's great physically and really helps me to relax. Ernie Harwell and I walked six miles today. Minneapolis is a great town: Clean; not too big, but big enough; crisp, sunny weather.

Ernie and I were blessed this morning with a reminder I wish all young people would remember. We saw three drunk men passed out alongside of a building before nine o'clock. It was sad—I thanked God for giving me the grace to do something with my life.

I thought of two words—*grace* and *mercy*. Grace is getting something you don't deserve. Mercy is not getting something that you do deserve. I thought about all the good things that have happened to me. If it weren't for the grace of God, that could have been me lying there.

I am so thankful I'm able to look at some of those things and see them with my own eyes and feel them with my own heart. If we ever lose sight of that, we lose everything. How lucky I am to be in baseball and be able to enjoy the good life.

Our workout lasted from 1:30 to 4:00. Doug Bair and Juan Berenguer pitched. Kirk Gibson hit a towering home run and Barbaro Garbey blasted four straight bullets. Garbey is going to be a good hitter—better than Glenn Wilson. I still can't believe we got Willie Hernandez and Dave Bergman for Wilson and John Wockenfuss. I worked with Howard Johnson today, trying to get him to spread his feet more at home plate so he can get more power into his hitting.

Our double play combination, Alan Trammell and Lou Whitaker, came up with a pair of gems today. Both players had ideas that were so simple and yet so true. Trammell said, "to be a winner, you really have to want it and hurt for it until it comes." Whitaker said, "you have to play the game and not let it play you." You know, when you think about it those ideas both can be applied to life: Play the game of life. Enjoy it, have some fun, and don't let it play you.

I think our team is shaping up just fine.

# THURSDAY, APRIL 5

## AT MINNESOTA

# GAME 2

## TIGERS 7, TWINS 3

### (2–0, TIED 1ST)

| DETROIT | ab | r | h | bi | MINNESOTA | ab | r | h | bi |
|---|---|---|---|---|---|---|---|---|---|
| Whitakr 2b | 4 | 1 | 0 | 0 | Eisnrch cf | 3 | 0 | 1 | 0 |
| Tramml ss | 5 | 2 | 4 | 1 | Teufel 2b | 4 | 0 | 0 | 0 |
| Evans 1b | 4 | 0 | 1 | 1 | Hrbek 1b | 4 | 0 | 0 | 0 |
| Bergmn 1b | 1 | 0 | 0 | 0 | Brnnsky rf | 4 | 1 | 1 | 0 |
| Parrish c | 2 | 1 | 0 | 0 | Bush dh | 2 | 2 | 1 | 0 |
| Herndon lf | 3 | 0 | 0 | 0 | Engle dh | 1 | 0 | 0 | 0 |
| Allen dh | 3 | 2 | 1 | 0 | Hatcher lf | 4 | 0 | 0 | 0 |
| Grubb dh | 1 | 0 | 0 | 0 | Gaetti 3b | 3 | 0 | 2 | 1 |
| Lemon cf | 4 | 0 | 2 | 1 | Reed c | 3 | 0 | 0 | 1 |
| Gibson rf | 4 | 1 | 1 | 3 | RWshtn ph | 1 | 0 | 0 | 0 |
| Brokns 3b | 3 | 0 | 0 | 0 | Faedo ss | 2 | 0 | 0 | 0 |
| Totals | 34 | 7 | 9 | 6 | Totals | 31 | 3 | 5 | 2 |

```
Detroit          001 301 200—7
Minnesota        020 001 000—3
```

Game winning RBI — Gibson (1). E—Whitaker, DP—Detroit 1. LOB—Detroit 5, Minnesota 5. 2B—Bush, Gaetti, Lemon. 3B—Trammell. HR—Trammell (1), Gibson (1). SB—Bergman (1) Trammell (1).

| | IP | H | R | ER | BB | SO |
|---|---|---|---|---|---|---|
| **Detroit** | | | | | | |
| Petry W,1-0 | 7 | 5 | 3 | 2 | 4 | 1 |
| Hernandz | 2 | 0 | 0 | 0 | 0 | 2 |
| **Minnesota** | | | | | | |
| Viola L,0-1 | 6 | 6 | 5 | 5 | 3 | 7 |
| Comstock | 2-3 | 2 | 2 | 2 | 1 | 0 |
| Pashnick | 2 1-3 | 1 | 0 | 0 | 1 | 0 |

BK—Pashnick. T—2:33. A—8,373.

Another beautiful morning for a walk, and what a beautiful ball game.

Danny Petry was outstanding today. Alan Trammell had four hits and Chet Lemon made three great catches—one was an unbelievable stab in left center. He must be the best centerfielder in either league.

Kirk Gibson really showed me something. He battled lefty pitcher Frank Viola for a game-winning, three-run homer to dead center in the fourth inning. I don't know if he'll ever become the great player he has the potential to be, but I will say that in my 31 years in baseball, I've never seen a player change his personality—totally change his direction and dedication—like Gibby has.

# FRIDAY, APRIL 6

## AT CHICAGO

# GAME 3

## TIGERS 3, WHITE SOX 2

### (3-0, TIED 1ST)

| DETROIT | | | | | CHICAGO | | | | |
|---|---|---|---|---|---|---|---|---|---|
| | ab | r | h | bi | | ab | r | h | bi |
| Whitaker 2b | 4 | 0 | 0 | 0 | RLaw cf | 4 | 0 | 0 | 0 |
| Trammell ss | 3 | 1 | 0 | 0 | Fisk c | 3 | 1 | 1 | 0 |
| Evans dh | 4 | 0 | 1 | 1 | Baines rf | 3 | 1 | 1 | 0 |
| Parrish c | 3 | 1 | 1 | 0 | Luzinski dh | 3 | 0 | 0 | 1 |
| Gibson rf | 2 | 1 | 0 | 0 | Paciorek 1b | 4 | 0 | 2 | 1 |
| Kuntz rf | 0 | 0 | 0 | 0 | Kittle lf | 3 | 0 | 0 | 0 |
| Herndon lf | 3 | 0 | 0 | 0 | VLaw 3b | 2 | 0 | 0 | 0 |
| Bergman 1b | 4 | 0 | 1 | 2 | Hairston ph | 1 | 0 | 1 | 0 |
| Lemon cf | 4 | 0 | 1 | 0 | Hulett 3b | 1 | 0 | 0 | 0 |
| Johnson 3b | 3 | 0 | 1 | 0 | Fletcher ss | 4 | 0 | 0 | 0 |
| Brookens 3b | 0 | 0 | 0 | 0 | Cruz 2b | 2 | 0 | 1 | 0 |
| Totals | 30 | 3 | 5 | 3 | Totals | 30 | 2 | 6 | 2 |

Detroit           300 000 000— 3
Chicago           000 100 010— 2

Game-winning RBI—Evans (1). DP—
Detroit 2, Chicago 2. LOB—Detroit 6,
Chicago 6. 2B—Paciorek 2, Fisk. 3B—
Lemon. SB—Trammell (2), Cruz (2). SF—
Luzinski.

| Detroit | IP | H | R | ER | BB | SO |
|---|---|---|---|---|---|---|
| Wilcox (W 1-0) | 7 | 4 | 1 | 1 | 4 | 2 |
| Hernandez (S 1) | 2 | 2 | 1 | 1 | 0 | 1 |
| Chicago | | | | | | |
| Dotson (L 0-1) | 8 | 5 | 3 | 3 | 6 | 3 |
| Agosto | 1-3 | 0 | 0 | 0 | 0 | 0 |
| Reed | 2-3 | 0 | 0 | 0 | 0 | 0 |

T—2:51. A—42,692.

This is a very special day. April sixth always will be the most important day of my life. It was on this day in 1983 when my son, Albert, drove off a cliff and fell 800 feet to the bottom of a canyon back home in California. He was unconscious for nine hours. Then, miraculously, he woke up and walked home. He had a broken sternum and cuts all over his body, but we were thankful he suffered no brain damage or internal injuries.

There's no way he should be here now—but God saved him. I told Albert that April sixth changed his daddy's life. I went home and looked down that canyon. I remember looking up and saying, "God, I don't know why you spared him, but I tell You this has changed my life."

I want to win as much as anyone. But nothing about this game can ever bother me after that. I get upset over a loss now, but only for the moment. I think I'm a much stronger person for that.

* * * *

Today's game was exciting: Chicago's home opener. The place was packed. The White Sox are good and their fans are great. However, it didn't take long to show them we're pretty decent, too.

Darrell Evans singled home a run and Dave Bergman came through with a two-run single in the first. Milt Wilcox threw 101 pitches in seven innings for the win. Willie Hernandez got the save.

I've only seen a little of Bergman, but he looks like he's got excellent hands. He seems to have a quick mind when he's talking about the game. He can hit well to leftfield and rip the inside pitch to right. This is only a prediction, but I'll say Dave turns out to be one of the biggest plusses on this team.

**Dave Bergman connects for a homer.** Photo by Doc Holcomb, courtesy of *The Detroit News*

# SATURDAY, APRIL 7

## AT CHICAGO

# GAME 4

## TIGERS 4, WHITE SOX 0

### (4-0, ½ GAME AHEAD)

| DETROIT | ab | r | h | bi | | CHICAGO | ab | r | h | bi |
|---|---|---|---|---|---|---|---|---|---|---|
| Whitakr 2b | 4 | 0 | 1 | 1 | | RLaw cf | 3 | 0 | 0 | 0 |
| Trammi ss | 4 | 0 | 1 | 0 | | Dybzisk ss | 0 | 0 | 0 | 0 |
| Garbey 1b | 3 | 0 | 0 | 0 | | Fisk c | 3 | 0 | 0 | 0 |
| Bergmn 1b | 1 | 0 | 0 | 0 | | Baines rf | 3 | 0 | 0 | 0 |
| LNParsh c | 3 | 1 | 0 | 0 | | Luzinsk dh | 2 | 0 | 0 | 0 |
| Herndon lf | 4 | 0 | 0 | 0 | | Stegmn pr | 0 | 0 | 0 | 0 |
| Allen dh | 3 | 0 | 0 | 0 | | Kittle lf | 4 | 0 | 0 | 0 |
| Grubb ph | 1 | 0 | 0 | 0 | | Paciork 1b | 1 | 0 | 0 | 0 |
| Lemon cf | 4 | 2 | 2 | 2 | | VLaw 3b | 1 | 0 | 0 | 0 |
| Gibson rf | 1 | 1 | 1 | 1 | | Walker ph | 1 | 0 | 0 | 0 |
| Brokns 3b | 2 | 0 | 0 | 0 | | Hulett 3b | 0 | 0 | 0 | 0 |
| | | | | | | Fletchr ss | 2 | 0 | 0 | 0 |
| | | | | | | Hairstn cf | 1 | 0 | 0 | 0 |
| | | | | | | JCruz 2b | 3 | 0 | 0 | 0 |
| Totals | 30 | 4 | 5 | 4 | | Totals | 26 | 0 | 0 | 0 |

Detroit      020 020 000— 4
Chicago    000 000 000— 0
   Game Winning RBI — Lemon (1).
DP—Detroit 1, Chicago 1. LOB—Detroit 3, Chicago 5. 2B—Lemon, Gibson. HR—Lemon (1). SB—RLaw (1), Trammell (3). S—Brookens.

| | IP | H | R | ER | BB | SO |
|---|---|---|---|---|---|---|
| **Detroit** | | | | | | |
| Morris W,2-0 | 9 | 0 | 0 | 0 | 6 | 8 |
| **Chicago** | | | | | | |
| Bannister L,0-1 | 6 | 4 | 4 | 4 | 2 | 3 |
| Brennan | 2 | 1 | 0 | 0 | 1 | 3 |
| Barojas | 1 | 0 | 0 | 0 | 0 | 1 |

T—2:44. A—24,616.

Michigan Avenue looked like a picture this morning. The prettiest sight in America. I had a great feeling and I knew something special was going to happen, but I never dreamed it would be a no-hitter.

The day belonged to Jack Morris and he shared it with the nation. The game was NBC's first telecast of the season. Jack really gave Joe Garagiola and Vin Scully something to talk about.

I was a little nervous when Jack walked the bases loaded to start the fourth. But he got out of it by starting a double play on Greg Luzinski before striking out Ron Kittle. After the seventh inning, there was just no way anyone was going to get a hit off of Jack.

He walked Luzinski with two out in the ninth and Dave Stegman pinch ran. Jack and Stegman had roomed together when Dave played for the Tigers. Jack just looked over and smiled at his old roommate and said, "You're not going anywhere." He didn't. Finally, Kittle struck out and the no-hitter was history.

Jack Morris is the best pitcher in baseball. He proved it today. After the game, White Sox manager Tony LaRussa came to our clubhouse to congratulate Jack. That really showed class. I called owner Tom Monaghan at home and put Jack on the line. I don't know which one of them was more excited.

I do know one thing—I'll remember this day the rest of my life.

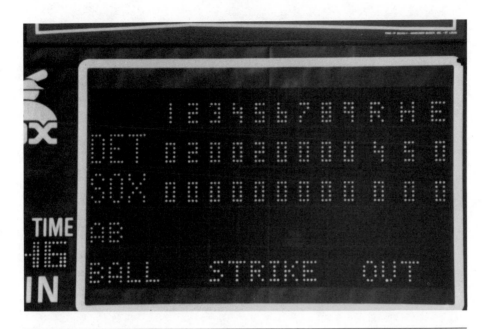

**The scoreboard tells it all.** Photo by Richard Witt

**A classic moment in Tiger history.** Photo by Richard Witt

15

# SUNDAY, APRIL 8

## AT CHICAGO

# GAME 5

## TIGERS 7, WHITE SOX 3

### (5-0, 1½ GAMES AHEAD)

| DETROIT | ab | r | h | bi | CHICAGO | ab | r | h | bi |
|---|---|---|---|---|---|---|---|---|---|
| Whitakr 2b | 5 | 0 | 2 | 1 | RLaw cf | 4 | 1 | 2 | 0 |
| Trammi ss | 4 | 0 | 1 | 0 | Fisk c | 2 | 0 | 0 | 0 |
| DEvns dh | 3 | 1 | 1 | 0 | MHill c | 0 | 0 | 0 | 0 |
| LNParsh c | 5 | 0 | 0 | 0 | Baines rf | 4 | 1 | 2 | 2 |
| Lowry c | 0 | 0 | 0 | 0 | Luzinsk dh | 4 | 0 | 0 | 0 |
| Gibson rf | 4 | 2 | 2 | 1 | Walker 1b | 3 | 0 | 0 | 0 |
| Kuntz rf | 1 | 0 | 0 | 0 | Hulett ph | 1 | 0 | 0 | 0 |
| Grubb lf | 1 | 1 | 0 | 0 | Kittle lf | 4 | 1 | 1 | 1 |
| Herndon lf | 1 | 1 | 0 | 0 | VLaw 3b | 2 | 0 | 0 | 0 |
| Bergmn 1b | 2 | 1 | 1 | 0 | Squires 3b | 1 | 0 | 0 | 0 |
| Garbey 1b | 3 | 1 | 2 | 3 | Paciork ph | 1 | 0 | 1 | 0 |
| Lemon cf | 3 | 0 | 1 | 1 | Fletchr ss | 3 | 0 | 1 | 0 |
| HJhnsn 3b | 3 | 0 | 1 | 1 | JCruz 2b | 3 | 0 | 0 | 0 |
| Brokns 3b | 1 | 0 | 0 | 0 | | | | | |
| Totals | 36 | 7 | 11 | 7 | Totals | 32 | 3 | 7 | 3 |

Detroit  020 120 200— 7
Chicago  011 000 010— 3

Game Winning RBI—Whitaker (1).
DP—Detroit 1, Chicago 1. LOB—Detroit 11, Chicago 5. 2B—Bergman, DaEvans, Garbey 2. HR—Gibson (2), Kittle (1), Baines (1). SB—Grubb (1), Trammell (4), Whitaker (1), Herndon (1). S—Lemon.

| | IP | H | R | ER | BB | SO |
|---|---|---|---|---|---|---|
| Detroit | | | | | | |
| Rozema | 4 | 5 | 2 | 2 | 1 | 1 |
| Lopez W, 1-0 | 4 | 1 | 1 | 1 | 1 | 4 |
| Hernandz | 1 | 1 | 0 | 0 | 0 | 1 |
| Chicago | | | | | | |
| Seaver L, 0-1 | 4 1-3 | 7 | 5 | 5 | 3 | 3 |
| Agosto | 1 | 1 | 0 | 0 | 4 | 0 |
| Barojas | 1 | 2 | 2 | 2 | 1 | 1 |
| Burns | 1 2-3 | 1 | 0 | 0 | 0 | 2 |
| RReed | 1 | 0 | 0 | 0 | 0 | 1 |

Rozema pitched to one batter in the fifth.
HBP—Fletcher by Rozema. T—3:17. A—20,478.

It was overcast as I walked down Michigan Avenue, but how could I feel anything but great? Before the game I had a long talk with Dave Rozema. I told him I didn't care how he pitched this year. But I was concerned with him becoming a better person. He's a super kid who just needs help and direction once in awhile. I told him he would walk with me each morning on our next road trip, so we will have a chance to talk.

Rozey pitched four good innings before his arm stiffened a little. Aurelio Lopez gave us four more good ones for the win, Willie Hernandez finished the game. Barbaro Garbey had two big hits and Kirk Gibson hit one nine miles into the upper deck. Our record stands 5-0—a pretty good road trip.

# MONDAY, APRIL 9

## AT DETROIT

## (5–0, 1½ GAMES AHEAD)

One day off before our home opener. I had a complete physical and the doctors said the walking was doing me good. Roger Craig and I walked in the afternoon. I marveled at how he thinks positively all the time. He keeps telling me how we have to walk that last mile with our players and make them feel good about themselves. When they feel good about themselves, they become better players.

I think our club should win between 100 and 110 games this year. We've got the talent and the team's attitude is great. Everything is going super. I guess God looks after those who can't help themselves. I'm living proof.

**Barbaro Garbey.**   Photo courtesy of Detroit Tigers     **Dave Rozema.**   Photo courtesy of Detroit Tigers

# TUESDAY, APRIL 10

## AT DETROIT

# GAME 6

## TIGERS 5, RANGERS 1

### (6-0, 2½ GAMES AHEAD)

| TEXAS | ab | r | h | bi | DETROIT | ab | r | h | bi |
|---|---|---|---|---|---|---|---|---|---|
| Sample lf | 4 | 0 | 0 | 0 | Whitakr 2b | 3 | 1 | 0 | 0 |
| BBell 3b | 4 | 1 | 1 | 0 | Tramml ss | 3 | 1 | 1 | 0 |
| GWrght cf | 4 | 0 | 0 | 0 | DEvns dh | 4 | 1 | 1 | 3 |
| LAPrsh dh | 4 | 0 | 1 | 1 | LNParsh c | 4 | 0 | 0 | 0 |
| Ward rf | 3 | 0 | 2 | 0 | Gibson rf | 4 | 1 | 1 | 0 |
| OBrien 1b | 3 | 0 | 0 | 0 | Herndon lf | 2 | 1 | 1 | 0 |
| Yost c | 3 | 0 | 0 | 0 | Bergmn 1b | 4 | 0 | 1 | 1 |
| Foley c | 1 | 0 | 0 | 0 | Lemon cf | 2 | 0 | 0 | 0 |
| Tollesn 2b | 2 | 0 | 0 | 0 | HJhnsn 3b | 1 | 0 | 0 | 1 |
| Wilkrsn ss | 2 | 0 | 0 | 0 | Brokns 3b | 0 | 0 | 0 | 0 |
| OJones ph | 1 | 0 | 0 | 0 | | | | | |
| Andersn ss | 0 | 0 | 0 | 0 | | | | | |
| Totals | 31 | 1 | 4 | 1 | Totals | 27 | 5 | 5 | 5 |

```
Texas................................100 000 000— 1
Detroit..............................401 000 00x— 5
```
Game Winning RBI — DaEvans (2).
LOB—Texas 6, Detroit 6. 2B—Herndon.
HR—DaEvans (2). SB—Herndon (2).

| Texas | IP | H | R | ER | BB | SO |
|---|---|---|---|---|---|---|
| DStewart L,0-2 | 2-3 | 2 | 4 | 4 | 5 | 0 |
| Schmidt | 4 1-3 | 2 | 1 | 1 | 0 | 3 |
| Henke | 2 | 1 | 0 | 0 | 1 | 1 |
| Bibby | 1 | 0 | 0 | 0 | 1 | 1 |
| Detroit | | | | | | |
| Petry W,2-0 | 9 | 4 | 1 | 1 | 3 | 7 |

HBP—Lemon by Henke. WP—Henke. T—
2:32. A—51,238.

Who would have dreamed we would take a 5-0 record into the home opener? I certainly didn't. The whole town is turned on. I've got to kick myself to stay on the ground.

It was sunny and about 50 degrees today; the best opening day weather I've had in my career. The park was totally sold out. I couldn't wait to get there this morning.

I visited with Bill Lajoie before going to the clubhouse. We talked about our road trip and some of the things going on with the team. What was happening down on the field was unbelievable. Except for the World Series, I'd never seen so many writers and TV cameras at a ballgame. A 5-0 start gets people crazy. Even I got caught up in the scene.

The game really took care of itself. Dan Petry pitched a four-hitter and Evans socked a three-run homer on his very first swing at Tiger Stadium. Kirk Gibson made a great running catch in the ninth.

The crowd went wild. No Tiger team since 1911 had started the season with six straight wins. After the game, I told the writers it meant just six games we couldn't lose. But everyone knew it meant more than that. Just ask the people who were dancing in the streets.

After the game, I went to a television party. I would rather have gone home for soup and grilled cheese sandwiches with my coaches, but I guess this is part of the game. And these fans deserve everything I can give them.

# WEDNESDAY, APRIL 11

## AT DETROIT

## (6–0, 2½ GAMES AHEAD)

Another day off. It seems like that's all we have. On my way home from my walk, a man stopped his truck and started walking with me. He told me how much our fast start meant to the city and that made me feel good.

When you're winning, you're on top of the world. I guess you know where you are when you're losing. That's the way life is. I really believe baseball affects the mood of a city. I saw it happen in Cincinnati and I really feel it here this year. People truly love baseball.

**Tiger slugger Darrell Evans.**  Photo by Clifton Boutelle

# THURSDAY, APRIL 12

## AT DETROIT

# GAME 7

## TIGERS 9, RANGERS 4

### (7-0, 3 GAMES AHEAD)

| TEXAS | ab r h bi | DETROIT | ab r h bi |
|---|---|---|---|
| Rivers lf | 4 1 2 1 | Whitakr 2b | 4 1 1 1 |
| Hostlr ph | 1 0 0 0 | Trammll ss | 3 3 2 1 |
| BBell 3b | 3 0 0 0 | Garbey 1b | 3 2 2 0 |
| GWrght cf | 5 0 3 1 | Bergmn 1b | 0 1 0 0 |
| LAPrsh dh | 5 0 0 0 | LNParsh c | 5 0 2 1 |
| Ward rf | 4 1 1 0 | Lowry c | 0 0 0 0 |
| BJones 1b | 4 1 2 2 | Herndon lf | 4 1 1 1 |
| Foley c | 3 0 0 0 | Lemon cf | 4 1 1 3 |
| Tollesn 2b | 4 1 1 0 | Allen dh | 4 0 2 1 |
| Wilkrsn ss | 4 0 1 0 | DEvns ph | 0 0 0 1 |
| | | Gibson rf | 5 0 1 0 |
| | | Brokns 3b | 4 0 0 0 |
| Totals | 37 4 10 4 | Totals | 36 9 12 9 |

Texas...............................001 000 120— 4
Detroit..............................200 104 11x— 9
Game Winning RBI — Herndon (1).
E—Wilkerson, Mo..is. LOB—Texas 9,
Detroit 11. 2B—Tolleson, Allen. HR— BJones
(1), Trammell (2), Lemon (2), Whitaker (1).
SB—Rivers (1), Trammell (5). SF—Da-
Evans.

| | IP | H | R | ER | BB | SO |
|---|---|---|---|---|---|---|
| Texas | | | | | | |
| Tanana L,0-1 | 6 | 10 | 7 | 4 | 4 | 5 |
| OJones | 1 | 2 | 2 | 2 | 2 | 1 |
| Henke | 1 | 0 | 0 | 0 | 0 | 0 |
| Detroit | | | | | | |
| Morris W,3-0 | 7 | 7 | 2 | 0 | 1 | 2 |
| Lopez | 1 | 2 | 2 | 2 | 1 | 0 |
| Hernandz | 1 | 1 | 0 | 0 | 1 | 0 |

OJones pitched to three batters in 8th.
HBP—Trammell by Tanana. WP—Morris. PB—LNParrish. T—2:48. A—19,154.

Another Jack Morris masterpiece. He went seven innings and allowed only two runs on a couple of bloops to left.

Larry Herndon singled home the game-winner in the first. He's had
two great seasons playing for Detroit and is one of the best deals Jim
Campbell ever made. Larry's quiet. He doesn't say much. In fact, he
probably won't say 100 words to me all year. But he's got a great
attitude: He comes to the park ready to play, never complains, never
talks about problems. He's just a great human being.

Seven straight wins is the best start in Tiger history. The record is
broken—it's good to get that out of the way. The goal now is to sustain
it. If we keep this up, we'll have a good lead in a couple of weeks.

# FRIDAY, APRIL 13

## AT BOSTON

# GAME 8

## TIGERS 13, RED SOX 9

### (8-0, 3 GAMES AHEAD)

| DETROIT | ab | r | h | bi | BOSTON | ab | r | h | bi |
|---|---|---|---|---|---|---|---|---|---|
| Whitakr 2b | 5 | 2 | 2 | 0 | Remy 2b | 5 | 1 | 3 | 1 |
| Tramml ss | 4 | 2 | 2 | 0 | DwEvns rf | 3 | 2 | 1 | 1 |
| Garbey 1b | 1 | 1 | 1 | 0 | Boggs 3b | 3 | 1 | 0 | 0 |
| Bergmn 1b | 4 | 1 | 2 | 1 | Rice lf | 5 | 1 | 2 | 2 |
| LNParsh c | 6 | 2 | 2 | 2 | Easler dh | 5 | 1 | 4 | 1 |
| Herndon lf | 4 | 1 | 2 | 2 | Armas cf | 4 | 1 | 1 | 0 |
| Lemon cf | 5 | 1 | 2 | 2 | Gedman c | 3 | 2 | 1 | 1 |
| Allen dh | 1 | 1 | 1 | 1 | Stapltn 1b | 3 | 0 | 1 | 0 |
| DEvns dh | 4 | 0 | 0 | 1 | Hoffmn ss | 2 | 0 | 0 | . |
| Kuntz rf | 5 | 1 | 1 | 1 | Miller ph | 1 | 0 | 0 | 0 |
| Brokns 3b | 5 | 1 | 2 | 1 | Gutirrz ss | 0 | 0 | 0 | 0 |
| | | | | | Nichols ph | 1 | 0 | 1 | 2 |
| | | | | | Jurak ss | 0 | 0 | 0 | 0 |
| Totals | 44 | 13 | 17 | 11 | Totals | 35 | 9 | 14 | 8 |

Detroit.............................800 100 040--13
Boston..............................510 000 030— 9
Game Winning RBI —Herndon (2).
E—Hoffman 2, Gedman. DP—Detroit 6, Boston 1. LOB—Detroit 9, Boston 6. 2B—Brookens, Trammell, Herndon 2, Whitaker, Nichols, Easler. HR—LNParrish (1), Gedman (1), DwEvans (1).

| | IP | H | R | ER | BB | SO |
|---|---|---|---|---|---|---|
| Detroit | | | | | | |
| Wilcox | 2-3 | 4 | 5 | 5 | 1 | 0 |
| Bair W,1-0 | 4 1-3 | 3 | 1 | 1 | 1 | 5 |
| Abbott | 2 | 2 | 0 | 0 | 1 | 0 |
| Hernandz | 2 | 5 | 3 | 3 | 2 | 2 |
| Boston | | | | | | |
| Hurst L,1-2 | 1-3 | 3 | 7 | 5 | 3 | 1 |
| MGBron | 5 1-3 | 7 | 2 | 2 | 1 | 3 |
| Stanley | 2 1-3 | 5 | 4 | 4 | 0 | 2 |
| Clear | 1 | 2 | 0 | 0 | 1 | 1 |

HBP—DwEvans by Wilcox, Thomas by Abbott. WP—MGBrown. T—3:11. A—35,179.

Our fourth team opener; we should be used to it. But Fenway Park in Boston is different. This is a great baseball town and a great city.

Another beautiful spring day: We walked through Commonwealth Park before the game. There's so much history in Boston, and so much youth. I guess that's what makes this city so alive.

Our bats were alive in the first inning of the game. We sent up 13 men and scored eight runs with help from some Red Sox errors.

We needed the runs, though. Wilcox couldn't get out of the first inning and gave up five runs to them. Then Doug Bair saved us with four strong innings.

Doug is throwing just like when I first got him at Cincinnati back in 1978. His confidence is back and he has a better slider. He will be very important in long relief to help us get to Lopez and Hernandez later in the game.

Parrish hit his first home run. That should get him going. Six of our guys had two hits apiece. The biggest thing was the six double plays we turned to tie a record. We have a great infield, a premier defense. Seems like we're always either tying or setting records lately.

Eight straight games without a loss. We'll just have to take it one step at a time and see what happens.

## SATURDAY, APRIL 14

### AT BOSTON

### (8–0, 3½ GAMES AHEAD)

We had another day off, so we worked out at Fenway. Dave Rozema looked good on the mound. Strange as it sounds, I think David will be a good pitching coach one day. Roger Craig—one of the best—will teach him a lot while he's here with us.

I still think we need three more lefthanded pitchers to be truly outstanding. When that happens, this will be a great team. We also have a great shortstop and second baseman in Doug Baker and Chris Pittaro on the way up from the farm club. They'll be ready when we need them.

## SUNDAY, APRIL 15

### AT BOSTON

### (8–0, 3 GAMES AHEAD)

It rained all day, so we're scheduled to play two games tomorrow. I spent a long time talking to Bill Lajoie on the phone about getting some lefthanded pitching. I enjoy talking to Bill because he has great baseball instincts.

Before the rain, we ran the players hard. If we can't play, they need the work.

The speaker at chapel service this morning was outstanding. He talked about how money meant nothing if it wasn't used properly. God has promised to give us enough for our needs.

I don't feel money is a big part of my life now. Maybe that's because I've made enough or maybe because I'm just lucky. I don't have a burning love for money. I do have a great love for people and for enjoying my days around the park and the players.

# MONDAY, APRIL 16

## AT BOSTON

## (8–0, 3 GAMES AHEAD)

Today's doubleheader was rained out, so we're still undefeated. We returned to Detroit this evening and I had dinner with [president and chief executive officer] Jim Campbell.

Throughout all my days with Cincinnati, everyone told me there was no better general manager in baseball than Jim. He's the one man in baseball everyone wants to work for. That's because he lets you do your job. He's a real man's man.

# TUESDAY, APRIL 17

## AT DETROIT

## (8–0, 2½ GAMES AHEAD)

It *snowed* like crazy today. I wished my kids could have seen it. The game was postponed. Who knows when we'll play again? At this rate, we'll go undefeated for the whole season.

I'm really happy because [Tiger owner] Tom Monaghan let me buy 400 shares of the club. I couldn't believe it. He has no idea how grateful I am. It feels great investing in something I really believe in.

# WEDNESDAY, APRIL 18

## AT DETROIT

# GAME 9

## TIGERS 4, ROYALS, 3
## (10 INNINGS)
## (9-0, 2½ GAMES AHEAD)

| KANSAS CITY | ab | r | h | bi | DETROIT | ab | r | h | bi |
|---|---|---|---|---|---|---|---|---|---|
| Cncpcn ss | 3 | 0 | 0 | 0 | Whitakr 2b | 5 | 0 | 0 | 0 |
| OSnchz ph | 1 | 0 | 0 | 0 | Tramml ss | 4 | 1 | 1 | 0 |
| Biancln ss | 1 | 0 | 0 | 0 | Garbey 1b | 3 | 0 | 1 | 0 |
| Sheridn cf | 5 | 1 | 2 | 0 | Bergmn 1b | 0 | 0 | 0 | 0 |
| Orta rf | 4 | 1 | 1 | 3 | LNParsh c | 5 | 1 | 3 | 1 |
| McRae dh | 4 | 0 | 1 | 0 | Herndon lf | 5 | 1 | 1 | 0 |
| Balboni 1b | 4 | 0 | 2 | 0 | Lemon cf | 4 | 0 | 2 | 1 |
| White 2b | 4 | 0 | 2 | 0 | Allen dh | 2 | 1 | 1 | 0 |
| WDavis lf | 4 | 0 | 0 | 0 | DEvns dh | 1 | 0 | 1 | 0 |
| Slaught c | 4 | 1 | 1 | 0 | Gibson rf | 3 | 0 | 0 | 0 |
| Pryor 3b | 3 | 0 | 0 | 0 | Brokns 3b | 3 | 0 | 2 | 1 |
| | | | | | HJhnsn 3b | 1 | 0 | 0 | 0 |
| Totals | 37 | 3 | 9 | 3 | Totals | 36 | 4 | 12 | 3 |

```
Kansas City .................... 000 000 030  0— 3
Detroit ........................ 010 100 100  1— 4
```
Two outs when winning run scored.
Game Winning RBI — None.
E—White. DP—Kansas City 1, Detroit 2.
LOB—Kansas City 5, Detroit 8. 2B— White,
Lemon 2, Brookens. 3B—Herndon. HR—
LNParrish (2), Orta (1). S—Allen, Bergman.

| | IP | H | R | ER | BB | SO |
|---|---|---|---|---|---|---|
| Kansas City | | | | | | |
| Black | 7 | 9 | 3 | 3 | 2 | 3 |
| Beckwith L,0-1 | 2 2-3 | 3 | 1 | 0 | 1 | 1 |
| Detroit | | | | | | |
| Morris | 9 | 9 | 3 | 3 | 0 | 3 |
| Hernandz W,1-0 | 1 | 0 | 0 | 0 | 0 | 1 |

It was frigid this evening, but we finally got to play. It took us 10 innings to make our record nine straight wins.

Jack Morris went nine before Willie Hernandez got the win. Jack wasn't real sharp, but we should have scored six runs for him. Instead, we left a man on third base with less than two out three times. I wasn't very pleased with this game. We played poorly. But you know things must be going your way when Frank White bobbles a ball in the tenth for the game winner.

Before the game I had a talk with the team. I told my players we are going to run a lot during the season. I think if we can stay in shape and avoid injuries, we'll be a better ball club. And I told the pitchers Roger Craig is more than my righthand man. He's my right hand, my left hand, and both my feet. What he says, goes. Except for during the game, Roger is completely in charge.

The manager takes responsibility for any mistakes during the game and I'll make all the decisions, so there's no need to blame Roger. Every player must know two things: they don't *have* to like the manager and they don't *have* to respect him. The manager has to earn that affection and respect.

# THURSDAY, APRIL 19

## AT DETROIT

# GAME 10

## ROYALS 5, TIGERS 2

### (9–1, 1½ GAMES AHEAD)

| KANSAS CITY | ab | r | h | bi | DETROIT | ab | r | h | bi |
|---|---|---|---|---|---|---|---|---|---|
| Cncpcn ss | 4 | 0 | 0 | 0 | Whitakr 2b | 4 | 1 | 1 | 0 |
| Sherldn cf | 4 | 1 | 1 | 0 | Tramml ss | 4 | 0 | 1 | 0 |
| Orta rf | 4 | 0 | 2 | 1 | DEvns dh | 4 | 0 | 2 | 0 |
| Motley rf | 0 | 0 | 0 | 0 | LNParsh c | 4 | 0 | 0 | 1 |
| McRae dh | 4 | 0 | 1 | 1 | Gibson rf | 3 | 1 | 2 | 1 |
| Balboni 1b | 3 | 1 | 0 | 0 | Herndon lf | 4 | 0 | 0 | 0 |
| White 2b | 4 | 2 | 2 | 2 | Bergmn 1b | 3 | 0 | 0 | 0 |
| Slaught c | 4 | 0 | 1 | 0 | Lemon cf | 3 | 0 | 1 | 0 |
| WDavis lf | 4 | 0 | 0 | 0 | HJhnsn 3b | 3 | 0 | 0 | 0 |
| Pryor 3b | 4 | 1 | 1 | 0 | | | | | |
| Totals | 35 | 5 | 8 | 4 | Totals | 32 | 2 | 7 | 2 |

```
Kansas City ......................... 002 001 020— 5
Detroit ............................... 100 000 001— 2
    Game Winning RBI — McRae (1).
    E—HJohnson 2. DP—Kansas City 1. LOB
—Kansas City 6, Detroit 5. 2B—DaE-vans.
HR—White (1), Gibson (3). SB— Trammell
(6), Lemon (1). S—Concepcion.
```

| | IP | H | R | ER | BB | SO |
|---|---|---|---|---|---|---|
| Kansas City | | | | | | |
| Sabrhgn W,1-0 | 6 | 6 | 1 | 1 | 2 | 4 |
| Quisnbry S,5 | 3 | 1 | 1 | 1 | 0 | 0 |
| Detroit | | | | | | |
| Petry L,2-1 | 8 | 8 | 5 | 4 | 2 | 4 |
| Lopez | 1 | 0 | 0 | 0 | 0 | 0 |

```
    WP—Saberhagen. T—2:27. A—12,100.
```

No one in Detroit wanted to see it end, but everyone knew it was coming. The American League record of 11 straight would have been nice to break, but that's not the most important thing this season.

The writers asked me afterward if I would finally wash my lucky undershirt. I told them I had already washed it five times during the streak.

Again, we left the tying run on third with less than two out, and Howard Johnson made two errors at third. Dan Petry pitched eight good innings, but we gave him no support.

I didn't mind the crowd booing after the game. The fans expect perfection because they pay for it. If you buy something in a store, you expect perfection. It's the same thing here.

The good thing was that nobody hung their head in the clubhouse after the loss. These are professionals—they can handle victory and defeat. That's what major league baseball is all about.

# FRIDAY, APRIL 20

## AT DETROIT

# GAME 11

## TIGERS 3, WHITE SOX 2

### (10-1, 2½ GAMES AHEAD)

| CHICAGO | ab | r | h | bi | DETROIT | ab | r | h | bi |
|---|---|---|---|---|---|---|---|---|---|
| RLaw cf | 4 | 0 | 2 | 0 | Whitakr 2b | 4 | 1 | 1 | 0 |
| Fletchr ss | 3 | 0 | 0 | 0 | Tramml ss | 4 | 0 | 1 | 0 |
| Hairstn ph | 1 | 0 | 0 | 0 | Garbey 1b | 3 | 1 | 2 | 0 |
| Dybzisk ss | 0 | 0 | 0 | 0 | Brgmn ph | 1 | 0 | 0 | 0 |
| Baines rf | 4 | 0 | 1 | 0 | LNParsh c | 5 | 0 | 3 | 1 |
| Luzinsk dh | 3 | 1 | 1 | 0 | Herndon lf | 2 | 1 | 1 | 1 |
| Walker 1b | 4 | 0 | 1 | 0 | Lemon cf | 4 | 0 | 1 | 0 |
| K Ittle lf | 4 | 1 | 1 | 2 | Allen dh | 3 | 0 | 0 | 0 |
| VLaw 3b | 4 | 0 | 1 | 0 | DEvns dh | 1 | 0 | 0 | 0 |
| MHill c | 3 | 0 | 0 | 0 | Gibson rf | 4 | 0 | 2 | 1 |
| JCruz 2b | 4 | 0 | 1 | 0 | Brokns 3b | 3 | 0 | 0 | 0 |
| | | | | | Grubb ph | 1 | 0 | 0 | 0 |
| | | | | | MCastil 3b | 0 | 0 | 0 | 0 |
| Totals | 34 | 2 | 8 | 2 | Totals | 35 | 3 | 11 | 3 |

Herndon awarded first base on catcher's interference.

Chicago.............................020 000 000— 2
Detroit..............................010 000 101— 3
Two outs when winning run scored.
   Game Winning RBI — LNParrish (1).
   E—MHill. DP—Detroit 1. LOB—Chicago 8, Detroit 11. 2B—RLaw. HR—Kittle (2). S—Trammell.

| | IP | H | R | ER | BB | SO |
|---|---|---|---|---|---|---|
| **Chicago** | | | | | | |
| Bannister | 6 1-3 | 8 | 2 | 2 | 1 | 5 |
| RReed L,0-1 | 2 1-3 | 3 | 1 | 1 | 1 | 0 |
| **Detroit** | | | | | | |
| Wilcox | 8 | 8 | 2 | 2 | 3 | 3 |
| Lopez W,2-0 | 1 | 0 | 0 | 0 | 0 | 1 |

   HBP—Garbey by Bannister. T—2:36. A—33 954.

We won a good one tonight. Milt Wilcox didn't get the win, but he pitched a great game for eight innings. He made a super play on a bunt and that really won the game.

Milt is one of the big keys to our ballclub. Milt's biggest problem is that he always misses five or six weeks during a season. He can't do that in 1984 if we are going to win this thing. He can miss a couple, but not five or six. If he stays healthy, he'll be a better than .500 pitcher and win 15 or 16 games. And in this business, just three more wins could be a big difference.

Aurelio Lopez pitched a perfect inning for the win. Lance Parrish singled home the winning run in the last of the ninth. I talked to Howard Johnson before the game to try to lift him up from yesterday. I also gave Gibby a pat on the back for the way he's been playing the outfield.

These fans are great. Almost 34,000 of them came out on a chilly night in April. They started the Wave—all the fans were standing up and sitting down by sections in the stands—and everyone in the dugout was watching the spectacle.

# SATURDAY, APRIL 21

## AT DETROIT

# GAME 12

## TIGERS 4, WHITE SOX 1

### (11–1, 3½ GAMES AHEAD)

| CHICAGO | ab | r | h | bi | | DETROIT | ab | r | h | bi |
|---|---|---|---|---|---|---|---|---|---|---|
| RLaw cf | 4 | 0 | 1 | 0 | | Whitakr 2b | 3 | 3 | 2 | 1 |
| Fisk c | 4 | 0 | 0 | 0 | | Trammll ss | 4 | 0 | 2 | 1 |
| Baines rf | 4 | 0 | 0 | 0 | | DaEvns 1b | 4 | 0 | 2 | 1 |
| Luzinsk dh | 4 | 1 | 1 | 0 | | Brokns 3b | 0 | 0 | 0 | 0 |
| Walker 1b | 4 | 0 | 3 | 1 | | LNParsh c | 4 | 0 | 1 | 0 |
| Paciork lf | 4 | 0 | 0 | 0 | | Gibson rf | 4 | 0 | 1 | 0 |
| Hulett 3b | 2 | 0 | 0 | 0 | | Herndon lf | 4 | 0 | 1 | 0 |
| Squires ph | 1 | 0 | 0 | 0 | | Grubb dh | 2 | 0 | 1 | 0 |
| VLaw 3b | 0 | 0 | 0 | 0 | | Lemon cf | 4 | 0 | 0 | 0 |
| Hairstn ph | 1 | 0 | 0 | 0 | | HJhnsn 3b | 2 | 1 | 0 | 0 |
| Fletchr ss | 2 | 0 | 0 | 0 | | Bergmn 1b | 0 | 0 | 0 | 0 |
| JCruz 2b | 1 | 0 | 0 | 0 | | | | | | |
| Totals | 31 | 1 | 5 | 1 | | Totals | 31 | 4 | 10 | 3 |

Chicago...........................000 000 001— 1
Detroit............................101 000 20x— 4
Game Winning RBI — Whitaker (2).
E—Herndon. DP—Detroit 1. LOB—
Chicago 6, Detroit 7. 2B—Walker 2, Trammell, Luzinski. HR—Whitaker (2). SB— Gibson (2). S—JCruz.

| | IP | H | R | ER | BB | SO |
|---|---|---|---|---|---|---|
| **Chicago** | | | | | | |
| Hoyt L, 2-1 | 8 | 10 | 4 | 4 | 4 | 5 |
| **Detroit** | | | | | | |
| Rozema W, 1-0 | 6 | 2 | 0 | 0 | 2 | 7 |
| Bair S, 1 | 3 | 3 | 1 | 1 | 0 | 3 |

T—2:35. A—34,395.

I'm really proud of our pitching. Dave Rozema shut out the White Sox for six innings and Doug Bair finished for the save.

Lou Whitaker led the first with a homer off Lamar Hoyt and Larry Herndon made a great running catch with a man on. Looks like we've got another streak going.

**A bunt for second baseman Lou Whitaker.**  Photo by Clifton Boutelle

# SUNDAY, APRIL 22

## AT DETROIT

# GAME 13

## TIGERS 9, WHITE SOX 1

### (12–1, 4½ GAMES AHEAD)

| CHICAGO | ab | r | h | bi |
|---|---|---|---|---|
| RLaw cf | 3 | 0 | 0 | 0 |
| Stegmn ph | 1 | 1 | 1 | 0 |
| Fisk c | 4 | 0 | 1 | 0 |
| Baines rf | 3 | 0 | 1 | 0 |
| MHill ph | 1 | 0 | 0 | 0 |
| Luzinsk dh | 3 | 0 | 0 | 0 |
| JCruz 2b | 0 | 0 | 0 | 0 |
| Paciork lf | 3 | 0 | 0 | 1 |
| Squires 1b | 3 | 0 | 1 | 0 |
| Kittle ph | 1 | 0 | 0 | 0 |
| VLaw 3b | 2 | 0 | 0 | 0 |
| Hairstn ph | 1 | 0 | 0 | 0 |
| Dybzisk 2b | 0 | 0 | 0 | 0 |
| Fletchr ss | 3 | 0 | 1 | 0 |
| Hulett 2b | 1 | 0 | 0 | 0 |
| Walker 1b | 2 | 0 | 0 | 0 |
| Totals | 31 | 1 | 5 | 1 |

| DETROIT | ab | r | h | bi |
|---|---|---|---|---|
| Whitakr 2b | 5 | 1 | 1 | 0 |
| Trammi ss | 4 | 3 | 2 | 1 |
| DEvns dh | 5 | 2 | 3 | 2 |
| Gibson rf | 4 | 1 | 1 | 2 |
| Grubb lf | 1 | 0 | 1 | 0 |
| Herndon lf | 3 | 0 | 2 | 0 |
| Bergmn 1b | 2 | 0 | 0 | 0 |
| Garbey 1b | 3 | 0 | 2 | 3 |
| HJhnsn 3b | 2 | 0 | 1 | 0 |
| Brokns 3b | 3 | 1 | 1 | 0 |
| Lemon cf | 4 | 1 | 4 | 1 |
| Lowry c | 3 | 0 | 0 | 0 |
| Totals | 39 | 9 | 18 | 9 |

Chicago.............................000 000 001— 1
Detroit.............................200 020 05x— 9

Game Winning RBI — Gibson (2).
DP—Chicago 1, Detroit 1. LOB—Chicago 5, Detroit 10. 2B—DaEvans 2. 3B— Brookens. HR—Gibson (4). S—Lowry. SF—Paciorek.

| Chicago | IP | H | R | ER | BB | SO |
|---|---|---|---|---|---|---|
| Brennan L,0-1 | 2 1-3 | 6 | 2 | 2 | 1 | 0 |
| Agosto | 2 1-3 | 3 | 2 | 2 | 2 | 3 |
| Barojas | 2 | 2 | 0 | 0 | 0 | 0 |
| Burns | 1 | 7 | 5 | 5 | 0 | 0 |
| Squires | 1-3 | 0 | 0 | 0 | 0 | 0 |
| Detroit | | | | | | |
| Berengur W,1-0 | 7 | 2 | 0 | 0 | 1 | 7 |
| Lopez | 1 | 1 | 0 | 0 | 0 | 1 |
| Hernandz | 1 | 2 | 1 | 1 | 1 | 2 |

T—2:58. A—10,603.

Today was Easter Sunday and, man, it was cold. We almost froze to death on our way to Mass.

Our bats were hot, though. We pounded 18 hits and even a 1½-hour snow delay couldn't stop us. Kirk Gibson hit another homer and is getting better all the time. We're so strong on our bench now that we can make a lot of moves and rest our players.

We must have hit the ball hard. Chicago even had put Mike Squires (usually a utility infielder) on the mound to finish the game.

# MONDAY, APRIL 23

## AT DETROIT

## (12–1, 4 GAMES AHEAD)

Our night game with Minnesota was rained out, so we're scheduled to play two tomorrow.

I walked 4½ miles in one hour this morning and was beat. But even feeling tired feels good when you're 12–1. I did a lot of thinking during the walk. By June 1, we'll probably have Ruppert Jones and Doug Baker up from Evansville. We've still got to come up with two left-handed pitchers though. I would love to get Gary Lavelle from San Francisco. If we can solve about five little problems, this will be a great club.

**Shortstop Alan Trammell at bat.**  Photo by Doc Holcomb, courtesy of *The Detroit News*

# TUESDAY, APRIL 24

## AT DETROIT

# GAMES 14 & 15

## TIGERS 6, TWINS 5
## TIGERS 4, TWINS 3

### (14–1, 5½ GAMES AHEAD)

| MINNESOTA | ab | r | h | bi | DETROIT | ab | r | h | bi |
|---|---|---|---|---|---|---|---|---|---|
| DBrown cf | 5 | 0 | 1 | 0 | Whitakr 2b | 5 | 1 | 2 | 1 |
| RWshtn ss | 4 | 0 | 0 | 0 | Tramml ss | 4 | 0 | 2 | 2 |
| Hrbek 1b | 4 | 1 | 1 | 1 | DEvns dh | 4 | 0 | 0 | 0 |
| Engle c | 2 | 2 | 0 | 0 | Gibson rf | 4 | 1 | 1 | 0 |
| Bush dh | 4 | 1 | 2 | 1 | Grubb lf | 3 | 0 | 0 | 0 |
| Brnnsky rf | 3 | 1 | 1 | 2 | Kuntz pr | 0 | 1 | 0 | 0 |
| Gaetti 3b | 3 | 0 | 1 | 0 | Bergmn 1b | 4 | 1 | 1 | 1 |
| Hatcher lf | 3 | 0 | 0 | 0 | HJhnsn 3b | 4 | 0 | 1 | 0 |
| Teufel 2b | 4 | 0 | 1 | 1 | Lemon cf | 2 | 1 | 1 | 1 |
| | | | | | Lowry c | 2 | 1 | 1 | 0 |
| | | | | | LNPrsh ph | 1 | 0 | 0 | 0 |
| Totals | 32 | 5 | 7 | 5 | Totals | 33 | 6 | 9 | 5 |

```
Minnesota ......................... 000 410 000— 5
Detroit ............................. 001 020 003— 6
    Two outs when winning run scored.
    Game Winning RBI — Whitaker (3).
    E—Trammell. DP—Minnesota 3, Detroit
3. LOB—Minnesota 5, Detroit 5. 2B— Bru-
nansky, Bush, Whitaker. 3B—Gibson. HR—
Hrbek (3), Lemon (3).
```

| | IP | H | R | ER | BB | SO |
|---|---|---|---|---|---|---|
| **Minnesota** | | | | | | |
| Williams | 7 | 6 | 3 | 3 | 2 | 4 |
| RDavis L,2-2 | 1 2-3 | 3 | 3 | 3 | 1 | 0 |
| **Detroit** | | | | | | |
| Morris W,4-0 | 9 | 7 | 5 | 5 | 5 | 1 |

```
    HBP—Lemon by Williams. WP—Morris,
RDavis. T—2:16.
```

| MINNESOTA | ab | r | h | bi | DETROIT | ab | r | h | bi |
|---|---|---|---|---|---|---|---|---|---|
| DBrown cf | 4 | 0 | 0 | 0 | Brokns 2b | 4 | 0 | 0 | 0 |
| RWshtn ss | 3 | 0 | 0 | 0 | Tramml ss | 2 | 2 | 1 | 0 |
| Hrbek 1b | 3 | 1 | 1 | 2 | Garbey 1b | 4 | 1 | 2 | 1 |
| Engle c | 3 | 0 | 1 | 0 | LNParsh c | 3 | 1 | 1 | 3 |
| Bush dh | 4 | 0 | 1 | 1 | Lowry c | 1 | 0 | 1 | 0 |
| Brnnsky rf | 4 | 0 | 1 | 0 | Herndon lf | 4 | 0 | 1 | 0 |
| Gaetti 3b | 4 | 0 | 0 | 0 | Lemon cf | 4 | 0 | 1 | 0 |
| Hatcher lf | 1 | 0 | 0 | 0 | Allen dh | 3 | 0 | 1 | 0 |
| Meier lf | 2 | 1 | 1 | 0 | DEvns ph | 1 | 0 | 0 | 0 |
| Teufel 2b | 3 | 1 | 1 | 0 | MCastll 3b | 3 | 0 | 0 | 0 |
| Eisnrch ph | 1 | 0 | 0 | 0 | Whitakr 2b | 0 | 0 | 0 | 0 |
| | | | | | Kuntz rf | 3 | 0 | 1 | 0 |
| | | | | | Gibson rf | 1 | 0 | 0 | 0 |
| Totals | 32 | 3 | 6 | 3 | Totals | 33 | 4 | 9 | 4 |

```
Minnesota ......................... 100 020 000— 3
Detroit ............................. 001 030 00x— 4
    Game Winning RBI — LNParrish (2).
    E—Gaetti, MCastillo, Trammell. DP—
Minnesota 1, Detroit 2. LOB—Minnesota 7,
Detroit 8. 2B—Lemon, Garbey. HR—LNPar-
rish (3).
```

| | IP | H | R | ER | BB | SO |
|---|---|---|---|---|---|---|
| **Minnesota** | | | | | | |
| Viola L,0-3 | 6 1-3 | 9 | 4 | 4 | 2 | 4 |
| Walters | 1 1-3 | 0 | 0 | 0 | 1 | 0 |
| Filson | 1-3 | 0 | 0 | 0 | 0 | 0 |
| **Detroit** | | | | | | |
| Petry | 3 | 2 | 1 | 1 | 2 | 1 |
| Abbott W,1-0 | 3 | 3 | 2 | 2 | 1 | 2 |
| Lopez S,1 | 3 | 1 | 0 | 0 | 2 | 3 |

```
    Petry pitched to one batter in the fourth.
    T—2:29. A—20,315.
```

There can't be a turning point this early in the season. But whenever you win a doubleheader, you feel something special. Even when you're riding a hot streak.

In the opener, Jack Morris went all the way for his fourth straight win on three runs in the ninth. Lou Whitaker singled home the winner.

We trailed, 3–1, in the fifth inning of the second game when Lance Parrish unloaded a three-run homer to put us ahead. Dan Petry left after three innings with a stiff shoulder, but I don't think it's serious. Glen Abbott went three innings for the win and Lopez went the last three for the save.

Our pitching was good. Our defense was good. We got the key hits when we needed them. That's the ticket.

# WEDNESDAY, APRIL 25

## AT TEXAS

# GAME 16

## TIGERS 9, RANGERS 4

### (15–1, 5½ GAMES AHEAD)

| DETROIT | ab | r | h | bi | TEXAS | ab | r | h | bi |
|---|---|---|---|---|---|---|---|---|---|
| Whitakr 2b | 4 | 1 | 3 | 0 | Sample lf | 4 | 0 | 1 | 0 |
| Tramml ss | 5 | 0 | 1 | 0 | Rivers dh | 3 | 0 | 1 | 0 |
| DaEvns 1b | 4 | 1 | 1 | 0 | Stein ph | 2 | 1 | 1 | 0 |
| Bergmn 1b | 0 | 0 | 0 | 0 | GWrght cf | 3 | 1 | 0 | 0 |
| LNParsh c | 5 | 1 | 1 | 3 | BBell 3b | 4 | 0 | 2 | 2 |
| Gibson rf | 4 | 0 | 1 | 0 | LAPrsh rf | 4 | 0 | 1 | 0 |
| Herndon lf | 5 | 1 | 0 | 0 | OBrien 1b | 4 | 1 | 1 | 0 |
| Grubb dh | 3 | 1 | 1 | 1 | Foley c | 2 | 1 | 2 | 2 |
| Garbey dh | 2 | 2 | 2 | 1 | Ward ph | 1 | 0 | 0 | 0 |
| Lemon cf | 3 | 1 | 1 | 1 | Toliesn 2b | 4 | 0 | 1 | 0 |
| HJhnsn 3b | 3 | 1 | 1 | 2 | Wilkrsn ss | 3 | 0 | 0 | 0 |
| Brokns 3b | 1 | 0 | 1 | 1 | Hosttlr ph | 1 | 0 | 1 | 0 |
| Totals | 39 | 9 | 13 | 9 | Totals | 35 | 4 | 11 | 4 |

```
Detroit ........................ 010  200  501— 9
Texas .......................... 000  020  020— 4
```

Game Winning RBI — Grubb (1).
E—Gibson. DP—Detroit 3. LOB—Detroit 8, Texas 7. 2B—Garbey, BBell. HR—Foley (1), Grubb (1), HJohnson (1), LNParrish (4). SB—Gibson 2 (3), Garbey (1).

| | IP | H | R | ER | BB | SO |
|---|---|---|---|---|---|---|
| **Detroit** | | | | | | |
| Wilcox W,2-0 | 6 | 6 | 2 | 2 | 2 | 2 |
| Hernandz S,2 | 3 | 5 | 2 | 2 | 1 | 3 |
| **Texas** | | | | | | |
| DStewart L,0-5 | 6 1-3 | 9 | 7 | 7 | 4 | 9 |
| Mason | 2-3 | 2 | 1 | 1 | 1 | 0 |
| Bibby | 2 | 2 | 1 | 1 | 0 | 0 |

T—2:38. A—25,883.

Arlington Stadium looks like a completely new ball park with a scoreboard running the entire length of the outfield. They tell me it cost $6 million. It looks really nice. The wind used to blow straight in from right and this park destroyed a lot of good hitters. Now it blows straight out and I predict there'll be a ton of homers hit from now on.

We went to the park early to work with Howard Johnson and Barbaro Garbey on defense. Both of them are improving. I talked again with Bill Lajoie about getting some lefties. I like to stir things up when we're winning. I believe when you're on a roll, you should still try to make yourself better. That's when you're in a position to do something. I must drive Bill and Jim Campbell crazy with all the deals I propose when we're winning. Jim calls me "Deal-a-Day Anderson." But we still end up sticking it to the other team when it counts.

We hit three home runs tonight. Lance Parrish hit his fourth. Johnson and Johnny Grubb each hit his first. Lou Whitaker made an unbelievable play at second base and Parrish threw out Mickey Rivers and Billy Sample. This club is playing the best I've seen in my life.

# THURSDAY, APRIL 26

## AT TEXAS

# GAME 17

## TIGERS 7, RANGERS 5

### (16–1, 6 GAMES AHEAD)

| DETROIT | ab | r | h | bi |
|---|---|---|---|---|
| Whitakr 2b | 5 | 1 | 2 | 0 |
| Trammll ss | 4 | 1 | 3 | 1 |
| Garbey 1b | 4 | 0 | 1 | 2 |
| LNParsh c | 5 | 1 | 1 | 1 |
| Herndon lf | 5 | 2 | 2 | 0 |
| Lemon cf | 4 | 1 | 2 | 2 |
| Brokns 3b | 4 | 0 | 1 | 1 |
| Allen dh | 1 | 1 | 0 | 0 |
| DEvns dh | 0 | 0 | 0 | 0 |
| Kuntz rf | 2 | 0 | 0 | 0 |
| Gibson rf | 2 | 0 | 1 | 0 |
| Totals | 36 | 7 | 13 | 7 |

| TEXAS | ab | r | h | bi |
|---|---|---|---|---|
| Sample lf | 5 | 1 | 2 | 0 |
| OBrien 1b | 5 | 1 | 2 | 3 |
| BJones rf | 4 | 1 | 3 | 1 |
| BBell 3b | 4 | 0 | 1 | 0 |
| LAPrsh dh | 4 | 0 | 0 | 0 |
| GWrght cf | 4 | 0 | 0 | 0 |
| Foley c | 3 | 1 | 1 | 1 |
| Tollesn 2b | 4 | 0 | 2 | 0 |
| Wilkrsn ss | 2 | 1 | 0 | 0 |
| Stein 2b | 1 | 0 | 0 | 0 |
| Rivers ph | 1 | 0 | 0 | 0 |
| Totals | 37 | 5 | 11 | 5 |

Detroit .............................. 401 100 100— 7
Texas ................................ 110 030 000— 5

Game Winning RBI — Garbey (1).
E—Brookens. DP—Detroit 2, Texas 2. LOB—Detroit 7, Texas 6. 2B—Whitaker, Herndon 2, Lemon. HR—BJones (2), Foley (2), OBrien (3), LNParrish (5). SB— Gibson (4).

| Detroit | IP | H | R | ER | BB | SO |
|---|---|---|---|---|---|---|
| Rozema | 4 1-3 | 7 | 5 | 5 | 0 | 1 |
| Bair W,2-0 | 2 | 4 | 0 | 0 | 1 | 1 |
| Lopez S,2 | 2 2-3 | 0 | 0 | 0 | 0 | 2 |
| Texas | | | | | | |
| Tanana L,2-2 | 3 2-3 | 8 | 6 | 6 | 3 | 2 |
| Schmidt | 3 1-3 | 3 | 1 | 1 | 1 | 3 |
| OJones | 2 | 2 | 0 | 0 | 1 | 2 |

WP—Tanana. BK—Tanana. T—2:50. A—13,559.

Even if we were 1–15 . . . what a life! I told that to Roger Craig while we were relaxing in the whirlpool after our walk. Baseball is unbelievable. It's like taking a water gun to rob a bank. Leave your name, address, and phone number, and the police don't bother you. This is the only game where you can be 70 years old and still feel like a kid. How did I get so lucky?

I'm still bugging Bill Lajoie about getting two lefties. We've got the right ingredients to put together a package. Bill can swing it. He's got a great baseball mind.

Today, we got four runs in the first inning and then held on. Dave Rozema stiffened a little, but Doug Bair was super. So was Aurelio Lopez. He's been so good, it's scary.

We swung the bats real well. Larry Herndon got a couple of hits, but I'm worried about him. He's pulling off the plate too much. We've got to straighten him out. We've got to get Rozema and Milt Wilcox pitching better, too.

Later on the plane I realized that this was seventh straight win on the road.

# FRIDAY, APRIL 27

## AT DETROIT

# GAME 18

## INDIANS 8, TIGERS 4
### (19 INNINGS)
### (16–2, 5 GAMES AHEAD)

| CLEVELAND | ab | r | h | bi | | DETROIT | ab | r | h | bi |
|---|---|---|---|---|---|---|---|---|---|---|
| Butler cf | 6 | 3 | 1 | 0 | | Whitakr 2b | 7 | 2 | 3 | 0 |
| Bernzrd 2b | 6 | 1 | 0 | 1 | | Trammi ss | 8 | 1 | 2 | 0 |
| Franco ss | 7 | 1 | 2 | 3 | | DaEvns 1b | 8 | 1 | 1 | 1 |
| Thrntn dh | 9 | 0 | 0 | 0 | | LNParsh c | 8 | 0 | 1 | 1 |
| Tabler 1b | 3 | 0 | 1 | 0 | | Gibson rf | 7 | 0 | 0 | 0 |
| Hargrv 1b | 4 | 0 | 1 | 3 | | Herndon lf | 7 | 0 | 1 | 0 |
| Hassey c | 4 | 0 | 0 | 1 | | Garbey 3b | 3 | 0 | 1 | 1 |
| Fischlin 3b | 2 | 0 | 0 | 0 | | Brokns 3b | 1 | 0 | 0 | 0 |
| Jacoby c | 6 | 0 | 1 | 0 | | Brgmn ph | 1 | 0 | 0 | 0 |
| Willard ph | 2 | 0 | 0 | 0 | | MCastil 3b | 0 | 0 | 0 | 0 |
| Vukvch rf | 7 | 2 | 3 | 0 | | Grubb ph | 1 | 0 | 0 | 0 |
| Nixon lf | 6 | 1 | 2 | 0 | | Abbott p | 0 | 0 | 0 | 0 |
| | | | | | | Lowry ph | 1 | 0 | 0 | 0 |
| | | | | | | Lemon cf | 1 | 0 | 0 | 0 |
| | | | | | | HJhnsn dh | 7 | 0 | 1 | 0 |
| Totals | 62 | 8 | 11 | 8 | | Totals | 66 | 4 | 10 | 3 |

```
Cleveland............120 000 000 100 000 000 4—8
Detroit.................300 000 000 100 000 000 0—4
```
Game Winning RBI — Bernazard (2).

E—Garbey, Abbott 2, Gibson. DP—
Cleveland 1, Detroit 1. LOB—Cleveland 13,
Detroit 9. 2B—Franco. SB—Butler (12). S—
Nixon 2, Bernazard, Butler. SF—Bernazard.

| | IP | H | R | ER | BB | SO |
|---|---|---|---|---|---|---|
| **Cleveland** | | | | | | |
| Sutcliffe | 9 | 8 | 4 | 4 | 3 | 3 |
| Camacho | 0 | 1 | 0 | 0 | 0 | 0 |
| Jeffcoat | 2-3 | 0 | 0 | 0 | 0 | 0 |
| Frazier | 2 1-3 | 0 | 0 | 0 | 0 | 2 |
| Waddell | 5 | 1 | 0 | 0 | 1 | 4 |
| Aponte W, 1-0 | 2 | 0 | 0 | 0 | 0 | 1 |
| **Detroit** | | | | | | |
| Berengur | 7 2-3 | 7 | 3 | 1 | 3 | 6 |
| Hernandz | 1 2-3 | 1 | 1 | 1 | 1 | 2 |
| Lopez | 4 2-3 | 1 | 0 | 0 | 4 | 2 |
| Abbott L, 1-1 | 5 | 2 | 4 | 0 | 2 | 2 |

Sutcliffe pitched to one batter in the 10th,
Camacho pitched to one batter in the 10th.
WP—Lopez. T—5:44. A—34,112.

I didn't walk today. I didn't get to bed until 5 A.M. after flying home from Texas. I slept for a few hours and then went to the park at one.

What a day . . . and what a night. We went 19 innings and then . . . pffft. All our pitchers threw well, but I honestly think we were pooped from the night before. Glenn Abbott made two errors in the 19th inning and Kirk Gibson dropped a fly ball. All three errors came on easy plays.

The game ended at 1:19 A.M. It was another short night for sleeping.

# SATURDAY, APRIL 28

## AT DETROIT

# GAME 19

## TIGERS 6, INDIANS 2

### (17-2, 5½ GAMES AHEAD)

| CLEVELAND | ab | r | h | bi | DETROIT | ab | r | h | bi |
|---|---|---|---|---|---|---|---|---|---|
| Butler cf | 3 | 0 | 0 | 0 | Whitakr 2b | 4 | 1 | 2 | 2 |
| Bernzrd 2b | 3 | 1 | 0 | 0 | Trammi ss | 3 | 1 | 1 | 2 |
| Fischlin 2b | 0 | 0 | 0 | 0 | DaEvns 1b | 4 | 0 | 1 | 1 |
| Franco ss | 2 | 1 | 0 | 0 | Brokns 3b | 0 | 0 | 0 | 0 |
| Tabler dh | 4 | 0 | 0 | 0 | Gibson rf | 3 | 0 | 1 | 0 |
| Hargrv 1b | 4 | 0 | 1 | 1 | Grubb dh | 2 | 0 | 0 | 0 |
| Jacoby 3b | 3 | 0 | 1 | 0 | Allen dh | 2 | 0 | 0 | 0 |
| Willard c | 3 | 0 | 1 | 0 | Herndon lf | 4 | 0 | 1 | 0 |
| Vukvch rf | 3 | 0 | 0 | 0 | Garbey 3b | 3 | 1 | 1 | 0 |
| Nixon lf | 3 | 0 | 0 | 0 | Bergmn 1b | 1 | 0 | 0 | 0 |
| | | | | | Lemon cf | 3 | 2 | 2 | 1 |
| | | | | | Lowry c | 2 | 1 | 1 | 0 |
| Totals | 28 | 2 | 3 | 1 | Totals | 31 | 6 | 10 | 6 |

```
Cleveland........................000 200 000— 2
Detroit..........................120 300 00x— 6
```

Game Winning RBI — DaEvans (3):

DP—Cleveland 1, Detroit 1. LOB— Cleveland 3, Detroit 4. 2B—Gibson, Trammell. HR —Lemon (4), Whitaker (3). SB— Trammell (7), Bernazard 2 (11), Franco (5). S—Lowry.

| | IP | H | R | ER | BB | SO |
|---|---|---|---|---|---|---|
| Cleveland | | | | | | |
| Behenna L,0-1 | 3 1-3 | 9 | 6 | 6 | 2 | 1 |
| Jeffcoat | 2 2-3 | 1 | 0 | 0 | 0 | 2 |
| Aponte | 2 | 0 | 0 | 0 | 0 | 3 |
| Detroit | | | | | | |
| Morris W,5-0 | 9 | 3 | 2 | 2 | 3 | 5 |

HBP—Franco by Morris WP—Morris. T —2:24. A—28,253.

I sent Morris home early last night. He was home by the 13th inning and asleep by the 17th. It paid off. He was super today. He allowed just three hits and should have even shut them out. He had the good stuff today. I think he has better stuff when he pitches on the fourth day.

I don't know if Trammell is the best player in all of baseball, but I've never seen a shortstop who can do as many things as well as he does. I've never seen a more complete player. He even stole another base today.

In all honesty, this is a better team than any of my Cincinnati clubs. It has better pitching, better all-around defense, and more all-around power. If everyone stays healthy, you'll see one of the great baseball teams of our time over the next five years.

**Ace pitcher Jack Morris flashes his form.** Photo by Doc Holcomb, courtesy of *The Detroit News*

35

# SUNDAY, APRIL 29

## AT DETROIT

# GAME 20

## TIGERS 6, INDIANS 1

### (18–2, 6 GAMES AHEAD)

| CLEVELAND | ab | r | h | bi | DETROIT | ab | r | h | bi |
|---|---|---|---|---|---|---|---|---|---|
| Butler cf | 3 | 1 | 0 | 0 | Whitakr 2b | 4 | 1 | 2 | 0 |
| Bernzrd 2b | 4 | 0 | 0 | 0 | Gibson rf | 4 | 1 | 3 | 3 |
| Franco ss | 4 | 0 | 1 | 1 | DEvns dh | 3 | 0 | 1 | 0 |
| Thrntn dh | 4 | 0 | 0 | 0 | LNParsh c | 4 | 0 | 1 | 1 |
| Tabler 1b | 3 | 0 | 0 | 0 | Lowry c | 0 | 0 | 0 | 0 |
| Hassey c | 3 | 0 | 0 | 0 | Herndon lf | 4 | 0 | 1 | 0 |
| Jacoby 3b | 1 | 0 | 0 | 0 | HJhnsn 3b | 3 | 0 | 0 | 0 |
| Perkins ph | 1 | 0 | 0 | 0 | Tramml ss | 1 | 1 | 1 | 0 |
| CCastill rf | 0 | 0 | 0 | 0 | Lemon cf | 3 | 1 | 0 | 0 |
| Vukvch rf | 3 | 0 | 1 | 0 | Bergmn 1b | 4 | 0 | 1 | 1 |
| Nixon lf | 2 | 0 | 0 | 0 | Brookns ss | 3 | 2 | 1 | 1 |
| Hargrv ph | 1 | 0 | 0 | 0 | | | | | |
| Fischlin 3b | 0 | 0 | 0 | 0 | | | | | |
| Totals | 29 | 1 | 2 | 1 | Totals | 33 | 6 | 11 | 6 |

```
Cleveland.....................000 000 001— 1
Detroit..........................003 010 02x— 6
```

Game Winning RBI — Gibson (3).
E—Franco, Vukovich. DP—Cleveland 1.
LOB—Cleveland 4, Detroit 7. 2B—Vukovich,
Franco, Gibson 2, LNParrish, Trammell.

| | IP | H | R | ER | BB | SO |
|---|---|---|---|---|---|---|
| **Cleveland** | | | | | | |
| Spillner L,0-1 | 5 | 6 | 4 | 2 | 3 | 2 |
| Camacho | 2 | 2 | 0 | 0 | 0 | 0 |
| Frazier | 1 | 3 | 2 | 2 | 1 | 0 |
| **Detroit** | | | | | | |
| Petry W,3-1 | 8 | 1 | 0 | 0 | 2 | 7 |
| Hernandz | 1 | 1 | 1 | 1 | 1 | 1 |

WP—Petry, Camacho. T—2:20. A— 24,-853.

Petry pitched today. Man, did he pitch!

Danny is coming so close to greatness now. He is a tremendous young man, and so dedicated. He's been his own worst enemy because he puts so much pressure on himself. I think he's finally learning now that no one is perfect.

He was close to perfection today, though. He had a no-hitter going until George Vukovich doubled to left center with one out in the eighth. I kidded Chet Lemon that he should have caught the ball, but there was no chance.

We played super defense. They actually could have had four hits that we stole from them. Brookens made two great plays. I didn't put Alan Trammell in until the seventh. He batted once and doubled. I thank God he got that hit. I didn't realize he had a 17-game streak going.

No Tiger team in history has ever had an 18–2 April. I never dreamed we would—May might even be better!

# MONDAY, APRIL 30

## EXHIBITION AT CINCINNATI

## (18–2, 6 GAMES AHEAD)

We flew to Cincinnati for the Annual Kid Glove Exhibition Game with the Reds. It's a great game for sandlot baseball, but I don't like to play all my guns.

We feasted in the clubhouse. My friend, Ted Gregory, brought us a mountain of ribs and there was a big cake that said "Welcome Home Main Spark." There are a lot of good people in the Cincinnati organization. That's why I think it'll be good again. But you know I had to be feeling chipper coming into town with a record of 18–2.

**Dan Petry shows his stuff.**   Photo by Doc Holcomb, courtesy of *The Detroit News*

# THE STARTERS

There's an old debate in baseball that guarantees a long night of arguments every time it's discussed. Some say your starting pitching is only as good as your bullpen. Others argue that the bullpen is only as good as the starting rotation allows it to be.

Everybody who saw the Tigers this year knows that with Willie Hernandez and Aurelio Lopez, our bullpen was without a doubt the best in the game this season. But you've got to have the horses at the start of the race who can bring you near that finish line.

I like to think of it this way: If you've got a fancy new tuxedo and a brand new pair of dancing shoes, they ain't going to do you no good if you can't get to the prom on time. What I mean is that your starting pitching had better get you near the end of the game so that your bullpen has a chance to strut its stuff.

That's why we were so fortunate in 1984. Our starting pitching was good enough to take us to where we were going. Then the bullpen was ready to stand up, slam the door in someone's face, and lock it so tight that even a burglar couldn't crack it.

I said it all along—there were two things that the Tigers of 1984 have that I never had in all my good years in Cincinnati—Jack Morris and Dan Petry. This is a legitimate one-two pitching power punch that other managers only dream of.

There was a lot more to our starting rotation than just Morris and Petry. But having the luxury of these guys pitching every fourth or fifth day eliminated the possibility of those eight and nine game losing streaks that can knock a team right out of the race. With a couple of horses like Morris and Petry, you can stop what would be a killing losing streak before it really gets a chance to start rolling. Every team is going to lose four or five in a row sometime during a 162-game season, but the team that can snap it right there is almost guaranteed to be in the race all year long.

That's the beauty of having Morris and Petry. They're like a traffic cop who can stop that rush of oncoming cars before they turn into a jam and throw the whole place out of whack.

39

Morris had one of the craziest seasons ever. He went from proving he was the best starting pitcher in the game, to a period of struggling and soul-searching, to finally, a return to normal; he solidified the rotation as the team made its drive in the stretch.

Morris started the season the way every kid dreams of life in the major leagues—winning all the time. I mean to tell you, Jack was incredible. In his second start of the season, he fired a no-hitter at Chicago. And he did it on national TV against the defending West Division champions to boot. By the end of May, he was 10–1 and his only loss was a 1–0 heartbreaker to the Boston Red Sox.

Just to give an example of how things were going, there was a fan sitting behind our dugout in Chicago the day Jack had the no-hitter. After the fifth inning, that fan kept yelling at Morris that he was working on a no-hitter, trying to jinx him and coax him into a mistake.

Jack walked back to the dugout after an inning late in the game and looked up into the stands and yelled at that fan, "I know I'm working on a no-hitter. And you better keep watching because I'm going to get it, too."

That's the kind of confidence Jack has. He's cocky, but not arrogant. All great pitchers are like that. In fact, I've never seen a good player who isn't cocky enough to know that he's good and then go out and do the job. People started talking about 30 victories and Jack was being compared to Denny McLain when he won 31 games for the 1968 World Champion Tigers.

All of a sudden, Jack ran into a little elbow problem and before you knew it, all the pressures of being on top of the baseball world started to close in. Jack withdrew inside of himself and at times let his temper get the best of him on the mound. For a period of more than a month, Jack refused to talk to the press. The articles that were written about him started to question his dedication to the game.

I had more meetings with Jack in my office than the United Nations has over a missile crisis. I'll never forget that afternoon late in August when I finally asked Jack to talk to the press as a favor to me. He looked at me with those calculating eyes all the good players seem to have and simply said, "For you, I'll do it."

Finally it was over and Jack got back to being the outstanding pitcher everyone knew he was.

I've met a lot of great horse trainers and they all say the same thing. You just can't go near a really great race horse. They start to get nervous and sometimes turn mean. All of them are like that; they're extremely high strung. That's exactly the way Jack is. He's strung tighter than rope.

**Jack Morris.** Photo courtesy of Detroit Tigers

**Dan Petry.** Photo courtesy of Detroit Tigers

**Milt Wilcox.** Photo courtesy of Detroit Tigers

**Juan Berenguer.** Photo courtesy of Detroit Tigers

Jack never tried to show up a player in his life. But he is so high strung, that sometimes his temper gets the best of him. He wants to win so badly that sometimes he forgets what he's doing.

In my meetings with Jack, I tried to explain that he must try to play within himself and his abilities. He must understand himself before he can understand the game. I told him not to promise me he'd never let his temper show again. If he promised that and then his temper got the best of him, he'd feel sorry the promise was broken and we'd never come close to an understanding.

All I know is that Jack Morris has taken the ball more than any other pitcher in the five years I've been here. And he wants to win so badly that it hurts. Anyone who wants to win that bad, can't be all wrong.

Petry is a different type of person in that once he blows his steam after a loss, he's ready for his next turn. Danny also wants to win badly, but he really is more concerned with having the team win than he is for putting another W under his belt. That's why he's going to get a lot of those Ws before he's finished. He's a rugged competitor who'll do anything to win.

Danny is only 25 years old and I can't believe how much he's matured over the year. He's progressed quicker than I thought. He's matured to the point where he doesn't let things affect his pitching. He might get beat—but he'll make you throw the kitchen sink at him to do it. He's a couple of years away from the greatness that should be his, but he's improved immeasurably.

Danny is a tremendously dedicated young man. Baseball is his only concern in life and he realizes he has to work hard to reach the high goals that he's set. He works hard physically; he doesn't drink and he doesn't smoke. He's got a beautiful young wife and has his priorities in order. That may not sound like a lot, but it makes a difference when you point your life in one direction and then follow through on everything to meet the goals you set.

Milt Wilcox is the one key to the starting rotation who really put all the pieces together. Throughout his career, Milt seemed to be stymied at 12 or 13 wins. Sometimes even veteran players don't realize that psychologically they accept a certain standard and relax when they reach it, never daring to take that one step beyond.

Milt took that dare this year and took a giant step beyond all of his past limitations. I always felt that Milt was capable of winning between 15 and 20 games if he just pushed himself to pitch a whole season. Despite some arm problems, this year he pushed himself as hard as I've ever seen a veteran push himself and got over that hump to notch the most wins he's ever had in a season.

Milt is not the power pitcher he was when he broke in with me at Cincinnati as a kid in 1970. He's more a pitcher who has a good concept of the game. He teases hitters; paints the corners of the plate. He sets up his fastball real nice.

Milt is the kind of pitcher hitters don't mind facing. Then they wonder what went wrong. Al Kaline told me that's the way Catfish Hunter was. You didn't mind facing him. Then came the eighth inning, and you realized you were 0-for-4.

We used several pitchers in the fourth spot before we finally settled on Juan Berenguer. Juan worked very, very hard at this. He never gave up and he deserved what he got.

Juan has unbelievable stuff. His fastball cranks up to 95 miles an hour at times. For him, it's a matter of keeping his control. Bill Lajoie deserves credit for Berenguer. He signed him and stuck with him. He saw a good strong arm and refused to give up on him.

On September 5, Juan threw what might have been the most important single pitching performance of the season. He shut out the Orioles, 1–0, after we had dropped two to the Birds at home. We were going to Toronto for a big three-game series after that, closing in on the Division title. Who knows what might have happened had Juan not turned in the most important performance of his career?

And while we're giving credit, it's time to recognize Roger Craig. He's more than a pitching coach. He's another manager in the dugout and, most importantly, he's a good friend.

I could have fallen over and died in the middle of the season and nothing would have changed. That's because Roger could have taken right over and kept the team on a roll. Roger is such a positive person. He takes the pitchers under his wing and makes them believe in themselves—and that's half the battle.

Roger became pretty well known for teaching the split finger fastball to our staff. But it's the confidence he generated that was the real key. We're going to miss Roger because he's decided to retire. I'm going to miss him as a friend.

# MAY

"This month will tell a story. If we can open up the gap some more, the party will be over for a lot of people."    **May 1, 1984**

# TUESDAY, MAY 1

## AT DETROIT

# GAME 21

## TIGERS 11, RED SOX 2

### (19–2, 6½ GAMES AHEAD)

| BOSTON | ab | r | h | bi | DETROIT | ab | r | h | bi |
|---|---|---|---|---|---|---|---|---|---|
| Remy 2b | 4 | 0 | 0 | 0 | Kuntz rf | 3 | 2 | 3 | 3 |
| DwEvns rf | 3 | 2 | 1 | 0 | Gibson rf | 2 | 0 | 0 | 0 |
| Boggs 3b | 4 | 0 | 1 | 0 | Tramml ss | 4 | 2 | 2 | 0 |
| Rice lf | 4 | 0 | 3 | 2 | Garbey 1b | 5 | 1 | 3 | 4 |
| Easler 1b | 4 | 0 | 1 | 0 | LNParsh c | 5 | 0 | 1 | 0 |
| Armas dh | 3 | 0 | 0 | 0 | Herndon lf | 5 | 1 | 1 | 0 |
| Gedman c | 3 | 0 | 0 | 0 | Lemon cf | 5 | 2 | 3 | 4 |
| Nichols cf | 3 | 0 | 1 | 0 | Brokns 2b | 4 | 1 | 1 | 0 |
| Hoffmn ss | 2 | 0 | 1 | 0 | Allen dh | 2 | 1 | 0 | 0 |
| Miller ph | 1 | 0 | 0 | 0 | DEvns dh | 2 | 0 | 1 | 0 |
| Gutirrz ss | 0 | 0 | 0 | 0 | MCastil 3b | 2 | 1 | 1 | 0 |
| | | | | | Whitakr 2b | 2 | 0 | 0 | 0 |
| Totals | 31 | 2 | 8 | 2 | Totals | 41 | 11 | 16 | 11 |

Boston................................100 100 000— 2
Detroit.................................040 200 14x—11
   Game Winning RBI — Kuntz (1).
   E—Hoffman, Gedman. DP—Detroit 3.
LOB—Boston 3, Detroit 8. 2B—MCastillo,
Kuntz, Garbey, Trammell. HR—Lemon 2 (6).
SB—Brookens (1), Allen (1).

| | IP | H | R | ER | BB | SO |
|---|---|---|---|---|---|---|
| Boston | | | | | | |
| Hurst L,3-3 | 3 1-3 | 9 | 6 | 2 | 1 | 4 |
| Boyd | 4 2-3 | 7 | 5 | 5 | 1 | 3 |
| Detroit | | | | | | |
| Wilcox W,3-0 | 8 | 7 | 2 | 1 | 1 | 5 |
| Lopez | 1 | 1 | 0 | 0 | 0 | 0 |

   BK—Hurst. PB—LNParrish. T—2:31. A—
17,495.

This month will tell a story. If we can open the gap some more, the party will be over for a lot of people. We'll have a good month if we can get Larry Herndon and Lance Parrish going.

We started off well. Our bats were booming and the Red Sox shouldn't even have scored. Their runs came from a wind-blown pop-up and passed ball by Parrish.

We started all righthanded hitters against Bruce Hurst. Rusty Kuntz, Barbaro Garbey, and Chet Lemon each had three hits. Lemon drilled two home runs—Chester is going to have the best year of his career.

Milt Wilcox went eight innings and threw well. Milt's got to have a big year for us to go all the way.

# WEDNESDAY, MAY 2

## AT DETROIT

# GAME 22

## RED SOX 5, TIGERS 4

### (19–3, 5½ GAMES AHEAD)

| BOSTON | ab | r | h | bi | DETROIT | ab | r | n | bi |
|---|---|---|---|---|---|---|---|---|---|
| Remy 2b | 2 | 1 | 0 | 0 | Whitakr 2b | 5 | 1 | 1 | 1 |
| DwEvns rf | 5 | 1 | 2 | 2 | Tramml ss | 5 | 0 | 0 | 0 |
| Boggs 3b | 4 | 1 | 0 | 0 | Gibson rf | 5 | 2 | 4 | 1 |
| Rice lf | 4 | 1 | 1 | 2 | DEvns dh | 5 | 0 | 1 | 1 |
| Easler dh | 3 | 1 | 1 | 0 | Grubb lf | 4 | 0 | 1 | 0 |
| Armas dh | 4 | 0 | 0 | 0 | Lemon cf | 4 | 0 | 1 | 0 |
| Gedman c | 3 | 0 | 1 | 0 | Bergmn 1b | 4 | 0 | 3 | 1 |
| Nichols cf | 4 | 0 | 2 | 1 | HJhnsn 3b | 4 | 0 | 1 | 0 |
| Hoffmn ss | 4 | 0 | 1 | 0 | Lowry c | 3 | 0 | 0 | 0 |
|  |  |  |  |  | Garbey ph | 1 | 1 | 1 | 0 |
| Totals | 33 | 5 | 8 | 5 | Totals | 40 | 4 | 13 | 4 |

Boston.............................202  001  000— 5
Detroit.............................000  001  012— 4

Game Winning RBI — DwEvans (1).
LOB—Boston 7, Detroit 10. 2B—Whitaker, Gibson. 3B—Gedman, Gibson. HR— DwEvans (2), Rice (2). SB—Easler (1), S—Remy.

|  | IP | H | R | ER | BB | SO |
|---|---|---|---|---|---|---|
| **Boston** |  |  |  |  |  |  |
| MBrown W,1-2 | 5 2-3 | 7 | 1 | 1 | 1 | 3 |
| Stanley S,4 | 3 1-3 | 6 | 3 | 3 | 0 | 3 |
| **Detroit** |  |  |  |  |  |  |
| Berengur L,1-1 | 6 | 5 | 5 | 5 | 5 | 3 |
| Bair | 2 | 2 | 0 | 0 | 0 | 3 |
| Hernandz | 1 | 1 | 0 | 0 | 0 | 0 |

T—2:33. A—23,085.

I spent the morning with a photographer from *Sports Illustrated*. He took pictures of me working on lineups in my kitchen, me and Billy Consolo on the golf course, and me and my wife Carol walking around the neighborhood.

The evening was spent getting beaten by Boston. We had the tying run on second with one out in the ninth, but this time there was no magic. We had 13 hits and at least as many opportunities to win. Kirk Gibson had four hits and Dave Bergman three. One good thing—when we lose, we go down hard. I believe it'll be this way most of the year. If you beat us, you beat a club that's fighting all the way. Our kids don't know how to quit. Overall, they play harder than any club I've ever managed.

# THURSDAY, MAY 3

## AT DETROIT

# GAME 23

## RED SOX 1, TIGERS 0

## (19-4, 5 GAMES AHEAD)

| BOSTON | ab | r | h | bi | DETROIT | ab | r | h | bi |
|---|---|---|---|---|---|---|---|---|---|
| Barrett 2b | 4 | 0 | 0 | 0 | Whitaker 2b | 4 | 0 | 1 | 0 |
| DW Evans rf | 4 | 1 | 1 | 1 | Trammell ss | 3 | 0 | 0 | 0 |
| Boggs 3b | 2 | 0 | 1 | 0 | Garbey 1b | 4 | 0 | 0 | 0 |
| Rice lf | 4 | 0 | 1 | 0 | Parrish c | 4 | 0 | 2 | 0 |
| Easler 1b | 4 | 0 | 0 | 0 | Herndon lf | 3 | 0 | 1 | 0 |
| Armas dh | 4 | 0 | 1 | 0 | Lemon cf | 4 | 0 | 0 | 0 |
| Gedman c | 3 | 0 | 0 | 0 | Gibson rf | 4 | 0 | 1 | 0 |
| Nichols cf | 4 | 0 | 0 | 0 | Brookens 3b | 2 | 0 | 1 | 0 |
| Gutierrez sh | 3 | 0 | 1 | 0 | Kuntz dh | 3 | 0 | 0 | 0 |
| Totals | 32 | 1 | 5 | 1 | Totals | 31 | 0 | 6 | 0 |

Boston.................................000 000 080— 1
Detroit.................................000 000 000— 0
Game-winning RBI—Dw. Evans (2). E—
Gutierrez. DP—Boston 1. LOB—Boston 7,
Detroit 7. HR—Dw. Evans (3).

| | IP | H | R | ER | BB | SO |
|---|---|---|---|---|---|---|
| **Boston** | | | | | | |
| Ojeda (W 2-2) | 9 | 6 | 0 | 0 | 3 | 10 |
| **Detroit** | | | | | | |
| Morris (L 5-1) | 9 | 5 | 1 | 1 | 3 | 8 |

T—2:18. A—22,617.

What do you say when you lose 1-0? "Congratulations," that's all.

Morris pitched a super game, but suffered his first loss. He only allowed five hits, but one was an eighth inning homer to Dwight Evans. Boston's Bobby Ojeda was outstanding. He struck out 10 and we managed only six singles against him. We had two men on in the ninth with one out when Lemon hit a ball to left that would have been gone if it weren't for the strong wind that was blowing in from the outfield.

I guess you can't play 162 games and always get the big hit. Branch Rickey was right when he said, "Every team loses 60 games before the season even starts. The good ones can count on 90 wins. It's those 12 games in the middle that make the difference."

I don't think I'll worry about four losses by May 3. We've been contenders in every game. We will be in most games this year because we catch the ball. Defensively, I've never seen a better club.

After the game we bussed to Cleveland. I can't believe I would ever say this, but I actually got tired of talking. It seems like the writers are with us even when we sleep.

# FRIDAY, MAY 4

## AT CLEVELAND

# GAME 24

## TIGERS 9, INDIANS 2

### (20-4, 5 GAMES AHEAD)

| DETROIT | ab | r | h | bi | CLEVELAND | ab | r | h | bi |
|---|---|---|---|---|---|---|---|---|---|
| Whitakr 2b | 5 | 2 | 4 | 0 | Butler cf | 4 | 0 | 1 | 0 |
| Grubb ph | 1 | 0 | 0 | 0 | Bernzrd 2b | 4 | 0 | 0 | 0 |
| MCastil 3b | 0 | 0 | 0 | 0 | Hargrv 1b | 4 | 1 | 2 | 0 |
| Trammi ss | 5 | 1 | 1 | 1 | Perkins dh | 2 | 1 | 1 | 0 |
| Gibson rf | 3 | 2 | 1 | 0 | Franco dh | 1 | 0 | 0 | 0 |
| LNParsh c | 3 | 0 | 0 | 2 | Hassey c | 3 | 0 | 1 | 1 |
| Lowry c | 0 | 0 | 0 | 0 | Willard c | 1 | 0 | 0 | 0 |
| DEvns dh | 4 | 2 | 1 | 0 | Jacoby 3b | 4 | 0 | 1 | 1 |
| Herndon lf | 5 | 0 | 3 | 2 | Vukvch rf | 3 | 0 | 1 | 0 |
| Allen lf | 0 | 0 | 0 | 0 | Fischlin ss | 4 | 0 | 1 | 0 |
| Bergmn 1b | 5 | 1 | 1 | 1 | Nixon lf | 2 | 0 | 0 | 0 |
| Lemon cf | 5 | 0 | 1 | 1 | CCastill lf | 1 | 0 | 0 | 0 |
| Kuntz cf | 0 | 0 | 0 | 0 | | | | | |
| HJhnsn 3b | 3 | 1 | 1 | 1 | | | | | |
| Brokns 3b | 2 | 0 | 0 | 0 | | | | | |
| Totals | 41 | 9 | 13 | 8 | Totals | 33 | 2 | 8 | 2 |

Detroit ............................. 200 120 130— 9
Cleveland ......................... 200 000 000— 2
    Game Winning RBI — HJohnson (2).
    E—Fischlin 2, Jacoby 2, Brookens, CCastillo. DP—Detroit 1. LOB—Detroit 11, Cleveland 12. 2B—Gibson, Herndon 2, Hargrove, Jacoby, Vukovich, Trammell. HR—HJohnson (2). S—Trammell. SF—LNParrish 2.

| | IP | H | R | ER | BB | SO |
|---|---|---|---|---|---|---|
| **Detroit** | | | | | | |
| Petry W,4-1 | 5 | 6 | 2 | 2 | 6 | 5 |
| Hernandz S,3 | 4 | 2 | 0 | 0 | 1 | 4 |
| **Cleveland** | | | | | | |
| Spillner L,0-2 | 5 | 8 | 5 | 5 | 3 | 1 |
| Aponte | 2 | 4 | 3 | 2 | 0 | 0 |
| Jeffcoat | 2-3 | 1 | 1 | 0 | 0 | 0 |
| Frazier | 1 1-3 | 0 | 0 | 0 | 0 | 2 |

    Spillner pitched to 1 batter in 6th, Aponte pitched to 2 batters in 8th.
    HBP—CCastillo by Hernandez. WP—Petry, Hernandez. T—3:06. A—8,497.

It rained this morning and I didn't think we would get a chance to play. There was a steady mist throughout all nine innings.

Dan Petry went five innings and got the win, but he wasn't sharp. He threw 98 pitches and walked anybody who didn't swing. He walked the bases loaded in the fourth, then struck out the side. I will say this—Danny's got guts.

Lou Whitaker got four hits and Lance Parrish knocked in two runs with two sacrifice flies. I was proud of him. That's what we've worked so hard on: to never allow a man to die on third with less than two outs.

Chet Lemon stole the show in the sixth. He snuffed a Cleveland rally by robbing Carmen Castillo of extra bases with a great catch against the wall. Chester is the best centerfielder I have seen in my 31 years in baseball. There are a lot of good players on this team, but he's just as good as any of them. He never says he's tired, never complains. His strong will reminds me of Pete Rose.

I can't say this was a pretty game. It was ugly. But when you win an ugly game, it usually means good things are going to come.

# SATURDAY, MAY 5

## AT CLEVELAND

# GAME 25

## TIGERS 6, INDIANS 5

### (21-4, 5 GAMES AHEAD)

| DETROIT | ab | r | h | bi | CLEVELAND | ab | r | h | bi |
|---|---|---|---|---|---|---|---|---|---|
| Whitakr 2b | 4 | 1 | 1 | 0 | Butler cf | 4 | 1 | 1 | 0 |
| Trammi ss | 4 | 1 | 1 | 0 | Bernzrd 2b | 3 | 1 | 0 | 0 |
| Garbey 1b | 5 | 0 | 0 | 0 | Franco ss | 4 | 0 | 0 | 0 |
| LNPrsh dh | 4 | 0 | 0 | 0 | Thrntn dh | 3 | 1 | 2 | 1 |
| Herndon lf | 4 | 0 | 0 | 0 | Hargrv 1b | 4 | 0 | 2 | 1 |
| Lemon cf | 4 | 3 | 4 | 3 | Fischlin pr | 0 | 0 | 0 | 0 |
| Gibson rf | 4 | 1 | 1 | 0 | Hassey c | 4 | 0 | 1 | 0 |
| Brokns 3b | 2 | 0 | 1 | 0 | Jacoby 3b | 3 | 1 | 1 | 1 |
| HJhnsn 3b | 1 | 0 | 1 | 1 | Vukvch rf | 4 | 1 | 2 | 2 |
| Bergmn 1b | 0 | 0 | 0 | 0 | Nixon lf | 2 | 0 | 0 | 0 |
| MCastill c | 2 | 0 | 0 | 0 | Willard ph | 1 | 0 | 0 | 0 |
| Grubb ph | 1 | 0 | 1 | 1 | Rhombg lf | 0 | 0 | 0 | 0 |
| Lowry c | 1 | 0 | 0 | 0 | Perkins ph | 1 | 0 | 0 | 0 |
| Totals | 36 | 6 | 10 | 5 | Totals | 33 | 5 | 9 | 5 |

```
Detroit............................. 200 102 010— 6
Cleveland........................... 220 000 001— 5
```
Game Winning RBI — Grubb (2).
E—Gibson, Franco. DP—Detroit 1. LOB —Detroit 7, Cleveland 4. 2B—Jacoby, Trammell. HR—Vukovich (1), Lemon (7). SB—Whitaker (2), Trammell (8), MCastillo (1), Gibson (5), HJohnson (1). SF—Thornton, HJohnson, Jacoby.

| | IP | H | R | ER | BB | SO |
|---|---|---|---|---|---|---|
| Detroit | | | | | | |
| Abbott W,2-1 | 5 1-3 | 6 | 4 | 4 | 1 | 0 |
| Bair | 1 2-3 | 0 | 0 | 0 | 0 | 1 |
| Lopez S,3 | 2 | 3 | 1 | 1 | 0 | 3 |
| Cleveland | | | | | | |
| Heaton L,2-3 | 5 | 7 | 5 | 4 | 3 | 2 |
| Waddell | 2 | 2 | 1 | 1 | 0 | 0 |
| Jeffcoat | 1 | 1 | 0 | 0 | 0 | 1 |
| Camacho | 1 | 0 | 0 | 0 | 0 | 0 |

Heaton pitched to 2 batters in 6th, Waddell pitched to 1 batter in 8th.
T—2:57. A—9,282.

Chet Lemon did it with his bat today. Four hits and three RBIs. He hit a long home run. He's playing as good as anyone possibly can. He's got a new saying: "We mad and they don't even know it." I think he's right. That's the way this whole team is playing.

Glenn Abbott gave us 5-1/3 innings. That's all we needed from him. Doug Bair was super in the middle and Aurelio Lopez finished it out for us.

Broderick Perkins hit a long foul with one on and two out in the ninth before Lopey struck him out. My heart was beating 200 miles an hour before that ball hooked foul.

Lance Parrish and Larry Herndon are both still struggling, but I think they'll be okay when the warm weather hits.

# SUNDAY, MAY 6

## AT CLEVELAND

# GAME 26

## TIGERS 6, INDIANS 5

### (12 INNINGS)
### (22-4, 5 GAMES AHEAD)

| DETROIT | ab | r | h | bi | CLEVELAND | ab | r | h | bi |
|---|---|---|---|---|---|---|---|---|---|
| Whitakr 2b | 5 | 0 | 1 | 2 | Butler cf | 6 | 0 | 0 | 0 |
| Trammi ss | 7 | 0 | 3 | 1 | Bernzrd 2b | 6 | 0 | 0 | 0 |
| Gibson rf | 7 | 0 | 1 | 1 | Franco ss | 6 | 0 | 1 | 0 |
| LNParsh c | 6 | 0 | 1 | 0 | Thrntn dh | 5 | 2 | 2 | 0 |
| DEvns dh | 5 | 0 | 0 | 0 | Rhmbg pr | 0 | 0 | 0 | 0 |
| Grubb lf | 3 | 2 | 2 | 1 | Hargrv 1b | 6 | 2 | 2 | 1 |
| Kuntz lf | 0 | 0 | 0 | 0 | Tabler lf | 3 | 1 | 3 | 2 |
| Lemon cf | 6 | 1 | 1 | 0 | Nixon lf | 2 | 0 | 1 | 0 |
| Bergmn 1b | 5 | 2 | 3 | 0 | CCastill ph | 1 | 0 | 0 | 0 |
| HJhnsn 3b | 1 | 1 | 0 | 1 | Jacoby 3b | 4 | 0 | 1 | 0 |
| Brokns 3b | 0 | 0 | 0 | 0 | Willard c | 3 | 0 | 0 | 0 |
| | | | | | Perkins ph | 0 | 0 | 0 | 0 |
| | | | | | Hassey c | 0 | 0 | 0 | 0 |
| | | | | | Vukvch rf | 4 | 0 | 2 | 1 |
| Totals | 45 | 6 | 12 | 6 | Totals | 46 | 5 | 12 | 4 |

```
Detroit...................000 001 040 001— 6
Cleveland.................010 220 000 000— 5
```
Game Winning RBI — Whitaker (4).
LOB—Detroit 15, Cleveland 10. 2B—Gibson, Jacoby, Thornton, Hargrove, Bergman. HR—Grubb (2). S—Brookens 2, Jacoby.

| Detroit | IP | H | R | ER | BB | SO |
|---|---|---|---|---|---|---|
| Wilcox | 5 | 8 | 5 | 4 | 3 | 5 |
| Rozema | 2 | 0 | 0 | 0 | 0 | 0 |
| Hernandz | 3 | 1 | 0 | 0 | 0 | 2 |
| Lopez W,3-0 | 2 | 3 | 0 | 0 | 1 | 1 |
| Cleveland | | | | | | |
| Blyleven | 7 1-3 | 7 | 3 | 3 | 5 | 7 |
| Frazier | 0 | 0 | 2 | 2 | 2 | 0 |
| Jeffcoat | 1-3 | 1 | 0 | 0 | 1 | 0 |
| Waddell | 1 2-3 | 2 | 0 | 0 | 1 | 0 |
| Camacho L,0-2 | 2 2-3 | 2 | 1 | 1 | 1 | 1 |

PB—LNParrish. T—4:20. A—16,125.

No question about this game—we should have lost. It was one of those you remember in September and realize how big a bonus it was.

Toronto and Baltimore felt good watching the scoreboard early in the afternoon. But their hearts must have sunk when they watched TV that night. I know the feeling. We had it the whole month of September last year when Baltimore kept coming back from impossible deficits.

We were losing, 5-1, after the seventh inning. We got four hits in the eighth and then won it in the twelfth on Lou Whitaker's single. We worked them for four walks in the eighth inning and that really won the game.

We also got seven scoreless innings from our bullpen. When Jack Morris doesn't pitch, we really need our pen. It's been outstanding. The bullpen is basically why we're leading the league in ERA . . . and in the standings.

We got big hits from Dave Bergman, Chet Lemon, Alan Trammell, Kirk Gibson, Lance Parrish, and Johnny Grubb. It's amazing how everyone is chipping in. Even though he has a cold and has to wear dark glasses because of sun-blindness, Bergman was tremendous.

What a game!

**Chet Lemon says, "We mad and they don't even know it."** Photo by Clifton Boutelle

# MONDAY, MAY 7

## AT KANSAS CITY

# GAME 27

## TIGERS 10, ROYALS 3

### (23-4, 5½ GAMES AHEAD)

| DETROIT | ab | r | h | bi |
|---|---|---|---|---|
| Whitakr 2b | 5 | 0 | 1 | 0 |
| Tramml ss | 5 | 2 | 3 | 1 |
| Gibson rf | 3 | 2 | 1 | 1 |
| LNParsh c | 4 | 0 | 1 | 0 |
| Lowry c | 0 | 0 | 0 | 0 |
| DaEvns 1b | 3 | 2 | 1 | 2 |
| Brokns 3b | 0 | 0 | 0 | 0 |
| MCastil 3b | 1 | 0 | 0 | 0 |
| Herndon lf | 5 | 1 | 1 | 0 |
| Allen lf | 0 | 0 | 0 | 0 |
| Grubb dh | 3 | 1 | 2 | 2 |
| HJhnsn dh | 1 | 1 | 0 | 0 |
| Lemon cf | 3 | 1 | 2 | 3 |
| Kuntz cf | 0 | 0 | 0 | 0 |
| Garbey 3b | 4 | 0 | 0 | 0 |
| Totals | 37 | 10 | 12 | 9 |

| KANSAS CITY | ab | r | h | bi |
|---|---|---|---|---|
| Sheridn cf | 3 | 1 | 0 | 0 |
| Motley rf | 5 | 0 | 1 | 0 |
| Orta lf | 4 | 1 | 1 | 1 |
| McRae dh | 4 | 0 | 0 | 0 |
| White 2b | 4 | 1 | 3 | 0 |
| Balboni 1b | 3 | 0 | 1 | 2 |
| Slaught c | 4 | 0 | 1 | 0 |
| Pryor 3b | 3 | 0 | 0 | 0 |
| UWshtn ss | 3 | 0 | 0 | 0 |
| Totals | 33 | 3 | 7 | 3 |

Detroit ............................ 000 203 230—10
Kansas City ..................... 000 200 100— 3
Game Winning RBI — Grubb (3).
E—Orta. DP—Kansas City 1. LOB—Detroit 6, Kansas City 9. 2B—Slaught, Trammell, Balboni, Orta, Grubb, Lemon, White. 3B—Lemon, Gibson. HR—DaEvans (3). SB—Gibson (6), Herndon (3). S— Pryor, Gibson.

| | IP | H | R | ER | BB | SO |
|---|---|---|---|---|---|---|
| **Detroit** | | | | | | |
| Berenguer W,2-1 | 6 2-3 | 6 | 3 | 3 | 4 | 2 |
| Bair S,2 | 2 1-3 | 1 | 0 | 0 | 1 | 1 |
| **Kansas City** | | | | | | |
| Gubicza L,0-3 | 6 | 5 | 5 | 5 | 4 | 6 |
| Splittorff | 2 | 7 | 5 | 5 | 0 | 0 |
| Huismann | 1 | 0 | 0 | 0 | 1 | 1 |

WP—Bair. PB—Slaught. T—3:02. A—19,-474.

Juan Berenguer gave us 6-2/3 good innings; then Doug Bair wrapped it up. That's six straight times Doug has done his job. Trammell got three hits and is up to .373. Lemon had two more RBIs and has 27 in 27 games.

We're swinging the bat again. We're catching the ball even better. I think that's the key to our club—defense. It's the best I've ever seen.

On my walk this morning, I talked to Ernie Harwell. We couldn't believe that yet another player had been arrested for drugs. I don't understand the Players Association. Why don't they prohibit anyone caught using drugs from playing baseball ever again?

I mean that. We have a handful of guys casting a shadow over everyone's name, making people outside of baseball think that the whole game is into drugs. I will never believe that drug abuse is a sickness like heart disease. Drug abuse is not a sickness; it's a weakness of people who can't face reality.

It seems like players who use drugs have all that money and don't know what to do with it. They forget that God has been good to them and they could set themselves up financially for life. I honestly believe that if they hadn't tied Bowie Kuhn's hands, he would have stopped all this nonsense. I feel strongly that any player caught using drugs should be banned from baseball. It's as simple as that.

We should have a program established in every major league city that requires players to visit junior highs and high schools to talk about the evil of drugs. If our own ballplayers keep getting arrested for drug abuse, nobody is going to believe a thing we say. If we don't clean up our own backyard, you'll see baseball take a tailspin. Let's get rid of all the weaklings.

**Juan Berenguer delivers a strike.** Photo by Doc Holcomb, courtesy of *The Detroit News*

# TUESDAY, MAY 8

## AT KANSAS CITY

# GAME 28

## TIGERS 5, ROYALS 2

### (24-4, 6 GAMES AHEAD)

| DETROIT | ab | r | h | bi | KANSAS CITY | ab | r | h | bi |
|---|---|---|---|---|---|---|---|---|---|
| Whitakr 2b | 3 | 1 | 0 | 0 | Sheridn cf | 4 | 0 | 0 | 0 |
| Tramml ss | 4 | 1 | 1 | 4 | Motley rf | 4 | 0 | 1 | 1 |
| Garbey 1b | 3 | 0 | 1 | 0 | Orta lf | 4 | 1 | 2 | 1 |
| LNParsh c | 4 | 0 | 1 | 0 | McRae dh | 4 | 0 | 1 | 0 |
| Herndon lf | 4 | 1 | 2 | 0 | White 2b | 4 | 0 | 2 | 0 |
| DEvns dh | 4 | 1 | 2 | 0 | Balboni 1b | 3 | 0 | 0 | 0 |
| Lemon cf | 4 | 1 | 2 | 1 | Slaught c | 3 | 0 | 0 | 0 |
| Gibson rf | 4 | 0 | 0 | 0 | Ashford 3b | 3 | 0 | 0 | 0 |
| Brokns 3b | 4 | 0 | 0 | 0 | UWshtn ss | 2 | 1 | 1 | 0 |
| Totals | 34 | 5 | 9 | 5 | Totals | 31 | 2 | 7 | 2 |

```
Detroit ............................. 000  000  500— 5
Kansas City ...................... 000  011  000— 2
```
Game Winning RBI — Trammell (1).
DP—Detroit 1, Kansas City 1. LOB—Detroit 4. 2B—UWashingtn. HR—Orta (2), Trammell (3). SB—UWashingtn (2).

| | IP | H | R | ER | BB | SO |
|---|---|---|---|---|---|---|
| **Detroit** | | | | | | |
| Morris W,6-1 | 9 | 7 | 2 | 2 | 2 | 5 |
| **Kansas City** | | | | | | |
| Black L,3-2 | 6 2-3 | 7 | 4 | 4 | 2 | 4 |
| Quisenberry | 2 1-3 | 2 | 1 | 1 | 0 | 2 |

WP—Morris. T—2:35. A—14,304.

I can tell we're on a roll. The coaches, our writers, and broadcasters went to a luncheon hosted by *The Sporting News*. It was packed and everyone wanted to talk to us . . . to see if we're for real.

We gave the Royals a taste of the Tigers this evening. Even Dan Quisenberry couldn't hold us in the seventh. With the bases loaded, Quisenberry came in to face Alan Trammell. With anyone else, that would have been it, but not with Trammell. Quisenberry threw a breaking pitch for a strike before Alan belted one over the leftfield fence. It was the first grand slam Quisenberry ever gave up. After the game, Quisenberry cracked, "The wind stopped just before that inning began. Sparky must have some pretty high connections."

Not really. But I do have a super ballclub. In the third inning the Royals had the bases loaded with one out. Don Slaught hit a shot to Trammell's right. He dove for the ball, fired to Lou Whitaker for one out, and then Whitaker threw Slaught out at first. It was the best double play I'd ever seen.

I never thought I would ever see a shortstop as great as Dave Concepcion. Now I've seen one better. I think Alan Trammell may be the best player in baseball, and he's also a great person. He's a great family man and will not allow big money to change his character. He will definitely be a Hall of Famer.

# WEDNESDAY, MAY 9

## AT KANSAS CITY

# GAME 29

## TIGERS 3, ROYALS 1

### (25–4, 7½ GAMES AHEAD)

| DETROIT | ab | r | h | bi | KANSAS CITY | ab | r | h | bi |
|---|---|---|---|---|---|---|---|---|---|
| Whitakr 2b | 5 | 0 | 2 | 1 | Motley rf | 5 | 0 | 0 | 0 |
| Tramml ss | 5 | 1 | 3 | 0 | Sheridn cf | 4 | 0 | 1 | 0 |
| Garbey 1b | 4 | 0 | 1 | 0 | Orta lf | 3 | 0 | 1 | 0 |
| LNParsh c | 2 | 0 | 0 | 0 | McRae dh | 3 | 0 | 1 | 0 |
| MCastill c | 2 | 0 | 1 | 1 | White 2b | 4 | 0 | 0 | 0 |
| Herndon lf | 4 | 0 | 0 | 0 | Balboni 1b | 4 | 1 | 2 | 0 |
| DEvns dh | 3 | 1 | 3 | 0 | Wathan c | 3 | 0 | 1 | 1 |
| Lemon cf | 4 | 0 | 0 | 0 | Pryor 3b | 3 | 0 | 1 | 0 |
| Kuntz rf | 3 | 1 | 2 | 1 | OSnchz ph | 1 | 0 | 0 | 0 |
| Gibson rf | 1 | 0 | 0 | 0 | Ashford 3b | 0 | 0 | 0 | 0 |
| Brokns 3b | 4 | 0 | 0 | 0 | UWshtn ss | 3 | 0 | 0 | 0 |
| | | | | | Roberts ph | 1 | 0 | 0 | 0 |
| | | | | | Cncpcn ss | 0 | 0 | 0 | 0 |
| Totals | 37 | 3 | 12 | 3 | Totals | 34 | 1 | 7 | 1 |

```
Detroit .............................. 020 010 000— 3
Kansas City ........................ 000 001 000— 1
```
Game Winning RBI — Kuntz (2).
E—DJackson, Trammell, Whitaker, Balboni. DP—Kansas City 2. LOB—Detroit 8, Kansas City 11. 2B—DaEvans, Kuntz, Balboni, Wathan.

| | IP | H | R | ER | BB | SO |
|---|---|---|---|---|---|---|
| **Detroit** | | | | | | |
| Petry W,5-1 | 6 2-3 | 7 | 1 | 1 | 4 | 5 |
| Lopez S,4 | 2 1-3 | 0 | 0 | 0 | 1 | 4 |
| **Kansas City** | | | | | | |
| DJackson L,0-4 | 6 | 9 | 3 | 2 | 1 | 2 |
| Huismann | 2 | 2 | 0 | 0 | 0 | 2 |
| Quisnbry | 1 | 1 | 0 | 0 | 0 | 0 |

WP—DJackson. T—2:48. A—15,709.

This was a great day for us. Dan Petry was on until he walked two men with two out in the seventh. But that's no problem with our bullpen. I brought in Aurelio Lopez and I never saw him throw harder. Lopey threw the hardest I've ever seen him throw for 2-2/3 innings. He struck out four and no one had a chance to hit off of him. Lopey never seems to be scared. When he's on top of his game, he's better than Clay Carroll used to be for me. And Carroll was some kind of pitcher.

Trammell had three hits again and I can't believe the plays he's making in the field. It's a laugh when people talk about who's the best shortstop in the game. Tram is head and shoulders over everyone. I mean *everyone*.

The writers made a big deal of us tying the 1955 Dodgers for the best 29-game start in history. 25–4 . . . that's great. But I keep telling my boys that this is an every night thing. I tell them we can't do it all in just one game. Don't hang your head if you lose. Don't try to make tomorrow come before it comes and don't bring yesterday with you. Just go out everyday and try to win.

# THURSDAY, MAY 10

## AT DETROIT

## (25–4, 7 GAMES AHEAD)

We had an day off in Detroit. This was our first chance to sleep in until early afternoon. We're on top of the world at 25–4. What a great feeling to relax at home and listen to all the nice things they're saying about us on radio and TV.

**Willie Hernandez saves the day.**   Photo by Doc Holcomb, courtesy of *The Detroit News*

# FRIDAY, MAY 11

## AT DETROIT

# GAME 30

## TIGERS 8, ANGELS 2

### (26-4, 7½ GAMES AHEAD)

| CALIFORNIA | ab | r | h | bi | DETROIT | ab | r | h | bi |
|---|---|---|---|---|---|---|---|---|---|
| Carew 1b | 5 | 0 | 1 | 0 | Whitakr 2b | 5 | 1 | 2 | 0 |
| Beniquz rf | 5 | 0 | 2 | 1 | Tramml ss | 4 | 0 | 0 | 0 |
| Lynn cf | 5 | 0 | 1 | 0 | Gibson rf | 5 | 2 | 2 | 1 |
| DeCncs 3b | 4 | 1 | 2 | 1 | DEvns dh | 4 | 2 | 2 | 2 |
| Picciolo 3b | 1 | 0 | 0 | 0 | Grubb lf | 2 | 0 | 1 | 0 |
| ReJksn dh | 4 | 0 | 0 | 0 | Herndon lf | 3 | 1 | 2 | 0 |
| Downing lf | 3 | 0 | 1 | 0 | Garbey 3b | 2 | 1 | 2 | 1 |
| Wilfong 2b | 4 | 0 | 1 | 0 | HJhnsn 1b | 0 | 0 | 0 | 0 |
| Narron c | 4 | 0 | 2 | 0 | Bergmn 1b | 3 | 1 | 2 | 3 |
| Schofild ss | 3 | 1 | 1 | 0 | Brokns 3b | 1 | 0 | 0 | 0 |
| | | | | | Lemon cf | 5 | 0 | 0 | 1 |
| | | | | | Kuntz cf | 0 | 0 | 0 | 0 |
| | | | | | Lowry c | 4 | 0 | 1 | 0 |
| Totals | 38 | 2 | 11 | 2 | Totals | 38 | 8 | 14 | 8 |

```
California.........................000  000  011— 2
Detroit ...........................020  302  10x— 8
```

Game Winning RBI — Bergman (1).
E—Schofield, Whitaker. DP—Detroit 1. LOB—California 11, Detroit 13. 2B—Lynn, DeCinces, Whitaker, Lowry, Herndon. 3B—Bergman. HR—DeCinces (6), Gibson (5). SB—Gibson (7). S—Lowry.

| | IP | H | R | ER | BB | SO |
|---|---|---|---|---|---|---|
| California | | | | | | |
| Witt L,4-2 | 3 2-3 | 7 | 5 | 5 | 3 | 4 |
| Curtis | 1 2-3 | 5 | 2 | 2 | 2 | 0 |
| Kaufman | 2 2-3 | 2 | 1 | 1 | 1 | 3 |
| Detroit | | | | | | |
| Wilcox W,4-0 | 6 | 6 | 0 | 0 | 1 | 5 |
| Hernandz S,4 | 3 | 5 | 2 | 2 | 0 | 0 |

HBP—Schofield by Wilcox. WP—Curtis.
T—2:55. A—44,187.

Tonight we got a chance to break the Dodgers' record. It was a summery day in spring and everyone has been talking about the Tigers. I was up early to appear on "Good Morning America" with our owner Tom Monaghan. Tom flew to New York to appear. I did the broadcast from the Detroit studio. I think I did most of the talking. I couldn't help it. It's about time this club got the national attention it deserves.

Over 44,000 people came to see us break the record. That's incredible attendance for May in Detroit. If we don't crack 2½ million this year, I'll be disappointed.

We didn't disappoint the fans tonight. Milt Wilcox gave us six shutout innings and Willie Hernandez finished again. The place went crazy. They were doing the Wave, screaming and jumping up and down in the stands. Friday nights at Tiger Stadium are a circus. Kirk Gibson, Barbaro Garbey, and Dave Bergman each had two hits. Bergman made two big plays in the field and tripled home the game-winner in the second.

# SATURDAY, MAY 12

## AT DETROIT

# GAME 31

## ANGELS 4, TIGERS 2

### (26–5, 7½ GAMES AHEAD)

```
CALIFORNIA              DETROIT
          ab r h bi              ab r h bi
Wilfong 2b  4 1 1 1   Whitakr 2b  4 0 2 0
Beniquz rf  4 1 0 0   Tramml ss   4 0 0 0
ReJksn dh   4 1 1 2   Garbey 1b   4 1 1 0
DeCncs 3b   5 1 3 0   Herndon lf  3 0 1 0
Downing lf  4 0 1 0   Lemon cf    4 1 2 1
Pettis cf   0 0 0 0   DEvns dh    3 0 0 0
Lynn cf     4 0 2 1   Brokns 3b   3 0 0 0
Narron 1b   4 0 0 0   Gibson rf   3 0 1 0
Boone c     4 0 2 0   MCastill c  2 0 0 0
Schofild ss 4 0 1 0   Kuntz ph    1 0 1 0
                      Lowry c     0 0 0 0
Totals     37 4 11 4  Totals     31 2 8 1
```

California........................000 020 110— 4
Detroit...........................010 100 000— 2
    Game Winning RBI — Lynn (4).
    E—Boone, Brookens, Berenguer. DP—
California 4, Detroit 2. LOB—California 10,
Detroit 4. 2B—DeCinces. HR—ReJackson
(7), Wilfong (3). SB—Lemon (2), DaEvans
(1).

```
                        IP   H R ER BB SO
California
John W,3-3              9     8 2  2  2  2
Detroit
Berengur L,2-2         6 2-3 10 3  3  3  6
Lopez                  2 1-3  1 1  1  0  0
```
HBP—ReJackson by Berenguer. WP—
Berenguer. T—2:22. A—38,514.

Today was a boo-boo. A big, bad boo-boo. And I was a big part of it.

We were on national television again and I must have put on a pretty good show.

Second base umpire Ted Hendry called an automatic double play on Chet Lemon after Larry Herndon went out of the baseline to take out the shortstop on a grounder in the ninth. I exploded when he told me Herndon was ten feet out of the line. I threw my hat and tried to throw home plate umpire Jim Evans off me after he grabbed me. I saw the replays after the game and admitted I was wrong. But not by ten feet.

That's not what beat us, though. Tommy John did. He was a master. He scattered eight hits and showed us why he's been so good for so long.

Reggie Jackson hit one over the right field roof. Amazing how Reggie always plays so good on national TV.

My mother watched the game back home in California. She called me and said, "Georgie, why did you act like that?"

# SUNDAY, MAY 13

## AT DETROIT

## RAINED OUT
## (26–5, 7½ GAMES AHEAD)

We started today's game, but rain finally stopped it. Jack Morris was pitching and now we have to move him back to Tuesday. I hate to do that because it can throw off a pitcher.

**Catcher Lance Parrish makes a close play at home.**  Photo by Doc Holcomb, courtesy of *The Detroit News*

# MONDAY, MAY 14

## AT DETROIT

# GAME 32

## TIGERS 7, MARINERS 5

### (27-5, 8 GAMES AHEAD)

| SEATTLE | ab | r | h | bi | | DETROIT | ab | r | h | bi |
|---|---|---|---|---|---|---|---|---|---|---|
| Percont 2b | 4 | 0 | 0 | 0 | | Whitakr 2b | 5 | 0 | 1 | 1 |
| SHndsn dh | 4 | 0 | 0 | 0 | | Trammi ss | 5 | 1 | 3 | 2 |
| GThoms lf | 5 | 1 | 1 | 0 | | Garbey 1b | 4 | 0 | 2 | 0 |
| Putnam 1b | 4 | 1 | 2 | 1 | | LNParsh c | 3 | 1 | 2 | 0 |
| Cowens rf | 3 | 2 | 3 | 2 | | Herndon lf | 4 | 0 | 2 | 0 |
| Bonnell cf | 2 | 1 | 0 | 0 | | Lemon cf | 4 | 0 | 1 | 1 |
| Coles 3b | 3 | 0 | 0 | 0 | | DEvns dh | 3 | 1 | 0 | 0 |
| Milborn 3b | 1 | 0 | 1 | 1 | | Kuntz rf | 4 | 3 | 3 | 1 |
| Kearney c | 4 | 0 | 0 | 0 | | Brokns 3b | 2 | 0 | 0 | 1 |
| Owen ss | 4 | 0 | 2 | 0 | | Bergmn 1b | 1 | 1 | 1 | 1 |
| Totals | 34 | 5 | 9 | 4 | | Totals | 35 | 7 | 15 | 7 |

```
Seattle .......................... 000  201  020—  5
Detroit .......................... 120  110  02x—  7
```

Game Winning RBI — Bergman (2).
E—Owen, Petry, Whitaker. DP—Seattle
2, Detroit 2. LOB—Seattle 7, Detroit 7. 2B—
GThomas, Kuntz. 3B—Bergman. HR—Trammell (4), Cowens (4), Kuntz (1). S—Bonnell.
SF—Brookens.

| | IP | H | R | ER | BB | SO |
|---|---|---|---|---|---|---|
| **Seattle** | | | | | | |
| VandBerg L,2-2 | 7 1-3 | 13 | 6 | 6 | 2 | 1 |
| Beard | 2-3 | 2 | 1 | 1 | 0 | 1 |
| **Detroit** | | | | | | |
| Petry | 5 | 6 | 3 | 3 | 2 | 1 |
| Bair | 2 | 1 | 2 | 2 | 2 | 1 |
| Lopez W,4-0 | 2 | 2 | 0 | 0 | 0 | 2 |

Petry pitched to 3 batters in the 6th.
BK—VandeBerg. T—3:05. A—18,830.

Here's one we shouldn't have won. Wins like this give you a cushion when you need it.

Seattle tied the score with two runs in the top of the eighth. Rusty Kuntz and Dave Bergman got it back in the last half of the inning. With one out, Kuntz doubled for his third hit. He's up to .440 now and is really doing a job. Then Bergman came off the bench for a triple. Whitaker singled home the insurance run.

Dan Petry and Doug Bair had rough outings. Aurelio Lopez pitched the last two innings for the win. It wasn't pretty, but it counted.

The worst part of the day came after the game. I tried to call my mother and father five times from the park. After the game, Mama called me to say Daddy was in the hospital. He's got a spot on his lung and it doesn't look good. It sure puts things into perspective; baseball seems so important until something like this happens.

# TUESDAY, MAY 15

## AT DETROIT

# GAME 33

## TIGERS 6, MARINERS 4

### (28–5, 8 GAMES AHEAD)

| SEATTLE | ab | r | h | bi | DETROIT | ab | r | h | bi |
|---|---|---|---|---|---|---|---|---|---|
| Perconte 2b | 4 | 0 | 0 | 0 | Whitaker 2b | 4 | 1 | 2 | 0 |
| DHendrsn ph | 1 | 0 | 0 | 0 | Trammell ss | 2 | 1 | 0 | 1 |
| Milbourne 3b | 4 | 1 | 1 | 0 | Gibson rf | 2 | 1 | 0 | 2 |
| GThomas lf | 2 | 0 | 0 | 0 | Evans dh | 3 | 1 | 1 | 1 |
| Putnam 1b | 3 | 0 | 0 | 1 | Grubb lf | 2 | 0 | 0 | 0 |
| Bradely c | 1 | 0 | 0 | 0 | Herndon lf | 3 | 0 | 1 | 0 |
| Cowens rf | 4 | 0 | 0 | 0 | Bergman 1b | 2 | 0 | 0 | 0 |
| Bonnell cf | 4 | 0 | 1 | 0 | Johnson 3b | 2 | 0 | 1 | 2 |
| SHendrsn dh | 3 | 1 | 1 | 0 | Brookens 3b | 1 | 0 | 0 | 0 |
| Kearney c | 4 | 1 | 1 | 0 | Lemon cf | 1 | 1 | 0 | 0 |
| Owen ss | 3 | 1 | 1 | 3 | Lowry c | 3 | 1 | 0 | 0 |
| Totals | 33 | 4 | 5 | 4 | Totals | 25 | 6 | 5 | 6 |

Seattle .................................. 100 000 300 — 4
Detroit .................................. 103 002 00x — 6

Game-winning RBI — Evans (4).

E—Johnson, Kearney, Whitaker, Perconte, Trammell. DP—Seattle 1, Detroit 2. LOB—Seattle 8, Detroit 11. HR—Owen (1). SB—Trammell (9), Owen (5). S— Lowry, Bergman. SF—Gibson 2.

| | IP | H | R | ER | BB | SO |
|---|---|---|---|---|---|---|
| **Seattle** | | | | | | |
| RThomas (L 3-2) | 2-2-3 | 3 | 4 | 3 | 6 | 2 |
| Mirabella | 3 2-3 | 1 | 2 | 0 | 3 | 4 |
| Stoddard | 1 2-3 | 1 | 0 | 0 | 3 | 2 |
| **Detroit** | | | | | | |
| Morris (W 7-1) | 7 | 3 | 4 | 3 | 5 | 4 |
| Hernandez (S 5) | 2 | 2 | 0 | 0 | 1 | 5 |

WP—Morris. PB—Lowry. T—3:32. A—21,782.

Today we had our second straight sloppy win. Jack Morris got another win, but I didn't like what I saw. Jack had a 6-1 lead and started to fool around. He just wasn't Jack Morris tonight. Willie Hernandez came in with a two-run lead and struck out five in the last two innings.

Alan Trammell threw a ball away. We were sloppy all around. I think I'll play all my righthanders tomorrow because we're just going through the motions now.

**Rusty Kuntz.**  Photo courtesy of Detroit Tigers       **Dave Bergman.**  Photo courtesy of Detroit Tigers

# WEDNESDAY, MAY 16

## AT DETROIT

# GAME 34

## TIGERS 10, MARINERS 1

### (29-5, 8 GAMES AHEAD)

| SEATTLE | ab | r | h | bi | DETROIT | ab | r | h | bi |
|---|---|---|---|---|---|---|---|---|---|
| Percont 2b | 3 | 0 | 1 | 0 | Whitakr 2b | 5 | 1 | 2 | 1 |
| SHndsn dh | 4 | 0 | 0 | 1 | Traml dh | 3 | 1 | 1 | 1 |
| Cowens rf | 4 | 0 | 0 | 0 | Grubb ph | 1 | 1 | 1 | 1 |
| Putnam 1b | 4 | 0 | 0 | 0 | Garbey 1b | 4 | 1 | 1 | 1 |
| Bonnell lf | 4 | 0 | 3 | 0 | Bergmn 1b | 0 | 1 | 0 | 0 |
| DHndsn cf | 4 | 0 | 0 | 0 | LNParsh c | 4 | 2 | 2 | 0 |
| Coles 3b | 2 | 0 | 0 | 0 | Lowry c | 1 | 1 | 1 | 1 |
| Kearney c | 3 | 0 | 1 | 0 | Herndon lf | 4 | 0 | 1 | 1 |
| Mercado c | 0 | 0 | 0 | 0 | Lemon cf | 5 | 0 | 2 | 0 |
| Owen ss | 1 | 1 | 1 | 0 | Kuntz rf | 4 | 2 | 1 | 2 |
| Ramos ss | 1 | 0 | 0 | 0 | MCastil 3b | 3 | 0 | 1 | 2 |
| | | | | | Brookns ss | 3 | 0 | 1 | 0 |
| Totals | 30 | 1 | 6 | 1 | Totals | 37 | 10 | 14 | 10 |

```
Seattle ............................ 001  000  000— 1
Detroit ........................... 501  010  03x— 10
```

Game Winning RBI — Trammell (2).
DP—Detroit 1. LOB—Seattle 5, Detroit 8.
2B—Bonnell 2, Owen, Lemon, Kuntz, Lowry.
3B—Trammell. HR—Grubb (3). SB—Kuntz
(1). S—Perconte.

| Seattle | IP | H | R | ER | BB | SO |
|---|---|---|---|---|---|---|
| MYoung L,2-3 | 4 2-3 | 11 | 7 | 7 | 4 | 3 |
| RThomas | 1-3 | 0 | 0 | 0 | 0 | 0 |
| Stoddard | 1 | 0 | 0 | 0 | 0 | 1 |
| Mirabella | 1 | 0 | 0 | 0 | 0 | 1 |
| Beard | 1 | 3 | 3 | 3 | 0 | 0 |
| Detroit | | | | | | |
| Wilcox W,5-0 | 6 | 4 | 1 | 1 | 2 | 5 |
| Bair | 1 | 1 | 0 | 0 | 0 | 0 |
| Hernandz | 1 | 0 | 0 | 0 | 0 | 0 |
| Lopez | 1 | 1 | 0 | 0 | 0 | 1 |

HBP—Bergman by Beard. WP—
MYoung, Beard. T—2:52. A—22,001.

Today I was on CBS Morning News—again with Tom Monaghan and again the same questions. That's all right, though; the nation is getting to know the Detroit Tigers.

We hammered Seattle tonight with a big five spot in the first inning. Alan Trammell had a stiff shoulder, but he tripled home the game-winner as a designated hitter in the first. Milt Wilcox was outstanding for six innings. He's getting his curve over and could win 20 this year.

But I really couldn't enjoy the game. My daughter, Shirlee, called to tell me about Daddy. There's a large tumor on his lung. She cried like a baby on the phone. I told Shirlee to say a prayer to herself and somehow, Grandpa will know.

I have to admit I felt like crying myself. I know why I love Daddy so much. He had no education and he was only a laborer, but everything he did, he did for his family.

Here I am on top of the baseball mountain, but without this one man who never went to school and never had any money, I would never be where I am.

I know in my heart that God loves us regardless of what we do. That's the same as with Daddy—he has loved all of us so much. He never had to tell me that—I knew it in my heart. I'm one of the luckiest people in the world to have been loved so much.

Please, God, help the doctors work this out.

# THURSDAY, MAY 17

## AT DETROIT

## (29–5, 7½ GAMES AHEAD)

What do you think about when your Daddy is dying? How do you keep your mind on anything else?

Walking with my wife Carol today, I thought of all the little things, all those meaningless little day-to-day things that really mean so much. Most of those things in my memory happened so long, long ago—yet it seems like yesterday.

I thought about playing ball across the street when Ralph's Market parking lot was the best stadium in the world. I remember how Daddy threw to me on the lawn and pulled so hard for us when we played American Legion ball. I even remembered when we lived in Bridgewater, South Dakota, next to the jail that was never locked.

The operation was scheduled for two o'clock Detroit time. I had a bad feeling about it.

The two o'clock operation never came. Instead there was a phone call from Mama. The sound of her voice told the whole story. Before the operation began, Daddy's heart gave out. He fell back on the table. He didn't suffer at all, and that would have made him happy. Daddy didn't want anyone to worry about him.

I dreaded telling Shirlee. I'll never forget her scream when I finally called her on the phone. She loved Grandpa so much.

I talked to Mama again to tell her Daddy was with God. When I go, I'm not sure where it will be, but Daddy's up with God. He never hurt a soul. He always told me, "Be nice to people. It'll never cost you a dime. Courtesy and honesty are free."

I'll never forget that lesson. I'll never be able to talk with Daddy or see his face again. But I'll never lose him.

Carol and I will fly to California tonight. I'll talk to Shirlee and try to explain that Grandpa can finally rest. I'm not sure I'll do my walking anymore. Too much time to think about all of the good people I've met.

Daddy is dead. He was 74.

# FRIDAY, MAY 18

## AT DETROIT

# GAME 35

## TIGERS 8, A'S 4

### (30–5, 7½ GAMES AHEAD)

| OAKLAND | ab | r | h | bi | DETROIT | ab | r | h | bi |
|---|---|---|---|---|---|---|---|---|---|
| Henderson lf | 2 | 0 | 1 | 0 | Whitaker 2b | 3 | 0 | 0 | 0 |
| Murphy cf | 3 | 1 | 1 | 1 | Trammell ss | 1 | 2 | 0 | 0 |
| Morgan 2b | 2 | 1 | 0 | 0 | Garbey 1b | 3 | 2 | 2 | 1 |
| Kingman dh | 3 | 1 | 1 | 0 | Parrish c | 3 | 1 | 2 | 2 |
| Lansford 3b | 2 | 0 | 1 | 0 | Herndon lf | 3 | 1 | 1 | 1 |
| Bochte 1b | 2 | 0 | 1 | 1 | Evans dh | 3 | 1 | 1 | 1 |
| Davis rf | 2 | 1 | 1 | 2 | Lemon cf | 2 | 1 | 1 | 0 |
| Heath c | 2 | 0 | 0 | 0 | Gibson rf | 3 | 0 | 1 | 2 |
| Phillips ss | 2 | 0 | 1 | 0 | Castillo 3b | 3 | 0 | 1 | 1 |
| Totals | 20 | 4 | 7 | 4 | Totals | 24 | 8 | 9 | 8 |

Oakland .................................001 300—4
Detroit ....................................511 10—8
(Game called one out top of 6th, rain)
Game-winning RBI—Parrish (3). DP—
Detroit 2. LOB—Oakland 2, Detroit 4. 2B—
Bochte. HR—Garbey (1), Davis (2), Evans (4), Murphy (5). SB— Trammell 2 (11), Garbey (2).

| | IP | H | R | ER | BB | SO |
|---|---|---|---|---|---|---|
| **Oakland** | | | | | | |
| Krueger (1-1) | 1 1-3 | 6 | 6 | 6 | 2 | 1 |
| Codiroll | 3 2-3 | 3 | 2 | 2 | 1 | 2 |
| **Detroit** | | | | | | |
| Petry (W 6-1) | 5 1-3 | 7 | 4 | 4 | 2 | 4 |

T—2:08. A—41,136.

Shirlee and I talked this morning. I think she understood. We spent the day in Riverside with Mama before visiting the funeral home late in the afternoon.

Daddy looked so peaceful. I knew he didn't suffer. That made me feel good. We put on Daddy's ring, the one he wore so proudly since 1949. I got it for being batboy on the Hollywood Stars championship team. He also wore his Detroit shirt that had a blue Tiger emblem. Mama said he was so proud of that shirt.

It seemed like thousands of people came by the house to say hello to Mama. They brought enough food to keep Mama out of the stores for weeks.

I checked on the Tiger score, just to see who won. We beat Oakland and I knew Daddy would have liked that.

\* \* \* \*

The Tigers won the game when it was called because of rain after 5½ innings. The Oakland team complained.

Dan Petry scattered seven hits for his seventh victory. Barbaro Garbey and Darrell Evans homered, and Lance Parrish knocked in a pair of runs.

# SATURDAY, MAY 19

## AT DETROIT

# GAME 36

## TIGERS 5, A'S 4

### (31-5, 7½ GAMES AHEAD)

| OAKLAND | ab | r | h | bi | DETROIT | ab | r | h | bi |
|---|---|---|---|---|---|---|---|---|---|
| RHndsn lf | 4 | 0 | 1 | 0 | Whitakr 2b | 4 | 1 | 2 | 2 |
| Murphy cf | 4 | 2 | 2 | 1 | Trammll ss | 4 | 0 | 0 | 0 |
| Morgan 2b | 5 | 0 | 1 | 0 | Gibson rf | 3 | 2 | 1 | 0 |
| Kngmn dh | 4 | 1 | 1 | 1 | LNParsh c | 3 | 1 | 2 | 0 |
| Lansfrd 3b | 2 | 1 | 0 | 0 | DEvns dh | 4 | 0 | 3 | 2 |
| Bochte 1b | 4 | 0 | 1 | 0 | Garbey 3b | 3 | 0 | 0 | 1 |
| MDavis rf | 3 | 0 | 2 | 2 | Brokns 3b | 0 | 0 | 0 | 0 |
| Heath c | 2 | 0 | 0 | 0 | Grubb lf | 2 | 0 | 1 | 0 |
| Hancck ph | 1 | 0 | 0 | 0 | Kuntz lf | 1 | 1 | 0 | 0 |
| Essian c | 0 | 0 | 0 | 0 | Lemon cf | 3 | 0 | 2 | 0 |
| Phillips ss | 3 | 0 | 1 | 0 | Bergmn 1b | 3 | 0 | 0 | 0 |
| Burghs ph | 1 | 0 | 0 | 0 | | | | | |
| Wagner ss | 0 | 0 | 0 | 0 | | | | | |
| Totals | 33 | 4 | 9 | 4 | Totals | 30 | 5 | 11 | 5 |

```
Oakland ..........................100 000 021— 4
Detroit .............................101 011 10x— 5
```
Game Winning RBI — Whitaker (5).
E—Heath. DP—Oakland 1.LOB—Detroit 9. 2B—MDavis. 3B—LNParrish. HR—Whitaker (4), Murphy (6). SB—Morgan (5), RHenderson (11), Gibson (8), Trammell (12). S—Bergman. SF—Kingman, Garbey.

| | IP | H | R | ER | BB | SO |
|---|---|---|---|---|---|---|
| **Oakland** | | | | | | |
| McCatty L,3-3 | 5 | 9 | 4 | 4 | 4 | 1 |
| Burgmeier | 1 | 0 | 0 | 0 | 1 | 1 |
| Atherton | 2 | 2 | 1 | 1 | 1 | 0 |
| **Detroit** | | | | | | |
| Morris W,8-1 | 7 1-3 | 8 | 3 | 3 | 6 | 6 |
| Lopez S,5 | 1 2-3 | 1 | 1 | 1 | 0 | 0 |

McCatty pitched to 2 batters in 6th.
T—3:00. A—42,906.

The funeral was at nine o'clock and the turnout was terrific. Mama whispered to Daddy, "I'm going to miss you, Ole Pal," and I knew what friendship was all about.

Daddy wore his ring and Tiger shirt proudly. I only wish he had a transistor radio because he loved listening to our games so much.

My two sisters will stay with Mama for awhile and then her life will go on alone. After awhile, I think I'll have her join us. We'll make sure the rest of her years are outstanding.

I checked the score again and would you believe we won another? A 5-4 thriller and now we're 31-5.

\* \* \* \*

The Tigers took a 5-1 load into the eighth and then held on for a one-run victory. Jack Morris notched his eighth victory and Aurelio Lopez finished for his fifth save.

Lou Whitaker belted a homer and Darrell Evans knocked in a pair of runs and collected three hits.

## SUNDAY, MAY 20

### AT DETROIT

# GAME 37

## TIGERS 4, A'S 3

### (32-5, 8½ GAMES AHEAD)

| OAKLAND | ab | r | h | bi | | DETROIT | ab | r | h | bi |
|---|---|---|---|---|---|---|---|---|---|---|
| RHndsn lf | 3 | 1 | 0 | 0 | | Whitakr 2b | 4 | 0 | 0 | 0 |
| Murphy cf | 4 | 0 | 0 | 0 | | Tramml ss | 4 | 0 | 1 | 0 |
| Morgan 2b | 4 | 0 | 0 | 1 | | Gibson rf | 4 | 1 | 1 | 0 |
| Kngmn dh | 4 | 0 | 0 | 0 | | DaEvns 1b | 4 | 1 | 1 | 0 |
| Lansfrd 3b | 4 | 0 | 1 | 0 | | Bergmn 1b | 0 | 0 | 0 | 0 |
| Bochte 1b | 2 | 1 | 1 | 0 | | Herndon lf | 4 | 0 | 2 | 0 |
| Almon 1b | 1 | 0 | 0 | 0 | | Grubb dh | 2 | 1 | 1 | 1 |
| MDavis rf | 2 | 0 | 0 | 0 | | LNPrsh dh | 1 | 0 | 1 | 0 |
| Essian c | 1 | 0 | 0 | 0 | | Lemon cf | 4 | 0 | 1 | 0 |
| Heath c | 3 | 1 | 2 | 2 | | Garbey 3b | 3 | 0 | 1 | 1 |
| Phillips ss | 2 | 0 | 0 | 0 | | Brokns 3b | 0 | 0 | 0 | 0 |
| Burghs ph | 1 | 0 | 0 | 0 | | Lowry c | 3 | 1 | 1 | 1 |
| Wagner ss | 0 | 0 | 0 | 0 | | | | | | |
| Totals | 31 | 3 | 4 | 3 | | Totals | 33 | 4 | 10 | 3 |

```
Oakland ..........................011  000  010— 3
Detroit ..........................210  100  00x— 4
     Game Winning RBI — None.
     E—RHenderson, Trammell. DP—Oak-
land 1, Detroit 1. LOB—Oakland 2, Detroit 6.
2B—Bochte. HR—Lowry (1), Heath (2). SB—
RHenderson (12).
```

| | IP | H | R | ER | BB | SO |
|---|---|---|---|---|---|---|
| **Oakland** | | | | | | |
| Sorensen L,1-6 | 6 2-3 | 9 | 4 | 2 | 1 | 3 |
| Conroy | 1 | 1 | 0 | 0 | 0 | 3 |
| Caudill | 1-3 | 0 | 0 | 0 | 0 | 0 |
| **Detroit** | | | | | | |
| Wilcox W,6-0 | 6 | 3 | 2 | 2 | 1 | 0 |
| Hernandez S,6 | 3 | 1 | 1 | 1 | 0 | 2 |

T—2:22. A—27,073.

We spent the day weeding at my son Albert's house before visiting my other son, Lee. We tuned in the news to find out the Tigers won another game. Milt Wilcox won his sixth straight without a loss with another strong six innings. Sixes must have been wild because Willie Hernandez notched his sixth save.

Dwight Lowry is a rookie catcher with us. He hit his first major league home run, so you know he'll never forget May 20.

I'm anxious to return to the team and will meet them in Anaheim on Tuesday. It seems so strange having to listen to the news to find out what my team did. 32-5 . . . it seems they're doing all right without me.

## MONDAY, MAY 21

### AT DETROIT

### (32-5, 8 GAMES AHEAD)

My last day away from the team. I had a long talk with Mama and then ordered pizza—Domino's, of course.

The team played an exhibition game against Cincinnati. We played all of our substitutes and still won, 3-2. That sure shows our depth.

# TUESDAY, MAY 22

## AT ANAHEIM

# GAME 38

## TIGERS 3, ANGELS 1

### (33–5, 8 GAMES AHEAD)

| DETROIT | ab | r | h | bi | CALIFORNIA | ab | r | h | bi |
|---|---|---|---|---|---|---|---|---|---|
| Whitaker 2b | 5 | 0 | 2 | 0 | Pettis cf | 4 | 0 | 0 | 0 |
| Trammell ss | 4 | 1 | 1 | 0 | Carew 1b | 3 | 1 | 2 | 1 |
| Gibson rf | 2 | 1 | 1 | 0 | Lynn rf | 4 | 0 | 1 | 0 |
| Parrish c | 3 | 0 | 1 | 1 | DeCinces 3b | 2 | 0 | 0 | 0 |
| Evans dh | 3 | 0 | 0 | 0 | Picciolo pr | 0 | 0 | 0 | 0 |
| Kuntz pr | 0 | 0 | 0 | 0 | ReJacksn dh | 3 | 0 | 0 | 0 |
| Herndon lf | 3 | 0 | 0 | 1 | Downing lf | 4 | 0 | 1 | 0 |
| Bergman 1b | 3 | 1 | 1 | 0 | Wilfong 2b | 4 | 0 | 1 | 0 |
| Lemon cf | 3 | 0 | 0 | 1 | Boone c | 4 | 0 | 0 | 0 |
| Johnson 3b | 3 | 0 | 1 | 0 | Schofield ss | 3 | 0 | 0 | 0 |
| BrTookens 3b | 1 | 0 | 0 | 0 | | | | | |
| Totals | 30 | 3 | 7 | 3 | Totals | 31 | 1 | 5 | 1 |

```
Detroit.........................110 000 010— 3
California......................100 000 000— 1
```

Game-winning RBI — Lemon (2).

E—Boone. DP—California 1. LOB— Detroit 7, California 7. 2B—Bergman, Lynn. HR —Carew (3). SB—Gibson (9). S —Parrish. SF —Herndon.

| | IP | H | R | ER | BB | SO |
|---|---|---|---|---|---|---|
| **Detroit** | | | | | | |
| Berenguer (W 3-2) | 6 | 3 | 1 | 1 | 3 | 9 |
| Lopez (S 6) | 3 | 2 | 0 | 0 | 1 | 4 |
| **California** | | | | | | |
| Witt (L 4-4) | 7 | 7 | 3 | 3 | 2 | 6 |
| Corbett | 2 | 0 | 0 | 0 | 1 | 0 |

Witt pitched to 2 batters in 8th.

HBP—by Witt (Bergman, Gibson). Balk —Berenguer, Lopez. PB—Boone. T—2:53. A —41,253.

This is the start of a nine-game West Coast swing. It should be a real test for us. Playing in California is always a little bit crazy. So many people call for tickets. The media always want interviews and I must have done 25 of them before the game. It was like a World Series.

When the game started, I finally felt relaxed just to be able to watch a game. That's something because I never relax during a game. And who ever would believe I could be tired of talking?

I told our PR man, Dan Ewald, to help funnel as many interviews as possible over to me. It's better to keep the writers and television people away from the players so they can concentrate and get their work done.

This game belonged to us. Juan Berenguer gave us six great innings and struck out nine batters. Aurelio Lopez finished the game for his sixth save of the season. That's 15 straight on the road. We're within one of tying the American League record and two within the major league mark.

This is the happiest I've ever been with a club for one reason: When I walk into the clubhouse, I don't have a problem. These guys act like the players did back in the fifties. They make a lot of money, but they don't act like it. They could have starred in *Happy Days*. Of course, I make sure I don't keep creeps around. Why should you spend seven months with a creep?

I really respect Gene Mauch. He was a great manager and now he's an executive with the Angels. He said an interesting thing before the game: "The hardest argument in baseball is with a pencil. To lose their lead, the Tigers will have to suffer a collapse even more dramatic than their start."

**Alan Trammell gets ready to bunt.** Photo by Doc Holcomb, courtesy of *The Detroit News*

# WEDNESDAY, MAY 23

## AT ANAHEIM

# GAME 39

## TIGERS 4, ANGELS 2

### (34-5, 8 GAMES AHEAD)

| DETROIT | ab | r | h | bi | CALIFORNIA | ab | r | h | bi |
|---|---|---|---|---|---|---|---|---|---|
| Kuntz rf | 1 | 0 | 1 | 0 | Pettis cf | 3 | 0 | 0 | 0 |
| K Gibson rf | 2 | 0 | 0 | 0 | Carew 1b | 4 | 0 | 0 | 0 |
| Tramml ss | 5 | 0 | 2 | 0 | Lynn rf | 4 | 1 | 1 | 0 |
| Garbey 1b | 5 | 1 | 1 | 0 | DeCncs 3b | 4 | 1 | 1 | 2 |
| LNParsh c | 5 | 1 | 2 | 2 | Downing lf | 4 | 0 | 0 | 0 |
| Herndon lf | 5 | 1 | 1 | 0 | ReJksn dh | 3 | 0 | 0 | 0 |
| Lemon cf | 2 | 1 | 2 | 0 | Wilfong 2b | 4 | 0 | 0 | 0 |
| Allen dh | 1 | 0 | 1 | 1 | Boone c | 3 | 0 | 1 | 0 |
| DEvns dh | 1 | 0 | 0 | 0 | Schofild ss | 1 | 0 | 1 | 0 |
| MCastil 3b | 3 | 0 | 2 | 1 | Beniqz ph | 1 | 0 | 1 | 0 |
| Whitakr 2b | 1 | 0 | 0 | 0 | Picciolo ss | 0 | 0 | 0 | 0 |
| Brokns 2b | 1 | 0 | 0 | 0 | | | | | |
| Bergmn 1b | 2 | 0 | 0 | 0 | | | | | |
| Totals | 34 | 4 | 12 | 4 | Totals | 31 | 2 | 5 | 2 |

```
Detroit ........................... 020  000  200—4
California ........................ 000  200  000—2
```
Game Winning RBI — Parrish (4).
LOB—Detroit 10, California 5. 2B—Trammell, Lemon. 3B—Schofield. HR—DeCinces (8), LNParrish (6). S—Brookens.

| | IP | H | R | ER | BB | SO |
|---|---|---|---|---|---|---|
| **Detroit** | | | | | | |
| Petry W,7-1 | 7 | 5 | 2 | 2 | 2 | 5 |
| Hernandz S,7 | 2 | 0 | 0 | 0 | 0 | 3 |
| **California** | | | | | | |
| John | 5 | 8 | 2 | 2 | 5 | 2 |
| LaCorte L,0-2 | 4 | 4 | 2 | 2 | 0 | 1 |

HBP—Schoefield by Petry, Allen by John. T—2:31. A—41,205.

The phone rang at 8:30 A.M. to start another string of interviews. I spent the rest of the day with Albert visiting Mama. I thought about what a great feeling it is to finally achieve friendship with your children.

Dan Petry pitched tonight. He always seems to throw a little something extra at Anaheim. He was raised only 10 minutes from the park, so lots of his friends and relatives always show up for the games.

Danny went seven strong innings for the win. Lance Parrish snapped a 2-2 tie with a two-run homer in the seventh. Willie Hernandez retired six straight batters for the save. In the ninth, he struck out Brian Downing, Reggie Jackson, and Rob Wilfong.

That tied us with the 1912 Washington Senators for the American League record of 16 straight road victories. Now that we're just one away from the major league mark, it would be nice to get it. It might be my only way to sneak in the back door of the Hall of Fame.

# THURSDAY, MAY 24

## AT ANAHEIM

# GAME 40

## TIGERS 5, ANGELS 1

### (35-5, 8½ GAMES AHEAD)

| DETROIT | | | | | CALIFORNIA | | | | |
|---|---|---|---|---|---|---|---|---|---|
| | ab | r | h | bi | | ab | r | h | bi |
| Whitakr 2b | 3 | 1 | 1 | 0 | Pettis cf | 4 | 0 | 0 | 0 |
| Tramml ss | 4 | 1 | 1 | 2 | Carew 1b | 4 | 1 | 1 | 0 |
| K Gibson rf | 4 | 1 | 1 | 0 | Lynn rf | 4 | 0 | 1 | 0 |
| LN Parsh c | 4 | 2 | 2 | 1 | DeCncs 3b | 4 | 0 | 1 | 0 |
| DEvns dh | 3 | 0 | 1 | 1 | Downing lf | 4 | 0 | 0 | 0 |
| Herndon lf | 4 | 0 | 0 | 0 | ReJksn dh | 2 | 0 | 0 | 0 |
| Bergmn 1b | 4 | 0 | 0 | 0 | Wilfong 2b | 2 | 0 | 1 | 0 |
| Lemon cf | 4 | 0 | 0 | 0 | Boone c | 3 | 0 | 0 | 0 |
| Garbey 3b | 3 | 0 | 1 | 0 | Picciolo ss | 2 | 0 | 0 | 0 |
| Brokns 3b | 0 | 0 | 0 | 0 | MCBrn ph | 1 | 0 | 0 | 0 |
| | | | | | Schofild ss | 0 | 0 | 0 | 0 |
| Totals | 33 | 5 | 7 | 4 | Totals | 30 | 1 | 4 | 0 |

Detroit............................000 401 000— 5
California.........................100 000 000— 1
Game Winning RBI — Trammell (3).
E—Garbey, Carew 2. DP—California 2.
LOB—Detroit 3, California 4. 2B—Wilfong.
HR—Trammell (5), LNParrish (7). SB—
Carew (1). S—Wilfong.

| | IP | H | R | ER | BB | SO |
|---|---|---|---|---|---|---|
| **Detroit** | | | | | | |
| Morris W,9-1 | 9 | 4 | 1 | 0 | 1 | 10 |
| **California** | | | | | | |
| Slaton L,1-2 | 5 2-3 | 6 | 5 | 5 | 2 | 1 |
| Kaufman | 2 1-3 | 1 | 0 | 0 | 0 | 1 |
| Corbett | 1 | 0 | 0 | 0 | 0 | 0 |
| T—2:19. A—43,580. | | | | | | |

I was having breakfast with my wife in the coffee shop this morning when I got a great lesson in humility. A man at another table kept staring at me. I thought that either he was offended by my pipe smoking or he wanted an autograph. He walked up and yelled, "Sparky Anderson, I'm from Dayton. When you managed Cincinnati I was a big fan of yours and I just want to thank you for all the happy times you gave us fans." I thanked him for the compliment. Then he went on, "By the way, what are you doing now?"

Here I am, managing the hottest sports team anywhere and someone asks me what I'm doing. If that doesn't tell you something about the records we're chasing, nothing will.

We tied the major league mark of 17 straight road victories set by the 1916 New York Giants. Our 35-5 start is the best ever for the first 40 games. I should try my luck in Las Vegas right now. This roll is really incredible!

Jack Morris pitched today and wanted to be part of baseball history. He sure made history of the Angels: one run on four hits for his ninth win. Alan Trammell and Lance Parrish—two southern California boys—hit homers.

Writers keep asking me to compare this team with my old Cincinnati Reds. This team has better pitching, defense, and depth. But it will take four or five years to find out if it can handle success as well as the Reds.

It's amazing how many Tiger fans we have out here. I guess when the auto industry in Michigan soured, a lot of people moved west. There were Tiger hats everywhere and they cheered every time we did something good.

We're not a bad team to pull for this year.

**Lance Parrish hits a big one.**   Photo courtesy of Detroit Tigers

# FRIDAY, MAY 25

## AT SEATTLE

# GAME 41

## MARINERS 7, TIGERS 3

### (35–6, 7½ GAMES AHEAD)

| DETROIT | ab | r | h | bi | SEATTLE | ab | r | h | bi |
|---|---|---|---|---|---|---|---|---|---|
| Brokns 2b | 4 | 0 | 0 | 0 | Percont 2b | 5 | 1 | 0 | 0 |
| Allen ph | 1 | 0 | 0 | 0 | Bonnell rf | 4 | 1 | 1 | 1 |
| Tramml ss | 5 | 1 | 2 | 1 | ADavis 1b | 4 | 1 | 3 | 3 |
| Garbey 1b | 4 | 0 | 0 | 0 | Putnam lf | 2 | 0 | 1 | 0 |
| LNParsh c | 4 | 0 | 0 | 0 | PBradly rf | 1 | 1 | 0 | 0 |
| Lowry c | 0 | 0 | 0 | 0 | Phelps dh | 4 | 0 | 1 | 0 |
| Herndon lf | 4 | 0 | 1 | 0 | DHndsn cf | 4 | 0 | 1 | 0 |
| DEvns dh | 2 | 1 | 2 | 0 | Milborn 3b | 4 | 1 | 2 | 1 |
| Lemon cf | 2 | 0 | 0 | 0 | Kearney c | 4 | 2 | 2 | 2 |
| Kuntz pr | 0 | 1 | 0 | 0 | Owen ss | 3 | 0 | 1 | 0 |
| KGibson rf | 4 | 0 | 1 | 0 | | | | | |
| MCastll 3b | 3 | 0 | 1 | 0 | | | | | |
| HJhnsn ph | 1 | 0 | 1 | 2 | | | | | |
| Totals | 34 | 3 | 8 | 3 | Totals | 35 | 7 | 12 | 7 |

```
Detroit ............................. 000 100 002— 3
Seattle ............................. 120 031 00x— 7
```

Game Winning RBI — ADavis (7).
E—Wilcox, Milbourne. DP—Detroit 1, Seattle 2. LOB—Detroit 8, Seattle 7. 2B—ADavis, Kearney, Trammell. HR—Trammell (6), Kearney (3), ADavis (11). S—Owen.

| Detroit | IP | H | R | ER | BB | SO |
|---|---|---|---|---|---|---|
| Wilcox L,6-1 | 4 2-3 | 9 | 6 | 5 | 1 | 2 |
| Bair | 1 1-3 | 1 | 1 | 1 | 0 | 1 |
| Rozema | 1 | 1 | 0 | 0 | 0 | 1 |
| Abbott | 1 | 1 | 0 | 0 | 0 | 0 |
| **Seattle** | | | | | | |
| VandBerg W,4-2 | 7 | 6 | 1 | 1 | 2 | 5 |
| Beard | 1 1-3 | 2 | 2 | 2 | 2 | 1 |
| Mirabella S,2 | 2-3 | 0 | 0 | 0 | 0 | 1 |

VandeBerg pitched to 1 batter in 8th.
HBP—Bonnell by Wilcox. WP—Vande-Berg 2, Wilcox. T—2:54. A—15,722.

The string snapped in Seattle. Seventeen straight wins on the road and then S-N-A-P. We all knew it was coming and we sure did the job up right. We stunk up the Dome. We couldn't do a thing right. We ran poorly, fielded poorly, and didn't hit a lick. I guess if you're going to get beat, you might as well do it right.

No excuses, but I honestly think our guys are worn out from all the media hype. We couldn't turn around in southern California without bumping into a microphone or camera. We're just mentally beat.

Milt Wilcox wasn't sharp at all. Seattle scored six runs off him before the fifth inning was over. It was his first loss.

This morning, Lance Parrish, Ernie Harwell, and I visited a nine-year-old boy from Michigan who's suffering from the second stage of cancer in the hospital out here. That boy was so thrilled to meet Lance. I'll never forget the look on his face.

**Kirk Gibson watches his home run ball.** Photo by Doc Holcomb, courtesy of *The Detroit News*

# SATURDAY, MAY 26

## AT SEATTLE

# GAME 42

## MARINERS 9, TIGERS 5

### (35-7, 6½ GAMES AHEAD)

| DETROIT | ab | r | h | bi |
|---|---|---|---|---|
| Whitakr 2b | 4 | 0 | 1 | 0 |
| Brokns 2b | 0 | 0 | 0 | 0 |
| Garbey ph | 1 | 0 | 1 | 1 |
| Tramml ss | 4 | 0 | 1 | 0 |
| MCastil 3b | 1 | 0 | 0 | 0 |
| KGibson rf | 4 | 1 | 2 | 1 |
| LNParsh c | 4 | 0 | 0 | 0 |
| Lowry c | 0 | 0 | 0 | 0 |
| DEvns dh | 4 | 0 | 0 | 0 |
| Herndon lf | 4 | 1 | 2 | 0 |
| Bergmn 1b | 4 | 1 | 2 | 0 |
| HJhnsn 3b | 4 | 1 | 2 | 1 |
| Kuntz cf | 3 | 1 | 2 | 2 |
| Totals | 37 | 5 | 13 | 5 |

| SEATTLE | ab | r | h | bi |
|---|---|---|---|---|
| Percont 2b | 5 | 0 | 2 | 0 |
| Phelps dh | 2 | 1 | 1 | 1 |
| SHndsn ph | 1 | 0 | 0 | 0 |
| ADavis 1b | 5 | 1 | 1 | 0 |
| Putnam lf | 3 | 1 | 1 | 1 |
| PBradly lf | 1 | 0 | 0 | 0 |
| Cowens rf | 4 | 1 | 1 | 0 |
| DHndsn cf | 4 | 0 | 1 | 2 |
| Coles 3b | 2 | 2 | 2 | 0 |
| Kearney c | 3 | 1 | 1 | 2 |
| Owen ss | 4 | 2 | 1 | 1 |
| Totals | 34 | 9 | 11 | 7 |

Detroit .................. 101 000 003— 5
Seattle ................. 400 102 20x— 9

Game Winning RBI — None.
E—Whitaker. DP—Seattle 1. LOB—Detroit 6, Seattle 6. 2B—Herndon, KGibson, HJohnson. HR—KGibson (6), Kuntz (2), Kearney (4). SB—Bergman (2), Perconte (8). S—Kearney. SF—Kuntz.

| | IP | H | R | ER | BB | SO |
|---|---|---|---|---|---|---|
| Detroit | | | | | | |
| Berengur L,3-3 | 1-3 | 5 | 4 | 4 | 1 | 0 |
| Bair | 3 2-3 | 2 | 1 | 1 | 1 | 3 |
| Rozema | 2 | 2 | 2 | 1 | 2 | 1 |
| Abbott | 1 | 2 | 2 | 2 | 0 | 0 |
| Hernandz | 1 | 0 | 0 | 0 | 0 | 0 |
| Seattle | | | | | | |
| MMoore W,2-3 | 5 | 6 | 2 | 2 | 0 | 5 |
| Stoddard | 3 1-3 | 7 | 3 | 3 | 0 | 3 |
| Mirabella | 2-3 | 0 | 0 | 0 | 0 | 0 |

WP—Berenguer. T—2:51. A—41,342.

We were awful again. It seemed like we had never left the Dome from the night before.

Kirk Gibson homered in the first, but the Mariners slapped four on us when they came to bat and we lost again. Juan Berenguer got the leadoff batter, then gave up a walk and five straight singles before I got him out of there.

I don't know what it is when you play a team like Seattle. It was the same thing when I managed Cincinnati. We would go into LA and sweep three from the Dodgers. Then we'd go down to San Diego and they would go through us like the Indians went through Custer. It's like the little kid on the block who stands up one day and kicks the bully right in the behind.

One thing I won't forget. They ran on us when it was 7-2. I'll remember that. They should let a sleeping dog lie.

# SUNDAY, MAY 27

## AT SEATTLE

# GAME 43

## MARINERS 6, TIGERS 1

### (35-8, 5 GAMES AHEAD)

| DETROIT | ab | r | h | bi | SEATTLE | ab | r | h | bi |
|---|---|---|---|---|---|---|---|---|---|
| Whitakr 2b | 4 | 0 | 1 | 0 | Percont 2b | 4 | 0 | 1 | 0 |
| Tramml ss | 4 | 0 | 3 | 0 | Phelps dh | 4 | 2 | 2 | 2 |
| Garbey 3b | 4 | 0 | 0 | 0 | ADavis 1b | 4 | 0 | 2 | 0 |
| LNPrsh dh | 4 | 0 | 2 | 0 | Putnam lf | 3 | 0 | 0 | 0 |
| Herndon lf | 4 | 0 | 0 | 0 | Cowens rf | 1 | 0 | 1 | 0 |
| Lemon cf | 3 | 1 | 1 | 1 | DHndsn cf | 1 | 1 | 1 | 0 |
| DaEvns 1b | 4 | 0 | 0 | 0 | PBradly cf | 1 | 1 | 0 | 0 |
| Kuntz rf | 1 | 0 | 1 | 0 | Bonnell rf | 4 | 1 | 2 | 1 |
| HJhnsn ph | 1 | 0 | 0 | 0 | Coles 3b | 4 | 0 | 1 | 1 |
| Lowry c | 0 | 0 | 0 | 0 | Kearney c | 4 | 1 | 3 | 1 |
| Allen ph | 1 | 0 | 1 | 0 | Owen ss | 4 | 0 | 1 | 1 |
| MCastill c | 2 | 0 | 1 | 0 | | | | | |
| KGibson rf | 2 | 0 | 0 | 0 | | | | | |
| Totals | 34 | 1 | 10 | 1 | Totals | 34 | 6 | 14 | 6 |

```
Detroit ............................010 000 000— 1
Seattle ...........................020 210 10x— 6
```

Game Winning RBI — Coles (1).
E—Garbey. DP—Detroit 1, Seattle 3. LOB—Detroit 8, Seattle 6. 2B—Trammell 2, Kearney 2, LNParrish. 3B—Bonnell, Owen. HR—Lemon (8), Phelps 2 (4). SB—PBradley (5).

| | IP | H | R | ER | BB | SO |
|---|---|---|---|---|---|---|
| **Detroit** | | | | | | |
| Petry L,7-2 | 4 | 9 | 4 | 2 | 1 | 4 |
| Lopez | 4 | 5 | 2 | 2 | 1 | 3 |
| **Seattle** | | | | | | |
| MYoung W,4-3 | 5 | 7 | 1 | 1 | 2 | 0 |
| Stanton | 3 | 2 | 0 | 0 | 0 | 5 |
| Mirabella | 1 | 1 | 0 | 0 | 0 | 1 |

MYoung pitched to 1 batter in 6th.
T—2:50. A—12,755.

Thank God we're leaving Seattle. It was almost embarrassing walking out of the park. They whopped on us again. I think if we had played them 10 straight games, they would have beat on our heads 10 straight times.

In these three days, the Mariners were the better club. Everything they did was right; everything we did was wrong. They tried five hit-and-runs and each time they hit a ball up the gap. Lemon hit a long home run, but it didn't mean a thing. We had 10 hits and they came back with 14.

Maybe our guys learned a good hard lesson. This game can be very humbling. The Blue Jays and Orioles are right on our heels and this game can change so fast. Every good club goes through this.

# MONDAY, MAY 28

## AT OAKLAND

# GAME 44

## TIGERS 6, A'S 2

### (36-8, 5½ GAMES AHEAD)

| DETROIT | ab | r | h | bi | OAKLAND | ab | r | h | bi |
|---|---|---|---|---|---|---|---|---|---|
| Whitakr 2b | 2 | 2 | 1 | 0 | RHndsn lf | 4 | 1 | 0 | 1 |
| Tramml ss | 4 | 1 | 3 | 1 | Murphy cf | 4 | 0 | 0 | 1 |
| KGibson rf | 4 | 1 | 1 | 1 | Morgan 2b | 4 | 0 | 1 | 0 |
| LNParsh c | 5 | 1 | 1 | 1 | Kngmn dh | 1 | 0 | 0 | 0 |
| DEvns dh | 3 | 1 | 1 | 0 | Burghs dh | 2 | 0 | 1 | 0 |
| Herndon lf | 4 | 0 | 0 | 1 | Almon ph | 1 | 0 | 0 | 0 |
| Bergmn 1b | 4 | 0 | 2 | 1 | Lansfrd 3b | 4 | 0 | 1 | 0 |
| Lemon cf | 4 | 0 | 0 | 1 | MDavis rf | 4 | 0 | 0 | 0 |
| HJhnsn 3b | 3 | 0 | 0 | 0 | Bochte 1b | 4 | 1 | 1 | 0 |
| Brokns 3b | 1 | 0 | 0 | 0 | Heath c | 3 | 0 | 1 | 0 |
| | | | | | Phillips ss | 3 | 0 | 1 | 0 |
| Totals | 34 | 6 | 9 | 6 | Totals | 34 | 2 | 6 | 2 |

```
Detroit ................................ 400 000 101 — 6
Oakland .............................. 001 001 000 — 2
```

Game Winning RBI — K Gibson (4).
E—Trammell, HJohnson, LNParrish. DP—Detroit 1. LOB—Detroit 11, Oakland 5. 2B—Heath, Trammell. HR—LNParrish (8). SB—RHenderson (19). SF—Lemon.

| Detroit | IP | H | R | ER | BB | SO |
|---|---|---|---|---|---|---|
| Morris W, 10-1 | 9 | 6 | 2 | 0 | 0 | 8 |
| Oakland | | | | | | |
| Codiroli L, 1-2 | 1-3 | 3 | 4 | 4 | 2 | 1 |
| JJones | 5 2-3 | 1 | 0 | 0 | 2 | 7 |
| Atherton | 1 2-3 | 3 | 1 | 1 | 4 | 1 |
| Conroy | 1 1-3 | 2 | 1 | 1 | 0 | 1 |

HBP—Herndon by Codiroli. WP—Morris. T—2:57. A—46,238.

Back to basics and Jack Morris. Jack was super today. He went the distance and is now 10-1. Right now, he's Cy Young. He doesn't just think he's good . . . he knows it. Jack knows how much his teammates depend on him. He should be even better when the weather gets hot and he can grip that split-finger fastball better.

I've got two pitchers here—Morris and Petry—the likes of whom I never had at Cincinnati. If I had three more Morrises, I would be a certified genius.

We scored four runs in the first inning and the rest was easy. Lance Parrish hit a 400-foot line-shot homer. If he would stop pulling off the ball, there's no telling what he could do. Lou Whitaker and Alan Trammell were on base eight times. They are the two keys to this team. What they do sets up everything else that follows.

We weren't sharp defensively but with Morris pitching, you can afford that.

Before the game a young radio woman interviewed me. She said that it was an honor to interview me because when she was conceived, her parents were talking baseball. I'm still trying to figure that one out.

# TUESDAY, MAY 29

## AT OAKLAND

# GAME 45

## A'S 8, TIGERS 5

### (36–9, 5½ GAMES AHEAD)

| DETROIT | ab | r | h | bi | OAKLAND | ab | r | h | bi |
|---|---|---|---|---|---|---|---|---|---|
| Whitakr 2b | 2 | 0 | 0 | 0 | RHndsn lf | 3 | 2 | 2 | 2 |
| Brokns 2b | 2 | 0 | 0 | 0 | Almon lf | 1 | 0 | 0 | 0 |
| Tramml ss | 4 | 1 | 1 | 0 | Murphy cf | 4 | 0 | 2 | 1 |
| Garbey 3b | 4 | 0 | 1 | 1 | Morgan 2b | 4 | 1 | 2 | 1 |
| LNParsh c | 4 | 1 | 1 | 0 | Kngmn dh | 5 | 1 | 2 | 1 |
| Herndon lf | 3 | 0 | 0 | 1 | Lansfrd 3b | 4 | 1 | 1 | 0 |
| DaEvns 1b | 4 | 0 | 0 | 0 | MDavis rf | 3 | 0 | 0 | 0 |
| Lemon cf | 4 | 1 | 2 | 2 | Bochte 1b | 4 | 1 | 2 | 0 |
| KGibson rf | 4 | 1 | 1 | 0 | Heath c | 4 | 1 | 2 | 3 |
| Kuntz dh | 2 | 1 | 0 | 1 | Phillips ss | 3 | 1 | 1 | 0 |
| Totals | 33 | 5 | 6 | 5 | Totals | 35 | 8 | 14 | 8 |

| | | | |
|---|---|---|---|
| Detroit | | 010 002 200— | 5 |
| Oakland | | 031 400 00x— | 8 |

Game Winning RBI — Heath (1).
E—Bochte. LOB—Detroit 3, Oakland 9.
2B—Bochte, Kingman, Garbey, Lansford.
3B—RHenderson. HR—Heath (3), Lemon
(9). SB—RHenderson (20), LNParrish (1),
Lemon (3), KGibson (10). S—MDavis.
SF—Murphy, Herndon.

| | IP | H | R | ER | BB | SO |
|---|---|---|---|---|---|---|
| Detroit | | | | | | |
| Wilcox L,6-2 | 3 1-3 | 7 | 7 | 7 | 3 | 1 |
| Bair | 1 2-3 | 4 | 1 | 1 | 0 | 0 |
| Rozema | 2 | 2 | 0 | 0 | 1 | 2 |
| Hernandz | 1 | 1 | 0 | 0 | 0 | 1 |
| Oakland | | | | | | |
| Krueger W,3-1 | 7 | 6 | 5 | 4 | 1 | 4 |
| Caudill S,10 | 2 | 0 | 0 | 0 | 0 | 2 |

T—2:42. A—22,499.

From the mountain to the valley. We got hammered today. Wilcox got upset by some calls and then Oakland waxed him with bullets.

After the game, I called my wife and laughed about what happened. I had felt so bad after our series in Seattle. Then I got right back up after winning last night. Now another bad loss.

A doctor once told me how lucky I am. He said most people only get a few real highs throughout their whole lives. In baseball, you experience a lot of highs and also a lot of lows. It keeps you young. In baseball, you're a kid forever.

# WEDNESDAY, MAY 30

## AT OAKLAND

# GAME 46

## TIGERS 2, A'S 1

### (37–9, 5½ GAMES AHEAD)

| DETROIT | ab | r | h | bi | OAKLAND | ab | r | h | bi |
|---|---|---|---|---|---|---|---|---|---|
| Whitakr 2b | 4 | 0 | 0 | 0 | RHndsn lf | 2 | 0 | 0 | 0 |
| Tramml ss | 3 | 0 | 0 | 1 | Murphy cf | 3 | 0 | 0 | 0 |
| KGibson rf | 4 | 1 | 1 | 1 | Morgan dh | 4 | 0 | 1 | 0 |
| LNParsh c | 3 | 0 | 1 | 0 | Lansfrd 3b | 2 | 0 | 0 | 1 |
| DEvns dh | 4 | 0 | 1 | 0 | MDavis rf | 4 | 0 | 0 | 0 |
| Grubb lf | 4 | 0 | 0 | 0 | Bochte 1b | 4 | 0 | 1 | 0 |
| Kuntz lf | 0 | 0 | 0 | 0 | Essian c | 4 | 0 | 1 | 0 |
| Lemon cf | 3 | 0 | 0 | 0 | Lopes pr | 0 | 0 | 0 | 0 |
| Bergmn 1b | 3 | 0 | 1 | 0 | Heath c | 0 | 0 | 0 | 0 |
| Garbey 3b | 3 | 1 | 1 | 0 | Phillips ss | 3 | 0 | 1 | 0 |
| Brokns 3b | 0 | 0 | 0 | 0 | Wagner 2b | 3 | 1 | 0 | 0 |
|  |  |  |  |  | Burghs ph | 1 | 0 | 0 | 0 |
|  |  |  |  |  | McCatty p | 0 | 0 | 0 | 0 |
| Totals | 32 | 2 | 5 | 2 | Totals | 30 | 1 | 4 | 1 |

```
Detroit ............................ 000  001  001— 2
Oakland ........................... 000  010  000— 1
```

Game Winning RBI — K Gibson (5).
E—Garbey, Phillips. DP—Oakland 1.
LOB—Detroit 4, Oakland 11. 3B—Garbey.
HR—KGibson (7). SB—RHenderson (21),
Lopes (5). S—Murphy, Phillips.

| | IP | H | R | ER | BB | SO |
|---|---|---|---|---|---|---|
| **Detroit** | | | | | | |
| Berengur. | 4 2-3 | 2 | 1 | 0 | 4 | 2 |
| Hernandz W,2-0 | 3 1-3 | 2 | 0 | 0 | 2 | 2 |
| Lopez S,7 | 1 | 0 | 0 | 0 | 0 | 0 |
| **Oakland** | | | | | | |
| McCatty L,3-4 | 8 1-3 | 5 | 2 | 2 | 1 | 2 |
| Atherton | 2-3 | 0 | 0 | 0 | 0 | 0 |

HBP—RHenderson by Berenguer. WP—
McCatty  T—2:34. A—15,224.

Thank God—and Kirk Gibson—we got another high today. Gibby hit a monstrous home run with one out in the ninth to give us a 2–1 win. He's an amazing player because he's always better when the chips are on the line. Some people are just like that. He's got a great sense of drama.

Juan Berenguer pitched well until he got wild in the fifth. We have a day off tomorrow, so I brought in Willie Hernandez right away. He slammed the door shut and then Aurelio Lopez locked it in the ninth.

We finished the West Coast trip at 5–4 and are 36–9. I would say that ain't too bad.

On the long flight home, I had time to think. The media hype has been unbelievable. I realize it's a part of the game. It's the show business part.

When I deal with the media, there are two people inside of me. There's Sparky Anderson—he's the one in baseball. He's a piece of show business. And there's also George Anderson. He's the real me. If you are really my friend, you will never call me Sparky.

# THURSDAY, MAY 31

## AT DETROIT

## (37–9, 5½ GAMES AHEAD)

One day off before it all begins—two big weeks with Baltimore and Toronto.

I went to the dentist to have a cap replaced. Never know, I might have to bite someone before these two weeks are over.

**Aurelio Lopez locks the door on the game.**   Photo by Clifton Boutelle

# JUNE

"After the game, some Baltimore writers asked if . . . the Tigers are for real. I told them 'Let's not ask "Can we play with them?" The question is "Can they play with us?" ' "  **June 10, 1984**

# FRIDAY, JUNE 1

## AT DETROIT

# GAME 47

## TIGERS 14, ORIOLES 2

### (38-9, 5½ GAMES AHEAD)

| BALTIMORE | ab | r | h | bi |
|---|---|---|---|---|
| Bumbry cf | 3 | 0 | 1 | 0 |
| Shelby cf | 1 | 0 | 0 | 0 |
| Dwyer rf | 4 | 0 | 0 | 0 |
| Ripken ss | 4 | 0 | 0 | 0 |
| Murray 1b | 4 | 0 | 0 | 0 |
| Gross 3b | 4 | 1 | 1 | 0 |
| Lowenstein lf | 2 | 1 | 1 | 2 |
| Young lf | 1 | 0 | 1 | 0 |
| Singleton dh | 4 | 0 | 2 | 0 |
| Dauer 2b | 3 | 0 | 1 | 0 |
| Dempsey c | 3 | 0 | 0 | 0 |
| Totals | 33 | 2 | 7 | 2 |

| DETROIT | ab | r | h | bi |
|---|---|---|---|---|
| Whitaker 2b | 3 | 1 | 1 | 1 |
| Trammell ss | 5 | 2 | 3 | 3 |
| Castillo 3b | 0 | 0 | 0 | 0 |
| Garbey 3b | 4 | 1 | 1 | 1 |
| Parrish c | 4 | 3 | 2 | 2 |
| Lowry c | 1 | 0 | 0 | 0 |
| Herndon lf | 5 | 1 | 2 | 1 |
| Evans 1b | 3 | 1 | 0 | 0 |
| Brookens 3b | 1 | 0 | 0 | 0 |
| Lemon cf | 4 | 2 | 2 | 3 |
| Bergman 1b | 1 | 0 | 0 | 0 |
| Gibson rf | 3 | 1 | 1 | 1 |
| Kuntz dh | 1 | 1 | 1 | 2 |
| Johnson dh | 2 | 1 | 0 | 0 |
| Totals | 37 | 14 | 13 | 14 |

Baltimore............................ 000 000 200 — 2
Detroit................................ 063 310 01x — 14
Game-winning RBI — Gibson (6).
E—Gross 2. DP—Detroit 1. LOB—Baltimore 5, Detroit 5. 2B—Herndon, Young. HR—Trammell (7), Lemon (10), Parrish (9), Lowenstein (3). SF—Whitaker, Garbey.

| Baltimore | IP | H | R | ER | BB | SO |
|---|---|---|---|---|---|---|
| McGregor (L 6-4) | 1 2-3 | 5 | 6 | 6 | 0 | 0 |
| Swaggerty | 2 1-3 | 3 | 6 | 5 | 2 | 2 |
| DMartinez | 4 | 5 | 2 | 2 | 1 | 4 |
| Detroit | | | | | | |
| Petry (W 8-2) | 6 | 3 | 0 | 0 | 1 | 1 |
| Bair (S 3) | 3 | 4 | 2 | 2 | 0 | 2 |

HBP—by McGregor (Gibson). T—2:28.
A—47,252.

The weather was great and the feeling in the air was electrifying. This city thinks it's the World Series. Writers from all over the country were here to talk with us and watch us play.

Were we ready for Baltimore? Just ask the Oriole players.

We slapped a six-spot on them in the second inning. Alan Trammell finished Scott McGregor with a home run. Chet Lemon and Lance Parrish also connected for homers. Dan Petry shut them out on three hits in six innings and Doug Bair finished.

More than 47,000 people were at the park to see us win today. The fans went crazy, but were well-behaved. It was incredible to hear all the car horns after the game.

I think Baltimore was confident that the pressure would get to us while they were here. We answered that.

# SATURDAY, JUNE 2

## AT DETROIT

# GAME 48

## ORIOLES 5, TIGERS 0

### (38–10, 4½ GAMES AHEAD)

| BALTIMORE | ab | r | h | bi |
|---|---|---|---|---|
| Bumbry cf | 3 | 1 | 1 | 0 |
| Shelby cf | 2 | 0 | 0 | 0 |
| Dwyer rf | 2 | 0 | 1 | 1 |
| GRonck rf | 2 | 0 | 1 | 0 |
| Ripken ss | 3 | 1 | 2 | 0 |
| EMurry 1b | 4 | 0 | 0 | 0 |
| Gross 3b | 3 | 1 | 1 | 2 |
| TCruz 3b | 1 | 0 | 0 | 0 |
| Lownstn lf | 3 | 1 | 1 | 0 |
| MKYoung lf | 1 | 0 | 0 | 0 |
| Singltn dh | 3 | 1 | 1 | 2 |
| Dauer 2b | 4 | 0 | 0 | 0 |
| Dempsy c | 4 | 0 | 1 | 0 |
| Totals | 35 | 5 | 9 | 5 |

| DETROIT | ab | r | h | bi |
|---|---|---|---|---|
| Whitakr 2b | 4 | 0 | 0 | 0 |
| Tramml ss | 4 | 0 | 1 | 0 |
| KGibson rf | 3 | 0 | 0 | 0 |
| LNParsh c | 3 | 0 | 0 | 0 |
| DEvns dh | 3 | 0 | 0 | 0 |
| Grubb lf | 3 | 0 | 0 | 0 |
| Lemon cf | 3 | 0 | 0 | 0 |
| Beromn 1b | 2 | 0 | 1 | 0 |
| HJhnsn 3b | 3 | 0 | 1 | 0 |
| Totals | 28 | 0 | 3 | 0 |

Baltimore........................ 122 000 000— 5
Detroit............................. 000 000 000— 0
Game Winning RBI — Dwyer (3).
LOB—Baltimore 6, Detroit 2. 2B—HJohnson, 3B—Bumbry. HR—Singleton (1), Gross (9). SF—Dwyer.

| | IP | H | R | ER | BB | SO |
|---|---|---|---|---|---|---|
| **Baltimore** | | | | | | |
| GDavis W,6-1 | 9 | 3 | 0 | 0 | 1 | 2 |
| **Detroit** | | | | | | |
| Morris L,10-2 | 6 | 7 | 5 | 5 | 1 | 1 |
| Hernandz | 1 2-3 | 2 | 0 | 0 | 1 | 3 |
| Lopez | 1 1-3 | 0 | 0 | 0 | 0 | 2 |

T—2:11. A—40,292.

We ran into another fine pitcher today. His name is Storm Davis and he could have won with one run. His fastball is unreal. On the other mound, Morris had trouble with the split finger pitch and the Orioles touched him for five runs in the first three innings.

Toronto won to move them to within 4½ games of us. This thing might get down-and-dirty all season. I honestly don't think Baltimore can win it this year but I do think our team may seesaw with Toronto before it's over.

**Tom Brookens hits his first home run of the season.** Photo by Doc Holcomb, courtesy of *The Detroit News*

# SUNDAY, JUNE 3

## AT DETROIT

# GAME 49

## ORIOLES 2, TIGERS 1

### (38–11, 4½ GAMES AHEAD)

| BALTIMORE | ab | r | h | bi | DETROIT | ab | r | h | bi |
|---|---|---|---|---|---|---|---|---|---|
| Bumbry cf | 3 | 1 | 1 | 0 | Whitakr 2b | 4 | 0 | 1 | 0 |
| Shelby cf | 0 | 0 | 0 | 0 | Tramml ss | 4 | 0 | 1 | 0 |
| Dwyer rf | 3 | 1 | 1 | 0 | Garbey 1b | 4 | 0 | 0 | 0 |
| Ripken ss | 2 | 0 | 0 | 1 | LNParsh c | 4 | 0 | 2 | 0 |
| EMurry 1b | 4 | 0 | 0 | 0 | Herndon lf | 4 | 0 | 1 | 0 |
| Gross 3b | 3 | 0 | 0 | 0 | Lemon cf | 4 | 0 | 1 | 0 |
| Lownstn lf | 1 | 0 | 1 | 1 | KGibsn dh | 4 | 0 | 0 | 0 |
| MKYong lf | 1 | 0 | 0 | 0 | Kuntz rf | 3 | 0 | 0 | 0 |
| Singltn dh | 3 | 0 | 0 | 0 | Brokns 3b | 4 | 1 | 1 | 1 |
| Dauer 2b | 4 | 0 | 2 | 0 | | | | | |
| Dempsy c | 4 | 0 | 0 | 0 | | | | | |
| Totals | 28 | 2 | 5 | 2 | Totals | 35 | 1 | 7 | 1 |

Baltimore .......................000 002 000— 2
Detroit ............................000 000 100— 1
 Game Winning RBI — Ripken (3). ●
 E—Ripken, Dauer, Garbey. DP—Baltimore 1, Detroit 4. LOB—Baltimore 7, Detroit 8. 2B—Lemon. HR—Brookens (1). SB—Trammell (13), Lowenstein (1). SF—Ripken.

| Baltimore | IP | H | R | ER | BB | SO |
|---|---|---|---|---|---|---|
| Flanagan W,4-4 | 9 | 7 | 1 | 1 | 1 | 6 |
| Detroit | | | | | | |
| Wilcox L,6-3 | 5 2-3 | 4 | 2 | 1 | 6 | 4 |
| Rozema | 3 1-3 | 1 | 0 | 0 | 1 | 2 |

 T—2:42. A—34,228.

Our bats went to sleep after those 14 runs Friday. Mike Flanagan went the distance for them. I didn't think he was throwing that well, but we kept popping balls up. We were struggling.

Milt Wilcox wasn't on at all. He walked six batters. You can't win that way.

Tom Brookens hit his first home run. He's struggled all year. He was 1 for 32 before that homer. I'm really pulling for Tom. He doesn't have great tools, but he gives you all he's got day after day. He'll do anything for the team. If I have to go to war, I want Tom with me.

This is no time for panic. Not with Toronto coming to town tomorrow.

# MONDAY, JUNE 4

## AT DETROIT

# GAME 50

## TIGERS 6, BLUE JAYS 3

### (10 INNINGS)

### (39–11, 5½ GAMES AHEAD)

| TORONTO | ab | r | h | bi | DETROIT | ab | r | h | bi |
|---|---|---|---|---|---|---|---|---|---|
| Garcia 2b | 5 | 0 | 2 | 0 | Whitaker 2b | 4 | 0 | 2 | 0 |
| Collins lf | 5 | 0 | 1 | 0 | Trammell ss | 5 | 0 | 1 | 0 |
| Moseby cf | 5 | 0 | 1 | 0 | Gibson rf | 3 | 0 | 0 | 0 |
| Upshaw 1b | 5 | 2 | 2 | 1 | Herndon lf | 1 | 0 | 0 | 0 |
| Aikens dh | 3 | 0 | 0 | 0 | Parrish c | 4 | 1 | 2 | 0 |
| Johnson dh | 2 | 0 | 0 | 0 | Evans dh | 3 | 0 | 0 | 0 |
| Bell rf | 3 | 1 | 2 | 2 | Grubb lf | 4 | 0 | 1 | 0 |
| Mulliniks 3b | 2 | 0 | 1 | 0 | Kuntz rf | 1 | 0 | 0 | 0 |
| Barfield ph | 1 | 0 | 0 | 0 | Lemon cf | 3 | 2 | 0 | 0 |
| Iorg 3b | 0 | 0 | 0 | 0 | Bergman 1b | 4 | 2 | 2 | 3 |
| Whitt c | 2 | 0 | 0 | 0 | Johnson 3b | 3 | 1 | 1 | 3 |
| Fernandz ph | 1 | 0 | 0 | 0 | Brookens 3b | 0 | 0 | 0 | 0 |
| Martinez c | 0 | 0 | 0 | 0 | | | | | |
| Griffin ss | 4 | 0 | 1 | 0 | | | | | |
| Totals | 38 | 3 | 10 | 3 | Totals | 35 | 6 | 9 | 6 |

Two out when winning run scored.

Toronto ............................ 010 002 000 0— 3
Detroit ............................ 000 000 300 3— 6
Game-winning RBI — Bergman (3).
DP—Toronto 2, Detroit 1. LOB—Toronto 8, Detroit 9. 2B—Whitaker, Parrish, Garcia, Moseby. HR—Upshaw (10), Bell (7), Johnson (3), Bergman (1). SB—Bell (6), Whitaker (3). S—Brookens, Evans.

| | IP | H | R | ER | BB | SO |
|---|---|---|---|---|---|---|
| **Toronto** | | | | | | |
| Stieb | 6 2-3 | 6 | 3 | 3 | 2 | 3 |
| Lamp | 2 | 1 | 0 | 0 | 2 | 1 |
| Key (L 2-3) | 2-3 | 1 | 1 | 1 | 0 | 0 |
| Jackson | 1-3 | 1 | 2 | 2 | 1 | 0 |
| **Detroit** | | | | | | |
| Berenguer | 6 2-3 | 8 | 3 | 3 | 2 | 7 |
| Hernandez | 3 | 2 | 0 | 0 | 1 | 3 |
| Lopez (W 5-0) | 1-3 | 0 | 0 | 0 | 0 | 0 |

HBP—by Stieb (Parrish, Lemon). PB—Whitt, Parrish. T—3:30. A—26,733.

Tonight I saw the greatest at bat in my life. It was a down-and-dirty fight and Dave Bergman won. Here's the scene: Two out in the last of the tenth, two men on, and the score tied at 3-3. Reliever Roy Lee Howell pitched to a full count. Then Bergie took over. Bergie fouled off seven pitches and then picked one practically off the ground and drilled it into the upper deck in right.

What a battle! Bergie was up there a full seven minutes. It seemed like a whole season. The house went wild.

We didn't tie the score until the seventh. Howard Johnson socked a three-run homer off starter Dave Stieb.

I'm pulling for HoJo. He's only 23 and has a great athletic body with great physical ability. But he's never been able to crack that line and walk across the river to be good. He stays on the bank. He's going to have to get good and wet to get to the other side. If he hits, he'll get better in the field. His confidence will soar. I hope this homer helped. Bill Lajoie has been in his corner all the way. I hope he's right.

This game kicked off ABC television's Monday night schedule. We gave NBC a no-hitter in April and now ABC got a real barn burner. I want us to become a regular on national TV. That's the way it was at Cincinnati. You would have thought we were a soap opera, we were on so much.

# TUESDAY, JUNE 5

## AT DETROIT

# GAME 51

## BLUE JAYS 8, TIGERS 4

### (39–12, 4½ GAMES AHEAD)

| TORONTO | ab | r | h | bi | DETROIT | ab | r | h | bi |
|---|---|---|---|---|---|---|---|---|---|
| Garcia 2b | 5 | 1 | 1 | 0 | Whitakr 2b | 1 | 2 | 1 | 1 |
| Collins lf | 5 | 0 | 1 | 0 | HJhnsn 3b | 2 | 0 | 0 | 0 |
| Moseby cf | 5 | 2 | 2 | 1 | Tramml ss | 1 | 0 | 1 | 0 |
| Upshaw 1b | 4 | 0 | 0 | 1 | KGibson rf | 4 | 0 | 2 | 1 |
| Aikens dh | 4 | 1 | 2 | 1 | Garbey rf | 1 | 0 | 0 | 0 |
| GBell rf | 3 | 1 | 1 | 0 | LNParsh c | 4 | 0 | 1 | 1 |
| Mulinks 3b | 4 | 1 | 1 | 0 | DEvns dh | 4 | 0 | 1 | 0 |
| Whitt c | 4 | 1 | 1 | 3 | Herndon lf | 5 | 0 | 1 | 0 |
| Griffin ss | 4 | 1 | 2 | 1 | Bergmn 1b | 3 | 1 | 0 | 0 |
| | | | | | Kuntz ph | 1 | 0 | 0 | 0 |
| | | | | | Lemon cf | 3 | 1 | 0 | 0 |
| | | | | | Brookns ss | 3 | 0 | 1 | 1 |
| Totals | 38 | 8 | 11 | 7 | Totals | 32 | 4 | 8 | 4 |

Toronto ..........................100 600 100— 8
Detroit ..........................101 200 000— 4

Game Winning RBI — Aikens (2).
E—Griffin, Lemon. DP—Toronto 2. LOB—Toronto 5, Detroit 12. 2B—Brookens. 3B—Moseby, Herndon. HR—Moseby (10), Aikens (1), Whitt (3), Griffin (2). SB—Garcia (24). SF—LNParrish, Whitaker.

| | IP | H | R | ER | BB | SO |
|---|---|---|---|---|---|---|
| **Toronto** | | | | | | |
| Alexandr | 3 2-3 | 5 | 4 | 4 | 4 | 0 |
| Acker W,1-2 | 4 | 2 | 0 | 0 | 2 | 2 |
| Key | 1 1-3 | 1 | 0 | 0 | 2 | 1 |
| **Detroit** | | | | | | |
| Abbott L,2-2 | 3 1-3 | 6 | 5 | 5 | 0 | 0 |
| Bair | 3 | 4 | 3 | 3 | 1 | 3 |
| Rozema | 2 2-3 | 1 | 0 | 0 | 1 | 1 |

HBP—Lemon by Acker. WP—Acker.
T—3:05. A—35,983.

When you leave 12 men on base, you don't deserve to win. What bothers me more than anything, is that we keep leaving runners at third with less than two out..

I'm concerned about Glenn Abbott—he got racked for five runs in the first four innings. I brought in Doug Bair in the fourth and he gave up back-to-back homers to Ernie Whitt and Alfredo Griffin. That was my fault—Doug wasn't ready and I rushed him.

**Sparky poses with ex-manager/sportscaster Earl Weaver.** Photo by Doc Holcomb, courtesy of *The Detroit News*

# WEDNESDAY, JUNE 6

## AT DETROIT

# GAME 52

## BLUE JAYS 6, TIGERS 3

### (39–13, 3½ GAMES AHEAD)

| TORONTO | ab | r | h | bi | DETROIT | ab | r | h | b |
|---|---|---|---|---|---|---|---|---|---|
| Garcia 2b | 5 | 0 | 0 | 0 | Whitakr 2b | 5 | 0 | 3 |  |
| Collins lf | 5 | 2 | 2 | 0 | Tramml ss | 5 | 0 | 1 |  |
| Moseby cf | 4 | 1 | 2 | 1 | KGibson rf | 5 | 0 | 1 |  |
| Upshaw 1b | 4 | 1 | 2 | 3 | LNParsh c | 5 | 0 | 0 |  |
| Aikens dh | 4 | 1 | 1 | 0 | DEvns dh | 3 | 1 | 0 | 0 |
| GBell rf | 4 | 1 | 2 | 1 | R Jones cf | 3 | 1 | 1 | 0 |
| Mullnks 3b | 4 | 0 | 1 | 0 | Herndon lf | 1 | 0 | 1 | 0 |
| Giorg 3b | 0 | 0 | 0 | 0 | Grubb lf | 2 | 0 | 0 |  |
| Whiff c | 3 | 0 | 1 | 0 | Bergmn 1b | 3 | 0 | 0 | 1 |
| Griffin ss | 4 | 0 | 2 | 0 | HJhnsn 3b | 3 | 1 | 2 | 0 |
| Totals | 37 | 6 | 13 | 5 | Totals | 35 | 3 | 9 | 3 |

```
Toronto............................ 012  020  010— 6
Detroit............................ 000  010  020— 3
```

Game Winning RBI — None.
DP—Toronto 1, Detroit 2. LOB—Toronto 6, Detroit 10. 2B—Collins, Moseby, HJohnson, Trammell, R Jones. HR—Upshaw (11), GBell (8). SB—Collins (14).

| | IP | H | R | ER | BB | SO |
|---|---|---|---|---|---|---|
| **Toronto** | | | | | | |
| Leal W,6-0 | 7 | 8 | 3 | 3 | 5 | 4 |
| Lamp | 2 | 1 | 0 | 0 | 0 | 0 |
| **Detroit** | | | | | | |
| Petry L,8-3 | 4 | 10 | 5 | 5 | 0 | 0 |
| Lopez | 4 | 2 | 1 | 1 | 2 | 2 |
| Hernandez | 1 | 1 | 0 | 0 | 0 | 1 |

Petry pitched to 2 batters in fifth, Leal pitched to 2 batters in eighth.
T—2:36. A—38,167.

We simply are not hitting. We aren't getting the ball out of the infield with runners in scoring position. The ball can't find the outfield. Our big bats aren't hitting. Our pitching has become inconsistent. Dan Petry gave up five runs and ten hits in four innings. He hasn't been consistent all year.

I don't like the writers saying the honeymoon is over. Nothing upsets me more than someone saying the pressure is beginning to build. I always thought pressure was for when you have kids, you're out of work, and there's no money in the bank.

# THURSDAY, JUNE 7

## AT DETROIT

# GAME 53

## TIGERS 5, BLUE JAYS 3

### (40–13, 4½ GAMES AHEAD)

| TORONTO | ab | r | h | bi | | DETROIT | ab | r | h | bi |
|---|---|---|---|---|---|---|---|---|---|---|
| Garcia 2b | 4 | 0 | 0 | 0 | | Whitakr 2b | 4 | 0 | 2 | 1 |
| Collins lf | 4 | 1 | 1 | 0 | | Tramml ss | 4 | 0 | 1 | 0 |
| Moseby cf | 4 | 1 | 1 | 1 | | KGibson rf | 4 | 0 | 1 | 0 |
| Upshaw 1b | 3 | 0 | 2 | 1 | | LNParsh c | 4 | 1 | 1 | 0 |
| Aikens dh | 4 | 0 | 0 | 0 | | DEvns dh | 3 | 1 | 0 | 0 |
| GBell rf | 4 | 0 | 0 | 0 | | Grubb lf | 2 | 1 | 1 | 0 |
| Mulinks 3b | 4 | 0 | 0 | 0 | | Kuntz cf | 1 | 0 | 0 | 0 |
| Whitt c | 4 | 0 | 1 | 0 | | RJones cf | 4 | 1 | 2 | 3 |
| Griffin ss | 3 | 1 | 2 | 0 | | Bergmn 1b | 3 | 0 | 0 | 1 |
| CJhnsn ph | 1 | 0 | 0 | 0 | | HJhnsn 3b | 3 | 1 | 1 | 0 |
| | | | | | | Brokns 3b | 1 | 0 | 0 | 0 |
| Totals | 35 | 3 | 7 | 2 | | Totals | 33 | 5 | 9 | 5 |

```
Toronto........................ 001 000 020— 3
Detroit......................... 010 004 00x— 5
```
Game Winning RBI — RJones (1).
E—Bergman 2, Garcia. LOB—Toronto 6, Detroit 7. 2B—Grubb, Griffin, Collins. HR—RJones (1). SB—KGibson (11), HJohnson (2). SF—Bergman.

| Toronto | IP | H | R | ER | BB | SO |
|---|---|---|---|---|---|---|
| Clancy L,4-6 | 5 2-3 | 8 | 5 | 5 | 2 | 3 |
| RLJckson | 2 1-3 | 1 | 0 | 0 | 0 | 3 |
| Detroit | | | | | | |
| Morris W,11-2 | 9 | 7 | 3 | 1 | 1 | 4 |

WP—Morris, RLJackson. T—2:38. A—40,879.

School's still in and we drew 41,000 to a Thursday afternoon game. These Detroit fans are something else!

We didn't disappoint them. We called up Ruppert Jones from Evansville yesterday. I put him in and he responded with a three-run game-winning homer in the sixth. The fans took to him right away. They cheered, "Rupe! Rupe! Rupe!" as he circled the bases.

Jack Morris was super and went all the way. Howard Johnson made a great play down the line over the bag at third. Tom Brookens topped it in the ninth with an unbelievable diving stop.

It was a long day. The "Today Show" shot actor Roy Scheider and me at the park at 8 A.M. Roy made a movie at Tiger Stadium last summer and we became pretty good friends.

# FRIDAY, JUNE 8

## AT BALTIMORE

# GAME 54

## TIGERS 3, ORIOLES 2

### (41–13, 5½ GAMES AHEAD)

| DETROIT | | | | | BALTIMORE | | | | |
|---|---|---|---|---|---|---|---|---|---|
| | ab | r | h | bi | | ab | r | h | bi |
| Whitaker 2b | 3 | 0 | 0 | 0 | Bumbry cf | 2 | 1 | 0 | 0 |
| Trammell ss | 3 | 0 | 1 | 1 | Shelby ph | 1 | 0 | 0 | 0 |
| Gibson rf | 5 | 1 | 1 | 0 | Dwyer rf | 2 | 0 | 1 | 0 |
| Parrish c | 5 | 0 | 2 | 1 | Roenicke ph | 1 | 0 | 1 | 0 |
| Evans dh | 3 | 0 | 1 | 0 | Ripken ss | 3 | 0 | 0 | 0 |
| Jones lf | 3 | 0 | 0 | 0 | Murray 1b | 2 | 0 | 0 | 1 |
| Kuntz ph | 1 | 0 | 1 | 0 | Gross 3b | 3 | 0 | 1 | 0 |
| Lemon cf | 4 | 0 | 2 | 0 | Ayala ph | 1 | 0 | 0 | 0 |
| Bergman 1b | 2 | 1 | 1 | 0 | Cruz 3b | 0 | 0 | 0 | 0 |
| Garbey ph | 1 | 0 | 0 | 0 | Lowenstein lf | 3 | 0 | 0 | 0 |
| Johnson 3b | 3 | 1 | 1 | 0 | Rayford ph | 1 | 0 | 0 | 0 |
| Brookens 3b | 0 | 0 | 0 | 0 | Singleton dh | 4 | 0 | 0 | 0 |
| | | | | | Dauer 2b | 3 | 1 | 1 | 0 |
| | | | | | Sakata pr | 1 | 0 | 1 | 0 |
| | | | | | Dempsey c | 3 | 0 | 1 | 0 |
| | | | | | Young ph | 1 | 0 | 0 | 0 |
| **Totals** | 33 | 3 | 10 | 2 | **Totals** | 31 | 2 | 6 | 1 |

Detroit ..................................... 100 000 200—0
Baltimore ............................... 001 001 000—0
Game-winning RBI—Trammell (4). E—
Dwyer, Trammell, TMartinez. DP— De-
troit 1, Baltimore 1. LOB—Detroit 10,
Baltimore 8. 2B—Dauer, Lemon, Johnson,
Evans. SB—Gibson (12). S—Dwyer,
Trammell, Whitaker. SF—Trammell,
Murray.

| | IP | H | R | ER | BB | SO |
|---|---|---|---|---|---|---|
| **Detroit** | | | | | | |
| Wilcox (W 7-3) | 6 | 4 | 2 | 2 | 2 | 1 |
| Bair | 1 | 0 | 0 | 0 | 0 | 1 |
| Hernandez (S 8) | 2 | 2 | 0 | 0 | 1 | 2 |
| **Baltimore** | | | | | | |
| Davis (L 6-2) | 6 1-3 | 8 | 3 | 2 | 2 | 3 |
| T.Martinez | 2 1-3 | 2 | 0 | 0 | 2 | 1 |
| Stewart | 1-3 | 0 | 0 | 0 | 0 | 1 |

WP—Wilcox. T—3:18. A—50,361.

It was an oven in Baltimore today. Almost 100 degrees and muggy. With this heat and seven straight games against Baltimore and Toronto, our guys will be tired at the end of the week.

Landing the first punch was very important. The Orioles know they're in for a war.

Milt Wilcox pitched his heart out for six innings. I took him out after we got the lead with two runs in the seventh. Doug Bair and Willie Hernandez took over.

Bair pitched one perfect inning and Hernandez two. Willie has been a savior. He, Aurelio Lopez, and Bair have been as good as anyone can be. Without those guys, we wouldn't be in first place. The bullpen is the key to our club. We'll win it with this bullpen.

Over 50,000 people showed up to see what these Tigers are all about. They did the Wave and they shook Tiger tails at us all night. But we went home with the win.

# SATURDAY, JUNE 9

## AT BALTIMORE

# GAME 55

## ORIOLES 4, TIGERS 0

## (41–14, 5½ GAMES AHEAD)

| DETROIT | | | | | BALTIMORE | | | | |
|---|---|---|---|---|---|---|---|---|---|
| | ab | r | h | bi | | ab | r | h | bi |
| Whitakr 2b | 4 | 0 | 1 | 0 | Bumbry cf | 4 | 0 | 1 | 0 |
| Tramml ss | 4 | 0 | 0 | 0 | Dwyer rf | 3 | 0 | 0 | 0 |
| Garbey lf | 4 | 0 | 2 | 0 | MK Yong lf | 0 | 0 | 0 | 0 |
| LNPrsh dh | 4 | 0 | 1 | 0 | Ripken ss | 3 | 1 | 1 | 1 |
| Lemon cf | 4 | 0 | 1 | 0 | EMurry 1b | 3 | 1 | 1 | 0 |
| DaEvns 1b | 3 | 0 | 1 | 0 | Gross 3b | 3 | 1 | 1 | 0 |
| Herndn ph | 1 | 0 | 0 | 0 | Lownstn lf | 3 | 0 | 1 | 2 |
| Kuntz rf | 3 | 0 | 1 | 0 | Singltn dh | 4 | 0 | 0 | 0 |
| MCastill c | 3 | 0 | 0 | 0 | Dauer 2b | 3 | 0 | 2 | 1 |
| Brokns 3b | 3 | 0 | 0 | 0 | Dempsy c | 2 | 1 | 0 | 0 |
| Totals | 33 | 0 | 7 | 0 | Totals | 28 | 4 | 7 | 4 |

```
Detroit............................ 000 000 000— 0
Baltimore........................ 001 003 00x— 4
```
Game Winning RBI — Ripken (4).
DP—Detroit 2, Baltimore 1. LOB—Detroit 6, Baltimore 6. 2B—EMurray, Lemon.

| | IP | H | R | ER | BB | SO |
|---|---|---|---|---|---|---|
| **Detroit** | | | | | | |
| Berenguer L,3-4 | 5 1-3 | 3 | 2 | 2 | 4 | 6 |
| Lopez | 1-3 | 3 | 2 | 2 | 1 | 0 |
| Willis | 2 1-3 | 1 | 0 | 0 | 1 | 0 |
| **Baltimore** | | | | | | |
| Flanagan W,5-4 | 9 | 7 | 0 | 0 | 0 | 2 |

T—2:41. A—44,404.

Today was another hot day, but our bats were ice cold. Mike Flanagan shut us out. I can't figure out how he does it, but he pitched a great game. That's the second time in a week he's beaten us.

Aurelio Lopez got hit hard for the first time all season. It was just one of those nights.

We called up Carl Willis yesterday and pitched him a little tonight. He's only 22. If ever I've seen a guy who'll be a great major league pitcher, he's the one. Over the years, he'll help with this club.

We didn't do anything bad tonight. We just didn't hit.

# SUNDAY, JUNE 10

## AT BALTIMORE

# GAMES 56 & 57

## TIGERS 10, ORIOLES 4
## TIGERS 8, ORIOLES 0

### (43-14, 7 GAMES AHEAD)

| DETROIT | ab | r | h | bi | BALTIMORE | ab | r | h | bi |
|---|---|---|---|---|---|---|---|---|---|
| Whitakr 2b | 4 | 5 | 3 | 0 | Bumbry cf | 3 | 0 | 1 | 0 |
| Trammll ss | 4 | 2 | 2 | 4 | Shelby cf | 2 | 0 | 1 | 0 |
| KGibson rf | 5 | 0 | 3 | 4 | Dwyer rf | 3 | 0 | 2 | 0 |
| DaEvns 1b | 3 | 0 | 1 | 2 | GRonck rf | 2 | 0 | 0 | 0 |
| Grubb dh | 2 | 0 | 0 | 0 | Ripken ss | 4 | 1 | 1 | 0 |
| Herndn dh | 3 | 0 | 0 | 0 | EMurry 1b | 4 | 1 | 1 | 2 |
| R Jones lf | 2 | 0 | 0 | 0 | Gross 3b | 3 | 0 | 0 | 0 |
| Garbey lf | 3 | 0 | 1 | 0 | TCruz 3b | 1 | 0 | 0 | 0 |
| Lemon cf | 4 | 1 | 0 | 0 | Lownstn lf | 3 | 0 | 0 | 0 |
| HJhnsn 3b | 3 | 0 | 2 | 0 | MKYng rf | 1 | 1 | 1 | 1 |
| Brokns 3b | 2 | 1 | 0 | 0 | Singltn lf | 4 | 1 | 3 | 1 |
| MCastill c | 4 | 1 | 1 | 0 | Dauer 2b | 3 | 0 | 0 | 0 |
| | | | | | Dempsy c | 2 | 0 | 1 | 0 |
| | | | | | Rayford c | 1 | 0 | 0 | 0 |
| Totals | 39 | 10 | 13 | 10 | Totals | 36 | 4 | 11 | 4 |

Lemon reached first on catcher's interference.

```
Detroit.......................... 102 020 140—10
Baltimore........................ 102 000 010— 4
```

Game Winning RBI — KGibson (7).
E—Dwyer, Gross, Dempsey, EMurray.
DP—Detroit 2, Baltimore 1. LOB—Detroit 7, Baltimore 7. 2B—Whitaker, Trammell. 3B—Trammell. HR—Singleton (2), EMurray (12), MKYoung (2). SB—KGibson (13), HJohnson (3). SF—DaEvans.

| | IP | H | R | ER | BB | SO |
|---|---|---|---|---|---|---|
| **Detroit** | | | | | | |
| Abbott | 2 2-3 | 7 | 3 | 3 | 1 | 0 |
| Bair W,3-0 | 3 1-3 | 1 | 0 | 0 | 1 | 3 |
| Hernandz S,9 | 3 | 3 | 1 | 1 | 0 | 0 |
| **Baltimore** | | | | | | |
| Boddicker L,7-5 | 4 1-3 | 7 | 5 | 4 | 1 | 3 |
| Underwd | 2 1-3 | 3 | 1 | 1 | 1 | 1 |
| SStewart | 1 1-3 | 2 | 4 | 0 | 1 | 0 |
| Swaggerty | 1 | 1 | 0 | 0 | 0 | 0 |

WP—TUnderwood, SStewart. T—2:48.

| DETROIT | ab | r | h | bi | BALTIMORE | ab | r | h | bi |
|---|---|---|---|---|---|---|---|---|---|
| Whitakr 2b | 3 | 1 | 0 | 1 | Bumbry lf | 4 | 0 | 0 | 0 |
| Trammll ss | 5 | 1 | 3 | 0 | Shelby cf | 4 | 0 | 0 | 0 |
| KGibson rf | 5 | 0 | 3 | 2 | Ripken ss | 3 | 0 | 1 | 0 |
| LNParsh c | 5 | 0 | 0 | 0 | EMurry 1b | 3 | 0 | 0 | 0 |
| DaEvns 1b | 3 | 0 | 0 | 0 | Gross 3b | 2 | 0 | 1 | 0 |
| Kuntz lf | 1 | 1 | 1 | 0 | Singltn dh | 3 | 0 | 0 | 0 |
| Grubb dh | 1 | 0 | 0 | 1 | MKYng rf | 3 | 0 | 0 | 0 |
| Herndn dh | 3 | 1 | 1 | 0 | Sakata 2b | 3 | 0 | 0 | 0 |
| Garbey lf | 4 | 1 | 1 | 1 | Rayford c | 3 | 0 | 1 | 0 |
| R Jones cf | 2 | 0 | 0 | 0 | | | | | |
| Lemon cf | 2 | 1 | 0 | 0 | | | | | |
| HJhnsn 3b | 3 | 1 | 3 | 2 | | | | | |
| Brokns 3b | 1 | 1 | 1 | 1 | | | | | |
| Totals | 38 | 8 | 13 | 8 | Totals | 28 | 0 | 3 | 0 |

```
Detroit.......................... 003 001 031— 8
Baltimore........................ 000 000 000— 0
```

Game Winning RBI — HJohnson (3).
E—Ripken. DP—Detroit 2, Baltimore 1. LOB—Detroit 9, Baltimore 2. 2B—KGibson, Gross, Garbey, Rayford. HR—HJohnson (4). SF—Whitaker.

| | IP | H | R | ER | BB | SO |
|---|---|---|---|---|---|---|
| **Detroit** | | | | | | |
| Petry W,9-3 | 9 | 3 | 0 | 0 | 1 | 4 |
| **Baltimore** | | | | | | |
| DMartinez L,1-3 | 5 | 6 | 3 | 3 | 2 | 2 |
| Underwd | 2-3 | 3 | 1 | 1 | 1 | 0 |
| Swaggerty | 2 | 2 | 3 | 1 | 1 | 0 |
| TMartinez | 1 1-3 | 2 | 1 | 1 | 0 | 2 |

HBP—Grubb by DMartinez. WP—TMartinez. T—2:44. A—51,764.

This has got to be one of the greatest days in Tiger history. It has to be when you go into Baltimore and sweep a doubleheader in front of 52,000. Our kids took it right to the World Champs and slapped them right in the face. Today I sensed our kids can compete under pressure. That's the one thing that worried me.

We played super all day long—hitting, pitching, and defense.

Kirk Gibson had six hits and six RBIs. Alan Trammell had five hits and knocked in four runs. Doug Bair came out of the bullpen to win the first game. Dan Petry was awesome with a three-hit shutout in the second.

Howard Johnson was the kid who really showed me something. He played well in the field and came up with five hits, including a long home run down the right field line. HoJo is starting to relax and let his talent come out. I think we'll wind up with a pretty good player here.

After the games, some Baltimore writers asked if this doubleheader proved the Tigers are for real. I told them somebody's missing the point. Who's chasing whom? I believe the Orioles are outstanding, but somewhere along the line, people are getting off the track. We're the ones in front. Let's not ask, "Can we play with them?" The question is, "Can they play with us?"

I know our guys won't wilt. We'll win this whole thing. We have excellent defense, a great bullpen, and three good starting pitchers. Right now, this is the best team in baseball.

**Howard Johnson makes the catch.**   Photo by Doc Holcomb, courtesy of *The Detroit News*

# MONDAY, JUNE 11

## AT TORONTO

# GAME 58

## TIGERS 5, BLUE JAYS 4

### (44–14, 8 GAMES AHEAD)

| DETROIT | ab | r | h | bi |
|---|---|---|---|---|
| Whitakr 2b | 4 | 1 | 1 | 2 |
| Tramml ss | 5 | 1 | 2 | 0 |
| KGibsn dh | 3 | 0 | 0 | 1 |
| LNParsh c | 4 | 0 | 1 | 0 |
| DaEvns 1b | 3 | 1 | 1 | 0 |
| Garbey 1b | 2 | 0 | 0 | 0 |
| Grubb rf | 2 | 1 | 1 | 0 |
| Kuntz rf | 1 | 0 | 0 | 0 |
| Lemon cf | 3 | 0 | 1 | 1 |
| RJones lf | 3 | 0 | 2 | 1 |
| Herndon lf | 1 | 0 | 0 | 0 |
| HJhnsn 3b | 3 | 1 | 1 | 0 |
| Brokns 3b | 0 | 0 | 0 | 0 |
| Totals | 34 | 5 | 10 | 5 |

| TORONTO | ab | r | h | bi |
|---|---|---|---|---|
| Garcia 2b | 4 | 1 | 2 | 0 |
| Collins lf | 4 | 1 | 1 | 3 |
| Moseby cf | 4 | 0 | 1 | 1 |
| Upshaw 1b | 4 | 0 | 1 | 0 |
| Aikens dh | 2 | 0 | 0 | 0 |
| CJhnsn dh | 2 | 0 | 0 | 0 |
| GBell rf | 4 | 0 | 1 | 0 |
| Mulinks 3b | 3 | 0 | 0 | 0 |
| Giorg 3b | 0 | 0 | 0 | 0 |
| Barfild ph | 1 | 0 | 0 | 0 |
| Whitt c | 3 | 1 | 2 | 0 |
| Ferndz ph | 1 | 0 | 0 | 0 |
| Griffin ss | 3 | 1 | 1 | 0 |
| BMrtnz ph | 1 | 0 | 0 | 0 |
| Totals | 36 | 4 | 9 | 4 |

Detroit ............................120 200 000— 5
Toronto ............................003 000 100— 4

Game Winning RBI — Whitaker (6).
E—Whitaker, Trammell. DP—Detroit 1. LOB—Detroit 9, Toronto 6. 2B—Grubb, RJones, LNParrish, Whitt, Lemon. 3B—Trammell. HR—Collins (2), Whitaker (5). SB—GBell (7). S—KGibson. SF—KGibson, Lemon.

| | IP | H | R | ER | BB | SO |
|---|---|---|---|---|---|---|
| **Detroit** | | | | | | |
| Rozema W,2-0 | 5 | 4 | 3 | 3 | 0 | 2 |
| Monge | 0 | 1 | 0 | 0 | 0 | 0 |
| Willis | 1 2-3 | 3 | 1 | 1 | 0 | 0 |
| Hernandz S,10 | 2 1-3 | 1 | 0 | 0 | 0 | 3 |
| **Toronto** | | | | | | |
| Leal L,6-1 | 6 | 9 | 5 | 5 | 2 | 7 |
| Key | 1 2-3 | 1 | 0 | 0 | 2 | 2 |
| Lamp | 1 1-3 | 0 | 0 | 0 | 0 | 2 |

Monge pitched to 1 batter in the 6th, Leal pitched to 1 batter in the 7th.
HBP—Garcia by Rozema. WP—Leal. T—3:04. A—35,062.

The Toronto papers called this "The June World Series." It's big, but we've got to keep our heads about this. There's a long way to go.

Toronto people are great. Very friendly and they enjoy the fact they have a major league team to root for. They tried the Wave against us, but an ocean couldn't have stopped our bullpen.

Willie Hernandez pitched another 2-1/3 scoreless innings for his tenth save. I thought Willie would be good; but no one in his right mind could have expected this. This might sound crazy, but even with all those RBIs, I wouldn't trade Willie for Eddie Murray. Willie is the best relief pitcher in the league right now. Maybe even in the major leagues.

Dave Rozema gave us five tough innings. With our bullpen that's all we need from him. We purchased Sid Monge from San Diego yesterday and I ran him out there. Carl Willis came in before Willie shut the door. I mean he slammed the door. S-L-A-M.

Ruppert Jones had two more hits. He can play and he's a good outfielder who can run. Chet Lemon made another great catch. He's having the best year of his career. Alan Trammell made two more outstanding plays to keep us out of trouble before it could begin. These are things that don't show up in box scores.

If we could just get Larry Herndon, Darrell Evans, and Lance Parrish hitting, we would really be awesome.

# TUESDAY, JUNE 12

## AT TORONTO

# GAME 59

## BLUE JAYS 12, TIGERS 3

### (44–15, 7 GAMES AHEAD)

| DETROIT | ab | r | h | bi | TORONTO | ab | r | h | bi |
|---|---|---|---|---|---|---|---|---|---|
| Whitakr 2b | 4 | 0 | 3 | 2 | Garcia 2b | 5 | 2 | 4 | 1 |
| Tramml ss | 2 | 0 | 0 | 0 | Collins lf | 2 | 2 | 2 | 1 |
| Brookns ss | 2 | 0 | 0 | 1 | Barfield rf | 2 | 0 | 1 | 0 |
| K Gibson rf | 4 | 0 | 0 | 0 | Moseby cf | 5 | 1 | 1 | 1 |
| LNParsh c | 3 | 0 | 0 | 0 | Upshaw 1b | 3 | 2 | 0 | 1 |
| MCastill c | 1 | 0 | 0 | 0 | Aikens dh | 2 | 0 | 1 | 1 |
| DaEvns 1b | 4 | 0 | 0 | 0 | C Jhnsn dh | 0 | 1 | 0 | 1 |
| Grubb dh | 4 | 0 | 2 | 0 | GBell rf | 4 | 0 | 3 | 2 |
| Lemon cf | 3 | 1 | 1 | 0 | Leach lf | 1 | 0 | 0 | 0 |
| Kuntz cf | 0 | 0 | 0 | 0 | Mulinks 3b | 2 | 0 | 0 | 0 |
| R Jones lf | 4 | 0 | 0 | 0 | Glorg 3b | 3 | 1 | 1 | 0 |
| HJhnsn 3b | 3 | 2 | 2 | 0 | Whitt c | 4 | 2 | 2 | 3 |
| | | | | | Griffin ss | 3 | 1 | 1 | 0 |
| | | | | | Fernndz ss | 2 | 0 | 0 | 0 |
| Totals | 34 | 3 | 8 | 3 | Totals | 38 | 12 | 16 | 11 |

Detroit .............................. 000 010 200— 3
Toronto ............................. 102 600 030—12

Game Winning RBI — Collins (6).
E—Griffin, DaEvans. DP—Detroit 1,
Toronto 2. LOB—Detroit 8, Toronto 9.
2B—Whitaker, Garcia, Grubb, GBell. 3B—
Collins, Whitaker. HR—Whitt (4). SB—
Collins (15). SF—CJohnson.

| | IP | H | R | ER | BB | SO |
|---|---|---|---|---|---|---|
| **Detroit** | | | | | | |
| Morris L, 11-3 | 3 | 8 | 6 | 6 | 2 | 3 |
| Monge | 4 | 6 | 3 | 2 | 1 | 2 |
| Lopez | 1 | 2 | 3 | 3 | 1 | 0 |
| **Toronto** | | | | | | |
| Clancy W, 5-6 | 7 2-3 | 7 | 3 | 3 | 4 | 5 |
| RL Jckson | 1 1-3 | 1 | 0 | 0 | 0 | 0 |

Morris pitched to 3 batters in the 4th.
HBP—Collins hit by Monge, Upshaw hit
by Monge. T—2:43. A—40,437.

It was Toronto's turn tonight. They kicked us all around the park. You don't worry about these kinds of losses because they're going to happen to everyone once in awhile. It's the first time we've really been mauled all year.

Jack Morris was lit up for six runs in three innings. He had nothing and never made a good pitch when he got two strikes on someone.

Sid Monge had trouble in his four innings. He's still nervous being around us. We have to build his confidence.

Maybe after this series some of the media will disappear until the fall. I can't believe all the writers who follow us everywhere. I honestly feel this has tired some of our players.

# WEDNESDAY, JUNE 13

## AT TORONTO

# GAME 60

## BLUE JAYS 7, TIGERS 3

### (44–16, 6 GAMES AHEAD)

| DETROIT | ab | r | h | bi | TORONTO | ab | r | h | bi |
|---|---|---|---|---|---|---|---|---|---|
| Whitakr 2b | 5 | 1 | 1 | 0 | Garcia 2b | 4 | 0 | 1 | 1 |
| Tramml ss | 5 | 1 | 0 | 0 | Collins lf | 4 | 1 | 1 | 1 |
| K Gibson rf | 3 | 0 | 1 | 0 | Moseby cf | 2 | 1 | 1 | 0 |
| Kuntz rf | 1 | 0 | 0 | 0 | Upshaw 1b | 4 | 1 | 2 | 2 |
| Brgmn ph | 1 | 0 | 0 | 0 | Aikens dh | 4 | 1 | 1 | 0 |
| LNParsh c | 4 | 1 | 1 | 1 | GBell rf | 4 | 0 | 0 | 0 |
| DaEvns 1b | 1 | 0 | 1 | 0 | Mullnks 3b | 4 | 1 | 3 | 1 |
| Grubb dh | 3 | 0 | 1 | 0 | Glorg 3b | 0 | 0 | 0 | 0 |
| Herndn dh | 1 | 0 | 0 | 0 | Whitt c | 3 | 0 | 0 | 1 |
| Lemon cf | 4 | 0 | 1 | 1 | Griffin ss | 4 | 2 | 2 | 1 |
| R Jones lf | 4 | 0 | 0 | 0 | | | | | |
| HJhnsn 3b | 4 | 0 | 1 | 0 | | | | | |
| Totals | 36 | 3 | 7 | 2 | Totals | 33 | 7 | 11 | 7 |

Detroit...........................000 000 030— 3
Toronto...........................020 020 30x— 7
Game Winning RBI — Mulliniks (1).
E—Mulliniks, Griffin. LOB—Detroit 9,
Toronto 5. 2B—Mulliniks 2, Griffin, Garcia,
Upshaw, LNParrish. SF—Whitt.

| | IP | H | R | ER | BB | SO |
|---|---|---|---|---|---|---|
| **Detroit** | | | | | | |
| Wilcox L,7-4 | 5 | 6 | 4 | 4 | 1 | 2 |
| Bair | 2 | 4 | 3 | 3 | 0 | 1 |
| Willis | 1 | 1 | 0 | 0 | 0 | 0 |
| **Toronto** | | | | | | |
| Stieb W,8-2 | 7 | 3 | 0 | 0 | 2 | 5 |
| Key | 2-3 | 3 | 3 | 1 | 1 | 0 |
| Lamp | 1 1-3 | 1 | 0 | 0 | 0 | 2 |

HBP—Moseby hit by Wilcox. T—2:28.
A—34,122.

We ended our two weeks with Toronto and Baltimore by getting our butts kicked. We split 14 games with them. We actually gained a half game on Toronto in the process.

But how can we be satisfied? We could have blown the lid off everything just by playing well. To tell the truth, we haven't played well in 20 games. We're not catching the ball the way we were and we're not hitting. All of our offense was concentrated in three games. We really played poorly the last two games. We better get our act together and we better make it quick. We're playing like zombies on the field.

So far, this team has not shown me it has the killer instinct. When a great team smells blood, it goes for the jugular. I hope before the season is over I'll see that. We have great talent and prime players, but they still haven't shown me they know how to put people away. Bury them. You can be a good team on talent alone. But you can't be great until you know how to go for the jugular.

# THURSDAY, JUNE 14

## AT MILWAUKEE

## (44–16, 6 GAMES AHEAD)

We didn't arrive in Milwaukee until late afternoon. At the elevator I signed autographs for some kids. I've never asked anyone for an autograph in my life. I probably never will. I've never known why anyone would want my autograph, but I always take time to sign and say thank you afterward. I thank them because they think enough of me to want my signature.

Photo by Doc Holcomb, courtesy of *The Detroit News*

**High fives for Lance Parrish and Alan Trammell.**

# FRIDAY, JUNE 15

## AT MILWAUKEE

# GAME 61

## TIGERS 3, BREWERS 2

### (45–16, 6 GAMES AHEAD)

| DETROIT | ab r h bi | MILWAUKEE | ab r h bi |
|---|---|---|---|
| Whitakr 2b | 5 0 1 0 | James rf | 4 2 3 0 |
| Tramml ss | 5 1 0 0 | Gantnr 2b | 4 0 3 2 |
| K Gibson rf | 5 1 1 0 | Yount ss | 4 0 0 0 |
| LN Parsh c | 3 1 2 1 | Cooper 1b | 4 0 1 0 |
| DaEvns 1b | 2 0 0 0 | Oglivie lf | 4 0 1 0 |
| Bergmn 1b | 0 0 0 0 | Smmns dh | 4 0 0 0 |
| Grubb dh | 2 0 0 1 | R Howel 3b | 2 0 0 0 |
| Herndon lf | 3 0 2 1 | Romero 3b | 1 0 0 0 |
| Kuntz cf | 0 0 0 0 | Sundbrg c | 3 0 0 0 |
| Lemon cf | 3 0 1 0 | Mannng cf | 2 0 0 0 |
| R Jones ph | 0 0 0 0 | R Clark cf | 1 0 0 0 |
| Garbey lf | 1 0 0 0 | | |
| H Jhnsn 3b | 4 0 0 0 | | |
| Brokns 3b | 0 0 0 0 | | |
| Totals | 33 3 7 3 | Totals | 33 2 8 2 |

```
Detroit ..........................010 000 020— 3
Milwaukee ....................001 001 000— 2
```
Game Winning RBI — Herndon (3).
E—Yount, Manning. DP—Detroit 1.
LOB—Detroit 9, Milwaukee 4. 2B—James,
Gantner. 3B—James. HR—LNParrish (10).
S—Grubb, LNParrish. SF—Grubb.

| | IP | H | R ER | BB SO |
|---|---|---|---|---|
| **Detroit** | | | | |
| Petry W, 10-3 | 7 | 7 | 2 2 | 0 2 |
| Hernandz S, 11 | 2 | 1 | 0 0 | 0 2 |
| **Milwaukee** | | | | |
| Cocanowr L, 5-6 | 7 1-3 | 7 | 3 1 | 3 3 |
| Waits | 1 2-3 | 0 | 0 0 | 0 2 |

T—2:42. A—32,074.

We got a couple of gifts today. Robin Yount bobbled Alan Trammell's grounder to open the eighth. Then Rick Manning dropped a sacrifice fly by John Grubb. Those guys don't make mistakes often, so we had to take advantage of them.

Larry Herndon got an infield single with the bases loaded in the eighth. But we're still not hitting with men on often enough to suit me.

Dan Petry battled for seven innings. Then it was Willie Hernandez again for the last two. He's got four saves in our last five wins.

Midnight is the trading deadline. I had a long talk with Bill Lajoie who is trying to swing a deal with Cleveland or Montreal. Nothing worked. We've got to come up with another pitcher or we'll run into problems down the line.

# SATURDAY, JUNE 16

## AT MILWAUKEE

# GAME 62

## TIGERS 6, BREWERS 0

### (46–16, 6 GAMES AHEAD)

| DETROIT | ab | r | h | bi | MILWAUKEE | ab | r | h | bi |
|---|---|---|---|---|---|---|---|---|---|
| Whitaker 2b | 5 | 0 | 1 | 0 | James rf | 4 | 0 | 0 | 0 |
| Trammell ss | 5 | 0 | 0 | 0 | Gantner 2b | 4 | 0 | 1 | 0 |
| Gibson rf | 4 | 2 | 2 | 0 | Yount ss | 3 | 0 | 2 | 0 |
| Parrish c | 4 | 1 | 1 | 0 | Cooper 1b | 4 | 0 | 0 | 0 |
| Evans dh | 3 | 1 | 1 | 4 | Ogilvie lf | 4 | 0 | 1 | 0 |
| Grubb lf | 3 | 0 | 0 | 0 | Simmons dh | 4 | 0 | 1 | 0 |
| Kuntz cf | 1 | 0 | 0 | 0 | Howell 3b | 3 | 0 | 0 | 0 |
| Bergman 1b | 4 | 1 | 3 | 0 | Sundberg c | 1 | 0 | 0 | 0 |
| Jones cf | 4 | 1 | 2 | 2 | Manning cf | 3 | 0 | 0 | 0 |
| Johnson 3b | 3 | 0 | 0 | 0 | | | | | |
| Brookens 3b | 1 | 0 | 0 | 0 | | | | | |
| Totals | 37 | 6 | 10 | 6 | Totals | 30 | 0 | 5 | 0 |

Detroit ............................... 002 103 000—6
Milwaukee ........................... 000 000 000—0
Game-winning RBI—Jones (2). E—Cooper. DP—Detroit 2. LOB— Detroit 5, Milwaukee 6. 3B—Gibson. HR— Jones (2), Evans (5). SF—Evans.

| | IP | H | R | ER | BB | SO |
|---|---|---|---|---|---|---|
| **Detroit** | | | | | | |
| Berenguer (W 4-4) | 9 | 5 | 5 | 0 | 3 | 1 |
| **Milwaukee** | | | | | | |
| Sutton (L 3-7) | 5 | 7 | 6 | 6 | 0 | 6 |
| Ladd | 3 | 2 | 0 | 0 | 0 | 2 |
| Tellmann | 1 | 1 | 0 | 0 | 0 | 0 |

Sutton pitched to 3 batters in 6th.
WP—Berenguer. PB—Parrish. T—2:30.
A—50,395.

Roger Craig and I walked for almost two hours around Lake Michigan this morning. He promised Juan Berenguer would pitch a good game tonight.

Roger was right. Juan got his second career shutout and we finally got him some runs. Darrell Evans hit a three-run homer. Maybe that'll get him going. Ruppert Jones really took one deep into the right field bleachers. Those were two clutch hits we desperately needed. Lou Whitaker and Alan Trammell have started to slow down a little and someone has to pick up the slack.

**Ruppert Jones.** Photo courtesy of Detroit Tigers

**Darrell Evans.** Photo courtesy of Detroit Tigers

# SUNDAY, JUNE 17

## AT MILWAUKEE

# GAME 63

## TIGERS 7, BREWERS 4

### (47–16, 6 GAMES AHEAD)

| DETROIT | | | | | MILWAUKEE | | | | |
|---|---|---|---|---|---|---|---|---|---|
| | ab | r | h | bi | | ab | r | h | bi |
| Kuntz rf | 3 | 1 | 0 | 0 | James rf | 3 | 0 | 0 | 0 |
| Tramml ss | 5 | 0 | 1 | 1 | Gantnr 2b | 4 | 0 | 1 | 0 |
| Garbey 1b | 5 | 1 | 1 | 0 | Yount ss | 3 | 1 | 1 | 0 |
| Bergmn 1b | 0 | 0 | 0 | 0 | Cooper 1b | 4 | 1 | 1 | 1 |
| LNPrsh dh | 5 | 1 | 2 | 0 | Oglivie lf | 3 | 1 | 0 | 0 |
| Lemon cf | 5 | 1 | 3 | 2 | Smmns dh | 4 | 1 | 3 | 0 |
| Herndon lf | 3 | 0 | 1 | 0 | Schroedr c | 3 | 0 | 0 | 1 |
| MCastill c | 3 | 1 | 0 | 0 | Ready 3b | 3 | 0 | 0 | 0 |
| Brokns 2b | 4 | 1 | 2 | 2 | RHowel ph | 1 | 0 | 0 | 1 |
| HJhnsn 3b | 3 | 1 | 1 | 1 | Mannng cf | 4 | 0 | 0 | 0 |
| Whitakr 2b | 1 | 0 | 0 | 0 | | | | | |
| Totals | 37 | 7 | 11 | 6 | Totals | 32 | 4 | 6 | 3 |

```
Detroit ..........................100 050 010— 7
Milwaukee ....................010 002 001— 4
```

Game Winning RBI — None.

E—McClure. LOB—Detroit 12, Milwaukee 5. 2B—Lemon, Gantner, Cooper, Simmons. 3B—Lemon, Brookens. SB—Simmons (1), Garbey (3), Lemon (4). S—HJohnson. SF—Schroeder.

| | IP | H | R | ER | BB | SO |
|---|---|---|---|---|---|---|
| **Detroit** | | | | | | |
| Rozema W,3-0 | 5 | 4 | 1 | 1 | 1 | 0 |
| Lopez S,8 | 4 | 2 | 3 | 3 | 2 | 2 |
| **Milwaukee** | | | | | | |
| McClure L,1-2 | 4 2-3 | 7 | 5 | 1 | 4 | 5 |
| Lazorko | 2 1-3 | 2 | 1 | 1 | 3 | 1 |
| Tellmann | 2 | 2 | 1 | 1 | 1 | 0 |

WP—Rozema, Lopez 2. T—2:51. A—44,902.

We brought out the brooms. We swept Milwaukee. This game was a big one because I used my righthanded lineup.

I don't know if anyone has paid close attention, but everyone on the team has played his part this year. This will pay off down the line because everyone feels part of the team. Our coaches have done a great job keeping everyone ready.

Tom Brookens played second and made a couple of big league plays. He also got a couple of hits. Everyone is pulling for Brookens.

Dave Rozema held them for five innings and it was easy for Aurelio Lopez to hold a five-run lead. Lopey needs more work and I might start using him in long relief.

We've got a little problem with Jack Morris. His elbow started to hurt during his last start. He will not pitch against New York. I want to be careful with him. We can't lose him for too long. Carl Willis will start tomorrow.

# MONDAY, JUNE 18

## AT DETROIT

# GAME 64

## YANKEES 2, TIGERS 1

### (47–17, 5½ GAMES AHEAD)

| NEW YORK | ab | r | h | bi | DETROIT | ab | r | h | bi |
|---|---|---|---|---|---|---|---|---|---|
| Rndlph 2b | 5 | 2 | 2 | 0 | Whitakr 2b | 3 | 0 | 1 | 0 |
| Wynegar c | 5 | 0 | 1 | 0 | Tramml ss | 4 | 0 | 0 | 0 |
| Mtngly 1b | 2 | 0 | 1 | 2 | KGibson rf | 4 | 1 | 2 | 1 |
| Baylor dh | 3 | 0 | 0 | 0 | LNParsh c | 4 | 0 | 0 | 0 |
| Winfield rf | 4 | 0 | 2 | 0 | DEvns dh | 3 | 0 | 0 | 0 |
| Kemp lf | 3 | 0 | 0 | 0 | Brokns pr | 0 | 0 | 0 | 0 |
| Dayett lf | 0 | 0 | 0 | 0 | Grubb ph | 0 | 0 | 0 | 0 |
| Smalley 3b | 4 | 0 | 0 | 0 | Kuntz pr | 0 | 0 | 0 | 0 |
| Griffey cf | 4 | 0 | 1 | 0 | Lemon cf | 2 | 0 | 0 | 0 |
| OMoren cf | 0 | 0 | 0 | 0 | Herndon lf | 4 | 0 | 0 | 0 |
| Mechm ss | 4 | 0 | 1 | 0 | Bergmn 1b | 3 | 0 | 0 | 0 |
| | | | | | Garbey 3b | 3 | 0 | 0 | 0 |
| Totals | 34 | 2 | 8 | 2 | Totals | 30 | 1 | 3 | 1 |

```
New York .......................... 100 010 000— 2
Detroit ............................. 100 000 000— 1
```
Game Winning RBI — Mattingly (4).
E—Mattingly. LOB—New York 9, Detroit 6. 2B—Mattingly, Randolph, Meacham. HR—KGibson (8). SF—Mattingly.

| | IP | H | R | ER | BB | SO |
|---|---|---|---|---|---|---|
| **New York** | | | | | | |
| Niekro W,10-3 | 8 2-3 | 3 | 1 | 1 | 4 | 6 |
| Rijo S,2 | 1-3 | 0 | 0 | 0 | 0 | 0 |
| **Detroit** | | | | | | |
| Wilcox L,7-5 | 7 | 7 | 2 | 2 | 3 | 7 |
| Hernandz | 2 | 1 | 0 | 0 | 0 | 0 |

T—2:54. A—40,315.

The way we're drawing, home and road, we're bound to set attendance records. We'll go over 2½ million at home and close to two million on the road.

We had over 40,000 for tonight's game with the Yankees. Too bad we didn't show them much. Wilcox pitched a good game, but two runs just don't get it done. Alan Trammell is in an awful slump—1 for 26. Larry Herndon hasn't hit anything all year. Lance Parrish has yet to explode.

Tonight, though, I have to give credit to the old man: Phil Niekro pitched one terrific game. Kirk Gibson homered in the first, but that was it, see you later.

# TUESDAY, JUNE 19

## AT DETROIT

# GAME 65

## TIGERS 7, YANKEES 6

### (48–17, 6½ GAMES AHEAD)

| NEW YORK | ab | r | h | bi | DETROIT | ab | r | h | bi |
|---|---|---|---|---|---|---|---|---|---|
| Rndlph 2b | 4 | 1 | 1 | 0 | Whitakr 2b | 4 | 1 | 1 | 0 |
| Wynegar c | 3 | 1 | 0 | 0 | Tramml ss | 4 | 0 | 1 | 0 |
| Mtngly 1b | 5 | 1 | 2 | 2 | Garbey 1b | 4 | 1 | 2 | 0 |
| Winfield rf | 4 | 1 | 3 | 0 | LNPrsh dh | 4 | 2 | 2 | 2 |
| Gamble dh | 3 | 0 | 0 | 0 | Lemon cf | 3 | 1 | 1 | 0 |
| Baylor ph | 1 | 0 | 0 | 0 | Herndon lf | 4 | 2 | 3 | 1 |
| Kemp lf | 4 | 1 | 1 | 1 | Kuntz rf | 4 | 0 | 1 | 2 |
| Smalley 3b | 5 | 1 | 1 | 1 | Brokns 3b | 3 | 0 | 1 | 1 |
| OMoren cf | 4 | 0 | 1 | 1 | KGibsn ph | 0 | 0 | 0 | 1 |
| Mechm ss | 4 | 0 | 0 | 0 | Bergmn 1b | 0 | 0 | 0 | 0 |
|  |  |  |  |  | MCastill c | 4 | 0 | 0 | 0 |
| Totals | 37 | 6 | 9 | 5 | Totals | 34 | 7 | 12 | 7 |

```
New York ..........................020  020  002— 6
Detroit ...........................200  000  14x— 7
```

Game Winning RBI — Kuntz (3).
E—Whitaker, Garbey. DP—New York 1, Detroit 1. LOB—New York 10, Detroit 5. 2B—Winfield, Lemon, Herndon, Brookens. 3B—Smalley. HR—LNParrish (11), Mattingly (11). SB—OMoreno (8). SF—KGibson.

| | IP | H | R | ER | BB | SO |
|---|---|---|---|---|---|---|
| **New York** | | | | | | |
| Guidry L,5-5 | 7 1-3 | 12 | 7 | 7 | 1 | 5 |
| Christnsen | 2-3 | 0 | 0 | 0 | 0 | 0 |
| **Detroit** | | | | | | |
| Willis | 4 1-3 | 9 | 4 | 4 | 0 | 3 |
| Bair | 2 2-3 | 0 | 0 | 0 | 4 | 1 |
| Lopez ,6-0 | 1 1-3 | 0 | 2 | 0 | 2 | 0 |
| Hernandz S,12 | 2-3 | 0 | 0 | 0 | 0 | 0 |

T—2:49. A—41,192.

People say I look so much older on TV when I'm standing in the dugout. I can't disagree—that ain't no picnic out there. I never relax when I'm managing the team.

Tonight's a good example. We couldn't really get to Ron Guidry until the eighth with four runs. Willie Hernandez came on in the ninth to save the win for Aurelio Lopez. I hate to think where we would be without Willie.

It was a rough game and a good one to win. Toronto won their game, so we had to keep pace.

Earlier this afternoon the Detroit Chamber of Commerce honored me at a luncheon with the Summit Award. I'm told it's their highest honor. I wish I could share it with the entire organization. They deserve the credit.

# WEDNESDAY, JUNE 20

## AT DETROIT

# GAME 66

## TIGERS 9, YANKEES 6

### (13 INNINGS)

### (49–17, 7½ GAMES AHEAD)

| NEW YORK | ab | r | h | bi | DETROIT | ab | r | h | bi |
|---|---|---|---|---|---|---|---|---|---|
| Rndlph 2b | 7 | 1 | 1 | 0 | Kuntz rf | 2 | 1 | 0 | 0 |
| Wynegar c | 6 | 1 | 2 | 1 | KGibson rf | 2 | 1 | 0 | 0 |
| Mtngly 1b | 6 | 0 | 2 | 1 | Trammll ss | 5 | 1 | 2 | 2 |
| Winfield rf | 6 | 2 | 3 | 2 | Garbey 1b | 4 | 1 | 2 | 1 |
| Gamble dh | 2 | 0 | 1 | 1 | Bergmn 1b | 2 | 0 | 0 | 0 |
| Harrah dh | 1 | 0 | 0 | 0 | LNPrsh dh | 6 | 2 | 2 | 1 |
| Griffey dh | 1 | 0 | 1 | 0 | Lemon cf | 5 | 1 | 4 | 2 |
| Kemp lf | 5 | 0 | 1 | 0 | Herndon lf | 4 | 0 | 0 | 0 |
| Smalley 3b | 5 | 0 | 1 | 0 | Grubb ph | 0 | 1 | 0 | 0 |
| OMoren cf | 2 | 1 | 1 | 0 | Brokns 2b | 2 | 0 | 0 | 0 |
| Baylor ph | 0 | 0 | 0 | 0 | Whitakr 2b | 3 | 0 | 0 | 0 |
| Dayett rf | 2 | 0 | 0 | 0 | HJhnsn 3b | 5 | 1 | 2 | 3 |
| Mechm ss | 6 | 1 | 1 | 1 | MCastill c | 5 | 0 | 0 | 0 |
| Totals | 49 | 6 | 14 | 6 | Totals | 45 | 9 | 12 | 9 |

```
New York.................. 220 000 011 000 0— 6
Detroit.................... 201 001 110 000 3— 9
```

Two out when winning run scored.
Game Winning RBI — HJohnson (4).
E—Bergman. DP—New York 2, Detroit 3.
LOB—New York 10, Detroit 6. 2B—Winfield,
Meacham, Lemon, Randolph. HR— Trammell (8), LNParrish (12), Winfield (8),
Lemon (11), HJohnson (5). SB—OMoreno
(9). S—Kemp, Whitaker, Lemon.

| | IP | H | R | ER | BB | SO |
|---|---|---|---|---|---|---|
| **New York** | | | | | | |
| Shirley | 5 | 7 | 4 | 4 | 2 | 0 |
| Christnsen | 2 | 3 | 2 | 2 | 2 | 3 |
| Fontenot | 5 | 0 | 0 | 0 | 1 | 3 |
| Rijo L,1-7 | 2-3 | 2 | 3 | 3 | 1 | 0 |
| **Detroit** | | | | | | |
| Petry | 6 | 10 | 4 | 4 | 2 | 1 |
| Lopez | 1 | 1 | 1 | 1 | 1 | 0 |
| Hernandz | 4 | 3 | 1 | 1 | 2 | 4 |
| Bair W,4-0 | 2 | 1 | 0 | 0 | 0 | 2 |

Shirley pitched to 1 batter in 6th, Lopez
pitched to 2 batter in 8th, Christiansen
pitched to 2 batters in 8th.
PB—MCastillo. T—3:51. A—41,972.

It took some scrambling, but we got the Yanks in the 13th. Howard Johnson belted a three-run shot into the upper deck with two out. I mean to say he shot it up there. S-H-O-T.

This kid is really coming along. His confidence is growing. He's getting better and better. He's finally gotten wet and is closing in on the other side of the river.

We also got homers from Alan Trammell, Lance Parrish, and Chet Lemon. It's sure good to see Trammell hitting again.

Doug Bair pitched the last two innings for the win. What have I been saying about our bullpen?

Thirteen innings on top of an extra long day. I went to Flint to play in a charity golf tournament for kids. I enjoyed doing that. But the media attention is more than I ever expected. Even in our big years at Cincinnati, it never went on for so long.

It's great for the club because we've become a national team in just three months. It's great for the city of Detroit. Sometimes I get to the point where I don't know how many times I can answer the same question over and over in a different way. I try to give everyone a different angle, but with so many people asking it's not that easy.

# THURSDAY, JUNE 21

## AT DETROIT

# GAME 67

## BREWERS 4, TIGERS 3

### (49–18, 6½ GAMES AHEAD)

| MILWAUKEE | ab | r | h | bi | DETROIT | ab | r | h | bi |
|---|---|---|---|---|---|---|---|---|---|
| James rf | 4 | 0 | 1 | 0 | Whitakr 2b | 4 | 0 | 0 | 0 |
| Gantnr 2b | 3 | 0 | 1 | 0 | Tramml ss | 4 | 0 | 0 | 0 |
| Yount ss | 3 | 1 | 0 | 0 | KGibson rf | 4 | 0 | 0 | 0 |
| Cooper 1b | 4 | 0 | 1 | 0 | DaEvns 1b | 2 | 1 | 1 | 0 |
| Oglivie lf | 4 | 0 | 1 | 1 | Brokns pr | 0 | 0 | 0 | 0 |
| Smmns dh | 4 | 0 | 1 | 0 | Grubb dh | 4 | 0 | 0 | 0 |
| Mannng pr | 0 | 0 | 0 | 0 | Kuntz pr | 0 | 0 | 0 | 0 |
| RClark cf | 3 | 1 | 1 | 0 | Lemon cf | 3 | 1 | 1 | 1 |
| Sundbrg c | 3 | 2 | 2 | 1 | HJhnsn 3b | 4 | 0 | 1 | 0 |
| Romero 3b | 3 | 0 | 1 | 1 | RJones lf | 2 | 0 | 0 | 0 |
| | | | | | Herndon lf | 1 | 1 | 1 | 2 |
| | | | | | MCastill c | 3 | 0 | 0 | 0 |
| Totals | 31 | 4 | 9 | 3 | Totals | 31 | 3 | 4 | 3 |

Milwaukee...................... 001 021 000— 4
Detroit............................ 000 000 300— 3
 Game Winning RBI — Sundberg (6).
 DP—Detroit 2. LOB—Milwaukee 5, Detroit 4. 2B—Sundberg, Oglivie, Lemon, Cooper. HR—Sundberg (3), Herndon (1). S—RClark. SF—Romero.

| | IP | H | R | ER | BB | SO |
|---|---|---|---|---|---|---|
| **Milwaukee** | | | | | | |
| Sutton W,4-7 | 6 1-3 | | | 2 | 3 | 6 |
| Waits | 1-3 | | 1 | 1 | 0 | 1 |
| Fingers S,12 | 2 1-3 | 1 | 0 | 0 | 0 | 2 |
| **Detroit** | | | | | | |
| Berengur L,4-5 | 5 1-3 | 7 | 4 | 4 | 2 | 1 |
| Monge | 2 2-3 | 1 | 0 | 0 | 1 | 0 |
| Lopez | 1 | 1 | 0 | 0 | 0 | 0 |
 WP—Berenguer. T—2:30. A—32,291.

The Brewers must have been mad from our sweep in Milwaukee. Don Sutton and Rollie Fingers stopped us today. Now there are two veteran pitchers. Fingers doesn't throw the way he used to, but he's awfully smart and still has that forkball.

Larry Herndon hit his first homer of the season. I hope that will help him out of his slump, because we can't win without him.

My daughter, Shirlee, is in town. Before the game we joked about Tom Selleck (who is seen on television wearing a Detroit cap) writing us into a *Magnum, P.I.* episode. We better win this thing before worrying about the good times.

# FRIDAY, JUNE 22

## AT DETROIT

# GAME 68

## TIGERS 7, BREWERS 3

### (50–18, 7½ GAMES AHEAD)

| MILWAUKEE | ab | r | h | bi | DETROIT | ab | r | h | bi |
|---|---|---|---|---|---|---|---|---|---|
| James rf | 5 | 1 | 1 | 0 | Kuntz rf | 0 | 1 | 0 | 0 |
| Gantnr 2b | 4 | 1 | 2 | 2 | KGibson rf | 3 | 0 | 1 | 2 |
| Yount ss | 3 | 0 | 0 | 0 | Tramml ss | 5 | 1 | 1 | 0 |
| Cooper 1b | 4 | 0 | 0 | 0 | Garbey dh | 4 | 1 | 1 | 1 |
| Oglivie lf | 4 | 1 | 1 | 1 | LNParsh c | 4 | 0 | 1 | 0 |
| Smmns dh | 4 | 0 | 0 | 0 | Lemon cf | 3 | 1 | 0 | 0 |
| RClark cf | 4 | 0 | 1 | 0 | Herndon lf | 4 | 1 | 1 | 2 |
| Sundbrg c | 2-0 | 1 | 0 | | DaEvns 1b | 3 | 0 | 1 | 1 |
| Romero 3b | 4 | 0 | 0 | 0 | Bergmn 1b | 0 | 0 | 0 | 0 |
| | | | | | HJhnsn 3b | 3 | 0 | 0 | 0 |
| | | | | | Whitakr 2b | 1 | 1 | 1 | 0 |
| | | | | | Brokns 2b | 2 | 1 | 2 | 1 |
| Totals | 34 | 3 | 6 | 3 | Totals | 32 | 7 | 9 | 7 |

Milwaukee ........................ 002 001 000— 3
Detroit ............................500 000 02x— 7
Game Winning RBI — Garbey (2).
E—HJohnson, KGibson. DP—Detroit 1.
LOB—Milwaukee 7, Detroit 7. 2B— LNParrish, KGibson. HR—Gantner (2), Oglivie (4). SB—Sundberg (1).

| | IP | H | R | ER | BB | SO |
|---|---|---|---|---|---|---|
| **Milwaukee** | | | | | | |
| McClure L, 1-3 | 1-3 | 3 | 5 | 5 | 2 | 0 |
| Lazorko | 4 2-3 | 3 | 0 | 0 | 2 | 3 |
| BGibson | 2 | 0 | 0 | 0 | 1 | 2 |
| Tellmann | 1 | 3 | 2 | 2 | 0 | 0 |
| **Detroit** | | | | | | |
| Rozema W, 4-0 | 6 | 5 | 3 | 3 | 1 | 1 |
| Willis | 2-3 | 0 | 0 | 0 | 1 | 0 |
| Hernandz S, 13 | 2 1-3 | 1 | 0 | 0 | 1 | 5 |

HBP—Brookens by Lazorko. T—2:53.
A—48,497.

Another wild Friday night: More than 48,000 at Tiger Stadium. Good thing we didn't disappoint them. Dave Rozema and Carl Willis pitched before Willie Hernandez slammed the door for the 13th time this season. Don't ask me to explain Willie— he just does the job.

Joe Altobelli called this morning to ask me to coach in the All-Star Game. I was scheduled to do radio commentary for CBS, but I had to call and cancel. It would have been nice with all the national attention we're getting. But baseball has brought me everything I have and my first responsibility must always be to the game.

# SATURDAY, JUNE 23

## AT DETROIT

# GAME 69

## TIGERS 5, BREWERS 1

### (51–18, 7½ GAMES AHEAD)

| MILWAUKEE | ab | r | h | bi | DETROIT | ab | r | h | bi |
|---|---|---|---|---|---|---|---|---|---|
| James rf | 4 | 0 | 1 | 0 | Whitakr 2b | 5 | 0 | 1 | 0 |
| Gantnr 2b | 3 | 0 | 0 | 1 | Tramml ss | 4 | 0 | 0 | 0 |
| Yount ss | 3 | 0 | 0 | 0 | KGibson rf | 4 | 2 | 3 | 1 |
| Cooper 1b | 4 | 0 | 1 | 0 | LNParsh c | 4 | 0 | 2 | 1 |
| Oglivie lf | 4 | 0 | 0 | 0 | DEvns dh | 2 | 0 | 0 | 0 |
| Smmns dh | 4 | 0 | 0 | 0 | Lemon cf | 4 | 0 | 0 | 0 |
| R Clark cf | 2 | 0 | 0 | 0 | Herndon lf | 4 | 1 | 2 | 0 |
| Schroedr c | 3 | 0 | 0 | 0 | Bergmn 1b | 4 | 1 | 2 | 0 |
| Romero 3b | 3 | 1 | 2 | 0 | HJhnsn 3b | 3 | 1 | 1 | 3 |
|  |  |  |  |  | MCastil 3b | 0 | 0 | 0 | 0 |
| Totals | 30 | 1 | 4 | 1 | Totals | 34 | 5 | 11 | 5 |

```
Milwaukee...................... 000  000  010— 1
Detroit........................... 131  000  00x— 5
```

Game Winning RBI — KGibson (8).
LOB—Milwaukee 5, Detroit 8. 2B—Bergman, LNParrish, Romero. HR—KGibson (9), HJohnson (6). SB—Whitaker (4), KGibson (14). S—MCastillo. SF—Gantner.

| | IP | H | R | ER | BB | SO |
|---|---|---|---|---|---|---|
| **Milwaukee** | | | | | | |
| Porter L,5-3 | 2 1-3 | 6 | 5 | 5 | 0 | 0 |
| Ladd | 3 2-3 | 3 | 0 | 0 | 1 | 2 |
| BGibson | 1 2-3 | 2 | 0 | 0 | 1 | 1 |
| Waits | 1-3 | 0 | 0 | 0 | 0 | 0 |
| **Detroit** | | | | | | |
| Wilcox W,8-5 | 8 | 4 | 1 | 1 | 2 | 4 |
| Bair | 1 | 0 | 0 | 0 | 0 | 1 |

T—2:33. A—44,680.

We hit them with five in the first three innings and coasted the rest of the way. Milt Wilcox was super. He didn't lose his shutout until the eighth, then Doug Bair finished them off.

I still can't believe the crowds we're drawing. Over 44,000 again today. I would be disappointed if we didn't average 40,000 from here on. That's the way first place is supposed to be.

Kirk Gibson hit a homer in the first and Howard Johnson hit one in the second. Johnson is coming on.

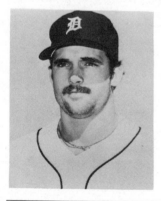

**Howard Johnson.** Photo courtesy of Detroit Tigers

**Larry Herndon.** Photo courtesy of Detroit Tigers

# SUNDAY, JUNE 24

## AT DETROIT

# GAME 70

## TIGERS 7, BREWERS 1

### (52–18, 8½ GAMES AHEAD)

| MILWAUKEE | ab | r | h | bi | DETROIT | ab | r | h | bi |
|---|---|---|---|---|---|---|---|---|---|
| James rf | 4 | 0 | 0 | 0 | Whitakr 2b | 4 | 1 | 1 | 0 |
| Gantnr 2b | 4 | 0 | 0 | 0 | Tramml ss | 3 | 1 | 1 | 0 |
| Yount ss | 4 | 0 | 0 | 0 | KGibson rf | 3 | 1 | 1 | 2 |
| Cooper 1b | 3 | 0 | 0 | 0 | LNParsh c | 4 | 2 | 3 | 2 |
| Oglivie lf | 3 | 0 | 0 | 0 | DEvns dh | 4 | 0 | 0 | 0 |
| Smmns dh | 3 | 0 | 0 | 0 | Grubb lf | 1 | 0 | 0 | 0 |
| RClark cf | 3 | 1 | 1 | 0 | Lemon cf | 2 | 1 | 1 | 0 |
| Sundbrg c | 3 | 0 | 1 | 1 | Bergmn 1b | 2 | 0 | 1 | 0 |
| Romero 3b | 3 | 0 | 1 | 0 | Garbey 1b | 2 | 0 | 0 | 0 |
| | | | | | R Jones cf | 4 | 1 | 1 | 3 |
| | | | | | H Jhnsn 3b | 2 | 0 | 0 | 0 |
| | | | | | MCastil 3b | 1 | 0 | 0 | 0 |
| Totals | 30 | 1 | 3 | 1 | Totals | 32 | 7 | 9 | 7 |

Milwaukee...................... 000 000 010— 1
Detroit........................... 010 006 00x— 7
Game Winning RBI — LNParrish (5).
E—Bergman. LOB—Milwaukee 2, Detroit 5. 2B—RClark, Sundberg. 3B—KGibson. HR—LNParrish (13), R Jones (3).

| | IP | H | R | ER | BB | SO |
|---|---|---|---|---|---|---|
| **Milwaukee** | | | | | | |
| Haas L, 4-6 | 5 | 5 | 5 | 5 | 3 | 3 |
| Waits | 1-3 | 1 | 1 | 1 | 0 | 1 |
| Tellmann | 2 2-3 | 3 | 1 | 1 | 1 | 2 |
| **Detroit** | | | | | | |
| Morris W, 12-3 | 6 | 1 | 0 | 0 | 0 | 4 |
| Lopez S, 9 | 3 | 2 | 1 | 1 | 0 | 0 |

Haas pitched to 4 batters in 6th.
T—2:?. A—39,067.

We got Jack Morris back after missing two turns. He shut them down on one hit in six innings. Aurelio Lopez finished for the save. Milwaukee technicians clocked Morris at 96 miles an hour.

Lance Parrish is starting to improve his swing a little—he hit a homer. Jones put one over the rightfield roof. Ruppert Jones gives us another dimension. That's what I was thinking about when we got him. Depending upon who's pitching, we can field two different teams. There's nothing better than having fresh people. The more people you can play, the better.

When you use a lot of players, you show you can win without certain people. There are fewer stars . . . fewer ego trips if players know you can win without them. On every good team there are only three players you can't win without.

We drew 165,000 for the four-game series. That's the best in the league this year. Even in Cincinnati we never had this kind of support. This city is unbelievable.

# MONDAY, JUNE 25

## AT NEW YORK

# GAME 71

## YANKEES 7, TIGERS 3

### (52–19, 9 GAMES AHEAD)

| DETROIT | ab | r | h | bi | NEW YORK | ab | r | h | bi |
|---|---|---|---|---|---|---|---|---|---|
| Kuntz rf | 4 | 0 | 0 | 0 | Rndlph 2b | 4 | 0 | 1 | 0 |
| Brgmn ph | 1 | 0 | 0 | 0 | Wynegar c | 3 | 2 | 2 | 0 |
| Tramml ss | 4 | 1 | 2 | 0 | Mtngly 1b | 5 | 2 | 3 | 1 |
| Garbey 1b | 5 | 1 | 2 | 2 | Winfield rf | 5 | 1 | 5 | 4 |
| LNPrsh dh | 5 | 0 | 0 | 0 | Gamble dh | 3 | 0 | 1 | 1 |
| Lemon cf | 3 | 1 | 2 | 0 | Baylor dh | 1 | 0 | 0 | 0 |
| Herndon lf | 3 | 0 | 1 | 0 | Kemp lf | 5 | 0 | 1 | 0 |
| KGibson rf | 1 | 0 | 0 | 0 | Dayett lf | 0 | 0 | 0 | 0 |
| Brokns 2b | 3 | 0 | 2 | 1 | Smalley 3b | 3 | 0 | 0 | 0 |
| Whitakr 2b | 1 | 0 | 0 | 0 | Griffey cf | 3 | 1 | 0 | 0 |
| MCastili c | 3 | 0 | 1 | 0 | Mechm ss | 3 | 1 | 1 | 0 |
| DEvns ph | 1 | 0 | 0 | 0 | | | | | |
| Hernndz p | 0 | 0 | 0 | 0 | | | | | |
| Willis p | 0 | 0 | 0 | 0 | | | | | |
| HJhnsn 3b | 4 | 0 | 0 | 0 | | | | | |
| Totals | 38 | 3 | 10 | 3 | Totals | 35 | 7 | 14 | 6 |

```
Detroit ...................000 100 200— 3
New York ...............)..000 010 33x— 7
```
Game Winning RBI — None.
E—Smalley, Brookens. DP—Detroit 1. LOB—Detroit 10, New York 11. 2B—Lemon, Brookens 2, Mattingly, Winfield. HR—Garbey (2). S—Meacham, Randolph.

| | IP | H | R | ER | BB | SO |
|---|---|---|---|---|---|---|
| Detroit | | | | | | |
| Petry | 6 1-3 | 11 | 3 | 3 | 2 | 2 |
| Bair L,4-1 | 0 | 1 | 1 | 0 | 0 | 0 |
| Hernandz | 1 | 2 | 3 | 3 | 3 | 1 |
| Willis | 2-3 | 0 | 0 | 0 | 0 | 0 |
| New York | | | | | | |
| Guidry W,6-5 | 7 | 9 | 3 | 3 | 1 | 5 |
| JHowell S,2 | 2 | 1 | 0 | 0 | 1 | 1 |

Bair pitched to one batter in 7th, Guidry pitched to one batter in 8th.
T—3:11. A—29,237.

Someone must be looking out for us. We lost a game and gained a half game in the standings after Toronto dropped two.

New York is always a tough place to play, but we didn't give ourselves a chance. We played terribly. We threw away a double play chance in the seventh and again in the eighth.

The Yankees can hit, especially their lefthanded players. Dave Winfield was 5 for 5. He's hitting .750 against us. I dread every time he comes to the plate.

# TUESDAY, JUNE 26

## AT NEW YORK

# GAME 72

## TIGERS 9, YANKEES 7

### (53–19, 10 GAMES AHEAD)

| DETROIT | ab | r | h | bi |
|---|---|---|---|---|
| Kuntz rf | 3 | 2 | 0 | 0 |
| KGibson rf | 1 | 0 | 0 | 0 |
| Trammll ss | 5 | 0 | 2 | 2 |
| Garbey 1b | 3 | 0 | 2 | 2 |
| DaEvns 1b | 1 | 1 | 1 | 1 |
| Bergmn 1b | 0 | 0 | 0 | 0 |
| LNPrsh dh | 6 | 1 | 2 | 2 |
| Lemon cf | 6 | 0 | 1 | 0 |
| Herndon lf | 5 | 1 | 2 | 0 |
| Brokns 2b | 5 | 2 | 3 | 0 |
| MCastill c | 4 | 1 | 2 | 0 |
| Grubb ph | 0 | 0 | 0 | 0 |
| Hernndz p | 0 | 0 | 0 | 0 |
| HJhnsn 3b | 4 | 1 | 1 | 2 |
| Whitakr 2b | 1 | 0 | 0 | 0 |
| Totals | 44 | 9 | 16 | 9 |

| NEW YORK | ab | r | h | bi |
|---|---|---|---|---|
| Rndlph 2b | 5 | 1 | 1 | 1 |
| Wynegar c | 4 | 1 | 1 | 2 |
| Mtngly 1b | 5 | 1 | 2 | 0 |
| Baylor dh | 5 | 1 | 2 | 2 |
| Gamble rf | 3 | 1 | 1 | 1 |
| Dayett rf | 1 | 0 | 0 | 0 |
| Kemp lf | 5 | 0 | 2 | 1 |
| Smalley 3b | 5 | 0 | 0 | 0 |
| Griffey cf | 4 | 1 | 1 | 0 |
| Mechm ss | 4 | 1 | 2 | 0 |
| Totals | 41 | 7 | 12 | 7 |

Detroit .......................... 040 000 030 2— 9
New York ...................... 003 012 100 0— 7

Game Winning RBI — LNParrish (6).
E—Smalley. LOB—Detroit 11, New York 8. 2B—Garbey, Randolph, Kemp. HR—Wynegar (4), Baylor (16), LNParrish (14). SB—HJohnson 2 (5), Gamble (1), Brookens (2). S—Meacham.

| Detroit | IP | H | R | ER | BB | SO |
|---|---|---|---|---|---|---|
| Berengur | 2 1-3 | 5 | 3 | 3 | 1 | 0 |
| Lopez | 3 2-3 | 4 | 3 | 3 | 2 | 5 |
| Monge | 1 1-3 | 2 | 1 | 1 | 0 | 2 |
| Hernandz W,3-0 | 2 2-3 | 1 | 0 | 0 | 0 | 2 |
| **New York** | | | | | | |
| Rawley | 1 2-3 | 4 | 4 | 4 | 3 | 1 |
| Shirley | 5 1-3 | 7 | 2 | 0 | 0 | 2 |
| Fontenot | 2-3 | 0 | 1 | 1 | 1 | 0 |
| Christnsen L,2-3 | 2 1-3 | 5 | 2 | 2 | 2 | 3 |

Shirley pitched to 2 batters in the 8th.
WP—Rawley 2. T—3:22. A—32,301.

Jim Campbell came to New York this morning. He, Ernie Harwell, broadcaster George Kell, and I were invited to the Stock Exchange. How can any human being survive those pressures? Millions of dollars are exchanged there within the snap of a finger and the place is a madhouse! I couldn't believe it. I must have signed autographs for a half hour straight. Here they are dealing in millions and I'm signing autographs for their kids and friends.

Tonight's game was a doozy. We came back with three runs in the seventh before Lance Parrish sent us home with a long home run in the tenth.

Willie Hernandez did it again for us with 2-2/3 scoreless innings. We're 10 ahead of Toronto now. I still wish we had one more starting pitcher.

# WEDNESDAY, JUNE 27

## AT NEW YORK

# GAME 73

## YANKEES 5, TIGERS 4

### (53–20, 10 GAMES AHEAD)

| DETROIT | ab | r | h | bi | NEW YORK | ab | r | h | bi |
|---|---|---|---|---|---|---|---|---|---|
| Kuntz rf | 3 | 1 | 0 | 0 | Rndlph 2b | 3 | 0 | 0 | 0 |
| Trammlss | 3 | 1 | 1 | 0 | Wynegar c | 3 | 1 | 1 | 0 |
| Garbey 1b | 3 | 1 | 1 | 2 | Mtngly 1b | 4 | 2 | 3 | 2 |
| Bergmn 1b | 0 | 0 | 0 | 0 | Baylor dh | 3 | 1 | 1 | 1 |
| LNParsh dh | 4 | 0 | 0 | 0 | Gamble rf | 3 | 0 | 0 | 0 |
| Lemon cf | 3 | 1 | 1 | 1 | Kemp lf | 4 | 0 | 0 | 1 |
| Herndon lf | 3 | 0 | 0 | 0 | Dayett lf | 0 | 0 | 0 | 0 |
| KGibsn ph | 1 | 0 | 1 | 0 | Smalley 3b | 3 | 0 | 1 | 1 |
| Brokns 2b | 3 | 0 | 1 | 1 | OMoren cf | 4 | 0 | 0 | 0 |
| DEvns ph | 1 | 0 | 0 | 0 | Mechm ss | 3 | 1 | 1 | 0 |
| MCastill c | 3 | 0 | 0 | 0 | | | | | |
| Grubb ph | 1 | 0 | 0 | 0 | | | | | |
| HJhnsn 3b | 2 | 0 | 0 | 0 | | | | | |
| Whitakr 2b | 0 | 0 | 0 | 0 | | | | | |
| Totals | 30 | 4 | 5 | 4 | Totals | 30 | 5 | 7 | 5 |

Detroit............................ 000 300 100— 4
New York.......................... 001 001 03x— 5
Game Winning RBI — Smalley (3).
E—Brookens. LOB—Detroit 4, New York
6. 2B—Trammell, Garbey, Lemon, Baylor.
HR—Mattingly (12). SB—Meacham (1),
Brookens (3). SF—Lemon, Smalley.

| | IP | H | R | ER | BB | SO |
|---|---|---|---|---|---|---|
| **Detroit** | | | | | | |
| Rozema | 6 | 5 | 2 | 2 | 2 | 0 |
| Willis L,0-1 | 1 | 2 | 3 | 3 | 1 | 0 |
| Bair | 1 | 0 | 0 | 0 | 1 | 0 |
| **New York** | | | | | | |
| Rasmusn | 7 2-3 | 4 | 4 | 4 | 4 | 3 |
| JHowell W,3-4 | 1 1-3 | 1 | 0 | 0 | 0 | 0 |

Willis pitched to 3 batters in the 8th.
T—2:36. A—30,428.

Thirty-one years in this game and I still can't figure it out. We gave away two games we should have won and then won the one we should have lost (last night's game).

We took a 4–2 lead into the eighth, but the Yankees pounced on Doug Bair and Carl Willis.

We still leave New York with a 10-game lead. All the New York writers want to talk pennant, but nothing doing. I'll never forget the 1969 Cubs. That was the greatest Lock–City job and they didn't win. Then there was the 1978 Red Sox, who lost a 14-game lead from mid-August. Until we're pressed, we can afford to rest some regulars from time to time. The biggest mistake a manager can make is not to use all his players.

Walking down the streets of Manhattan I couldn't help but wonder: How does a kid from South Dakota get invited to coach an All-Star Game, turn down CBS for a commentator's job, and manage the hottest pro team in sports?

Please, don't wake me up.

# THURSDAY, JUNE 28

## AT DETROIT

## (53–20, 9½ GAMES AHEAD)

A day off in Detroit: I got to bed at 4 A.M. and was up at 7:30 to play in Al Kaline's charity golf tournament. Like everyone on the team, I'm very tired. But I slept better after hearing that Toronto lost.

**Ruppert Jones beats the throw.** Photo by Doc Holcomb, courtesy of *The Detroit News*

# FRIDAY, JUNE 29

## AT DETROIT

# GAMES 74 & 75

## TWINS 5, TIGERS 3
## TIGERS 7, TWINS 5

### (54–21, 10 GAMES AHEAD)

| MINNESOTA | ab | r | h | bi | | DETROIT | ab | r | h | bi |
|---|---|---|---|---|---|---|---|---|---|---|
| Puckett cf | 5 | 1 | 2 | 0 | | Whitakr 2b | 5 | 0 | 3 | 0 |
| Hatcher lf | 4 | 1 | 1 | 0 | | Trammll ss | 3 | 0 | 1 | 1 |
| Hrbek 1b | 5 | 0 | 3 | 2 | | KGibson rf | 3 | 1 | 0 | 0 |
| Engle c | 5 | 0 | 1 | 1 | | Herndon lf | 1 | 0 | 0 | 0 |
| Bush dh | 3 | 1 | 2 | 0 | | LNParsh c | 5 | 0 | 1 | 2 |
| Teufel 2b | 5 | 0 | 0 | 0 | | Grubb dh | 4 | 0 | 1 | 0 |
| David rf | 4 | 1 | 1 | 2 | | Lemon cf | 4 | 0 | 1 | 0 |
| Brnnsky rf | 0 | 0 | 0 | 0 | | Bergmn 1b | 4 | 0 | 0 | 0 |
| Gaetti 3b | 4 | 0 | 1 | 0 | | RJones lf | 2 | 1 | 2 | 0 |
| Jimenez ss | 3 | 1 | 1 | 0 | | Kuntz rf | 1 | 0 | 1 | 0 |
| | | | | | | Garbey ph | 1 | 0 | 0 | 0 |
| | | | | | | HJhnsn 3b | 4 | 1 | 1 | 0 |
| Totals | 38 | 5 | 12 | 5 | | Totals | 37 | 3 | 11 | 3 |

Minnesota ..................... 020 021 000— 5
Detroit ........................ 003 000 000— 3
Game Winning RBI — Engle (4).
E—LNParrish, H.Johnson. DP—Detroit 2. LOB—Minnesota 10, Detroit 10. 2B— Hrbek 2, Bush, LNParrish. HR—David (1). SF—Trammell.

| | IP | H | R | ER | BB | SO |
|---|---|---|---|---|---|---|
| Minnesota | | | | | | |
| Williams W,3-3 | 6 | 7 | 3 | 3 | 0 | 0 |
| Filson | 2-3 | 1 | 0 | 0 | 1 | 1 |
| Lysander | 2 | 3 | 0 | 0 | 0 | 3 |
| RDavis S,15 | 1-3 | 0 | 0 | 0 | 1 | 0 |
| Detroit | | | | | | |
| Morris L,12-4 | 5 2-3 | 10 | 5 | 5 | 3 | 2 |
| Balr | 3 1-3 | 2 | 0 | 0 | 1 | 0 |

T—2:50.

| MINNESOTA | ab | r | h | bi | | DETROIT | ab | r | h | bi |
|---|---|---|---|---|---|---|---|---|---|---|
| Puckett cf | 3 | 0 | 1 | 0 | | Whitakr 2b | 5 | 0 | 2 | 0 |
| DBrown cf | 2 | 0 | 1 | 0 | | Trammll ss | 4 | 3 | 1 | 0 |
| Hatcher lf | 5 | 0 | 0 | 0 | | KGibson rf | 4 | 2 | 2 | 4 |
| Hrbek 1b | 3 | 2 | 1 | 0 | | LNParsh c | 4 | 0 | 1 | 1 |
| Bush dh | 2 | 1 | 1 | 0 | | Grubb dh | 1 | 0 | 0 | 0 |
| Engle dh | 1 | 0 | 0 | 0 | | Herndn dh | 3 | 0 | 0 | 0 |
| Brnnsky rf | 4 | 1 | 1 | 3 | | Lemon cf | 4 | 1 | 1 | 1 |
| Teufel 2b | 4 | 0 | 1 | 0 | | RJones lf | 2 | 1 | 1 | 1 |
| Gaetti 3b | 3 | 0 | 1 | 1 | | Kuntz lf | 2 | 0 | 1 | 0 |
| Laudner c | 4 | 1 | 1 | 1 | | Bergmn 1b | 1 | 0 | 0 | 0 |
| RWshtn ss | 4 | 0 | 1 | 0 | | Garbey 1b | 2 | 0 | 0 | 0 |
| | | | | | | HJhnsn 3b | 4 | 0 | 2 | 0 |
| | | | | | | Brokns 3b | 0 | 0 | 0 | 0 |
| Totals | 35 | 5 | 9 | 5 | | Totals | 36 | 7 | 11 | 7 |

Minnesota ......................... 000 311 000— 5
Detroit ........................... 220 000 102— 7
One out when winning run scored.
Game Winning RBI — KGibson (9).
LOB—Minnesota 8, Detroit 7. 2B— RWashingtn, LNParrish. HR—KGibson 2 (11), Lemon (12), RJones (4), Brunansky (5). SB—Trammell (14). SF—Gaetti.

| | IP | H | R | ER | BB | SO |
|---|---|---|---|---|---|---|
| Minnesota | | | | | | |
| Smithson | 1 1-3 | 5 | 4 | 4 | 0 | 1 |
| Whthouse | 3 2-3 | 3 | 0 | 0 | 1 | 5 |
| Lysander | 3 | 2 | 1 | 1 | 0 | 0 |
| Filson L,4-2 | 1-3 | 1 | 2 | 2 | 1 | 0 |
| Detroit | | | | | | |
| Wilcox | 5 | 5 | 5 | 5 | 1 | 4 |
| Lopez | 2 1-3 | 3 | 0 | 0 | 2 | 0 |
| Hernandz W,4-0 | 1 2-3 | 1 | 0 | 0 | 0 | 1 |

Wilcox pitched to 2 batters in 6th. Whitehouse pitched to 1 batter in 6th.
HBP—Hrbek by Wilcox, KGibson by Whitehouse. T—3:00. A—44,619.

What did I tell you about things going right? We split a doubleheader with Minnesota and gained a half game on the Blue Jays.

In the first game, Minnesota beat Jack Morris for the first time after 11 straight wins. He didn't have anything and didn't deserve to win. Minnesota has a good young team.

We bounded back in the second, thanks to Kirk Gibson. Gibby popped a two-run homer in the first inning and then ended the game with a two-run shot in the ninth. He is an amazing player when the chips are on the line.

Chet Lemon and Ruppert Jones hit back-to-back homers. It seems every homer Jones hits means something special.

# SATURDAY, JUNE 30

## AT DETROIT

# GAME 76

## TIGERS 4, TWINS 3

### (55–21, 10 GAMES AHEAD)

| MINNESOTA | ab | r | h | bi | DETROIT | ab | r | h | bi |
|---|---|---|---|---|---|---|---|---|---|
| Puckett cf | 5 | 0 | 0 | 0 | Whitakr 2b | 3 | 0 | 1 | 0 |
| Hatcher lf | 4 | 0 | 1 | 0 | Tramml ss | 4 | 0 | 1 | 0 |
| Hrbek 1b | 4 | 0 | 1 | 0 | KGibson rf | 4 | 1 | 0 | 0 |
| Bush dh | 3 | 1 | 0 | 0 | LNParsh c | 4 | 0 | 1 | 0 |
| Engle c | 4 | 1 | 1 | 0 | RJones dh | 3 | 0 | 0 | 1 |
| Brnnsky rf | 4 | 1 | 1 | 1 | Lemon cf | 4 | 1 | 2 | 0 |
| Teufel 2b | 3 | 0 | 1 | 2 | Herndon lf | 4 | 1 | 1 | 0 |
| Gaetti 3b | 3 | 0 | 1 | 0 | Bergmn 1b | 3 | 1 | 2 | 2 |
| RWshtn ss | 3 | 0 | 1 | 0 | Brokns 3b | 1 | 0 | 1 | 0 |
| David ph | 0 | 0 | 0 | 0 | HJhnsn 3b | 2 | 0 | 1 | 0 |
| Laudnr ph | 1 | 0 | 0 | 0 | Garbey 1b | 1 | 0 | 0 | 0 |
| Totals | 34 | 3 | 7 | 3 | Totals | 33 | 4 | 10 | 3 |

```
Minnesota .................. 000  012  000— 3
Detroit ...................... 010  100  11x— 4
```
Game Winning RBI — None.
E—Engle. LOB—Minnesota 7, Detroit 11. 2B—Lemon, HJohnson, Engle, Teufel. HR—Bergman (2), Brunansky (12). SB—KGibson (15). SF—RJones.

| | IP | H | R | ER | BB | SO |
|---|---|---|---|---|---|---|
| **Minnesota** | | | | | | |
| Schrom L, 1-3 | 7 | 9 | 4 | 3 | 4 | 3 |
| Whthouse | 0 | 1 | 0 | 0 | 0 | 0 |
| RDavis | 1 | 0 | 0 | 0 | 1 | 1 |
| **Detroit** | | | | | | |
| Petry W, 11-3 | 8 1-3 | 7 | 3 | 3 | 3 | 10 |
| Hernandz S, 14 | 2-3 | 0 | 0 | 0 | 0 | 1 |

Schrom pitched to 1 batter in 8th, Whitehouse pitched to 1 batter in 8th.
WP—RDavis 2. T—2:43. A—48,095.

Over 48,000 people tonight. We had to scratch it out. Dan Petry battled for 8-1/3 innings before Mr. Lock—Willie Hernandez—sealed it shut.

We used a Ron Davis wild pitch in the eighth for the win, but who cares as long as it's another **W** on the board.

I'm still trying to convince everyone we need another starting pitcher. It'll be a scuffle without at least one more strong arm.

# UP THE MIDDLE PLUS ONE

*Alan Trammell* is the complete major leaguer. Taking into consideration his speed, power, defense, hitting, and instincts, right now he might be the best player in the game.

*Lou Whitaker* is a young hitter who thrives in the clutch. He has outstanding hands and extremely quick feet around second base.

*Chet Lemon* is the best centerfielder in either league today. He isn't the fastest, but he's the best because he works harder at it than anyone.

*Lance Parrish* is the man. I honestly believe he's the best all-around catcher in the game and he's just starting to come on strong.

How's that for openers when you talk about strength up the middle?

The old baseball adage says a team is only as strong as its players up the middle. Those four guys should leave no doubt as to why we finished at the top this year.

Make no mistake about it. Without our bullpen this year, even these four guys wouldn't have been able to carry the load. But there isn't another foursome like this anywhere; just look around. People think I'm crazy when I say this, but you can take the other 25 teams and put them together and still not come up with a group as strong as this.

Except for Lemon, all three won Gold Gloves in 1983. If the four of them don't make it this time, then there really ain't no justice.

Together, Whitaker and Trammell are a pure delight to watch working around the bag. The people in Detroit have been enjoying them for years. Finally the nation received some of that pleasure this season.

Whitaker is one of the most confident young hitters in the game. He loves it when the crowd chants "Lou . . . Lou . . . Lou" as he goes to the plate and he's got just enough showmanship to respond to pressure situations. Great hand action should make him a solid .300 hitter for the rest of his career.

Trammell is the man who has amazed me more than anyone. I always thought Dave Concepcion was untouchable. But when you take everything into consideration, we may be seeing someone even better than him. Alan is the most improved player over a five-year span that I have

**Alan Trammell.**   Photo courtesy of Detroit Tigers

**Lou Whitaker.**   Photo courtesy of Detroit Tigers

**Chet Lemon.**   Photo courtesy of Detroit Tigers

**Lance Parrish.**   Photo courtesy of Detroit Tigers

seen in baseball. I have never seen a player get stronger and stronger, better and better, and improve his mind the way Alan has done since I arrived at Detroit in 1979.

Alan is only 26 and I'm positive he'll be playing another 12 to 15 years. He takes outstanding care of himself and has a great body. He'll probably wind up his career as a third baseman because he'll end up hitting enough home runs to justify his position there. But for right now, I'll take him at shortstop and claim he's the best.

Trammell and Whitaker are as good a doubleplay team as you're going to see now. The difference between them and my pair at Cincinnati (Dave Concepcion and Joe Morgan) is that David and Joe had more baseball savvy. David and Joe had a natural feel for the game. The way they played hitters and the anticipation in their minds became hypnotic. They knew at every moment what was happening on the field.

Alan and Lou haven't reached that point yet. But from pure physical baseball talent, they're the best in the game. At the top of their game, they're as exciting as a couple of dancers. They make you watch and shake your head in disbelief. If they mature and learn those little things, they have a chance to be the best ever.

Lemon in center is a pure joy to have around. I never had the chance to watch Willie Mays in his glory years, and I thought Paul Blair never could be beat, but after watching Chester the last several years, I have to say without a doubt, he's the best centerfielder I've seen in my 31 years in the game.

Chester is a Pete Rose type. He never complains. He's always there and he plays each game as if it were the seventh game of the World Series. Chester doesn't know any other way to play and that's his greatest asset.

Chester's strength is physical, and that comes from one thing—not drinking or smoking. Combine all that with his little boy desire to want to play every day and it is no wonder Chester has all those fans who sit in the bleachers in the palm of his hand.

Parrish is an amazing physical specimen who is the closest thing to Superman we have on this team. Only time will tell whether he finishes with the numbers Johnny Bench put on the board, but there is no question he's much stronger than John was. No one works harder physically than Lance. After a game for up to an hour, he's busy pumping iron and doing various stretching exercises. Lance is totally dedicated to tuning his body.

**Kirk Gibson.** Photo courtesy of Detroit Tigers

There's a lot more to Lance, however, than all those muscles the girls love to see. He's a great human being who is dedicated to his family. This never shows in the box scores and some of his teammates may not know, but that's a quality that benefits any great athlete.

Lance is a tireless worker who always asks "why." Whenever you ask him to do something, he always asks why. He'll do whatever it is, but he wants to know why. Anytime you have a player who wants to know the ins and outs of the game, you've got yourself a winner.

And speaking of winners, there's one who stands above everyone else on this club. He's not part of the middle. But he's a force all by himself.

Kirk Gibson, to me, is what this game is all about. It's about winning and the pain it takes to get there. Gibby is one of those truly rare players who can go 0 for 20 during a five-game winning streak and be the happiest man in the clubhouse. Now that's the highest compliment I can give any player. Other players like to win. But a loss is easy to take if they get three hits by themselves. If Gibby gets three hits and we lose, Gibby might tear the clubhouse down.

Gibby gets the highest rating as a player from me. I hope that other players learn from his presence. In my 31 years in baseball, I've never seen a player change his direction so completely. His personality, his drive, his dedication are unsurpassed. With Gibby on the right side of our middle, their strength is that much stronger.

# JULY

"Five hundred ball just won't cut it. Our guys . . . have to kick themselves in the rear and play better."                    **July 8, 1984**

# SUNDAY, JULY 1

## AT DETROIT

# GAME 77

## TWINS 9, TIGERS 0

### (55–22, 9 GAMES AHEAD)

| MINNESOTA | ab | r | h | bi | DETROIT | ab | r | h | bi |
|---|---|---|---|---|---|---|---|---|---|
| Puckett cf | 4 | 1 | 0 | 1 | Kuntz rf | 4 | 0 | 1 | 0 |
| Hatcher lf | 4 | 1 | 1 | 0 | Tramml ss | 4 | 0 | 0 | 0 |
| DBrown lf | 1 | 0 | 0 | 0 | Garbey 1b | 4 | 0 | 0 | 0 |
| Hrbek 1b | 5 | 2 | 3 | 4 | LNPrsh dh | 3 | 0 | 1 | 0 |
| Bush dh | 4 | 1 | 1 | 0 | Lemon cf | 2 | 0 | 1 | 0 |
| Teufel 2b | 4 | 1 | 2 | 1 | Herndon lf | 3 | 0 | 0 | 0 |
| Gaetti 3b | 4 | 1 | 1 | 0 | Brokns 2b | 3 | 0 | 0 | 0 |
| David rf | 2 | 1 | 1 | 1 | HJhnsn 3b | 3 | 0 | 1 | 0 |
| Laudner c | 4 | 0 | 0 | 0 | MCastill c | 3 | 0 | 0 | 0 |
| Jimenez ss | 3 | 1 | 2 | 2 | | | | | |
| Totals | 35 | 9 | 11 | 9 | Totals | 29 | 0 | 4 | 0 |

Minnesota..................... 002 221 002— 9
Detroit.......................... 000 000 000— 0
Game Winning RBI — Jimenez (1).
E—Brookens, Jimenez, MCastillo, Monge. DP—Minnesota 1, Detroit 2. LOB—Minnesota 4, Detroit 3. 2B—Kuntz, Jimenez, Gaetti, HJohnson, Hrbek. HR—Hrbek (8). SF—Puckett, David.

| Minnesota | IP | H | R | ER | BB | SO |
|---|---|---|---|---|---|---|
| Viola W,8-7 | 9 | 4 | 0 | 0 | 1 | 3 |
| Detroit | | | | | | |
| Berenguer L,4-6 | 5 | 7 | 6 | 5 | 1 | 2 |
| Willis | 2 | 3 | 1 | 1 | 1 | 1 |
| Monge | 2 | 1 | 2 | 0 | 1 | 1 |

T—2:21. A—43,484.

An ugly day. You couldn't put enough perfume on this game to make it smell halfway decent.

What bothers me is that we played so well to get the big lead and now we're just going through the motions. Here it is July 1 and we have five or six guys who act like they're dead. I don't understand it, but I'll guarantee you right now this baloney is going to stop.

Regulars cannot miss more than 10 or 15 games a year. A catcher maybe 20 to 25. I'm getting my regulars back in there and playing a set lineup. The exception is Alan Trammell. His arm is hurting. I'll call up Doug Baker from Evansville and use Tram at DH. Maybe after a couple of days, he'll be ready.

I'm getting a little concerned with our starting pitchers. It's fine to work your bullpen, but you shouldn't kill people. If you don't get some consistency from your starters, you'll tear your bullpen to shreds.

Juan Berenguer pitched today and had us down 6-0 before leaving after five. When he gets into trouble, he can't seem to pitch his way out.

# MONDAY, JULY 2

## AT CHICAGO

# GAME 78

## WHITE SOX 7, TIGERS 1

### (55–23, 9 GAMES AHEAD)

| DETROIT | ab | r | h | bi | CHICAGO | ab | r | h | bi |
|---|---|---|---|---|---|---|---|---|---|
| Whitakr 2b | 4 | 0 | 0 | 0 | RLaw cf | 3 | 0 | 0 | 0 |
| Traml dh | 3 | 0 | 2 | 0 | Fletchr ss | 4 | 2 | 1 | 0 |
| Garbey 1b | 4 | 0 | 0 | 0 | Baines rf | 3 | 1 | 2 | 2 |
| LNParsh c | 3 | 1 | 0 | 0 | GWalkr 1b | 4 | 2 | 1 | 0 |
| MCastill c | 0 | 0 | 0 | 0 | Squires 1b | 0 | 0 | 0 | 0 |
| Lemon cf | 4 | 0 | 1 | 0 | Kittle lf | 3 | 2 | 2 | 2 |
| Herndon lf | 4 | 0 | 1 | 1 | Stegman lf | 0 | 0 | 0 | 0 |
| KGibson rf | 3 | 0 | 0 | 0 | Luzinsk dh | 3 | 0 | 1 | 2 |
| Brokns 3b | 4 | 0 | 1 | 0 | VLaw 3b | 2 | 0 | 0 | 0 |
| Baker ss | 3 | 0 | 0 | 0 | Hairstn ph | 1 | 0 | 1 | 1 |
| | | | | | Dybzisk 3b | 0 | 0 | 0 | 0 |
| | | | | | MHill c | 4 | 0 | 0 | 0 |
| | | | | | JCruz 2b | 4 | 0 | 0 | 0 |
| Totals | 32 | 1 | 5 | 1 | Totals | 31 | 7 | 8 | 7 |

Detroit ...........................000 001 000— 1
Chicago .........................200 203 00x— 7
  Game Winning RBI — Baines (8).
  E—Fletcher, Whitaker, Lopez. DP—Detroit 3. LOB—Detroit 7, Chicago 5. 2B—Trammell. HR—Baines (13), Kittle (19).

| | IP | H | R | ER | BB | SO |
|---|---|---|---|---|---|---|
| **Detroit** | | | | | | |
| Rozema L,4-1 | 4 | 5 | 4 | 4 | 2 | 0 |
| Lopez | 2 | 2 | 3 | 0 | 1 | 0 |
| Monge | 2 | 1 | 0 | 0 | 2 | 0 |
| **Chicago** | | | | | | |
| FBannistr W,5-6 | 9 | 5 | 1 | 1 | 3 | 6 |

  T—2:29. A—32,768.

We are looking bad. Doug Baker played well at short, but it's a lot different without Alan Trammell in the field. Tram got two hits as the DH. But using him at that spot takes away our maneuverability in the lineup. It keeps John Grubb and Dave Bergman on the bench and limits them to maybe one pinch hit. We've got to have flexibility. Tram has pain in his arm and shoulder. That doesn't sound good.

The White Sox beat up on Dave Rozema early. This starting pitching situation is really concerning me now.

Ron Kittle hit and impressive one over the left field roof. That's how I used to hit them . . . before I shrank.

# TUESDAY, JULY 3

## AT CHICAGO

# GAME 79

## WHITE SOX 9, TIGERS 5

### (55-24, 8 GAMES AHEAD)

| DETROIT | ab | r | h | bi | CHICAGO | ab | r | h | bi |
|---|---|---|---|---|---|---|---|---|---|
| Whitakr 2b | 5 | 1 | 1 | 0 | RLaw cf | 5 | 0 | 2 | 1 |
| Traml dh | 5 | 0 | 1 | 0 | Fletchr ss | 5 | 0 | 1 | 0 |
| KGibson rf | 3 | 1 | 2 | 0 | Baines rf | 3 | 1 | 0 | 0 |
| LNParsh c | 4 | 1 | 1 | 3 | GWalkr 1b | 3 | 2 | 2 | 0 |
| RJones lf | 4 | 1 | 1 | 1 | Stegman lf | 0 | 0 | 0 | 0 |
| Lemon cf | 3 | 0 | 0 | 0 | Kittle lf | 3 | 1 | 0 | 0 |
| Bergmn 1b | 3 | 0 | 0 | 0 | Squires 1b | 0 | 0 | 0 | 0 |
| HJhnsn 3b | 4 | 1 | 1 | 1 | Luzinsk dh | 4 | 2 | 2 | 4 |
| Baker ss | 3 | 0 | 0 | 0 | VLaw 3b | 4 | 1 | 2 | 1 |
| DEvns ph | 1 | 0 | 0 | 0 | MHill c | 4 | 2 | 2 | 2 |
| | | | | | JCruz 2b | 4 | 0 | 1 | 1 |
| Totals | 35 | 5 | 7 | 5 | Totals | 35 | 9 | 12 | 9 |

Detroit............................. 300 002 000— 5
Chicago............................. 000 530 01x— 9
Game Winning RBI — JCruz (5).
E—Baines. DP—Detroit 1. LOB—Detroit 6, Chicago 5. 2B—MHill, RLaw. HR—LNParrish (15), Luzinski (4), RJones (5), HJohnson (7), MHill (2). SB—Bergman (3), KGibson (16).

| | IP | H | R | ER | BB | SO |
|---|---|---|---|---|---|---|
| **Detroit** | | | | | | |
| Morris L, 12-5 | 4 1-3 | 9 | 8 | 8 | 2 | 1 |
| Bair | 2 2-3 | 2 | 0 | 0 | 1 | 2 |
| Hernandz | 1 | 1 | 1 | 1 | 0 | 1 |
| **Chicago** | | | | | | |
| Seaver W, 7-6 | 6 | 5 | 5 | 5 | 3 | 7 |
| Agosto | 1-3 | 2 | 0 | 0 | 0 | 0 |
| RReed S, 4 | 2 2-3 | 0 | 0 | 0 | 1 | 2 |

T—2:42. A—42,094

We're paying for all the good stuff that happened to us earlier this season. I thought we had straightened it out after Lance Parrish hit a three-run homer off Tom Seaver in the first.

But Jack Morris started giving up runs, hits, and walks like it was Christmas. I have never seen Morris hit so hard as he has been in his last two starts. I don't know what's wrong with him, but we better get him settled. He's the big man on the staff. We simply have to have him win.

The U.S. Olympic team played an exhibition before our game. I visited with old friend Rod Dedeaux who is coaching the team. I was a batboy for Rod at the University of Southern California many years ago.

# WEDNESDAY, JULY 4

## AT CHICAGO

# GAME 80

## WHITE SOX 8, TIGERS 2

### (55–25, 7 GAMES AHEAD)

| DETROIT | ab | r | h | bi | CHICAGO | ab | r | h | bi |
|---|---|---|---|---|---|---|---|---|---|
| Whitakr 2b | 4 | 0 | 1 | 0 | RLaw cf | 2 | 1 | 0 | 0 |
| Traml dh | 4 | 0 | 1 | 0 | Boston cf | 0 | 0 | 0 | 0 |
| KGibson rf | 4 | 0 | 1 | 0 | Fletchr ss | 3 | 0 | 0 | 0 |
| LNParsh c | 3 | 0 | 0 | 0 | Baines rf | 2 | 1 | 2 | 1 |
| MCastili c | 1 | 0 | 0 | 0 | GWalkr 1b | 4 | 1 | 2 | 0 |
| DaEvns 1b | 3 | 1 | 1 | 1 | Stegman lf | 0 | 0 | 0 | 0 |
| Lemon cf | 3 | 0 | 0 | 0 | Hairston lf | 1 | 2 | 0 | 0 |
| R Jones lf | 1 | 0 | 0 | 0 | Squires 1b | 0 | 0 | 0 | 0 |
| HJhnsn 3b | 3 | 0 | 0 | 0 | Luzinsk dh | 4 | 1 | 1 | 2 |
| Baker ss | 2 | 0 | 0 | 0 | VLaw 3b | 4 | 1 | 1 | 2 |
| Brookns ss | 0 | 0 | 0 | 0 | MHill c | 3 | 1 | 0 | 0 |
| Grubb ph | 1 | 1 | 1 | 1 | JCruz 2b | 4 | 0 | 2 | 3 |
| Totals | 29 | 2 | 5 | 2 | Totals | 27 | 8 | 8 | 8 |

```
Detroit ...........................000 000 011— 2
Chicago ..........................000 006 20x— 8
```
Game Winning RBI — Baines (9).
DP—Detroit 4, Chicago 3. LOB—Detroit 2, Chicago 5. 2B—Trammell, GWalker 2, Baines, Whitaker. 3B—JCruz. HR—Luzinski (5), DaEvans (6), Grubb (4). S—Fletcher.

| Detroit | IP | H | R | ER | BB | SO |
|---|---|---|---|---|---|---|
| Wilcox L,8-6 | 5 2-3 | 5 | 6 | 6 | 7 | 2 |
| Lopez | 1-3 | 1 | 0 | 0 | 1 | 0 |
| Monge | 2 | 2 | 2 | 2 | 1 | 1 |
| Chicago | | | | | | |
| Dotson W,11-4 | 8 | 3 | 1 | 1 | 2 | 2 |
| A Jones | 1 | 2 | 1 | 1 | 0 | 1 |

T—2:34. A—87,665.

Happy Fourth of July. It must be for some, but not for the Tigers.

The White Sox beat up on us again. Milt Wilcox was sailing along fine until the sixth. Then pop . . . pop . . . pop, and we're out of it, 6-0.

Early in the year, we did all the little things that had to get done to win games; now the other teams are doing them to us.

I've been through these spells before. They happen to all good teams. I know things can get better, but I'm concerned with our young players because this experience is new to them. I hope they can cope with adversity because it's going to happen. I don't want them falling back and refusing to fight. I want to see them stand up, spit in the other guy's eye, and fight back.

# THURSDAY, JULY 5

## AT ARLINGTON

# GAME 81

## TIGERS 7, RANGERS 4

### (56–25, 7 GAMES AHEAD)

| DETROIT | ab | r | h | bi | TEXAS | ab | r | h | bi |
|---|---|---|---|---|---|---|---|---|---|
| Whitakr 2b | 4 | 1 | 1 | 2 | Sample cf | 5 | 0 | 0 | 0 |
| Tramml ss | 5 | 1 | 2 | 2 | OBrien 1b | 4 | 1 | 0 | 0 |
| KGibson rf | 3 | 1 | 1 | 3 | BBell 3b | 4 | 1 | 2 | 0 |
| LNParsh c | 5 | 0 | 1 | 0 | LAPrsh dh | 4 | 1 | 1 | 0 |
| DEvns dh | 4 | 1 | 1 | 0 | BJones rf | 3 | 1 | 1 | 0 |
| Lemon cf | 4 | 0 | 1 | 0 | Ward lf | 4 | 0 | 2 | 3 |
| Herndon lf | 4 | 1 | 2 | 0 | Scott c | 4 | 0 | 2 | 1 |
| Bergmn 1b | 4 | 0 | 0 | 0 | Wilkrsn ss | 3 | 0 | 1 | 0 |
| HJhnsn 3b | 3 | 1 | 1 | 0 | Tollesn 2b | 3 | 0 | 0 | 0 |
| Grubb ph | 0 | 0 | 0 | 0 | | | | | |
| Brokns 3b | 0 | 1 | 0 | 0 | | | | | |
| Totals | 36 | 7 | 10 | 7 | Totals | 34 | 4 | 9 | 4 |

Detroit........................... 000 010 006— 7
Texas............................... 000 202 000— 4
Game Winning RBI — KGibson (10).
DP—Detroit 2, Texas 1. LOB—Detroit 6,
Texas 7. 2B—Ward, Trammell. HR—
KGibson (12).

| Detroit | IP | H | R | ER | BB | SO |
|---|---|---|---|---|---|---|
| Petry | 5 2-3 | 8 | 4 | 4 | 2 | 6 |
| Bair | 1 1-3 | 0 | 0 | 0 | 1 | 0 |
| Lopez W, 7-0 | 1 2-3 | 1 | 0 | 0 | 0 | 0 |
| Hernandz S, 15 | 1-3 | 0 | 0 | 0 | 0 | 1 |
| Texas | | | | | | |
| Hough L, 8-7 | 9 | 10 | 7 | 7 | 3 | 7 |

HBP—KGibson by Hough, Tolleson by
Lopez. WP—Hough, Petry, Bair. T—2:26.
A—15,151.

Arlington is an unlikely place to witness a miracle. But if this wasn't a miracle tonight, then my hair isn't white.

With three runs down and two out in the ninth, we stood up and scored six to steal the game. That game was so far in the grave, dirt had been thrown on it and grass was growing.

•With the bases loaded, Lou Whitaker singled to close the gap to one. Alan Trammell—back at short—singled home the tying run. Then Kirk Gibson drilled a shot over the fence down the right field line. If you were to lie down at night and try to envision something to get us out of our spin, you would invent a game like this.

# FRIDAY, JULY 6

## AT ARLINGTON

# GAME 82

## RANGERS 5, TIGERS 3

### (56–26, 6 GAMES AHEAD)

| DETROIT | ab | r | h | bi | TEXAS | ab | r | h | bi |
|---|---|---|---|---|---|---|---|---|---|
| Brokns 2b | 4 | 0 | 0 | 0 | Dunbar lf | 5 | 1 | 2 | 0 |
| Whitkr ph | 1 | 0 | 1 | 0 | Rivers dh | 4 | 1 | 1 | 0 |
| Tramml ss | 4 | 0 | 1 | 0 | BBell 3b | 4 | 0 | 1 | 2 |
| Garbey dh | 3 | 0 | 0 | 0 | LAPrsh rf | 4 | 2 | 3 | 1 |
| Grubb ph | 1 | 0 | 0 | 0 | OBrien 1b | 3 | 0 | 2 | 1 |
| Baker pr | 0 | 0 | 0 | 0 | Ward cf | 2 | 0 | 0 | 0 |
| LNParsh c | 3 | 1 | 0 | 0 | Scott c | 4 | 0 | 0 | 0 |
| Lemon cf | 4 | 1 | 2 | 0 | Tollesn 2b | 4 | 0 | 0 | 0 |
| DaEvns 1b | 3 | 1 | 2 | 3 | Wilkrsn ss | 4 | 1 | 3 | 0 |
| Herndon lf | 4 | 0 | 0 | 0 | | | | | |
| KGibson rf | 4 | 0 | 1 | 0 | | | | | |
| HJhnsn 3b | 4 | 0 | 1 | 0 | | | | | |
| Totals | 35 | 3 | 8 | 3 | Totals | 34 | 5 | 12 | 4 |

```
Detroit ..........................000 000 030— 3
Texas ............................003 010 10x— 5
```
Game Winning RBI — BBell (4).
DP—Detroit 1. LOB—Detroit 10, Texas 8. 2B—BBell, LAParrish, OBrien. 3B—Lemon. HR—LAParrish (13), DaEvans (7). SB—Brookens (4).

| Detroit | IP | H | R | ER | BB | SO |
|---|---|---|---|---|---|---|
| Berengur L,4-7 | 2 2-3 | 5 | 3 | 3 | 2 | 2 |
| Monge | 1 | 2 | 0 | 0 | 0 | 1 |
| Lopez | 4 1-3 | 5 | 2 | 2 | 1 | 3 |
| Texas | | | | | | |
| Mason W,6-6 | 7 | 4 | 0 | 0 | 3 | 3 |
| Noles | 1 2-3 | 3 | 3 | 3 | 1 | 1 |
| Schmidt S,4 | 1-3 | 1 | 0 | 0 | 1 | 0 |

WP—Mason, Berenguer. BK—Berenguer. T—2:42. A—22,376.

The lightning that struck last night stayed somewhere up in the sky. Our pitching situation has really gotten us into a bind. The All-Star break will help a little. But if we don't come up with a couple of reliable starters, we're going to have some problems.

Juan Berenguer got ripped again. I don't know what his problem is; all I know is he's not getting anyone out.

Topping things off, I was called by the American League office (they want Jack Morris to pitch in the All-Star game). If I pitch Morris Sunday, he can't pitch in the All-Star Game. Now I've got to come up with a reason for why Jack won't pitch Sunday.

Maybe he needs the rest and skipping one start will help turn things around for him. The writers are making a big thing of this and we don't need any more problems than what we already have.

# SATURDAY, JULY 7

## AT ARLINGTON

# GAME 83

## TIGERS 5, RANGERS 2

### (57–26, 7 GAMES AHEAD)

| DETROIT | ab | r | h | bi | TEXAS | ab | r | h | bi |
|---|---|---|---|---|---|---|---|---|---|
| Whitakr 2b | 4 | 0 | 1 | 1 | Dunbar dh | 4 | 1 | 1 | 0 |
| Tramml ss | 4 | 0 | 1 | 1 | Tollesn ph | 0 | 0 | 0 | 0 |
| KGibson rf | 4 | 0 | 0 | 0 | OBrien 1b | 5 | 1 | 2 | 0 |
| LNParsh c | 5 | 2 | 2 | 1 | BBell 3b | 5 | 0 | 1 | 0 |
| DEvns dh | 4 | 1 | 0 | 0 | LAPrsh rf | 5 | 0 | 2 | 2 |
| RJones c | 4 | 1 | 3 | 1 | Ward lf | 2 | 0 | 0 | 0 |
| Bergmn 1b | 3 | 1 | 0 | 0 | Sample cf | 4 | 0 | 0 | 0 |
| Herndon lf | 4 | 0 | 0 | 0 | Stein 2b | 4 | 0 | 1 | 0 |
| HJhnsn 3b | 3 | 0 | 0 | 1 | Wilkrsn ss | 3 | 0 | 2 | 0 |
| Brokns 3b | 0 | 0 | 0 | 0 | Yost c | 4 | 0 | 1 | 0 |
| Totals | 35 | 5 | 7 | 5 | Totals | 36 | 2 | 10 | 2 |

```
Detroit ..........................000  400  100— 5
Texas ............................100  010  000— 2
```
Game Winning RBI — HJohnson (5).
E—KGibson, OBrien. DP—Detroit 1.
LOB—Detroit 9, Texas 11. 2B—LAParrish.
HR—LNParrish (16). SB—KGibson (17) .

| | IP | H | R | ER | BB | SO |
|---|---|---|---|---|---|---|
| **Detroit** | | | | | | |
| Rozema W,5-1 | 6 | 9 | 2 | 1 | 1 | 3 |
| Hernandez S,16 | 3 | 1 | 0 | 0 | 3 | 5 |
| **Texas** | | | | | | |
| Darwin L,5-5 | 3 2-3 | 4 | 4 | 4 | 4 | 3 |
| McLaughlin | 3 1-3 | 3 | 1 | 1 | 1 | 1 |
| OJones | 2 | 0 | 0 | 0 | 1 | 0 |

WP—Darwin, Rozema. T—2:41. A—
2⁹,262.

It's a good thing we won because that's the only thing that went right today. Dave Rozema battled for six innings and Willie Hernandez sewed it up for save number 16.

There was more action in the clubhouse after the game than during it. I announced tomorrow's starter and Jack is upset because he wants to pitch tomorrow. The sportswriters are mad because he's missing a start.

But I think we owe something to baseball tradition. I called Jack into my office to explain the situation. Thirty years from now, he'll love telling his grandchildren how he pitched in the 1984 All-Star Game. Hey, this is our game and we owe everything to it.

Besides, when am I going to get another chance to rest him nine straight days? The opportunity is now and I'm going to take it.

I'll be glad when this thing passes. The All-Star Game couldn't have come at a better time.

# SUNDAY, JULY 8

## AT ARLINGTON

# GAME 84

## RANGERS 9, TIGERS 7

### (57–27, 7 GAMES AHEAD)

| DETROIT | ab | r | h | bi | TEXAS | ab | r | h | bi |
|---|---|---|---|---|---|---|---|---|---|
| Brokns 2b | 3 | 1 | 1 | 0 | Wilkrsn ss | 5 | 2 | 2 | 0 |
| Whitakr 2b | 2 | 0 | 0 | 0 | OBrien 1b | 4 | 1 | 1 | 0 |
| Tramml ss | 3 | 1 | 1 | 0 | BBell 3b | 5 | 1 | 2 | 2 |
| Baker ss | 1 | 0 | 0 | 0 | LAPrsh rf | 4 | 1 | 2 | 1 |
| Bergmn 1b | 1 | 0 | 0 | 0 | BJones dh | 4 | 2 | 2 | 2 |
| KGibson rf | 3 | 2 | 0 | 0 | Ward cf | 4 | 1 | 1 | 1 |
| LNPrsh dh | 4 | 0 | 1 | 0 | Dunbar lf | 4 | 1 | 2 | 1 |
| Lemon cf | 5 | 0 | 2 | 3 | Sample cf | 0 | 0 | 0 | 0 |
| Herndon lf | 3 | 1 | 1 | 0 | Scott c | 4 | 0 | 3 | 2 |
| R Jones lf | 1 | 0 | 0 | 0 | Tollesn 2b | 4 | 0 | 0 | 0 |
| Garbey 1b | 3 | 1 | 0 | 0 | | | | | |
| DaEvns 3b | 1 | 0 | 0 | 0 | | | | | |
| HJhnsn 3b | 4 | 1 | 2 | 3 | | | | | |
| MCastill c | 3 | 0 | 0 | 0 | | | | | |
| Grubb ph | 1 | 0 | 1 | 0 | | | | | |
| Lopez p | 0 | 0 | 0 | 0 | | | | | |
| Totals | 38 | 7 | 9 | 6 | Totals | 38 | 9 | 15 | 9 |

```
Detroit .......................000 204 100— 7
Texas .........................025 100 01x— 9
```
Game Winning RBI — B.Jones (2).
E—Tolleson, Garbey, Wilkerson. DP—
Detroit 1, Texas 1. LOB—Detroit 8, Texas
6. 2B—LAParrish 2, BBell, Dunbar, Lem-
on, Wilkerson. HR—HJohnson (8).

| | IP | H | R | ER | BB | SO |
|---|---|---|---|---|---|---|
| **Detroit** | | | | | | |
| Bair L,4-2 | 2 2-3 | 8 | 6 | 6 | 0 | 0 |
| Berengur | 3 1-3 | 5 | 2 | 2 | 0 | 1 |
| Lopez | 2 | 2 | 1 | 1 | 1 | 1 |
| **Texas** | | | | | | |
| Tanana W,9-8 | 6 | 6 | 6 | 2 | 1 | 5 |
| OJones | 2 | 3 | 1 | 0 | 1 | 0 |
| Schmidt S,5 | 1 | 0 | 0 | 0 | 1 | 0 |

HBP—KGibson by Tanana. T—2:37. A—
16,010.

We are staggering. But at least we're going into the All-Star break with a seven-game lead. The break may not save us, but it sure will give us a much-needed rest.

Doug Bair started so that I could rest my regular starters. If our starters aren't rested after the break, it won't matter if we have a 12- or 13-game lead.

We're playing sloppy all the way around. We're throwing to the wrong bases and not getting that one big hit that could turn things around. Now Lou Whitaker has a sore wrist and Alan Trammell had to leave the game after making a throw. We can't lose those two for long.

Since our 35-5 start we're 22-22, and .500 ball just won't cut it. We're going to have a team meeting in Minnesota when we all get there. Our guys don't seem to realize the opportunity they have. They've got to kick themselves in the rear and play better than .500 ball.

Two clubs are starting to worry me: the Yankees and Red Sox are killers. Before this is over, Boston will beat on some heads. They won't win it, but they'll work some people over real good.

# MONDAY, JULY 9

## AT SAN FRANCISCO

## (ALL-STAR BREAK)

## (57–27, 7 GAMES AHEAD)

From Texas to San Francisco, what a change! A day off would have been nice, but the honor of participating in an All-Star Game is something you just don't pass up. This is my seventh and each one has been a thrill.

The workout at Candlestick was filled with writers. I must have shook a million hands and done a million interviews. Everyone wants to talk about the Tigers.

# TUESDAY, JULY 10

## AT SAN FRANCISCO

## (ALL-STAR GAME)

## (57–27, 7 GAMES AHEAD)

The National League won, 3–1. The hitters had a hard time fighting the Candlestick wind and that late afternoon sun.

I coached third base but kept wondering about Alan Trammell's arm. This thing could be serious. Everyone has to pitch in. These last three months will be a war.

# WEDNESDAY, JULY 11

## AT SAN FRANCISCO

## (ALL-STAR BREAK)

## (57–27, 7 GAMES AHEAD)

I did a Ford commercial before flying to Minnesota. A limo longer than a city block took PR director Dan Ewald and me to a paradise in the mountains where the ad was shot. If God is living in the United States, it must be up there. In the distance, we could see the city of San Francisco under the clouds. The city looked like a miniature chess set.

**Lou Whitaker makes the tag.**  Photo by Doc Holcomb, courtesy of *The Detroit News*

# THURSDAY, JULY 12

## AT MINNESOTA

# GAME 85

## TWINS 4, TIGERS 2

### (57–28, 7 GAMES AHEAD)

| DETROIT | ab | r | h | bi | MINNESOTA | ab | r | h | bi |
|---|---|---|---|---|---|---|---|---|---|
| Whitakr 2b | 4 | 0 | 0 | 0 | Puckett cf | 4 | 0 | 1 | 1 |
| HJhnsn 3b | 4 | 0 | 0 | 0 | DBrown lf | 4 | 0 | 0 | 0 |
| Garbey dh | 4 | 1 | 2 | 1 | Hrbek 1b | 4 | 0 | 1 | 0 |
| LNParsh c | 4 | 0 | 0 | 0 | Engle c | 4 | 1 | 1 | 0 |
| Lemon cf | 3 | 1 | 1 | 0 | Bush dh | 4 | 1 | 1 | 0 |
| DaEvns 1b | 4 | 0 | 0 | 0 | Brnnsky rf | 4 | 0 | 1 | 1 |
| Herndon lf | 3 | 0 | 1 | 0 | Teufel 2b | 4 | 0 | 0 | 0 |
| R Jones ph | 1 | 0 | 0 | 0 | Gaetti 3b | 3 | 1 | 2 | 1 |
| K Gibson rf | 4 | 0 | 2 | 0 | Jimenez ss | 3 | 1 | 2 | 1 |
| Baker ss | 3 | 0 | 0 | 0 | | | | | |
| Grubb ph | 1 | 0 | 1 | 1 | | | | | |
| Totals | 35 | 2 | 7 | 2 | Totals | 34 | 4 | 9 | 4 |

```
Detroit.......................... 000  001  001— 2
Minnesota..................... 000  000  31x— 4
```

Game Winning RBI — Jimenez (2).

E—Gaetti, Whitaker. LOB—Detroit 8, Minnesota 6. 2B—Jimenez, Brunansky, Bush, Gaetti. HR—Garbey (3).

| Detroit | IP | H | R | ER | BB | SO |
|---|---|---|---|---|---|---|
| Petry L, 11-4 | 7 1-3 | 9 | 4 | 3 | 0 | 2 |
| Bair | 2-3 | 0 | 0 | 0 | 0 | 1 |
| Minnesota | | | | | | |
| Viola W, 10-7 | 8 | 5 | 1 | 1 | 1 | 5 |
| R Davis S, 17 | 1 | 2 | 1 | 1 | 1 | 1 |

T—2:18. A—29,729.

The war has resumed. We had the team meeting, but it didn't seem to help. We couldn't generate any hits at the plate, and we threw the ball around like it was a pick-up football game.

We're going to put Alan Trammell on the disabled list and go with the kid, Doug Baker, at short. I hope our guys can tighten their belts and dig in.

# FRIDAY, JULY 13

## AT MINNESOTA

# GAME 86

## TIGERS 5, TWINS 3

### (11 INNINGS)

### (58–28, 7 GAMES AHEAD)

| DETROIT | ab | r | h | bi | MINNESOTA | ab | r | h | bi |
|---|---|---|---|---|---|---|---|---|---|
| Whitakr 2b | 4 | 2 | 2 | 2 | Puckett cf | 4 | 0 | 1 | 0 |
| HJhnsn 3b | 5 | 0 | 0 | 0 | DBrown lf | 5 | 0 | 2 | 0 |
| KGibson rf | 4 | 0 | 0 | 1 | Hrbek 1b | 5 | 1 | 1 | 0 |
| LNParsh c | 4 | 0 | 2 | 1 | Engle c | 5 | 0 | 2 | 1 |
| DaEvns 1b | 3 | 0 | 1 | 0 | Bush dh | 3 | 0 | 0 | 0 |
| Bergmn 1b | 0 | 0 | 0 | 0 | Hatchr dh | 2 | 0 | 1 | 0 |
| Lemon cf | 4 | 0 | 2 | 0 | Brnnsky rf | 4 | 0 | 0 | 0 |
| R Jones dh | 5 | 0 | 0 | 0 | Teufel 2b | 4 | 0 | 0 | 0 |
| Herndon lf | 5 | 0 | 0 | 0 | Gaetti 3b | 4 | 1 | 2 | 0 |
| Baker ss | 2 | 1 | 1 | 0 | Jimenez ss | 3 | 1 | 1 | 0 |
| Grubb ph | 1 | 1 | 1 | 1 | RWshtn ss | 1 | 0 | 0 | 0 |
| Brookns ss | 2 | 1 | 2 | 0 | David ph | 1 | 0 | 0 | 0 |
| Totals | 39 | 5 | 11 | 5 | Totals | 41 | 3 | 10 | 1 |

```
Detroit ....................000 002 010 02— 5
Minnesota ................000 020 010 00— 3
```

Game Winning RBI — Whitaker (7).
E—Morris, Baker. DP—Detroit 1, Minnesota 1. LOB—Detroit 9, Minnesota 9. 2B—Gaetti, Whitaker, LNParrish, Hrbek, Brookens. 3B—Brookens. HR—Grubb (5), Whitaker (6). S—Puckett, HJohnson. SF—KGibson.

| | IP | H | R | ER | BB | SO |
|---|---|---|---|---|---|---|
| **Detroit** | | | | | | |
| Morris | 7 1-3 | 8 | 3 | 1 | 0 | 4 |
| Hernandz W,5-0 | 2 2-3 | 1 | 0 | 0 | 2 | 1 |
| Lopez S,10 | 1 | 1 | 0 | 0 | 1 | 1 |
| **Minnesota** | | | | | | |
| Butcher | 7 | 7 | 3 | 3 | 2 | 4 |
| Whthouse | 2-3 | 0 | 0 | 0 | 2 | 0 |
| Lysander L,0-1 | 3 1-3 | 4 | 2 | 2 | 2 | 3 |

Butcher pitched to 2 batters in 8th.
PB—LNParrish. T—3:11. A—30,050.

One of the best games of the season. There were lots of mistakes on both sides but each team fought back time after time.

Jack Morris didn't get the win, but at least he pitched decently after one of his temper tantrums. Darrell Evans had to go to the mound to straighten him out.

Lou Whitaker won the game with a bloop inside-the-park home run in the eleventh. The play that made it possible, though, came from Kirk Gibson. He threw out Tim Teufel at the plate with two out in the ninth. It was beautiful, and it really showed what Gibson is all about. Gibby didn't get a hit tonight, but you should have seen him after the game. He was like a kid at Christmas. Gibby really doesn't care what he does personally, as long as the team wins. That's the difference between him and most other players in the game. Gibby is a real winner.

# SATURDAY, JULY 14

## AT MINNESOTA

# GAME 87

## TIGERS 6, TWINS 5

### (12 INNINGS)

### (59–28, 7 GAMES AHEAD)

| DETROIT | ab | r | h | bi | MINNESOTA | ab | r | h | bi |
|---|---|---|---|---|---|---|---|---|---|
| Whitakr 2b | 5 | 0 | 1 | 0 | Puckett cf | 5 | 1 | 1 | 0 |
| Garbey dh | 6 | 1 | 2 | 1 | Hatcher lf | 5 | 0 | 1 | 0 |
| KGibson rf | 6 | 1 | 1 | 0 | Hrbek 1b | 5 | 1 | 2 | 1 |
| LNParsh c | 5 | 2 | 1 | 2 | Engle c | 5 | 1 | 0 | 0 |
| Lemon cf | 5 | 0 | 2 | 1 | Bush dh | 4 | 1 | 2 | 2 |
| DaEvns 1b | 4 | 0 | 0 | 0 | DBrwn ph | 1 | 0 | 0 | 0 |
| Herndon lf | 2 | 0 | 0 | 0 | Brnnsky rf | 5 | 0 | 1 | 1 |
| R Jones ph | 1 | 0 | 1 | 0 | Gaetti 3b | 5 | 0 | 1 | 0 |
| Baker ss | 0 | 0 | 0 | 0 | Teufel 2b | 5 | 1 | 1 | 1 |
| Bergmn 1b | 2 | 1 | 1 | 2 | Jimenez ss | 3 | 0 | 0 | 0 |
| Brookns ss | 2 | 0 | 0 | 0 | David ph | 0 | 0 | 0 | 0 |
| Grubb lf | 1 | 0 | 0 | 0 | Laudnr ph | 1 | 0 | 0 | 0 |
| Kuntz lf | 2 | 0 | 0 | 0 | RWshtn ss | 1 | 0 | 0 | 0 |
| HJhnsn 3b | 5 | 1 | 2 | 0 | | | | | |
| Totals | 46 | 6 | 11 | 6 | Totals | 45 | 5 | 9 | 5 |

```
Detroit ..................000 003 001 002— 6
Minnesota ...............200 002 000 001— 5
```

Game Winning RBI — Lemon (3).

E—HJohnson. LOB—Detroit 11, Minnesota 4. 2B—HJohnson 2, KGibson, Hatcher, Lemon, Hrbek, Gaetti. HR— LNParrish (17), Bush (7), Bergman (3), Teufel (9). SB—Garbey (4). SF—Bergman.

| | IP | H | R | ER | BB | SO |
|---|---|---|---|---|---|---|
| **Detroit** | | | | | | |
| Wilcox | 5 2-3 | 8 | 4 | 4 | 0 | 2 |
| Bair | 3 1-3 | 0 | 0 | 0 | 0 | 2 |
| Hernandz W,6-0 | 3 | 1 | 1. | 1 | 0 | 1 |
| **Minnesota** | | | | | | |
| Filson | 6 | 5 | 3 | 3 | 0 | 1 |
| Lysander | 1-3 | 1 | 0 | 0 | 0 | 0 |
| Whthouse | 2-3 | 0 | 0 | 0 | 1 | 1 |
| RDavis | 3 | 3 | 1 | 1 | 3 | 4 |
| Walters L,0-3 | 1 1-3 | 2 | 2 | 2 | 1 | 0 |
| BCastilo | 2-3 | 0 | 0 | 0 | 1 | 0 |

WP—RDavis. T—3:40. A—46,017.

It's amazing how the good players always wind up in the middle of the action. Today it was Gibson again. This time he *scored* the big run instead of throwing it out.

Gibson led off the twelfth with a double. Two batters later, Lemon singled and Dave Engle tried to block Gibby at the plate. Engle rode his shoulder into Gibby, but never made the tag.

That's two straight extra inning games. The rest we got during the All-Star break is getting used up in a hurry.

# SUNDAY, JULY 15

## AT MINNESOTA

# GAME 88

## TIGERS 6, TWINS 2

### (60–28, 7 GAMES AHEAD)

| DETROIT | ab | r | h | bi | MINNESOTA | ab | r | h | bi |
|---|---|---|---|---|---|---|---|---|---|
| Whitakr 2b | 5 | 1 | 4 | 1 | Puckett cf | 5 | 1 | 1 | 0 |
| R Jones lf | 3 | 0 | 1 | 0 | Hatcher lf | 4 | 0 | 1 | 0 |
| Herndon lf | 2 | 0 | 0 | 0 | Hrbek 1b | 4 | 0 | 2 | 1 |
| Grubb rf | 3 | 1 | 1 | 0 | Engle c | 4 | 0 | 0 | 0 |
| Kuntz ph | 0 | 0 | 0 | 0 | Bush dh | 3 | 1 | 0 | 0 |
| K Gibson rf | 1 | 0 | 1 | 0 | Gaetti 3b | 4 | 0 | 2 | 1 |
| L N Parsh c | 5 | 0 | 0 | 0 | Meier rf | 4 | 0 | 1 | 0 |
| D Evns dh | 5 | 1 | 2 | 3 | Teufel 2b | 4 | 0 | 1 | 0 |
| Lemon cf | 5 | 1 | 2 | 0 | Jimenez ss | 2 | 0 | 0 | 0 |
| Bergmn 1b | 4 | 1 | 2 | 1 | David ph | 1 | 0 | 0 | 0 |
| H Jhnsn 3b | 4 | 0 | 2 | 1 | R Wshtn ss | 1 | 0 | 1 | 0 |
| Baker ss | 4 | 1 | 0 | 0 | | | | | |
| Totals | 41 | 6 | 15 | 6 | Totals | 36 | 2 | 9 | 2 |

```
Detroit........................ 021 012 000— 6
Minnesota...................... 100 001 000— 2
```

Game Winning RBI — Whitaker (8).
E—Gaetti, Whitaker 2. DP—Detroit 2.
LOB—Detroit 12, Minnesota 8. 2B—
Hrbek, Lemon 2, H Johnson, Whitaker 2,
DaE-vans, Bergman, K Gibson. HR—DaE-
vans (8). SB—Bush (1).

| | IP | H | R | ER | BB | SO |
|---|---|---|---|---|---|---|
| **Detroit** | | | | | | |
| Rozema W,6-1 | 5 1-3 | 8 | 2 | 1 | 1 | 5 |
| Lopez S,11 | 3 2-3 | 1 | 0 | 0 | 0 | 5 |
| **Minnesota** | | | | | | |
| Schrom L,2-4 | 4 2-3 | 10 | 4 | 3 | 1 | 2 |
| Whthouse | 2-3 | 1 | 2 | 2 | 1 | 0 |
| Walters | 3 2-3 | 4 | 0 | 0 | 2 | 2 |

BK—Rozema T—3:00 A—27,965.

This was a little more normal and sets us up well for Chicago. Dave Rozema gave us his usual six and Aurelio Lopez finished for the save.

Darrell Evans hit a three-run homer and I hope this finally gets him going. I'm going to leave him in against both right and lefthanders. We've got to see what he can do.

We're going home to play Chicago while we're on a three-game winning streak, which is good when you're up against all those White Sox bombers.

Photo by Doc Holcomb, courtesy of *The Detroit News*

Lance Parrish gets a high five from Darrell Evans after a home run.

# MONDAY, JULY 16

## AT DETROIT

# GAME 89

## TIGERS 7, WHITE SOX 1

### (61–28, 8 GAMES AHEAD)

| CHICAGO | ab | r | h | bi | DETROIT | ab | r | h | bi |
|---|---|---|---|---|---|---|---|---|---|
| RLaw cf | 3 | 0 | 0 | 0 | Whitakr 2b | 4 | 1 | 1 | 1 |
| Fisk c | 3 | 0 | 0 | 0 | RJones lf | 3 | 1 | 1 | 1 |
| Baines rf | 4 | 0 | 0 | 0 | Kuntz lf | 1 | 0 | 0 | 0 |
| GWalkr 1b | 4 | 0 | 0 | 0 | KGibson rf | 3 | 2 | 2 | 3 |
| Luzinsk dh | 4 | 0 | 2 | 0 | LNParsh c | 3 | 1 | 0 | 0 |
| Kittle lf | 4 | 1 | 2 | 1 | DEvns dh | 4 | 0 | 1 | 1 |
| VLaw 3b | 2 | 0 | 0 | 0 | Lemon cf | 4 | 1 | 2 | 0 |
| Hairstn ph | 1 | 0 | 0 | 0 | Bergmn 1b | 2 | 0 | 1 | 1 |
| Dybzisk 3b | 0 | 0 | 0 | 0 | HJhnsn 3b | 4 | 1 | 1 | 0 |
| Squires ph | 1 | 0 | 0 | 0 | Baker ss | 3 | 0 | 0 | 0 |
| Fletchr ss | 3 | 0 | 0 | 0 | | | | | |
| JCruz 2b | 3 | 0 | 1 | 0 | | | | | |
| Totals | 32 | 1 | 5 | 1 | Totals | 31 | 7 | 9 | 7 |

Chicago .......................... 000 000 001— 1
Detroit .......................... 100 040 02x— 7
  Game Winning RBI — KGibson (11).
  DP—Chicago 1. LOB—Chicago 6, Detroit 4. 2B—JCruz. 3B—KGibson. HR—KGibson (13), Kittle (21). SB—RLaw (15). SF—Bergman.

| | IP | H | R | ER | BB | SO |
|---|---|---|---|---|---|---|
| Chicago | | | | | | |
| Hoyt L,8-10 | 5 1-3 | 8 | 5 | 5 | 1 | 6 |
| Burns | 1 2-3 | 0 | 2 | 2 | 1 | 1 |
| Spillner | 1 | 1 | 0 | 0 | 0 | 0 |
| Detroit | | | | | | |
| Abbott W,3-2 | 9 | 5 | 1 | 1 | 1 | 0 |

  Burns pitched to 2 batters in the 8th.
  HBP—Fisk by Abbott, LNParrish by Burns. T—2:29. A—41,935.

The boys wanted revenge after being swept at Chicago. Lance Parrish wanted a little more after being hit by a pitch from White Sox pitcher Britt Burns. Burns was ejected and Lance was convinced he was instructed to throw at him. Lance confronted Tony LaRussa, saying they ought to throw him out of baseball.

I don't like all this nonsense with throwing at batters. It distracts from the game. We did wind up with a big win. Glenn Abbott pitched a complete game in his first start since being recalled. He retired the first 13 hitters.

Kirk Gibson hit a homer and knocked in three runs. He's starting to carry the team.

My mother is in from California for this home stand. She's doing fine after Daddy's death. Once the season is over, Carol and I are going to have Mama move in with us.

# TUESDAY, JULY 17

## AT DETROIT

# GAME 90

## TIGERS 3, WHITE SOX 2

### (62–28, 9 GAMES AHEAD)

| CHICAGO | ab | r | h | bi |
|---|---|---|---|---|
| Fletchr ss | 3 | 0 | 0 | 0 |
| RLaw cf | 1 | 0 | 0 | 0 |
| Hairstn cf | 4 | 2 | 2 | 1 |
| Dybzisk ss | 0 | 0 | 0 | 0 |
| Baines rf | 4 | 0 | 1 | 1 |
| Luzinsk dh | 4 | 0 | 1 | 0 |
| GWalkr 1b | 4 | 0 | 0 | 0 |
| Kittle lf | 3 | 0 | 0 | 0 |
| VLaw 3b | 2 | 0 | 1 | 0 |
| MHill c | 3 | 0 | 0 | 0 |
| JCruz 2b | 3 | 0 | 0 | 0 |
| Totals | 31 | 2 | 5 | 2 |

| DETROIT | ab | r | h | bi |
|---|---|---|---|---|
| Whitakr 2b | 4 | 0 | 1 | 0 |
| R Jones cf | 4 | 1 | 1 | 0 |
| KGibson rf | 2 | 0 | 0 | 1 |
| LNParsh c | 3 | 1 | 2 | 0 |
| DEvns dh | 3 | 1 | 1 | 2 |
| Grubb lf | 3 | 0 | 2 | 0 |
| Kuntz cf | 0 | 0 | 0 | 0 |
| Bergmn 1b | 3 | 0 | 0 | 0 |
| HJhnsn 3b | 3 | 0 | 0 | 0 |
| Baker ss | 3 | 0 | 0 | 0 |
| Totals | 28 | 3 | 7 | 3 |

```
Chicago .....................001 001 000— 2
Detroit .....................300 000 00x— 3
```
Game Winning RBI — KGibson (12).
DP—Chicago 1, Detroit 1. LOB—Chicago 3, Detroit 2. 2B—Hairston, LNParrish, Whitaker. HR—DaEvans (9), Hairston (4). SF—KGibson.

| Chicago | IP | H | R | ER | BB | SO |
|---|---|---|---|---|---|---|
| GNelson L,1-2 | 9 | 7 | 3 | 3 | 0 | 3 |
| Detroit | | | | | | |
| Petry W,12-4 | 7 2-3 | 5 | 2 | 2 | 1 | 5 |
| Hernandz S,17 | 1 1-3 | 0 | 0 | 0 | 0 | 3 |

PB—MHill. T—2:03. A—34,579.

Dan Petry gave us one fine game tonight. Danny said he wanted this one real bad because of what the Sox did to Lance Parrish last night.

He probably could have finished, but I didn't want to take the chance with all those left-handers coming up in the eighth and ninth. I brought in Willie Hernandez and he retired four straight batters—three on strikes. This guy is not for real.

Roger Craig assured me before the game that our pitching staff was only going through a slump. It's natural for a long season and every team goes through it. Now it looks like we might be snapping out of it.

Kirk Gibson singled home the game-winner in the first and Darrell Evans hit a two-run homer.

# WEDNESDAY, JULY 18

## AT DETROIT

# GAME 91

## WHITE SOX 10, TIGERS 6

### (62–29, 8 GAMES AHEAD)

| CHICAGO | ab | r | h | bi | DETROIT | ab | r | h | bi |
|---|---|---|---|---|---|---|---|---|---|
| RLaw cf | 6 | 1 | 1 | 2 | Kuntz cf | 3 | 1 | 2 | 1 |
| Hairston lf | 5 | 2 | 2 | 2 | Garbey 1b | 5 | 0 | 0 | 0 |
| Stegman lf | 0 | 0 | 0 | 0 | KGibson rf | 5 | 1 | 1 | 0 |
| Baines rf | 2 | 0 | 0 | 0 | LNPrsh dh | 3 | 2 | 2 | 1 |
| Luzinsk dh | 5 | 1 | 4 | 2 | Herndon lf | 3 | 0 | 1 | 3 |
| GWalkr 1b | 5 | 1 | 2 | 1 | RJones lf | 1 | 0 | 0 | 0 |
| Squires 1b | 0 | 1 | 0 | 0 | HJhnsn 3b | 4 | 0 | 0 | 0 |
| VLaw 3b | 5 | 1 | 3 | 0 | Brokns 2b | 4 | 0 | 0 | 0 |
| MHill c | 4 | 1 | 1 | 0 | MCastill c | 3 | 1 | 2 | 0 |
| Fletchr ss | 5 | 1 | 3 | 2 | Baker ss | 4 | 1 | 1 | 1 |
| JCruz 2b | 3 | 1 | 0 | 1 | | | | | |
| Totals | 40 | 10 | 16 | 10 | Totals | 35 | 6 | 9 | 6 |

Chicago ........................ 130 030 021—10
Detroit .......................... 300 200 100— 6
   Game Winning RBI — Fletcher (9).
   DP—Chicago 1, Detroit 2. LOB—Chicago 9, Detroit 6. 2B—Fletcher, MCastillo, Kuntz, Luzinski. 3B—Herndon. HR—LNParrish (18), Hairston (5). SB—Luzinski (4), RLaw (16), GWalker (4), VLaw (1). SF—JCruz.

| Chicago | IP | H | R | ER | BB | SO |
|---|---|---|---|---|---|---|
| FBannistr W,7-6 | 6 2-3 | 8 | 5 | 5 | 2 | 5 |
| AJones | 0 | 1 | 1 | 1 | 0 | 0 |
| Agosto S,3 | 2 1-3 | 0 | 0 | 0 | 2 | 1 |
| Detroit | | | | | | |
| Morris L,12-6 | 4 | 10 | 7 | 7 | 2 | 1 |
| Bair | 1 | 1 | 0 | 0 | 1 | 0 |
| Monge | 1 | 1 | 0 | 0 | 0 | 1 |
| Berenguer | 1 1-3 | 2 | 2 | 2 | 2 | 1 |
| Lopez | 1 2-3 | 2 | 1 | 1 | 0 | 0 |

   Morris pitched to 3 batters in 5th.
   T—2:59. A—39,051.

Jack Morris was ripped. He blamed the umpires for some bad calls and let his temper get the best of him.

Roger Craig has been Jack's biggest ally, but after the game he said, "Jack is acting like a baby. Obviously Morris has a lot of growing up to do. We're going to win this thing, but we need Jack's help. He has to pitch better and act more like a man than he did tonight. He blamed the umpire for some calls. His temper got the best of him and upset his game plan.

"It's upsetting to the whole club when he does that. You can't act like that all your life."

Those are strong words from Roger, but they're true. If I worried about every player who got upset, I'd be a raving maniac by now.

# THURSDAY, JULY 19

## AT DETROIT

# GAME 92

## TIGERS 9, RANGERS 2

### (63–29, 8 GAMES AHEAD)

| TEXAS | ab | r | h | bi | DETROIT | ab | r | h | bi |
|---|---|---|---|---|---|---|---|---|---|
| Ward cf | 4 | 1 | 1 | 0 | Whitakr 2b | 5 | 2 | 3 | 0 |
| Rivers lf | 4 | 0 | 2 | 0 | R Jones cf | 4 | 3 | 4 | 1 |
| BBell 3b | 4 | 1 | 2 | 1 | KGibson rf | 3 | 1 | 1 | 2 |
| LAPrsh rf | 4 | 0 | 1 | 0 | LNParsh c | 5 | 1 | 1 | 3 |
| OBrien 1b | 4 | 0 | 0 | 0 | DEvns dh | 3 | 1 | 0 | 0 |
| Dunbar dh | 4 | 0 | 3 | 0 | Grubb lf | 3 | 0 | 2 | 0 |
| Scott c | 4 | 0 | 1 | 1 | Kuntz cf | 1 | 0 | 0 | 0 |
| Wilkrsn ss | 4 | 0 | 0 | 0 | HJhnsn 3b | 3 | 0 | 2 | 0 |
| Tollesn 2b | 3 | 0 | 0 | 0 | Bergmn 1b | 4 | 0 | 0 | 1 |
| | | | | | Baker ss | 3 | 1 | 0 | 0 |
| Totals | 35 | 2 | 10 | 2 | Totals | 34 | 9 | 13 | 7 |

```
Texas............................ 000 000 110— 2
Detroit.......................... 030 012 03x— 9
```
Game Winning RBI — R Jones (3).
DP—Texas 3, Detroit 2. LOB—Texas 6, Detroit 9. 2B—R Jones 2, LAParrish. HR—KGibson (14), LNParrish (19).

| | IP | H | R | ER | BB | SO |
|---|---|---|---|---|---|---|
| **Texas** | | | | | | |
| DStewart L,4-11 | 4 | 7 | 4 | 3 | 7 | 0 |
| OJones | 3 | 3 | 2 | 2 | 1 | 0 |
| McLaghlin | 1 | 3 | 3 | 3 | 0 | 0 |
| **Detroit** | | | | | | |
| Wilcox W,9-6 | 7 1-3 | 8 | 2 | 2 | 0 | 7 |
| Hernandz | 2-3 | 1 | 0 | 0 | 0 | 1 |
| Lopez | 1 | 1 | 0 | 0 | 0 | 1 |

DStewart pitched to 3 batters in the 5th.
WP—DStewart. PB—Scott. T—2:32. A—26,908.

We had a clubhouse meeting before the game. Jack Morris resigned as team player representative and Darrell Evans accepted the job. Morris also has refused to grant interviews to the press. Like I said, you can't worry about things like this or it'll drive you nuts.

In today's game, we jumped to an early lead and Milt Wilcox coasted the rest of the way for the win.

# FRIDAY, JULY 20

## AT DETROIT

# GAME 93

## TIGERS 3, RANGERS 1

### (64–29, 8 GAMES AHEAD)

| TEXAS | ab | r | h | bi | DETROIT | ab | r | h | bi |
|---|---|---|---|---|---|---|---|---|---|
| Dunbar lf | 4 | 0 | 1 | 0 | Whitakr 2b | 3 | 0 | 0 | 0 |
| Ward cf | 4 | 0 | 0 | 0 | Kuntz rf | 3 | 0 | 0 | 0 |
| OBrien 1b | 4 | 0 | 1 | 0 | Garbey dh | 4 | 1 | 1 | 2 |
| LAPrsh dh | 4 | 0 | 1 | 0 | LNParsh c | 4 | 0 | 0 | 0 |
| BBell 3b | 4 | 1 | 2 | 0 | Lemon cf | 4 | 1 | 3 | 1 |
| Foley c | 3 | 0 | 0 | 0 | Herndon lf | 4 | 0 | 0 | 0 |
| Sample ph | 1 | 0 | 0 | 0 | DaEvns 1b | 3 | 0 | 2 | 0 |
| GWright rf | 3 | 0 | 1 | 1 | Bergmn 1b | 0 | 0 | 0 | 0 |
| Stein 2b | 3 | 0 | 0 | 0 | Brookns ss | 3 | 0 | 1 | 0 |
| Wilkrsn ss | 3 | 0 | 0 | 0 | HJhnsn 3b | 3 | 1 | 1 | 0 |
| Totals | 33 | 1 | 6 | 1 | Totals | 31 | 3 | 8 | 3 |

Texas..........................000 100 000— 1
Detroit........................002 100 00x— 3
Game Winning RBI — Garbey (3).
LOB—Texas 5, Detroit 6. 2B—BBell, Brookens. HR—Garbey (4), Lemon (13). S—Whitaker.

| Texas | IP | H | R | ER | BB | SO |
|---|---|---|---|---|---|---|
| Tanana L,9-9 | 8 | 8 | 3 | 3 | 1 | 5 |
| **Detroit** | | | | | | |
| Rozema W,7-1 | 8 | 6 | 1 | 1 | 0 | 4 |
| Hernandz S,18 | 1 | 0 | 0 | 0 | 0 | 1 |

T—2:16. A—39,484.

Dave Rozema could have gone all the way for the first time this season. But I'm still not thinking complete games with that guy (Willie Hernandez) in the bullpen.

Willie has to pitch to stay sharp and if I can nurse Rozema through some extra innings this year our pitching will be stronger. Willie set them down—one, two, three.

Barbaro Garbey homered in the third to snap a 4 for 34 slump.

# SATURDAY, JULY 21

## AT DETROIT

# GAME 94

## TIGERS 7, RANGERS 6

### (65–29, 9 GAMES AHEAD)

| TEXAS | ab | r | h | bi | DETROIT | ab | r | h | bi |
|---|---|---|---|---|---|---|---|---|---|
| Rivers lf | 4 | 1 | 1 | 2 | Whitakr 2b | 4 | 0 | 0 | 0 |
| Yost ph | 1 | 0 | 0 | 0 | R Jones lf | 4 | 1 | 2 | 1 |
| OBrien 1b | 5 | 1 | 1 | 2 | KGibson rf | 2 | 1 | 0 | 0 |
| BBell 3b | 4 | 1 | 1 | 1 | LNParsh c | 4 | 0 | 0 | 0 |
| LAPrsh rf | 4 | 0 | 0 | 0 | DEvns dh | 2 | 2 | 0 | 0 |
| Dunbar dh | 3 | 0 | 0 | 1 | Lemon cf | 4 | 1 | 2 | 2 |
| Sample ph | 1 | 0 | 0 | 0 | HJhnsn 3b | 4 | 1 | 2 | 2 |
| Foley c | 3 | 0 | 1 | 0 | Bergmn 1b | 4 | 0 | 2 | 1 |
| Ward ph | 1 | 0 | 0 | 0 | Brookns ss | 3 | 1 | 0 | 0 |
| Scott c | 0 | 0 | 0 | 0 | | | | | |
| GWrght cf | 4 | 0 | 1 | 0 | | | | | |
| Wilkrsn ss | 4 | 1 | 1 | 0 | | | | | |
| Tollesn 2b | 4 | 2 | 3 | 0 | | | | | |
| Totals | 38 | 6 | 9 | 6 | Totals | 31 | 7 | 8 | 6 |

```
Texas ...........................005  000  100— 6
Detroit ........................020  050  00x— 7
```

Game Winning RBI — HJohnson (6).

E—LAParrish, Brookens, KGibson, Lemon. DP—Texas 1. LOB—Texas 5, Detroit 5. 2B—Lemon. 3B—Rivers. HR—O'Brien (11). SB—KGibson (18), HJohnson 2 (7), Toileson (20), Rivers (3).

| Texas | IP | H | R | ER | BB | SO |
|---|---|---|---|---|---|---|
| Noles L, 1-1 | 4 2-3 | 7 | 7 | 6 | 5 | 2 |
| Darwin | 3 1-3 | 1 | 0 | 0 | 0 | 4 |
| **Detroit** | | | | | | |
| Abbott | 2 1-3 | 5 | 5 | 4 | 0 | 0 |
| Monge W, 1-0 | 4 | 3 | 1 | 0 | 0 | 4 |
| Bair | 2-3 | 0 | 0 | 0 | 0 | 1 |
| Hernandz S, 19 | 2 | 1 | 0 | 0 | 0 | 2 |

WP—Monge, Noles. BK—Noles. T—2:38. A—46,219.

If someone had told me before the season started we'd draw more than 46,000 for a game with the Rangers, I would have told him he was nuts. This is a great baseball city, though. A great city, period.

The U.S. Olympic team played an exhibition game with the Japanese All-Stars before our game. Our U.S. team has some good-looking youngsters and they should make us proud.

The Rangers hit Glenn Abbott hard. He couldn't complete the third inning. Our bats carried us this game—along with our bullpen.

Willie Hernandez got his 19th save. You can't say enough good things about the way Willie had pitched. Clay Carroll in all of his good years at Cincinnati for me never did a job like this man is doing.

Sid Monge pitched four strong innings and only gave up one run. He got the win and that should make him finally feel part of the team.

We got a couple of big hits, especially one from Howard Johnson. This kid now is a legitimate major leaguer.

I liked this game. We played well in the sense that we battled hard. We fought to come back and we fought to win.

# SUNDAY, JULY 22

## AT DETROIT

# GAME 95

## TIGERS 2, RANGERS 0

### (66–29, 9 GAMES AHEAD)

| TEXAS | ab | r | h | bi | DETROIT | ab | r | h | bi |
|---|---|---|---|---|---|---|---|---|---|
| Rivers lf | 4 | 0 | 1 | 0 | Bergmn 1b | 3 | 2 | 1 | 1 |
| Wilkrsn ss | 3 | 0 | 1 | 0 | R Jones lf | 3 | 0 | 0 | 0 |
| Foley ph | 1 | 0 | 0 | 0 | K Gibson rf | 4 | 0 | 1 | 0 |
| OBrien 1b | 4 | 0 | 1 | 0 | LN Parsh c | 3 | 0 | 0 | 0 |
| LAPrsh dh | 3 | 0 | 1 | 0 | DEvns dh | 3 | 0 | 0 | 0 |
| BBell 3b | 3 | 0 | 0 | 0 | Lemon cf | 2 | 0 | 0 | 0 |
| Ward cf | 3 | 0 | 0 | 0 | HJhnsn 3b | 3 | 0 | 0 | 0 |
| GWright rf | 3 | 0 | 0 | 0 | Brokns 2b | 3 | 0 | 1 | 0 |
| Scott c | 3 | 0 | 0 | 0 | Baker ss | 3 | 0 | 0 | 0 |
| Tollesn 2b | 2 | 0 | 0 | 0 | | | | | |
| Totals | 29 | 0 | 4 | 0 | Totals | 27 | 2 | 3 | 1 |

```
Texas............................. 000  000  000— 0
Detroit.......................... 101  000  00x— 2
```
Game Winning RBI — Bergman (4).
DP—Detroit 1. LOB—Texas 3, Detroit 4.
HR—Bergman (4).

| | IP | H | R | ER | BB | SO |
|---|---|---|---|---|---|---|
| **Texas** | | | | | | |
| Hough L, 10-8 | 8 | 3 | 2 | 2 | 3 | 8 |
| **Detroit** | | | | | | |
| Petry W, 13-4 | 8 2-3 | 4 | 0 | 0 | 1 | 8 |
| Hernandz S, 20 | 1-3 | 0 | 0 | 0 | 0 | 0 |

WP—Hough. BK—Hough. T—2:11. A—37,846.

People always wonder what we say when I go to the mound for a pitcher. I'll fill you in on today's meeting:

Dan Petry was pitching a three-hit shutout with one man on, two out, and the Tigers leading, 2-0, in the top of the ninth. Pete O'Brien was the batter.

I walked to the mound to talk to Danny.

"It must be more than 100 degrees out here," I said.

"Yep," Petry answered.

"It sure is hot," I said.

"Yep," Petry answered.

"You've thrown a lot of pitches. How do you feel?" I said.

"How do you think I feel?" Petry answered.

"Well, you're going to feel worse soon because you're leaving," I said.

The crowd booed me. All 38,000 of them, because they wanted Danny to get that shutout. I don't blame them. They're great fans and Danny is such a great guy.

But the object is to win, not make friends. If I kept Danny in and O'Brien hits a home run to tie, then I've done everyone an injustice. It means we earned a 2-0 win and I destroyed it. With Willie Hernandez in the bullpen that's not going to happen. That's why clubs win pennants.

Willie came in and got O'Brien to pop out on the first pitch.

Petry seems to have better stuff every time out. He believes in himself and knows he's one of the best pitchers around. He's strong and keeps himself in excellent shape. He'll be an outstanding pitcher for many years to come.

Dave Bergman led off the game with a home run and we scored our other run on a wild pitch.

I rested Lou Whitaker for the second time this week. No one on our club can say they are tired because we have rested our players more this year than any club I've ever managed.

Alan Trammell is still out and it's tough playing without him. We're still nine games ahead, though, even with the injuries. If we can stay like this until everyone is back and healthy, we'll be all right.

Before the game I said good-bye to Mama. She's going back to California tomorrow and we're going off to Cleveland.

**Dan Petry smokes one by.**   Photo by Doc Holcomb, courtesy of *The Detroit News*

# MONDAY, JULY 23

## AT CLEVELAND

# GAME 96

## TIGERS 4, INDIANS 1

### (67–29, 10½ GAMES AHEAD)

| DETROIT | ab | r | h | bi | CLEVELAND | ab | r | h | bi |
|---|---|---|---|---|---|---|---|---|---|
| Whitakr 2b | 4 | 1 | 1 | 0 | Butler cf | 5 | 0 | 1 | 0 |
| R Jones cf | 4 | 0 | 1 | 1 | Franco ss | 4 | 0 | 0 | 0 |
| K Gibson rf | 4 | 1 | 2 | 2 | Hargrv 1b | 4 | 0 | 0 | 0 |
| LN Parsh c | 4 | 1 | 1 | 1 | Thrntn dh | 4 | 1 | 1 | 1 |
| DEvns dh | 4 | 0 | 0 | 0 | Hall lf | 3 | 0 | 0 | 0 |
| Grubb lf | 3 | 0 | 1 | 0 | Vukvch rf | 2 | 0 | 0 | 0 |
| Lemon cf | 1 | 0 | 0 | 0 | Bando c | 4 | 0 | 2 | 0 |
| H Jhnsn 3b | 4 | 0 | 0 | 0 | Jacoby 3b | 2 | 0 | 0 | 0 |
| Bergmn 1b | 2 | 1 | 0 | 0 | Bernzrd 2b | 3 | 0 | 2 | 0 |
| Baker ss | 1 | 0 | 0 | 0 | Willard ph | 1 | 0 | 0 | 0 |
|  |  |  |  |  | Fischlin 2b | 0 | 0 | 0 | 0 |
| Totals | 31 | 4 | 6 | 4 | Totals | 32 | 1 | 6 | 1 |

Detroit ..........................300 010 000— 4
Cleveland ......................000 000 001— 1
  Game Winning RBI — K Gibson (13).
  E—Bando. DP—Detroit 1. LOB—Detroit 4, Cleveland 13. HR—K Gibson (15), LN Parrish (20), Thornton (22). SB—Whitaker (5). S—Baker 2.

| Detroit | IP | H | R | ER | BB | SO |
|---|---|---|---|---|---|---|
| Morris W, 13-6 | 6 | 5 | 0 | 0 | 5 | 5 |
| Lopez | 1 1-3 | 0 | 0 | 0 | 4 | 0 |
| Bair S, 4 | 1 2-3 | 1 | 1 | 1 | 0 | 1 |
| Cleveland |  |  |  |  |  |  |
| Blyleven L, 9-4 | 9 | 6 | 4 | 4 | 2 | 3 |

  WP—Morris 2. T—3:09. A—16,576.

We are in for two very tough weeks. I'm looking down the road at nine games with Boston and I know that won't be a picnic.

We sure got a break tonight. We wound up walking nine guys and still won the game. That ain't supposed to happen.

Jack Morris was in trouble every inning he pitched and still left with six scoreless innings. Jack walked five and his pitches were all over the place. He threw 124 pitches before I took him out. But he hasn't thrown harder all year and that made us all feel good.

Kirk Gibson and Lance Parrish hit back-to-back homers in the first inning and that was all we really needed for the win.

# TUESDAY, JULY 24

## AT CLEVELAND

# GAME 97

## TIGERS 9, INDIANS 5

### (68–29, 11½ GAMES AHEAD)

| DETROIT | ab | r | h | bi | CLEVELAND | ab | r | h | bi |
|---|---|---|---|---|---|---|---|---|---|
| Whitakr 2b | 5 | 3 | 3 | 1 | Butler cf | 3 | 0 | 1 | 1 |
| R Jones lf | 2 | 0 | 1 | 0 | Carter cf | 2 | 0 | 1 | 1 |
| Herndon lf | 4 | 1 | 2 | 2 | Franco ss | 4 | 0 | 1 | 1 |
| K Gibson rf | 5 | 2 | 2 | 2 | Hargrv 1b | 4 | 0 | 0 | 0 |
| L N Parsh c | 3 | 0 | 1 | 2 | Thrntn dh | 4 | 0 | 0 | 0 |
| D Evns dh | 3 | 0 | 0 | 1 | Hall lf | 3 | 1 | 0 | 0 |
| Lemon cf | 5 | 0 | 0 | 0 | Tabler lf | 1 | 0 | 0 | 0 |
| H Jhnsn 3b | 4 | 0 | 1 | 0 | Vukvch rf | 3 | 1 | 1 | 0 |
| Bergmn 1b | 4 | 1 | 1 | 1 | C Castill rf | 1 | 0 | 0 | 0 |
| Baker ss | 5 | 2 | 4 | 0 | Willard c | 3 | 0 | 0 | 0 |
| | | | | | Bando ph | 1 | 1 | 1 | 1 |
| | | | | | Jacoby 3b | 3 | 1 | 1 | 1 |
| | | | | | Bernzrd 2b | 4 | 1 | 2 | 0 |
| Totals | 40 | 9 | 15 | 9 | Totals | 36 | 5 | 8 | 5 |

Detroit ........................ 100 403 010— 9
Cleveland ..................... 000 010 301— 5
Game Winning RBI — Whitaker (9).
E—Franco, Bergman, Whitaker. DP—Cleveland 2. LOB—Detroit 12, Cleveland 5. 2B—Herndon, Whitaker, Jacoby. HR—Whitaker (7), Bergman (5), K Gibson (16), Bando (6). SB—R Jones (1), K Gibson (19). SF—L N Parrish.

| | IP | H | R | ER | BB | SO |
|---|---|---|---|---|---|---|
| **Detroit** | | | | | | |
| Wilcox W, 10-6 | 6 2-3 | 6 | 4 | 0 | 1 | 4 |
| Hernandz | 2 1-3 | 2 | 1 | 1 | 0 | 2 |
| **Cleveland** | | | | | | |
| Farr L, 1-7 | 3 | 5 | 4 | 4 | 4 | 2 |
| Eastrly | 2 1-3 | 5 | 4 | 4 | 0 | 2 |
| Schulze | 3 1-3 | 5 | 1 | 1 | 3 | 0 |
| Jeffcoat | 1-3 | 0 | 0 | 0 | 0 | 0 |

Farr piched to 3 batters in the fourth.
WP—Easterly, Schulze. BK—Schulze.
T—3:21. A—15.578.

We're on another roll. This is six wins in a row since our debacle in Chicago. Everyone is contributing. I think we'll settle in and play pretty good baseball. I think our guys have made up their minds to make an all-out thrust and get this thing over with.

We got a big lead for Milt Wilcox tonight and he pitched his heart out for 6-2/3 innings. I hated to bring in Willie Hernandez, but at this point, I won't let any game that looks like we have won slip away. We've got 65 more games to play. If we win 33 of them, it's all over. That'll be 101 wins and that's enough for any team.

# WEDNESDAY, JULY 25

## AT CLEVELAND

# GAME 98

## INDIANS 4, TIGERS 1

### (68–30, 11½ GAMES AHEAD)

| DETROIT | ab | r | h | bi | CLEVELAND | ab | r | h | bi |
|---|---|---|---|---|---|---|---|---|---|
| Whitakr 2b | 4 | 0 | 0 | 0 | Butler cf | 4 | 1 | 2 | 0 |
| R Jones cf | 3 | 0 | 1 | 0 | Carter lf | 4 | 0 | 0 | 0 |
| K Gibson rf | 2 | 0 | 1 | 0 | Franco ss | 4 | 0 | 1 | 1 |
| LN Parsh c | 4 | 0 | 0 | 0 | Thrntn dh | 3 | 0 | 0 | 0 |
| D Evns dh | 4 | 1 | 2 | 1 | Hall rf | 4 | 0 | 0 | 0 |
| Grubb lf | 4 | 0 | 0 | 0 | Tabler 1b | 3 | 1 | 2 | 1 |
| H Jhnsn 3b | 3 | 0 | 1 | 0 | Hargrv 1b | 1 | 0 | 0 | 0 |
| Bergmn 1b | 3 | 0 | 1 | 0 | Bando c | 3 | 1 | 1 | 0 |
| Baker ss | 2 | 0 | 0 | 0 | Jacoby 3b | 4 | 1 | 1 | 1 |
| Garbey ph | 1 | 0 | 0 | 0 | Bernzrd 2b | 3 | 0 | 1 | 1 |
| Brookns ss | 1 | 0 | 0 | 0 | | | | | |
| Totals | 31 | 1 | 6 | 1 | Totals | 33 | 4 | 8 | 4 |

```
Detroit...................... 010  000  000— 1
Cleveland.................... 001  100  20x— 4
```

Game Winning RBI — Tabler (3).
E—Baker, Smith. LOB—Detroit 8, Cleveland 7. 2B—DaEvans, Bando. HR—DaEvans (10), Tabler (4).

| | IP | H | R | ER | BB | SO |
|---|---|---|---|---|---|---|
| **Detroit** | | | | | | |
| Rozema L,7-2 | 6 1-3 | 7 | 4 | 3 | 0 | 4 |
| Monge | 0 | 1 | 0 | 0 | 0 | 0 |
| Lopez | 1 2-3 | 0 | 0 | 0 | 2 | 1 |
| **Cleveland** | | | | | | |
| Smith W,4-2 | 7 1-3 | 5 | 1 | 1 | 5 | 6 |
| Camacho S,12 | 1 2-3 | 1 | 0 | 0 | 0 | 1 |

Monge pitched to 1 batter in 7th.
PB—Bando, LNParrish. T—2:48. A—15,516.

Cleveland's got a pretty good-looking rookie in Roy Smith. He stopped us cold. Dave Rozema pitched a decent game, but we couldn't put anything on the scoreboard. Our lone run was a homer by Darrell Evans.

Toronto got beat in 13 innings, so we didn't lose any ground but I want the lead to be bigger. I'm smart enough to know one thing—if we lose seven in a row and Toronto wins seven straight, it's a race again.

But right now we are in a position where they can't win. We can only lose.

# THURSDAY, JULY 26

## AT CLEVELAND

## POSTPONED, RAIN

### (68–30, 11½ GAMES AHEAD)

The rain-out tonight will be made up next Tuesday with a twi-nighter in Detroit. I don't mind the day off right now, but that gives us four doubleheaders in eight days. Two of those doubleheaders are with Boston and right now I don't think there's a better club in baseball than the Red Sox.

We've got a twi-nighter with the Red Sox in Detroit tomorrow. We'd have to win both to notch 70 wins in our first 100 games. My first year at Cincinnati in 1970 we jumped to a 70–30 start. I thought everything in the big leagues was so easy. Boy, have I learned a lesson. I never thought I'd even see the chance to be 70–30 ever again.

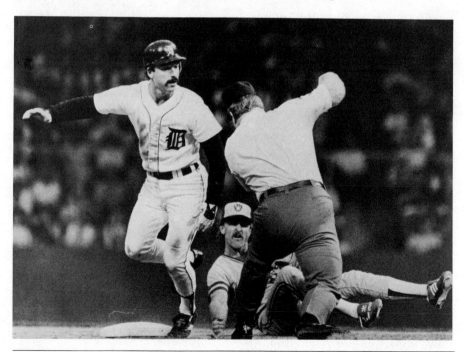

**Tom Brookens is safe at second.**  Photo by Doc Holcomb, courtesy of *The Detroit News*

# FRIDAY, JULY 27

## AT DETROIT

# GAMES 99 & 100

## TIGERS 9, RED SOX 1
## RED SOX 4, TIGERS 0

### (69–31, 12 GAMES AHEAD)

| BOSTON | ab | r | h | bi | DETROIT | ab | r | h | bi |
|---|---|---|---|---|---|---|---|---|---|
| Boggs 3b | 3 | 0 | 0 | 0 | Whitakr 2b | 5 | 0 | 1 | 0 |
| DwEvns rf | 4 | 0 | 1 | 0 | Garbey 1b | 3 | 1 | 1 | 0 |
| Rice lf | 4 | 0 | 2 | 0 | Bergmn 1b | 1 | 1 | 1 | 2 |
| Armas cf | 4 | 0 | 1 | 0 | Lemon cf | 3 | 2 | 1 | 1 |
| Easler dh | 3 | 0 | 1 | 0 | LNPrsh dh | 3 | 2 | 1 | 2 |
| Bucknr 1b | 4 | 0 | 0 | 0 | Herndon lf | 3 | 0 | 1 | 0 |
| Gedman c | 4 | 1 | 1 | 1 | R Jones lf | 1 | 0 | 1 | 2 |
| Barrett 2b | 2 | 0 | 0 | 0 | KGibson rf | 3 | 0 | 0 | 0 |
| Miller ph | 1 | 0 | 0 | 0 | HJhnsn 3b | 4 | 1 | 1 | 0 |
| Gutirrz ss | 3 | 0 | 0 | 0 | Brookns ss | 3 | 1 | 0 | 0 |
| Nichols ph | 1 | 0 | 0 | 0 | MCastill c | 4 | 1 | 1 | 0 |
| Totals | 33 | 1 | 6 | 1 | Totals | 33 | 9 | 9 | 7 |

Boston.......................... 000 000 001— 1
Detroit.......................... 200 002 50x— 9
Game Winning RBI — Lemon (4).
E—DwEvans. LOB—Boston 8, Detroit 4.
2B—Garbey, Bergman. HR—Lemon (14),
LNParrish (21), Gedman (11). SB—
LNParrish (2).

| Boston | IP | H | R | ER | BB | SO |
|---|---|---|---|---|---|---|
| Hurst L, 10-6 | 6 | 6 | 6 | 6 | 2 | 1 |
| Crawford | 2 | 3 | 3 | 2 | 2 | 1 |
| Detroit | | | | | | |
| Petry W, 14-4 | 9 | 6 | 1 | 1 | 3 | 3 |

Hurst pitched to 2 batters in the 7th.
T—2:30.

| BOSTON | ab | r | h | bi | DETROIT | ab | r | h | bi |
|---|---|---|---|---|---|---|---|---|---|
| Boggs 3b | 5 | 0 | 4 | 1 | Kuntz rf | 4 | 0 | 1 | 0 |
| DwEvns rf | 5 | 1 | 2 | 1 | Garbey 1b | 3 | 0 | 0 | 0 |
| Miller rf | 0 | 0 | 0 | 0 | Lemon cf | 4 | 0 | 1 | 0 |
| Rice lf | 5 | 1 | 1 | 0 | LNPrsh dh | 4 | 0 | 0 | 0 |
| Armas cf | 5 | 0 | 1 | 0 | Herndon lf | 4 | 0 | 1 | 0 |
| Easler dh | 5 | 0 | 1 | 1 | HJhnsn 3b | 3 | 0 | 0 | 0 |
| Bucknr 1b | 4 | 0 | 2 | 1 | Brokns 2b | 2 | 0 | 0 | 0 |
| Gedman c | 4 | 0 | 0 | 0 | MCastll c | 3 | 0 | 0 | 0 |
| Barrett 2b | 3 | 1 | 3 | 0 | Baker ss | 3 | 0 | 0 | 0 |
| Gutirrz ss | 3 | 1 | 1 | 0 | | | | | |
| Totals | 39 | 4 | 15 | 4 | Totals | 30 | 0 | 3 | 0 |

Boston .......................... 200 200 000— 4
Detroit ......................... 000 000 000— 0
Game Winning RBI — Easler (7).
DP—Detroit 1. LOB—Boston 10, Detroit
5. 2B—DwEvans. S—Gutierrez.

| Boston | IP | H | R | ER | BB | SO |
|---|---|---|---|---|---|---|
| Ojeda W, 9-7 | 9 | 3 | 0 | 0 | 2 | 5 |
| Detroit | | | | | | |
| Abbott L, 3-3 | 3 1-3 | 10 | 4 | 4 | 1 | 1 |
| Berengur | 2 2-3 | 3 | 0 | 0 | 0 | 3 |
| Monge | 1 | 0 | 0 | 0 | 0 | 0 |
| Bair | 1 | 2 | 0 | 0 | 0 | 0 |
| Lopez | 1 | 0 | 0 | 0 | 0 | 1 |

PB—MCastillo. T—2:22. A—49,607.

The 70–30 mark went untouched. Sweeping Boston now would be like hitting our centerfield scoreboard. At this moment, the Red Sox have the best team in the American League.

They've got so much power and outstanding young pitching. When they start a lefthander against us, we have hardly any power at all. We are one of the worst clubs right now against righthanded pitching.

Dan Petry pitched the first game and lost his shutout on a ninth inning homer by Rich Gedman. Petry is pitching stronger every time out. It won't surprise me to see him get a lot of Cy Young votes.

In the second game, Glenn Abbott gave up 10 hits and didn't even finish the fourth inning. Eight of the hits were flares or ground balls in the infield. Boston will find those holes against so-so pitching.

We split and still gained a half-game on Toronto. Thank you, Texas.

# SATURDAY, JULY 28

## AT DETROIT

# GAME 101

## RED SOX 3, TIGERS 2

### (69–32, 12 GAMES AHEAD)

| BOSTON | ab | r | h | bi | DETROIT | ab | r | h | bi |
|--------|----|----|----|----|---------|----|----|----|----|
| Boggs 3b | 4 | 0 | 0 | 0 | Whitakr 2b | 4 | 1 | 2 | 1 |
| DwEvns rf | 2 | 2 | 1 | 1 | Garbey dh | 3 | 0 | 0 | 0 |
| Rice lf | 5 | 1 | 2 | 0 | Grubb dh | 2 | 0 | 0 | 0 |
| Armas cf | 4 | 0 | 1 | 0 | KGibson rf | 5 | 0 | 2 | 0 |
| Easler dh | 4 | 0 | 1 | 0 | LNParsh c | 3 | 0 | 1 | 0 |
| Bucknr 1b | 3 | 0 | 1 | 0 | Lemon cf | 3 | 0 | 2 | 0 |
| Gedman c | 3 | 0 | 1 | 0 | Herndon lf | 2 | 1 | 1 | 0 |
| Nichols ph | 1 | 0 | 0 | 0 | RJones lf | 3 | 0 | 0 | 0 |
| Allenson c | 0 | 0 | 0 | 0 | DaEvns 1b | 4 | 0 | 1 | 1 |
| Barrett 2b | 4 | 0 | 1 | 0 | Baker ss | 0 | 0 | 0 | 0 |
| Gutirrz ss | 4 | 0 | 0 | 0 | HJhnsn 3b | 1 | 0 | 0 | 0 |
|  |  |  |  |  | Brookns ss | 2 | 0 | 0 | 0 |
|  |  |  |  |  | Bergmn 1b | 1 | 0 | 0 | 0 |
| Totals | 34 | 3 | 8 | 1 | Totals | 33 | 2 | 9 | 2 |

```
Boston .....................000 010 020— 3
Detroit ....................110 000 000— 2
```

Game Winning RBI — None.
E—HJohnson. DP—Boston 1, Detroit 1. LOB—Boston 9, Detroit 13. 2B—K.Gibson, DeEvans. 3B—Herndon. HR—Whitaker (3), DwEvans (20). S—H.Johnson.

| | IP | H | R | ER | BB | SO |
|--|----|----|----|----|----|----|
| **Boston** | | | | | | |
| J.Johnson | 5 | 6 | 2 | 2 | 4 | 8 |
| Stanley W, 7-6 | 2 | 2 | 0 | 0 | 1 | 0 |
| Clear | 2 | 1 | 0 | 0 | 3 | 2 |
| **Detroit** | | | | | | |
| Morris L, 13-7 | 7 | 8 | 3 | 2 | 3 | 7 |
| Hernandz | 2 | 0 | 0 | 0 | 1 | 2 |

J.Johnson pitched to 1 batter in 6th. Morris pitched to 3 batters in 8th.
HBP—Buckner by Hernandez. WP—Stanley. T—2:59. A—49,372.

More than 49,000 people came tonight and we played giveaway. The game should have been ours and we slopped it away.

To make things worse, I got terrible news before the game. Roger Craig told me he will retire after this year. I've often said that Roger is the best pitching coach in the game. He knows so much about pitching and baseball and knows how to build the confidence of everyone on the staff.

I don't blame Roger. In fact, I'm happy for him and sometimes wish it were me. I'm at a point in this game now that with all the money and egos I have to deal with, it's a constant headache. He can draw his pension, settle down and enjoy life while he's still young enough to do things.

We didn't do anything right in tonight's game. We took a 2–1 lead into the eighth and threw away two balls to hand Boston the win. Kirk Gibson didn't back up one of those wild throws in right field and we paid for it. We had chances to tie in the eighth and ninth but didn't grab them. Our pitching has been good, but not our hitting.

**Pitching Coach Roger Craig.**   Photo courtesy of Detroit Tigers

# SUNDAY, JULY 29

## AT DETROIT

# GAME 102

## TIGERS 3, RED SOX 0

### (70–32, 12 GAMES AHEAD)

| BOSTON | ab | r | h | bi | DETROIT | ab | r | h | bi |
|---|---|---|---|---|---|---|---|---|---|
| Boggs 3b | 4 | 0 | 1 | 0 | Whitakr 2b | 3 | 0 | 0 | 0 |
| DwEvns rf | 3 | 0 | 0 | 0 | R Jones lf | 4 | 1 | 1 | 0 |
| Rice lf | 3 | 0 | 0 | 0 | KGibson rf | 4 | 0 | 0 | 0 |
| Armas cf | 3 | 0 | 0 | 0 | LNParsh c | 3 | 0 | 1 | 1 |
| Easler dh | 3 | 0 | 0 | 0 | DEvns dh | 3 | 1 | 0 | 0 |
| Bucknr 1b | 3 | 0 | 0 | 0 | Lemon cf | 3 | 1 | 1 | 0 |
| Gedman c | 3 | 0 | 0 | 0 | HJhnsn 3b | 3 | 0 | 0 | 0 |
| Barrett 2b | 3 | 0 | 1 | 0 | Bergmn 1b | 2 | 0 | 0 | 0 |
| Gutirrz ss | 2 | 0 | 1 | 0 | Baker ss | 3 | 0 | 1 | 1 |
| Nichols ph | 1 | 0 | 0 | 0 | | | | | |
| Totals | 28 | 0 | 3 | 0 | Totals | 28 | 3 | 4 | 2 |

Boston............................ 000 000 000— 0
Detroit............................ 020 000 01x— 3
Game Winning RBI — None.
E—Boggs, Buckner. DP—Detroit 2.
LOB—Boston 1, Detroit 5. 3B—R Jones.
SF—LNParrish.

| Boston | IP | H | R | ER | BB | SO |
|---|---|---|---|---|---|---|
| Boyd L,5-8 | 8 | 4 | 3 | 1 | 3 | 10 |
| Detroit | | | | | | |
| Wilcox W,11-6 | 8 | 3 | 0 | 0 | 0 | 4 |
| Hernandz S,21 | 1 | 0 | 0 | 0 | 0 | 0 |

T—2:09. A—42,013.

This may have been the best game all season we've had for the pitcher dominating the other team's hitters. Milt Wilcox literally took the bats out of Boston's hands. They didn't hit any ball hard. Milt kept them off balance all day.

We are in first place simply because of our pitching, our bench, and our defense. Our bullpen has been untouchable.

This was a great one to win because Boston came to town 16½ games out and they're leaving the same way. That's great because I think they're the only club that could make a move on us. I don't think Toronto or Baltimore can make a run at it at this point.

Before the game, Jim Campbell, Bill Lajoie, and I talked about the Trammell situation. I'm inclined to take Alan off the disabled list Tuesday and use him as the designated hitter. We need his bat. We don't have anyone to hit lefthanded pitching.

# MONDAY, JULY 30

## AT DETROIT

### (70–32, 12½ GAMES AHEAD)

This day off definitely was one of my better days in a long, long time. It was great to get away from the park and take a breather from the games and all the media.

I played golf in Lance Parrish's charity tournament for kids. It took more than seven hours to play, but it was relaxing.

To top off a great day, Kansas City beat Toronto and now we're 12½ up.

**Doug Baker.** Photo courtesy of Detroit Tigers

# TUESDAY, JULY 31

## AT DETROIT

# GAMES 103 & 104

## TIGERS 5, INDIANS 1
## INDIANS 6, TIGERS 4

### (71–33, 12 GAMES AHEAD)

| CLEVELAND | ab | r | h | bi | DETROIT | ab | r | h | bi |
|---|---|---|---|---|---|---|---|---|---|
| Butler cf | 4 | 0 | 0 | 0 | Whitakr 2b | 3 | 0 | 1 | 1 |
| Franco ss | 4 | 0 | 0 | 0 | R Jones cf | 2 | 1 | 1 | 1 |
| Hargrv 1b | 4 | 0 | 1 | 0 | Herndon lf | 1 | 0 | 0 | 0 |
| Thrntn dh | 4 | 0 | 0 | 0 | K Gibson rf | 4 | 0 | 2 | 0 |
| Vukvch rf | 4 | 0 | 0 | 0 | LNParsh c | 3 | 0 | 0 | 0 |
| Hall lf | 3 | 1 | 2 | 0 | DEvns dh | 4 | 0 | 0 | 0 |
| Bando c | 3 | 0 | 1 | 0 | Grubb lf | 1 | 1 | 1 | 0 |
| Jacoby 3b | 2 | 0 | 0 | 0 | Lemon cf | 3 | 0 | 0 | 0 |
| Perkins ph | 0 | 0 | 0 | 0 | HJhnsn 3b | 4 | 1 | 1 | 0 |
| ischlin 3b | 0 | 0 | 0 | 0 | Bergmn 1b | 3 | 1 | 1 | 0 |
| rnzrd 2b | 3 | 0 | 0 | 1 | Baker ss | 3 | 1 | 1 | 3 |
| tals | 31 | 1 | 4 | 1 | Totals | 31 | 5 | 8 | 5 |

Cleveland .................. 000 000 100— 1
Detroit ...................... 050 000 00x— 5
Game Winning RBI — Baker (1).
E—Hargrove. LOB—Cleveland 6, Detroit 6. 2B—K Gibson. 3B—Baker, Hall. HR—R Jones (6). SF—Whitaker.

| | IP | H | R | ER | BB | SO |
|---|---|---|---|---|---|---|
| **Cleveland** | | | | | | |
| RSmith L,4-3 | 11-3 | 5 | 5 | 5 | 2 | 1 |
| Eastrly | 62-3 | 3 | 0 | 0 | 1 | 8 |
| **Detroit** | | | | | | |
| Berengur W,5-7 | 61-3 | 4 | 1 | 1 | 2 | 4 |
| Bair | 22-3 | 0 | 0 | 0 | 0 | 1 |

HBP—Perkins by Berenguer. T—2:30.

| CLEVELAND | ab | r | h | bi | DETROIT | ab | r | h | bi |
|---|---|---|---|---|---|---|---|---|---|
| Carter cf | 5 | 0 | 0 | 0 | Whitakr 2b | 5 | 1 | 2 | 1 |
| Franco ss | 4 | 2 | 2 | 0 | Traml dh | 5 | 0 | 0 | 0 |
| Hall lf | 4 | 2 | 2 | 0 | Lemon cf | 5 | 0 | 0 | 0 |
| Butler cf | 0 | 0 | 0 | 0 | LNParsh c | 4 | 1 | 1 | 1 |
| Tabler 1b | 4 | 2 | 2 | 4 | Herndon lf | 3 | 1 | 2 | 0 |
| Hargrv 1b | 0 | 0 | 0 | 0 | Garbey 1b | 4 | 0 | 3 | 0 |
| Vukvch rf | 3 | 0 | 2 | 1 | Kuntz rf | 2 | 0 | 0 | 1 |
| Jacoby 3b | 3 | 0 | 0 | 1 | K Gibson rf | 1 | 0 | 0 | 0 |
| Perkins dh | 4 | 0 | 2 | 0 | HJhnsn 3b | 3 | 1 | 1 | 1 |
| Bernzrd pr | 0 | 0 | 0 | 0 | Brookns ss | 3 | 0 | 1 | 0 |
| Willard c | 4 | 0 | 1 | 0 | Bergmn 1b | 1 | 0 | 0 | 0 |
| Fischlin 2b | 4 | 0 | 0 | 0 | | | | | |
| Totals | 35 | 6 | 11 | 6 | Totals | 36 | 4 | 10 | 4 |

Cleveland .................. 303 000 000— 6
Detroit ...................... 100 120 000— 4
Game Winning RBI — Tabler (5).
E—Kuntz. DP—Detroit 2. LOB—Cleveland 4, Detroit 9. 2B—Whitaker 2, HJohnson, Garbey. HR—Tabler (5). SB—Butler (32), Willard (1). SF—Jacoby, HJohnson.

| | IP | H | R | ER | BB | SO |
|---|---|---|---|---|---|---|
| **Cleveland** | | | | | | |
| Heaton W,8-10 | 5 | 9 | 4 | 4 | 3 | 4 |
| Waddell S,5 | 4 | 1 | 0 | 0 | 0 | 4 |
| **Detroit** | | | | | | |
| Rozema L,7-3 | 21-3 | 7 | 6 | 4 | 0 | 0 |
| Lopez | 62-3 | 4 | 0 | 0 | 1 | 5 |

T—2:50. A—32,158.

We activated Alan Trammell after the first game and sent Doug Baker down. Baker is a good kid who will be a good player, but we need that righthanded hitting because right now, ours stinks.

Right now, this club is swinging the bat like a second division team. You hate to see that when you've got 29 more games to win to reach 100. I think 100 will win this thing.

In the opener, Juan Berenguer pitched super. He went into the seventh before giving up a run. Doug Bair was perfect in relief.

In the second game, Dave Rozema fell behind by three in the first inning and our hitting simply couldn't get us back. We had the chances, but couldn't click. We simply have to get our guys hitting.

# AUGUST

"After the game . . . I closed the door to everyone but me and the players. . . . I told them I've never witnessed such great character in a team."
August 7, 1984

# WEDNESDAY, AUGUST 1

## AT DETROIT

# GAME 105

## INDIANS 4, TIGERS 2

### (71–34, 11 GAMES AHEAD)

| CLEVELAND | ab | r | h | bi | | DETROIT | ab | r | h | bi |
|---|---|---|---|---|---|---|---|---|---|---|
| Butler cf | 5 | 0 | 1 | 1 | | Whitakr 2b | 4 | 0 | 1 | 0 |
| Franco ss | 5 | 1 | 2 | 0 | | R Jones lf | 4 | 0 | 0 | 0 |
| Tabler 1b | 3 | 0 | 1 | 1 | | K Gibson rf | 4 | 0 | 0 | 0 |
| Thrntn dh | 3 | 0 | 0 | 0 | | LN Parsh c | 3 | 0 | 0 | 0 |
| Hall lf | 3 | 0 | 0 | 0 | | Grubb dh | 4 | 0 | 0 | 0 |
| Carter lf | 1 | 0 | 0 | 0 | | Lemon cf | 3 | 1 | 1 | 0 |
| Vukvch rf | 4 | 2 | 2 | 2 | | Bergmn 1b | 3 | 1 | 1 | 2 |
| Willard c | 4 | 0 | 0 | 0 | | H Jhnsn 3b | 2 | 0 | 0 | 0 |
| Jacoby 3b | 4 | 1 | 2 | 0 | | Brookns ss | 2 | 0 | 0 | 0 |
| Bernzrd 2b | 3 | 0 | 0 | 0 | | Traml ph | 1 | 0 | 0 | 0 |
| | | | | | | M Castll 3b | 0 | 0 | 0 | 0 |
| **Totals** | 35 | 4 | 8 | 4 | | **Totals** | 30 | 2 | 3 | 2 |

```
Cleveland......................011 000 101— 4
Detroit............................000 020 000— 2
```

Game Winning RBI — Vukovich (4).
E—Brookens 2. LOB—Cleveland 7, Detroit 3. 2B—Franco, Lemon. 3B—Jacoby. HR—Vukovich 2 (4), Bergman (6). SB—Franco (12), Thornton (5).

| | IP | H | R | ER | BB | SO |
|---|---|---|---|---|---|---|
| **Cleveland** | | | | | | |
| Farr W, 2-7 | 6 1-3 | 2 | 2 | 2 | 2 | 8 |
| Camacho S, 13 | 2 2-3 | 1 | 0 | 0 | 0 | 1 |
| **Detroit** | | | | | | |
| Petry L, 14-5 | 7 1-3 | 6 | 3 | 2 | 1 | 5 |
| Hernandz | 1 2-3 | 2 | 1 | 1 | 2 | 2 |

WP—Petry. T—2:46. A—27,271

This was no way to start the next to last month of the season. In fact, the way we're hitting, I'd like to forget August 1 altogether.

If we could be hitting the way we are pitching, we'd be at least 15 games up right now and have this thing wrapped up.

Steve Farr, the Indian's pitcher, came into the game with a 1-7 record and shut us down on two hits. He pitched like Dan Petry, and Danny pitched a good game. It's a shame to waste one like that.

# THURSDAY, AUGUST 2

## AT DETROIT

# GAME 106

## TIGERS 2, INDIANS 1

### (72–34, 11½ GAMES AHEAD)

| CLEVELAND | ab | r | h | bi | DETROIT | ab | r | h | bi |
|---|---|---|---|---|---|---|---|---|---|
| Butler cf | 4 | 0 | 1 | 0 | Whitakr 2b | 3 | 1 | 1 | 2 |
| Franco ss | 4 | 0 | 1 | 0 | Traml dh | 4 | 0 | 1 | 0 |
| Tabler lf | 4 | 0 | 1 | 0 | KGibson rf | 3 | 0 | 0 | 0 |
| Thrntn dh | 4 | 1 | 1 | 1 | LNParsh c | 4 | 0 | 3 | 0 |
| Vukvch rf | 3 | 0 | 0 | 0 | RJones lf | 3 | 0 | 0 | 0 |
| Carter ph | 1 | 0 | 1 | 0 | Lemon cf | 3 | 0 | 0 | 0 |
| Hargrv 1b | 3 | 0 | 1 | 0 | Bergmn 1b | 4 | 1 | 1 | 0 |
| CCastill ph | 1 | 0 | 0 | 0 | HJhnsn 3b | 4 | 0 | 1 | 0 |
| Bando c | 4 | 0 | 0 | 0 | Brookns ss | 1 | 0 | 0 | 0 |
| Jacoby 3b | 4 | 0 | 2 | 0 | | | | | |
| Bernzrd 2b | 2 | 0 | 0 | 0 | | | | | |
| Hall ph | 1 | 0 | 0 | 0 | | | | | |
| Fischlin 2b | 0 | 0 | 0 | 0 | | | | | |
| Totals | 35 | 1 | 8 | 1 | Totals | 29 | 2 | 7 | 2 |

Cleveland........................ 000 100 000— 1
Detroit........................... 000 020 00x— 2
Game Winning RBI — Whitaker (10).
E—Bergman. DP—Cleveland 1, Detroit 1. LOB—Cleveland 7, Detroit 9. 2B—HJohnson. 3B—Jacoby. HR—Thornton (23), Whitaker (9). S—Brookens.

| | IP | H | R | ER | BB | SO |
|---|---|---|---|---|---|---|
| Cleveland | | | | | | |
| Blyleven L, 10-5 | 6 | 7 | 2 | 2 | 3 | 2 |
| Jeffcoat | 1-3 | 0 | 0 | 0 | 0 | 0 |
| Waddell | 1 2-3 | 0 | 0 | 0 | 2 | 0 |
| Detroit | | | | | | |
| Morris W, 14-7 | 8 | 7 | 1 | 1 | 0 | 1 |
| Hernandz S, 22 | 1 | 1 | 0 | 0 | 0 | 0 |

Blyleven pitched to 2 batters in 7th.
T—2:39. A—28,700.

Our guys are talking lock now. That's good if they can back up what they're saying. Lance Parrish said he has no doubts we'll win the division. Actually, that's good if Lance really puts his mind to it. He's a leader and can make other players follow him. He got three hits tonight, and usually that will get Lance out of a slump.

At this point, I know one thing. We can't lose the division, we can only give it away.

Jack Morris pitched a strange game. He had good stuff and he walked none, but he struck out only one. He wasn't throwing real hard; I don't know why. He may be tired, but there's no reason he should be.

We won the game on Lou Whitaker's two-run homer in the fifth.

# FRIDAY, AUGUST 3

## AT DETROIT

# GAME 107

## ROYALS 9, TIGERS 6

### (72–35, 10½ GAMES AHEAD)

| KANSAS CITY | ab | r | h | bi | DETROIT | ab | r | h | bi |
|---|---|---|---|---|---|---|---|---|---|
| Wilson cf | 5 | 1 | 2 | 2 | Whitakr 2b | 5 | 3 | 4 | 0 |
| Sheridn rf | 5 | 0 | 1 | 0 | Traml dh | 4 | 2 | 1 | 2 |
| Brett 3b | 4 | 0 | 0 | 1 | Lemon cf | 4 | 0 | 2 | 1 |
| Wathan 1b | 0 | 0 | 0 | 0 | LNParsh c | 4 | 0 | 1 | 2 |
| Orta dh | 5 | 1 | 2 | 0 | Garbey 1b | 2 | 0 | 0 | 0 |
| Motley lf | 3 | 1 | 0 | 0 | Bergmn 1b | 2 | 0 | 0 | 0 |
| Balboni 1b | 2 | 1 | 0 | 0 | Herndon lf | 3 | 0 | 1 | 0 |
| Pryor 3b | 1 | 0 | 0 | 0 | R Jones lf | 1 | 0 | 0 | 0 |
| White 2b | 4 | 3 | 2 | 4 | KGibson rf | 4 | 0 | 0 | 0 |
| Slaught c | 4 | 1 | 1 | 0 | Brookns ss | 3 | 1 | 1 | 1 |
| Cncpcn ss | 4 | 1 | 3 | 1 | Grubb ph | 1 | 0 | 0 | 0 |
|  |  |  |  |  | MCastil 3b | 2 | 0 | 0 | 0 |
|  |  |  |  |  | HJhnsn 3b | 2 | 0 | 0 | 0 |
| Totals | 37 | 9 | 11 | 8 | Totals | 37 | 6 | 10 | 6 |

```
Kansas City ..................001 700 010— 9
Detroit .........................002 030 100— 6
```

Game Winning RBI — White (6).
E—MCastillo, KGibson. LOB—Kansas City 4, Detroit 5. 2B—Whitaker. 3B—Wilson, LNParrish. HR—Trammell (9), White (11), Brookens (2). SF—Brett.

| | IP | H | R | ER | BB | SO |
|---|---|---|---|---|---|---|
| **Kansas City** | | | | | | |
| Black | 4 2-3 | 7 | 5 | 5 | 1 | 3 |
| Sabrhgn W,5-8 | 1 2-3 | 1 | 1 | 1 | 0 | 0 |
| Quisnbry S,28 | 2 2-3 | 2 | 0 | 0 | 0 | 0 |
| **Detroit** | | | | | | |
| Wilcox L,11-7 | 3 | 6 | 6 | 6 | 1 | 5 |
| Lopez | 6 | 5 | 3 | 2 | 0 | 5 |

Wicox pitched to 5 batters in 4th.
HBP—Motley (by Wilcox). WP—Wilcox. T—2:37. A—39,480.

The Royals got to Milt Wilcox in the fourth and I came back with Aurelio Lopez. People don't realize that Lopez pitches better the more he works. I really didn't think Lopez would go this long, but we came to within two runs in the seventh.

We played poorly in the field. I think some of our guys are looking ahead to those three straight doubleheaders we've got coming up starting Sunday. I see a few rocky roads ahead.

# SATURDAY, AUGUST 4

## AT DETROIT

# GAME 108

## ROYALS 9, TIGERS 5

### (72–36, 9½ GAMES AHEAD)

| KANSAS CITY | ab | r | h | bi | DETROIT | ab | r | h | bi |
|---|---|---|---|---|---|---|---|---|---|
| Wilson cf | 4 | 1 | 1 | 0 | Whitakr 2b | 4 | 0 | 0 | 0 |
| Sheridn rf | 5 | 1 | 3 | 2 | Traml dh | 4 | 1 | 0 | 0 |
| Brett 3b | 5 | 0 | 0 | 1 | KGibson rf | 5 | 2 | 3 | 2 |
| Pryor 3b | 0 | 0 | 0 | 0 | LNParsh c | 5 | 0 | 1 | 0 |
| Orta dh | 3 | 0 | 2 | 1 | R Jones lf | 5 | 1 | 2 | 3 |
| McRae dh | 2 | 0 | 0 | 0 | Lemon cf | 4 | 0 | 0 | 0 |
| Diorg 1b | 4 | 2 | 2 | 0 | Bergmn 1b | 3 | 0 | 1 | 0 |
| Wathan 1b | 0 | 0 | 0 | 0 | HJhnsn 3b | 1 | 0 | 0 | 0 |
| Motley lf | 4 | 2 | 1 | 1 | Brookns ss | 2 | 1 | 0 | 0 |
| White 2b | 5 | 1 | 1 | 0 | DaEvns 3b | 2 | 0 | 0 | 0 |
| Slaught c | 4 | 1 | 3 | 2 | | | | | |
| Cncpcn ss | 4 | 1 | 2 | 2 | | | | | |
| Totals | 40 | 9 | 15 | 9 | Totals | 35 | 5 | 7 | 5 |

```
Kansas City.................... 200  004  300— 9
Detroit........................ 002  020  100— 5
```

Game Winning RBI — Sheridan (8).
E—Diorg. DP—Detroit 2. LOB—Kansas City 8, Detroit 9. 2B—Sheridan, Diorg, Slaught. 3B—KGibson 2. HR—R Jones (7). SB—K Gibson (20).

| Kansas City | IP | H | R | ER | BB | SO |
|---|---|---|---|---|---|---|
| Gubicza | 4 1-3 | 5 | 4 | 3 | 4 | 3 |
| Beckwith W,4-2 | 4 2-3 | 2 | 1 | 1 | 2 | 2 |
| **Detroit** | | | | | | |
| Abbott | 5 1-3 | 8 | 4 | 4 | 0 | 1 |
| Bair L,4-3 | 1-3 | 2 | 2 | 2 | 2 | 0 |
| Monge | 2-3 | 2 | 3 | 3 | 1 | 1 |
| Lopez | 1 2-3 | 3 | 0 | 0 | 0 | 2 |
| Hernandz | 1 | 0 | 0 | 0 | 1 | 2 |

WP—Abbott. T—2:57. A—41,714.

Now I pray. That's all I have left to do. Our pitching is shattered and we have three straight doubleheaders staring us right in the face.

Glenn Abbott couldn't get through the sixth inning. Doug Bair and Sid Monge were hammered. No way on God's earth I wanted to bring in Aurelio Lopez tonight. But there was no alternative. Our pitching staff is flat worn out. Tomorrow we've got Dave Rozema starting one game and Juan Berenguer the other. Where we go from there, who knows?

After the game a writer suggested that we needed another arm. How about three or four?

# SUNDAY, AUGUST 5

## AT DETROIT

# GAMES 109 & 110

## ROYALS 5, TIGERS 4
## ROYALS 4, TIGERS 0

### (72–38, 8 GAMES AHEAD)

| KANSAS CITY | ab | r | h | bi | DETROIT | ab | r | h | bi |
|---|---|---|---|---|---|---|---|---|---|
| Wilson cf | 5 | 0 | 1 | 0 | Whitakr 2b | 4 | 0 | 1 | 0 |
| Sheridn rf | 4 | 1 | 2 | 0 | Traml dh | 3 | 1 | 1 | 1 |
| Brett 3b | 5 | 0 | 0 | 0 | Lemon cf | 5 | 0 | 0 | 0 |
| Pryor 3b | 0 | 0 | 0 | 0 | LNParsh c | 4 | 1 | 0 | 0 |
| Orta dh | 5 | 2 | 3 | 0 | Garbey 1b | 3 | 1 | 1 | 1 |
| DIorg 1b | 5 | 0 | 3 | 2 | Bergmn 1b | 1 | 0 | 0 | 0 |
| Motley lf | 5 | 1 | 1 | 1 | Herndon lf | 2 | 0 | 2 | 2 |
| White 2b | 4 | 1 | 2 | 1 | R Jones lf | 1 | 0 | 0 | 0 |
| Cncpcn ss | 4 | 0 | 3 | 0 | KGibson rf | 4 | 0 | 1 | 0 |
| Wathan c | 4 | 0 | 1 | 1 | HJhnsn 3b | 4 | 0 | 0 | 0 |
|  |  |  |  |  | Brookns ss | 2 | 0 | 1 | 0 |
|  |  |  |  |  | DEvns ph | 0 | 1 | 0 | 0 |
| Totals | 41 | 5 | 16 | 5 | Totals | 33 | 4 | 7 | 4 |

Kansas City.................. 000 201 002— 5
Detroit........................ 000 003 001— 4

Game Winning RBI — Iorg (1).
E—Brett. DP—Kansas City 2, Detroit 2. LOB—Kansas City 10, Detroit 8. 2B—Herndon 2, Orta, DIorg. HR—White (12).

| Kansas City | IP | H | R | ER | BB | SO |
|---|---|---|---|---|---|---|
| M Jones | 6 | 4 | 3 | 2 | 4 | 4 |
| Sabrhgn W,6-8 | 2 | 0 | 0 | 0 | 1 | 0 |
| Quisnbry S,29 | 1 | 3 | 1 | 1 | 1 | 0 |
| Detroit |  |  |  |  |  |  |
| Rozema | 6 | 10 | 3 | 3 | 1 | 2 |
| Hernandz L,6-1 | 3 | 6 | 2 | 2 | 0 | 1 |

| KANSAS CITY | ab | r | h | bi | DETROIT | ab | r | h | bi |
|---|---|---|---|---|---|---|---|---|---|
| Wilson cf | 4 | 1 | 2 | 0 | Whitakr 2b | 3 | 0 | 0 | 0 |
| Sheridn rf | 4 | 1 | 2 | 2 | Traml dh | 3 | 0 | 2 | 0 |
| Brett 3b | 4 | 1 | 1 | 0 | Lemon cf | 4 | 0 | 1 | 0 |
| Pryor 3b | 0 | 0 | 0 | 0 | Herndon lf | 4 | 0 | 1 | 0 |
| Orta dh | 4 | 1 | 1 | 0 | Garbey 1b | 3 | 0 | 0 | 0 |
| DIorg 1b | 4 | 0 | 0 | 1 | Brgmn ph | 1 | 0 | 0 | 0 |
| Wathan 1b | 0 | 0 | 0 | 0 | KGibson rf | 4 | 0 | 1 | 0 |
| Motley lf | 4 | 0 | 1 | 1 | HJhnsn 3b | 4 | 0 | 1 | 0 |
| White 2b | 4 | 0 | 0 | 0 | Brookns ss | 2 | 0 | 0 | 0 |
| Slaught c | 4 | 0 | 0 | 0 | DEvns ph | 1 | 0 | 0 | 0 |
| Cncpcn ss | 4 | 0 | 1 | 0 | MCastill c | 2 | 0 | 0 | 0 |
|  |  |  |  |  | LNParsh c | 1 | 0 | 0 | 0 |
| Totals | 36 | 4 | 8 | 4 | Totals | 32 | 0 | 6 | 0 |

Kansas City.................. 400 000 000— 4
Detroit........................ 000 000 000— 0

Game Winning RBI — Sheridan (9).
E—Brett, Leibrandt, Whitaker. DP—Kansas City 2. LOB—Kansas City 7, Detroit 8. 2B—Trammell (6). SB—Wilson 2 (27).

| Kansas City | IP | H | R | ER | BB | SO |
|---|---|---|---|---|---|---|
| Lebrndt W,6-4 | 8 | 5 | 0 | 0 | 3 | 2 |
| Quisnbry | 1 | 1 | 0 | 0 | 0 | 0 |
| Detroit |  |  |  |  |  |  |
| Berengur L,5-8 | 9 | 8 | 4 | 4 | 2 | 8 |

BK—Leibrandt. T—2:37. A—42,761.

Mark this date down. My lowest point of the season. Ups and downs are part of the game, but I have never felt lower than today.

We had two losses to Kansas City; four over the weekend. I just can't stand to see everything we built crumble under all these doubleheaders.

One thing I'll say, our pitchers gave them a battle. Dave Rozema gave us six innings and left at 3–3. That's when I gambled and brought in Willie Hernandez. Willie didn't deserve the fate he got. But he suffered his first loss when Dane Iorg blooped a double over Ruppert Jones's head in left.

In the second game, Juan Berenguer went the distance. We needed someone to take charge on the mound. He took the loss, but what a job he did. He only gave up four runs and we just didn't give him any help.

Thank God we've got that eight-game lead.

157

# MONDAY, AUGUST 6

## AT BOSTON

# GAMES 111 & 112

## TIGERS 9, RED SOX 7
## RED SOX 10, TIGERS 2

### (73–39, 8½ GAMES AHEAD)

| DETROIT | ab | r | h | bi | | BOSTON | ab | r | h | bi |
|---|---|---|---|---|---|---|---|---|---|---|
| Whitakr 2b | 5 | 2 | 2 | 1 | | Boggs 3b | 4 | 0 | 2 | 0 |
| Traml dh | 5 | 0 | 2 | 0 | | DwEvns lf | 5 | 1 | 1 | 0 |
| Lemon cf | 5 | 2 | 3 | 3 | | Rice lf | 4 | 1 | 1 | 2 |
| LNParsh c | 5 | 1 | 2 | 3 | | Armas cf | 5 | 2 | 1 | 0 |
| Herndon lf | 3 | 1 | 1 | 0 | | Easler dh | 4 | 0 | 1 | 0 |
| R Jones lf | 2 | 0 | 0 | 0 | | Bucknr 1b | 5 | 2 | 2 | 3 |
| KGibson rf | 4 | 0 | 0 | 0 | | Gedman c | 5 | 1 | 3 | 1 |
| Garbey 3b | 3 | 0 | 2 | 1 | | Barrett 2b | 4 | 0 | 4 | 1 |
| HJhnsn 3b | 1 | 0 | 0 | 0 | | Gutirrz ss | 2 | 0 | 1 | 0 |
| DaEvns 1b | 3 | 1 | 1 | 0 | | Miller ph | 1 | 0 | 0 | 0 |
| Bergmn 1b | 1 | 0 | 1 | 0 | | Hoffmn ss | 1 | 0 | 0 | 0 |
| Brookns ss | 4 | 2 | 1 | 1 | | | | | | |
| Totals | 41 | 9 | 15 | 9 | | Totals | 40 | 7 | 16 | 7 |

Detroit .......................... 000 252 000 — 9
Boston .......................... 000 240 100 — 7

Game Winning RBI — Whitaker (11).
E—Garbey. DP—Detroit 1, Boston 1. LOB—Detroit 9, Boston 11. 2B—DaEvans, Trammell, DwEvans. HR—LNParrish (22), Lemon (15), Brookens (3), Buckner (5), Rice (18), Gedman (14). S—Gutierrez.

| Detroit | IP | H | R | ER | BB | SO |
|---|---|---|---|---|---|---|
| Petry | 4 2-3 | 11 | 6 | 4 | 2 | 7 |
| Lopez W,8-0 | 2 2-3 | 4 | 1 | 1 | 2 | 3 |
| Hernandz S,23 | 1 2-3 | 1 | 0 | 0 | 0 | 1 |
| **Boston** | | | | | | |
| Ojeda L,9-9 | 4 1-3 | 6 | 6 | 6 | 2 | 5 |
| Gale | 2-3 | 3 | 2 | 2 | 1 | 0 |
| Stanley | 4 | 6 | 1 | 1 | 1 | 2 |

Gale pitched to 1 batter in 6th.
T—3:17. A—0.000

| DETROIT | ab | r | h | bi | | BOSTON | ab | r | h | bi |
|---|---|---|---|---|---|---|---|---|---|---|
| Whitakr 2b | 3 | 0 | 1 | 0 | | Boggs 3b | 5 | 4 | 4 | 3 |
| Grubb lf | 1 | 0 | 0 | 0 | | DwEvns rf | 3 | 1 | 1 | 0 |
| Traml dh | 5 | 0 | 1 | 0 | | Nichols rf | 1 | 0 | 1 | 0 |
| KGibson rf | 3 | 0 | 1 | 1 | | Rice lf | 5 | 1 | 1 | 2 |
| LNParsh c | 3 | 0 | 0 | 0 | | Armas cf | 4 | 2 | 3 | 1 |
| MCastill c | 1 | 0 | 0 | 0 | | Easler dh | 4 | 1 | 3 | 3 |
| DaEvns 1b | 4 | 0 | 0 | 0 | | Bucknr 1b | 4 | 0 | 1 | 1 |
| R Jones lf | 4 | 0 | 0 | 0 | | Miller 1b | 0 | 0 | 0 | 0 |
| Lemon cf | 3 | 0 | 0 | 0 | | Gedman c | 4 | 0 | 2 | 0 |
| Garbey 2b | 1 | 0 | 0 | 0 | | Allenson c | 0 | 0 | 0 | 0 |
| HJhnsn 3b | 3 | 1 | 1 | 1 | | Barrett 2b | 4 | 0 | 0 | 0 |
| Brookns ss | 4 | 1 | 2 | 0 | | Gutirrz ss | 3 | 1 | 0 | 0 |
| Totals | 35 | 2 | 6 | 2 | | Totals | 37 | 10 | 15 | 10 |

Detroit .......................... 001 000 100 — 2
Boston .......................... 420 301 00x — 10

Game Winning RBI — Rice (10).
E—Gutierrez 2, Brookens. DP—Detroit 2. LOB—Detroit 9, Boston 5. 2B—DwEvans, Armas, Buckner, Boggs. HR—HJohnson (9), Boggs 2 (5).

| Detroit | IP | H | R | ER | BB | SO |
|---|---|---|---|---|---|---|
| Willis L,0-2 | 1-3 | 5 | 4 | 4 | 0 | 0 |
| Bair | 4 2-3 | 6 | 5 | 5 | 1 | 0 |
| Monge | 3 | 4 | 1 | 1 | 1 | 0 |
| **Boston** | | | | | | |
| Clemens W,6-4 | 8 | 6 | 2 | 2 | 2 | 9 |
| Crawford | 1 | 0 | 0 | 0 | 1 | 0 |

T—2:55. A—31,055

I never thought I'd say this, but tonight's split was more than I could have imagined. I'm convinced right now that there isn't a better club in either league than the Boston Red Sox.

We got Petry the lead in the opener, but he almost gave it back. Danny's just tired.

I had to call on Aurelio Lopez again. This guy is simply amazing. Everybody talks about Willie Hernandez and I can't argue with that. But Lopez is something else. I've never known a pitcher who can work as often and as long as he can. It was a battle all the way and finally we hung on.

In the second game, they hammered us in the first inning and only had to wait until the second to nail the coffin shut. We pitched Carl Willis, Sid Monge, and Doug Bair. We could have pitched Cy Young and it wouldn't have helped. This Boston team is tough. Willis was called up to give us an arm. All we got was one-third of an inning from him.

We've got another doubleheader tomorrow and a single game Wednesday. If we can win one of three here, I think it will help. Our doubleheader string will be over. We have the most worn out pitching staff I ever have seen.

**Jack Morris winds up.**  Photo courtesy of Detroit Tigers

# TUESDAY, AUGUST 7

## AT BOSTON

# GAMES 113 & 114

## RED SOX 12, TIGERS 7
## TIGERS 7, RED SOX 5

### (2ND GAME 11 INNINGS)
### (74–40, 9 GAMES AHEAD)

| DETROIT | ab | r | h | bi | BOSTON | ab | r | h | bi |
|---|---|---|---|---|---|---|---|---|---|
| Whitakr 2b | 5 | 0 | 0 | 0 | Boggs 3b | 4 | 1 | 2 | 1 |
| Traml dh | 5 | 1 | 1 | 1 | DwEvns rf | 5 | 1 | 2 | 0 |
| Lemon cf | 2 | 2 | 0 | 0 | Rice lf | 3 | 2 | 0 | 0 |
| Grubb lf | 0 | 0 | 0 | 0 | Nichols lf | 0 | 0 | 0 | 0 |
| LNParsh c | 4 | 1 | 2 | 1 | Armas cf | 5 | 3 | 2 | 5 |
| Herndon lf | 3 | 1 | 1 | 0 | Easler dh | 5 | 1 | 2 | 1 |
| R Jones lf | 1 | 0 | 0 | 0 | Bucknr 1b | 4 | 2 | 2 | 5 |
| Garbey 1b | 3 | 0 | 1 | 2 | Gedman c | 4 | 1 | 1 | 0 |
| DaEvns 3b | 2 | 0 | 0 | 0 | Barrett 2b | 4 | 0 | 1 | 0 |
| KGibson rf | 4 | 0 | 3 | 1 | Gutirrz ss | 3 | 1 | 1 | 0 |
| Brookns ss | 3 | 1 | 0 | 0 | | | | | |
| Bergmn 1b | 1 | 0 | 0 | 0 | | | | | |
| HJhnsn 3b | 4 | 1 | 2 | 2 | | | | | |
| Totals | 37 | 7 | 10 | 7 | Totals | 37 | 12 | 13 | 12 |

```
Detroit .....................121 020 100— 7
Boston .......................550 011 000—12
```

Game Winning RBI — Buckner (2).
E—Gutierrez, Brookens. DP—Detroit 1.
LOB—Detroit 8, Boston 5. 2B—Herndon,
Boggs, Gedman, Armas, Easler. HR—
Trammell (10), HJohnson (10), LNParrish
(23), Buckner 2 (7), Armas (31).

| | IP | H | R | ER | BB | SO |
|---|---|---|---|---|---|---|
| **Detroit** | | | | | | |
| Morris L, 14-8 | 1 1-3 | 6 | 9 | 8 | 2 | 1 |
| Monge | 4 2-3 | 6 | 3 | 3 | 1 | 1 |
| Willis | 2 | 1 | 0 | 0 | 1 | 0 |
| **Boston** | | | | | | |
| Hurst W, 11-6 | 6 | 10 | 7 | 7 | 3 | 7 |
| Clear S,5 | 3 | 0 | 0 | 0 | 2 | 4 |

Hurst pitched to 2 batters in 7th.
WP—Morris. T—2:49. A—0,000.

| DETROIT | ab | r | h | bi | BOSTON | ab | r | h | bi |
|---|---|---|---|---|---|---|---|---|---|
| Whitakr 2b | 6 | 0 | 1 | 0 | Boggs 3b | 5 | 0 | 1 | 1 |
| Traml dh | 5 | 0 | 2 | 0 | DwEvns rf | 5 | 1 | 1 | 3 |
| Lemon cf | 6 | 1 | 0 | 0 | Rice lf | 5 | 1 | 2 | 1 |
| LNParsh c | 5 | 2 | 2 | 3 | Armas cf | 5 | 0 | 1 | 0 |
| Herndon lf | 3 | 1 | 1 | 1 | Easler dh | 5 | 0 | 0 | 0 |
| R Jones lf | 3 | 0 | 1 | 0 | Bucknr 1b | 5 | 0 | 1 | 0 |
| Garbey 1b | 3 | 0 | 2 | 0 | Newman c | 4 | 0 | 0 | 0 |
| DaEvns 3b | 3 | 0 | 1 | 0 | Barrett 2b | 4 | 2 | 1 | 0 |
| KGibson rf | 4 | 1 | 1 | 1 | Gutirrz ss | 2 | 0 | 2 | 0 |
| Brookns ss | 3 | 0 | 0 | 0 | Miller ph | 1 | 1 | 1 | 0 |
| Bergmn 1b | 2 | 1 | 1 | 0 | Hoffmn ss | 0 | 0 | 0 | 0 |
| HJhnsn ss | 5 | 1 | 2 | 0 | Gedmn pb | 1 | 0 | 0 | 0 |
| | | | | | Jurak ss | 0 | 0 | 0 | 0 |
| Totals | 48 | 7 | 14 | 5 | Totals | 42 | 5 | 10 | 5 |

```
Detroit .....................010 210 001 02— 7
Boston .......................000 010 400 00— 5
```

Game Winning RBI — LNParrish (7).
E—Garbey, Buckner. DP—Detroit 1.
LOB—Detroit 11, Boston 5. 2B—Bergman,
Rice, Barrett, Boggs, R Jones. 3B—HJohn-
son. HR—Herndon (2), LNParrish 2 (25),
KGibson (17), DwEvans (22), Rice (19).
SB—Whitaker (6).

| | IP | H | R | ER | BB | SO |
|---|---|---|---|---|---|---|
| **Detroit** | | | | | | |
| Wilcox | 6 2-3 | 10 | 5 | 5 | 1 | 5 |
| Lopez W,9-0 | 3 1-3 | 0 | 0 | 0 | 0 | 5 |
| Hernandz S,24 | 1 | 0 | 0 | 0 | 0 | 2 |
| **Boston** | | | | | | |
| JJohnson | 5 | 6 | 4 | 4 | 0 | 9 |
| Crawford | 2 | 3 | 0 | 0 | 0 | 1 |
| Stanley | 1 1-3 | 2 | 1 | 0 | 0 | 2 |
| Clear | 2-3 | 0 | 0 | 0 | 2 | 2 |
| Gale L, 1-3 | 2 | 3 | 2 | 2 | 1 | 1 |

WP—JJohnson. PB—Newman. T—3:33.
A—32,120.

When we win this season, we're going to
look back to August 7 and look at that second game. If ever there was a turning
point, this was it.

With all the doubleheaders we've played,
our pitching was racked. I mean stripped
to the bone. We had a 4-1 lead in the
seventh before Red Sox Dwight Evans hit a
three-run homer to tie, and Jim Rice followed with another homer to go ahead.

Then our boys became men. All of a
sudden it looked like they were fighting to
win and not just to survive. There's a big
difference. You should have heard them in
the dugout. We scratched out a run in the
ninth to tie. Then Lance Parrish ended all
the nonsense with a long two-run homer in
the eleventh.

Aurelio Lopez came in after Rice hit the
homer and retired 10 straight men. Willie
Hernandez came in after Parrish con-

nected and set down three straight for his 24th save. Chet Lemon made a catch on Red Sox designated hitter Mike Easler in the fourth that was better than Willie Mays's catch off Vic Wertz in the 1954 World Series.

After the game I did something I had never done in my career before. Not here; not at Cincinnati; not anywhere. I closed the door to everyone but me and the players for 15 seconds. I told them I've never witnessed such great character in a team. There's no victory in my career that surpasses it. How could it after what these players have been through?

My pitchers were dead tired and getting pounded, Boston was beating on us left and right, but we split 2-2 and I came away with more respect for these players than I thought I ever could have.

Boston could get 50 runs in the final game, I could get mugged on the way back to the hotel tonight and I wouldn't care. That's how proud I feel.

We've still got to figure out Jack Morris's problem. He couldn't even give us two innings in the opener. Bill Buckner took him for a grand slam in the first inning and Tony Armas repeated the trick in the second. Jack has got to start pitching some ball games for us. He hasn't given us anything the last four or five times out. We can't let him wear our bullpen out.

**The dugout greets Lance Parrish after another homer.** Photo by Doc Holcomb, courtesy of *The Detroit News*

# WEDNESDAY, AUGUST 8

## AT BOSTON

# GAME 115

## RED SOX 8, TIGERS 0

### (74–41, 8 GAMES AHEAD)

| DETROIT | ab | r | h | bi | BOSTON | ab | r | h | bi |
|---|---|---|---|---|---|---|---|---|---|
| Whitakr 2b | 4 | 0 | 1 | 0 | Boggs 3b | 5 | 0 | 1 | 0 |
| Traml dh | 4 | 0 | 1 | 0 | Jurak 3b | 0 | 0 | 0 | 0 |
| KGibson rf | 4 | 0 | 1 | 0 | DwEvns rf | 4 | 1 | 1 | 0 |
| LNParsh c | 4 | 0 | 0 | 0 | Miller rf | 1 | 0 | 0 | 0 |
| DaEvns 3b | 3 | 0 | 0 | 0 | Rice lf | 4 | 1 | 1 | 1 |
| RJones cf | 4 | 0 | 1 | 0 | Nichols lf | 0 | 0 | 0 | 0 |
| Grubb lf | 3 | 0 | 2 | 0 | Armas c | 5 | 0 | 1 | 0 |
| Bergmn 1b | 3 | 0 | 0 | 0 | Easler dh | 4 | 3 | 3 | 0 |
| HJhnsn ss | 3 | 0 | 1 | 0 | Buckner 1b | 4 | 2 | 2 | 1 |
| | | | | | Gedman c | 3 | 1 | 2 | 5 |
| | | | | | Barrett 2b | 4 | 0 | 2 | 0 |
| | | | | | Gutirrz ss | 3 | 0 | 1 | 1 |
| Totals | 32 | 0 | 7 | 0 | Totals | 37 | 8 | 14 | 8 |

Detroit............................ 000 000 000— 0
Boston........................... 502 000 10x— 8
   Game Winning RBI — Rice (11).
   E—HJohnson 2. DP—Detroit 1, Boston 2. LOB—Detroit 6, Boston 8. 2B—Rice, DwEvans, Boggs. HR—Gedman (15). SF—Gedman, Gutierrez.

| | IP | H | R | ER | BB | SO |
|---|---|---|---|---|---|---|
| **Detroit** | | | | | | |
| Abbott L.,3-4 | 2-3 | 5 | 5 | 0 | 0 | 1 |
| Berengur | 5 1-3 | 6 | 2 | 1 | 0 | 4 |
| Rozema | 2 | 3 | 1 | 1 | 1 | 1 |
| **Boston** | | | | | | |
| Boyd W,7-8 | 9 | 7 | 0 | 0 | 1 | 2 |

   T—2:28. A—32,563.

I've got a big job ahead of me. Somehow we've got to pull these guys through this thing because we have a chance to be a good club for years to come if we can just get through this.

If we win this thing, these guys will be the happiest people in the world and they'll experience first-hand that all the money in the world cannot replace that unique feeling of winning. But they've got to get down into the trenches, get good and dirty, and fight like trapped tigers.

Tonight we played with no enthusiasm—like a wet rag. I knew we were in deep trouble before we went to the park. Because of all the doubleheaders, we had to come up with another pitcher, and the only way we had a chance was to score a lot of runs.

We didn't. We didn't touch the plate. Chet Lemon had a sore shoulder and couldn't play. Alan Trammell is still out and I'm really fearful he may not play the rest of the season. Thank God after next week's doubleheader with California, we have only single games the rest of the way. We'll just have to play one game at a time and shoot everything we've got at them everyday.

# THURSDAY, AUGUST 9

## AT KANSAS CITY

## (74–41, 8 GAMES AHEAD)

We needed this day off. Man, did we need it. I got to the hotel, ordered room service, and didn't budge. It was so relaxing to be away from the players and everyone. It starts to get to me when the players whine and cry about different things like bus rides, plane rides, playing and not playing. You reach a point where you just want to get away from it all.

Photo by Doc Holcomb, courtesy of *The Detroit News*

**The Tigers' Latin connection—Aurelio Lopez and Willie Hernandez.**

# FRIDAY, AUGUST 10

## AT KANSAS CITY

# GAME 116

## TIGERS 5, ROYALS 4

### (75–41, 7½ GAMES AHEAD)

| DETROIT | ab | r | h | bi | KANSAS CITY | ab | r | h | bi |
|---|---|---|---|---|---|---|---|---|---|
| Whitakr 2b | 5 | 0 | 1 | 1 | Wilson cf | 3 | 2 | 0 | 1 |
| Traml dh | 4 | 0 | 2 | 0 | Sheridn r | 5 | 0 | 0 | 0 |
| Lemon cf | 4 | 0 | 0 | 0 | Brett 3b | 4 | 1 | 3 | 3 |
| LNParsh c | 3 | 0 | 0 | 0 | Orta dh | 3 | 0 | 1 | 0 |
| Herndon lf | 3 | 0 | 1 | 0 | Dlorg 1b | 4 | 0 | 0 | 0 |
| R Jones lf | 1 | 1 | 1 | 1 | White 2b | 3 | 0 | 2 | 0 |
| Garbey 1b | 3 | 1 | 1 | 0 | Slaught c | 4 | 0 | 0 | 0 |
| DaEvns 1b | 1 | 0 | 0 | 0 | LJones lf | 4 | 1 | 1 | 0 |
| KGibson rf | 3 | 2 | 1 | 1 | Cncpcn ss | 1 | 0 | 1 | 0 |
| HJhnsn 3b | 4 | 0 | 0 | 0 | UWshtn ss | 1 | 0 | 0 | 0 |
| Brookns ss | 4 | 1 | 2 | 2 | McRae ph | 1 | 0 | 0 | 0 |
| Totals | 35 | 5 | 9 | 5 | Totals | 33 | 4 | 8 | 4 |

```
Detroit ..........................030 001 010— 5
Kansas City ...................100 030 000— 4
```

Game Winning RBI — R Jones (4).
E—KGibson, LNParrish, UWashingtn. DP—Kansas City 1. LOB—Detroit 6, Kansas City 7. 2B—Brett 2, Trammell. 3B—Brookens. HR—Brett (10), KGibson (18), RJones (8). SB—Wilson 2 (31), White (3). S—Wilson.

| | IP | H | R | ER | BB | SO |
|---|---|---|---|---|---|---|
| **Detroit** | | | | | | |
| Petry | 6 2-3 | 7 | 4 | 4 | 2 | 5 |
| Lopez W, 10-0 | 1 1-3 | 1 | 0 | 0 | 1 | 0 |
| Hernandz S, 25 | 1 | 0 | 0 | 0 | 0 | 0 |
| **Kansas City** | | | | | | |
| MJones | 6 1-3 | 8 | 4 | 4 | 3 | 5 |
| Beckwith L, 5-3 | 2 2-3 | 1 | 1 | 1 | 0 | 1 |

HBP—Concepcion by Petry. T—2:54. A—32,181.

This ball club is dead tired from all those doubleheaders. Just to show how tired, the Royals stole three bases against Lance Parrish. Now that just doesn't happen.

That's why I'm going to shoot every cannon I've got any time we have a chance win. I won't let one slip by. I'll use everybody. If a game gets out of hand early, we'll have to let it go.

Aurelio Lopez and Willie Hernandez relieved again tonight. These guys belong in *Ripley's Believe It or Not*. They just don't fail. Dan Petry threw the ball well for 6-2/3 innings. He made a couple of mistakes, but he was popping the ball.

Kirk Gibson tied the game with a homer in the seventh. Ruppert Jones pinch hit for Larry Herndon in the eighth and won it with a homer. What a great addition Ruppert has turned out to be.

# SATURDAY, AUGUST 11

## AT KANSAS CITY

# GAME 117

## TIGERS 9, ROYALS 5

### (76–41, 8 GAMES AHEAD)

| KANSAS CITY | ab | r | h | bi | DETROIT | ab | r | h | bi |
|---|---|---|---|---|---|---|---|---|---|
| Wilson cf | 4 | 1 | 1 | 0 | Whitakr 2b | 4 | 0 | 0 | 0 |
| Sheridn rf | 5 | 1 | 3 | 2 | Traml dh | 4 | 1 | 0 | 0 |
| Brett 3b | 5 | 0 | 0 | 1 | KGibson rf | 5 | 2 | 3 | 2 |
| Pryor 3b | 0 | 0 | 0 | 0 | LNParsh c | 5 | 0 | 1 | 0 |
| Orta dh | 3 | 0 | 2 | 1 | RJones lf | 5 | 1 | 2 | 3 |
| McRae dh | 2 | 0 | 0 | 0 | Lemon cf | 4 | 0 | 0 | 0 |
| DIorg 1b | 4 | 2 | 2 | 0 | Bergmn 1b | 3 | 0 | 1 | 0 |
| Wathan 1b | 0 | 0 | 0 | 0 | HJhnsn 3b | 1 | 0 | 0 | 0 |
| Motley lf | 4 | 2 | 1 | 1 | Brookns ss | 2 | 1 | 0 | 0 |
| White 2b | 5 | 1 | 1 | 0 | DaEvns 3b | 2 | 0 | 0 | 0 |
| Slaught c | 4 | 1 | 3 | 2 | | | | | |
| Cncpcn ss | 4 | 1 | 2 | 2 | | | | | |
| Totals | 40 | 9 | 15 | 9 | Totals | 35 | 5 | 7 | 5 |

```
Kansas City         200  004  300— 9
Detroit             002  020  100— 5
```

Game Winning RBI — Sheridan (8).
E—DIorg. DP—Detroit 2. LOB—Kansas City 8, Detroit 9. 2B—Sheridan, DIorg, Slaught. 3B—KGibson 2. HR—RJones (7). SB—KGibson (20).

| Kansas City | IP | H | R | ER | BB | SO |
|---|---|---|---|---|---|---|
| Gubicza | 4 1-3 | 5 | 4 | 3 | 4 | 3 |
| Beckwith W,4-2 | 4 2-3 | 2 | 1 | 1 | 2 | 2 |
| **Detroit** | | | | | | |
| Abbott | 5 1-3 | 8 | 4 | 4 | 0 | 1 |
| Bair L,4-3 | 1-3 | 2 | 2 | 2 | 2 | 0 |
| Monge | 2-3 | 2 | 3 | 3 | 1 | 1 |
| Lopez | 1 2-3 | 3 | 0 | 0 | 0 | 1 |
| Hernandz | 1 | 0 | 0 | 0 | 1 | 2 |

WP—Abbott. T—2:57. A—41,714.

Before the game I held another meeting with the players. I told them very simply that they had to win 25 more games. They must play as hard as they possibly can everyday and then leave the win or loss right there. Start over new each day.

It worked tonight. Especially for Jack Morris. He threw the ball well and he needed that. Jack gets so mentally down at times that he really needed a game like this. Jack and Dan Petry each have 10 more starts. They will each need to win at least six more for us to win this thing.

Kirk Gibson hit another homer. What a player he's been for the last month. Not just on the field but also on the bench and in the clubhouse. He keeps driving people. He's got this way about him—he's a flat-out winner.

Lance Parrish had a big two-run homer. Larry Herndon hit his first leftfield homer of the season. That may have been the first ball all year that he's really driven to leftfield. I hope that brings him out of it.

# SUNDAY, AUGUST 12

## AT KANSAS CITY

# GAME 118

## TIGERS 8, ROYALS 4
### (77–41, 9 GAMES AHEAD)

| DETROIT | ab | r | h | bi | KANSAS CITY | ab | r | h | bi |
|---|---|---|---|---|---|---|---|---|---|
| Whitakr 2b | 4 | 1 | 1 | 1 | Wilson cf | 5 | 0 | 1 | 2 |
| Traml dh | 5 | 1 | 2 | 2 | Sheridn rf | 4 | 0 | 0 | 0 |
| K Gibson rf | 2 | 0 | 0 | 0 | Brett 3b | 2 | 0 | 1 | 0 |
| LNParsh c | 4 | 1 | 0 | 0 | Pryor 3b | 1 | 0 | 0 | 0 |
| DaEvns 1b | 3 | 2 | 1 | 2 | Orta dh | 4 | 1 | 1 | 0 |
| Bergmn 1b | 0 | 0 | 0 | 0 | Diorg 1b | 4 | 1 | 1 | 0 |
| R Jones lf | 2 | 1 | 1 | 2 | White 2b | 3 | 0 | 1 | 1 |
| Herndon lf | 3 | 1 | 2 | 0 | L Jones lf | 3 | 1 | 0 | 0 |
| Lemon cf | 4 | 0 | 0 | 0 | Wathan c | 2 | 0 | 0 | 0 |
| HJhnsn 3b | 2 | 0 | 0 | 0 | Slaught c | 1 | 1 | 1 | 1 |
| Garbey ph | 1 | 0 | 0 | 1 | Blancln ss | 2 | 0 | 0 | 0 |
| Brokns 3b | 1 | 0 | 1 | 0 | Motley ph | 1 | 0 | 0 | 0 |
| Baker ss | 4 | 1 | 0 | 0 | UWshtn ss | 0 | 0 | 0 | 0 |
|  |  |  |  |  | McRae ph | 1 | 0 | 0 | 0 |
| Totals | 35 | 8 | 8 | 8 | Totals | 33 | 4 | 6 | 4 |

```
Detroit........................... 400  001  030— 8
Kansas City................... 000  000  400— 4
```
Game Winning RBI — DaEvans (5).
E—Herndon. LOB—Detroit 8, Kansas City 6. 2B—Herndon, Orta, Slaught, Whitaker, Trammell, White. 3B—DaEvans. HR—R Jones (9). SF—White.

| | IP | H | R | ER | BB | SO |
|---|---|---|---|---|---|---|
| **Detroit** | | | | | | |
| Wilcox W, 12-7 | 6 1-3 | 3 | 3 | 3 | 2 | 2 |
| Lopez | 2-3 | 2 | 1 | 1 | 0 | 1 |
| Hernandz | 2 | 1 | 0 | 0 | 1 | 0 |
| **Kansas City** | | | | | | |
| Sabrhgn L, 6-9 | 5 | 3 | 4 | 4 | 3 | 4 |
| Gura | 2 | 1 | 1 | 1 | 4 | 1 |
| Quisnbry | 1 | 4 | 3 | 3 | 1 | 1 |
| Huismann | 1 | 0 | 0 | 0 | 0 | 0 |

T—2:47. A—32,753.

The lowest point of the season for me was that first weekend in August when the Royals swept four from us at home. I just never would have believed they could ever do that to us. That's what makes this sweep here so special. If anyone had told me before we left that we'd be 5-3 on this trip, I don't know what I would have said—probably "I love you."

I learned a lot about our club on this trip. I learned that they will get in the trenches and fight. I learned they have character.

Today's game was tougher than the 8-4 score shows. We had a 5-0 lead at one point and then had to fight off their charge. Our guys busted their tails again. That's three days in a row they have really scrapped.

Darrell Evans got a big triple and Ruppert Jones hit another homer. Larry Herndon got two more hits and has inched into the .260s. He can make a big difference.

# MONDAY, AUGUST 13

## AT COOPERSTOWN
## (EXHIBITION GAME)

### (77–41, 9½ GAMES AHEAD)

We played an exhibition game against Atlanta and won, 7–5. It's always nice to win, but it didn't mean anything. We played our extras and brought up three minor league pitchers.

Being in Cooperstown, though, really makes you think about a lot of things. We only spent the afternoon there, so we didn't have a chance to get to the Museum, but you can really feel the presence of Babe Ruth and Ty Cobb and Lou Gehrig and all the ghosts who make up the tradition of this great game. How can anyone ever put on a uniform and not dream of someday making the Hall of Fame?

Cooperstown is a beautiful little town: the mountains, the lake, the trees. They have a beautiful, big old hotel there with no phones and no television in the rooms. I'd love to spend a few days here.

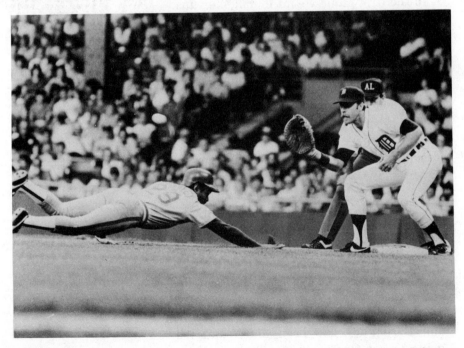

**Dave Bergman gets the throw at first.** Photo by Doc Holcomb, courtesy of *The Detroit News*

# TUESDAY, AUGUST 14

## AT DETROIT

# GAMES 119 & 120

## ANGELS 6, TIGERS 4
## ANGELS 12, TIGERS 1
### (77–43, 7½ GAMES AHEAD)

| CALIFORNIA | ab | r | h | bi | DETROIT | ab | r | h | bi |
|---|---|---|---|---|---|---|---|---|---|
| Beniquz rf | 5 | 3 | 4 | 0 | Whitakr 2b | 4 | 1 | 2 | 1 |
| Wilfong 2b | 3 | 0 | 1 | 0 | Traml dh | 4 | 1 | 2 | 1 |
| Grich 2b | 0 | 0 | 0 | 0 | KGibson rf | 5 | 0 | 1 | 0 |
| Lynn cf | 2 | 1 | 0 | 1 | LNParsh c | 5 | 1 | 2 | 1 |
| DeCncs 3b | 5 | 0 | 2 | 2 | DaEvns 1b | 4 | 0 | 1 | 0 |
| Downing lf | 4 | 0 | 1 | 2 | Bergmn 1b | 0 | 0 | 0 | 0 |
| Pettis cf | 1 | 0 | 0 | 0 | R Jones lf | 3 | 0 | 0 | 0 |
| ReJksn dh | 3 | 0 | 0 | 0 | Lemon cf | 2 | 0 | 0 | 0 |
| Narron 1b | 3 | 0 | 0 | 0 | HJhnsn 3b | 4 | 1 | 1 | 1 |
| Schofild ss | 3 | 0 | 0 | 0 | Baker ss | 3 | 0 | 0 | 0 |
| MCBrn ph | 1 | 0 | 0 | 0 | Grubb ph | 1 | 0 | 1 | 0 |
| Picciolo ss | 0 | 0 | 0 | 0 | Brokns pr | 0 | 0 | 0 | 0 |
| Boone c | 4 | 2 | 2 | 1 | | | | | |
| Totals | 34 | 6 | 10 | 6 | Totals | 35 | 4 | 10 | 4 |

California ..................... 200 010 102—6
Detroit ......................... 002 001 100—4

Game Winning RBI — DeCinces (10).
DP—California 1, Detroit 1. LOB—California 8, Detroit 9. 2B—Beniquez. HR—Whitaker (10), Trammell (11), DeCinces (27), Boone (3), HJohnson (11). SB—DeCinces (4). S—Wilfong, Grich, Trammell.

| California | IP | H | R | ER | BB | SO |
|---|---|---|---|---|---|---|
| Witt | 6 1-3 | 8 | 4 | 4 | 2 | 4 |
| Aase W,2-1 | 1 2-3 | 2 | 0 | 0 | 2 | 0 |
| L Sánchez S,11 | 1 | 0 | 0 | 0 | 0 | 0 |
| **Detroit** | | | | | | |
| Berengur | 6 | 5 | 3 | 3 | 3 | 6 |
| Lopez | 1 | 2 | 1 | 1 | 1 | 0 |
| Hernandz L,6-2 | 2 | 3 | 2 | 2 | 1 | 0 |

WP—Berenguer 2. T—2:53. A—..

| CALIFORNIA | ab | r | h | bi | DETROIT | ab | r | h | bi |
|---|---|---|---|---|---|---|---|---|---|
| Beniquz rf | 3 | 1 | 1 | 0 | Whitakr 2b | 2 | 0 | 0 | 0 |
| Pettis cf | 1 | 1 | 0 | 0 | Brokns 2b | 2 | 0 | 0 | 0 |
| Wilfong 2b | 5 | 2 | 3 | 1 | Traml dh | 3 | 1 | 1 | 0 |
| Lynn cf | 3 | 1 | 1 | 2 | KGibson rf | 2 | 0 | 1 | 0 |
| MCBron rf | 1 | 1 | 1 | 0 | Garbey lf | 1 | 0 | 1 | 0 |
| DeCncs 3b | 3 | 1 | 2 | 4 | LNParsh c | 2 | 0 | 1 | 0 |
| Grich 3b | 1 | 1 | 1 | 3 | MCastill c | 2 | 0 | 0 | 0 |
| Downing lf | 4 | 1 | 1 | 0 | DaEvns 1b | 4 | 0 | 1 | 1 |
| DMiller lf | 0 | 0 | 0 | 0 | R Jones lf | 4 | 0 | 1 | 0 |
| ReJksn dh | 5 | 1 | 3 | 1 | Lemon cf | 2 | 0 | 0 | 0 |
| Narron 1b | 4 | 0 | 0 | 0 | Grubb rf | 2 | 0 | 0 | 0 |
| Schofild ss | 5 | 0 | 0 | 0 | HJhnsn 3b | 3 | 0 | 1 | 0 |
| Boone c | 4 | 2 | 2 | 0 | Baker ss | 3 | 0 | 0 | 0 |
| | | | | | Herndn ph | 1 | 0 | 0 | 0 |
| Totals | 39 | 12 | 15 | 11 | Totals | 33 | 1 | 7 | 1 |

California ..................... 107 002 002—12
Detroit ......................... 000 000 010—1

Game Winning RBI — DeCinces (11).
DP—California 1, Detroit 2. LOB—California 5, Detroit 8. 3B—ReJackson. HR—DeCinces (14), Grich (10). SF—Grich.

| California | IP | H | R | ER | BB | SO |
|---|---|---|---|---|---|---|
| Kison W,3-1 | 6 | 3 | 0 | 0 | 2 | 5 |
| Corbett | 2 | 4 | 1 | 0 | 1 | 0 |
| Curtis | 1 | 0 | 0 | 0 | 0 | 0 |
| **Detroit** | | | | | | |
| Rozema L,7-4 | 2 | 7 | 5 | 5 | 0 | 2 |
| Bair | 3 1-3 | 5 | 5 | 5 | 3 | 2 |
| Monge | 3 2-3 | 3 | 2 | 2 | 1 | 5 |

Rozema pitched to four batters in 3rd.
HBP—HJohnson by Corbett. WP—Bair.
T—2:33. A—38,597.

There was only one good thing about today—our doubleheaders are over. We had six of them in the last 15 days. With this one, we really went out with a thud.

It was brutal. Flat-out painful.

In the first game we hit four home runs, and that's how many runs we scored—four. Willie Hernandez got beat in the ninth inning and that's something I never thought I'd see. It wasn't his fault, though. We had runners going all over the place except over home plate.

The second game was embarrassing. Dave Rozema lasted two innings and was knocked all over the park. Our pitching is in sad shape. It's been in rough shape the last six weeks, and now these doubleheaders have killed us. We released Glenn Abbott yesterday. Rozema isn't throwing anything, Sid Monge isn't showing anything, and Doug Bair is having a tough time.

We have 42 games to go and we must win at least 21. It won't be easy. I'll have to go with four starters—Morris, Petry, Wilcox, and Berenguer. It's been tough and it's going to get tougher. I can see right now that it'll be a race right down to the end.

168

# WEDNESDAY, AUGUST 15

## AT DETROIT

# GAME 121

## TIGERS 8, ANGELS 3

(78–43, 9 GAMES AHEAD)

| CALIFORNIA | ab | r | h | bi | DETROIT | ab | r | h | bi |
|---|---|---|---|---|---|---|---|---|---|
| Pettis cf | 4 | 0 | 2 | 1 | Whtaker 2b | 5 | 2 | 1 | 1 |
| Wilfong 2b | 4 | 0 | 1 | 0 | Trammll dh | 5 | 0 | 1 | 0 |
| Lynn rf | 4 | 1 | 1 | 1 | Garbey 1b | 3 | 0 | 3 | 0 |
| DeCinces 3b | 4 | 1 | 1 | 1 | Bergmn 1b | 2 | 0 | 2 | 3 |
| Jackson dh | 4 | 0 | 1 | 0 | Parrish c | 4 | 0 | 0 | 0 |
| Beniquez lf | 4 | 0 | 0 | 0 | Herndon lf | 3 | 1 | 1 | 0 |
| Sconiers 1b | 3 | 0 | 1 | 0 | Jones lf | 1 | 0 | 0 | 0 |
| Grich ph | 1 | 0 | 0 | 0 | Lemon cf | 4 | 1 | 1 | 0 |
| Narron c | 3 | 0 | 1 | 0 | Gibson rf | 3 | 3 | 2 | 0 |
| Schofield ss | 1 | 1 | 0 | 0 | Brookens ss | 3 | 0 | 3 | 2 |
| Brown ph | 1 | 0 | 0 | 0 | Johnson 3b | 3 | 1 | 0 | 1 |
| Picciolo ss | 0 | 0 | 0 | 0 | Baker ss | 0 | 0 | 0 | 0 |
| Totals | 33 | 3 | 8 | ? | Totals | 36 | 8 | 14 | 7 |

```
California      001 100 010— 3
Detroit         010 201 13x— 8
```

Game-winning RBI — Johnson (7).

E—wilfong, Sconiers. DP—California 1, Detroit 2. LOB—California 4, Detroit 8. 2B—Pettis, Wilfong, Whitaker, Gibson. 3B—Pettis, Bergman 2. HR—DeCinces (15), Lynn (15). SB—Sconiers (1), Johnson (8). S—Brookens.

| California | IP | H | R | ER | BB | SO |
|---|---|---|---|---|---|---|
| John (L 7-10) | 6 | 10 | 4 | 3 | 1 | 3 |
| Kaufman | 1-3 | 2 | 1 | 1 | 1 | 1 |
| Curtis | 1 | 1 | 3 | 1 | 1 | 0 |
| Sanchez | 2-3 | 1 | 0 | 0 | 0 | 0 |
| Detroit |  |  |  |  |  |  |
| Petry (W 15-5) | 8 | 8 | 3 | 3 | 1 | 5 |
| Hernandez | 1 | 0 | 0 | 0 | 0 | 0 |

T—2:46. A—33,940.

Pete Rose was named player-manager of the Cincinnati Reds. It caught me by surprise. I sent him a telegram: "Peter Edward, now you will have to wait a few more years before you enter the Hall of Fame. You also will find out what it's like not to sleep at night. You know I will always be pulling for you."

There is no one else on the face of the earth like Peter Edward Rose. No one really knows him. No one really can figure him out. But there will never be another.

At the game, the writers asked me a lot of questions about Rose. I was happy for him . . . and happy for us. We bounced back with Dan Petry and Willie Hernandez. Willie only needed 11 pitches to finish the game—one, two, three in the ninth.

Dave Bergman got two triples and knocked in three runs. He turned the game around. Tom Brookens has been super substituting at shortstop. He also gave us three hits tonight. Cleveland zapped Toronto in a doubleheader, so we're back to nine up. Can you figure that, how things change so quickly?

# THURSDAY, AUGUST 16

## AT DETROIT

# GAME 122

## TIGERS 8, ANGELS 7

### (79-43, 10 GAMES AHEAD)

| CALIFORNIA | ab | r | h | bi | | DETROIT | ab | r | h | bi |
|---|---|---|---|---|---|---|---|---|---|---|
| Pettis cf | 3 | 1 | 1 | 0 | | Whitakr 2b | 5 | 1 | 1 | 0 |
| Wilfong 2b | 5 | 1 | 1 | 0 | | Traml dh | 5 | 0 | 2 | 2 |
| Grich 2b | 1 | 0 | 0 | 0 | | KGibson rf | 4 | 2 | 2 | 2 |
| Lynn rf | 4 | 2 | 1 | 1 | | LNParsh c | 6 | 0 | 2 | 1 |
| DeCncs 3b | 6 | 1 | 2 | 1 | | DaEvns 1b | 4 | 0 | 0 | 1 |
| Downing lf | 5 | 1 | 3 | 5 | | RJones lf | 5 | 0 | 1 | 0 |
| ReJksn dh | 5 | 0 | 1 | 0 | | Lemon cf | 6 | 1 | 2 | 0 |
| Sconirs 1b | 4 | 0 | 0 | 0 | | HJhnsn 3b | 6 | 2 | 1 | 0 |
| MCBrn ph | 1 | 0 | 0 | 0 | | Brookns ss | 2 | 1 | 1 | 0 |
| Narron 1b | 1 | 0 | 0 | 0 | | Grubb ph | 0 | 0 | 0 | 0 |
| Schofild ss | 4 | 0 | 2 | 0 | | Baker ss | 1 | 1 | 0 | 0 |
| Beniqz ph | 1 | 0 | 0 | 0 | | Garbey ph | 1 | 0 | 1 | 1 |
| Picciolo ss | 0 | 0 | 0 | 0 | | | | | | |
| Boone c | 4 | 1 | 1 | 0 | | | | | | |
| Totals | 44 | 7 | 12 | 7 | | Totals | 45 | 8 | 13 | 7 |

```
California............... 003 400 000 000— 7
Detroit................... 230 000 020 001— 8
```
One out when winning run scored.
Game Winning RBI — Garbey (4).
E—Romanick. DP—California 1, Detroit 2. LOB—California 9, Detroit 12. 2B—Whitaker, Brookens, RJones, KGibson, Garbey. 3B—KGibson. HR—Downing (17). SB—Pettis (43), KGibson (21). S—Trammell, Pettis, KGibson.

| | IP | H | R | ER | BB | SO |
|---|---|---|---|---|---|---|
| **California** | | | | | | |
| Romanick | 1 2-3 | 5 | 5 | 4 | 2 | 1 |
| Kaufman | 3 1-3 | 2 | 0 | 0 | 0 | 0 |
| Corbett | 2 1-3 | 2 | 2 | 2 | 2 | 1 |
| Aase | 3 2-3 | 2 | 0 | 0 | 3 | 5 |
| Curtis L,0-1 | 1-3 | 2 | 1 | 1 | 0 | 0 |
| **Detroit** | | | | | | |
| Morris | 3 2-3 | 9 | 7 | 7 | 4 | 4 |
| Bair | 3 1-3 | 1 | 0 | 0 | 3 | 0 |
| Lopez | 1 1-3 | 2 | 0 | 0 | 0 | 0 |
| Hernandz W,7-2 | 3 2-3 | 0 | 0 | 0 | 0 | 6 |

BK—Kaufman. PB—LNParrish. T—4:02. A—37,779.

We had to win this one. We had a 5-0 lead with Jack Morris pitching and we almost blew it. That can't happen—not if we're going to win it all. When you give your ace five runs at this point of the season, he's supposed to shut them down. We can't expect to win this thing if this keeps happening.

Our guys battled, though. Alan Trammell tied the game with a single in the eighth, and Barbaro Garbey won it with a double in the 12th. Willie Hernandez out did even himself. Eleven batters came up and 11 men went down. Incredible!

We're back up to a 10-game lead, but we just can't have our top pitchers folding when they get a big lead. I know Morris is having his problems and still not talking to the press, but every man has to bear his own cross. It didn't stop us from winning. If you want something badly enough, you have to go get it. Why do you think I don't sleep some nights? I want to win this so bad I can taste it.

Right now we have a 9-1 record in extra inning games and are 21-8 in one-run games. Those are the reasons that teams win pennants. We don't lead in any department except one. We win the close games . . . the crucial ones.

# FRIDAY, AUGUST 17

## AT DETROIT

# GAME 123

## TIGERS 6, MARINERS 2

### (80–43, 10 GAMES AHEAD)

| SEATTLE | ab | r | h | bi | | DETROIT | ab | r | h | bi |
|---|---|---|---|---|---|---|---|---|---|---|
| Percont 2b | 5 | 0 | 0 | 0 | | Whitakr 2b | 2 | 1 | 0 | 0 |
| PBradly cf | 4 | 1 | 2 | 0 | | Brokns 2b | 1 | 1 | 1 | 1 |
| ADavis 1b | 4 | 0 | 2 | 1 | | Trammi ss | 4 | 1 | 2 | 1 |
| Phelps dh | 3 | 0 | 0 | 0 | | KGibson rf | 4 | 1 | 2 | 2 |
| Cowens rf | 5 | 0 | 0 | 0 | | LNParsh c | 4 | 0 | 0 | 0 |
| SHendsn lf | 4 | 1 | 1 | 0 | | RJones lf | 4 | 1 | 2 | 1 |
| Milborn 3b | 4 | 0 | 1 | 0 | | DEvns dh | 4 | 0 | 1 | 1 |
| Kearney c | 4 | 0 | 1 | 1 | | Bergmn 1b | 4 | 0 | 1 | 0 |
| Owen ss | 4 | 0 | 1 | 0 | | Lemon cf | 3 | 1 | 0 | 0 |
| | | | | | | HJhnsn 3b | 3 | 0 | 0 | 0 |
| Totals | 37 | 2 | 8 | 2 | | Totals | 33 | 6 | 9 | 6 |

```
Seattle ........................... 000  001  001— 2
Detroit ........................... 202  002  00x— 6
```

Game Winning RBI — KGibson (14).
E—Milbourne, MMoore, Brookens, Trammell. LOB—Seattle 12, Detroit 6. 2B—KGibson, Brookens, Trammell, ADavis. SB—KGibson (22), Lemon (5).

| | IP | H | R | ER | BB | SO |
|---|---|---|---|---|---|---|
| **Seattle** | | | | | | |
| MMoore L, 5-12 | 5 2-3 | 9 | 6 | 6 | 2 | 4 |
| Mirabella | 1 2-3 | 0 | 0 | 0 | 0 | 2 |
| Stanton | 2-3 | 0 | 0 | 0 | 0 | 1 |
| **Detroit** | | | | | | |
| Wilcox W, 13-7 | 8 | 7 | 1 | 1 | 3 | 5 |
| Lopez | 1 | 1 | 1 | 1 | 1 | 1 |

HBP—Lemon by MMoore. WP—MMoore. T—3:08. A—36.496.

We broke the club attendance record tonight. It used to be 2,031,847, set back in 1968. Before this thing is over, we'll top that by more than a half million.

We gave them something to cheer about, too. Alan Trammell returned to shortstop for the first time in 39 games. He was throwing all right and, believe me, getting him back may be one of the most significant things of our season.

Alan got a couple of hits. So did Kirk Gibson and Ruppert Jones. Gibson is a cat. He's a fighter. He reminds me of Pete Rose. Milt Wilcox pitched his way out of a couple of problems and gave us eight innings.

Remember that sweep job that the Mariners gave us back in May in Seattle? I think *the boys* did tonight.

# SATURDAY, AUGUST 18

## AT DETROIT

# GAME 124

## TIGERS 4, MARINERS 3

### (81–43, 11 GAMES AHEAD)

| SEATTLE | ab | r | h | bi | DETROIT | ab | r | h | bi |
|---|---|---|---|---|---|---|---|---|---|
| Percont 2b | 4 | 0 | 0 | 0 | Brokns 2b | 1 | 0 | 0 | 0 |
| PBradly cf | 0 | 1 | 0 | | Baker 2b | 2 | 0 | 0 | 0 |
| Milborn ph | 1 | 0 | 0 | 0 | Tramm'l ss | 3 | 1 | 1 | 0 |
| ADavis 1b | 3 | 1 | 0 | 0 | Garbey 1b | 3 | 0 | 0 | 0 |
| Phelps dh | 3 | 1 | 0 | 0 | Bergmn 1b | 1 | 0 | 0 | 0 |
| Cowens rf | 3 | 0 | 0 | 0 | LNPrsh dh | 3 | 2 | 1 | 0 |
| Caldern lf | 2 | 0 | 0 | 0 | Herndon lf | 4 | 0 | 1 | 1 |
| SHndsn ph | 1 | 0 | 1 | 2 | KGibson rf | 4 | 1 | 1 | 3 |
| Presley 3b | 3 | 0 | 0 | 0 | Kuntz cf | 3 | 0 | 0 | 0 |
| Bonnell ph | 1 | 0 | 0 | 0 | HJhnsn 3b | 2 | 0 | 0 | 0 |
| Kearney c | 3 | 0 | 0 | 0 | MCastill c | 1 | 0 | 1 | 0 |
| Owen ss | 3 | 1 | 1 | 0 | | | | | |
| Totals | 30 | 3 | 4 | 2 | Totals | 27 | 4 | 5 | 4 |

Seattle ..........................001 000 002— 3
Detroit .............. ............010 003 00x— 4
 Game Winning RBI — K Gibson (15).
 E—Berenguer. DP—Detroit 1. LOB—
Seattle 4, Detroit 5. 2B—LNParrish,
MCastillo. HR—KGibson (20). SB—Herndon (4), Trammell (15), HJohnson (9),
Baker (1) S—MCastillo.

| | IP | H | R | ER | BB | SO |
|---|---|---|---|---|---|---|
| **Seattle** | | | | | | |
| Geisel L,0-1 | 5 2-3 | 5 | 4 | 4 | 3 | 5 |
| Beard | 2 1-3 | 0 | 0 | 0 | 2 | 1 |
| **Detroit** | | | | | | |
| Berengur W,6-8 | 8 1-3 | 3 | 3 | 2 | 4 | 12 |
| Hernandz S,26 | 2-3 | 1 | 0 | 0 | 0 | 0 |

 T—2:41. A—36,719.

Juan Berenguer pitched the game of his career. It certainly was the best game we've had pitched in the last two months. He struck out 12 and could have had a shutout. I want Juan to build his confidence, but I brought in Willie Hernandez in the ninth anyway. The game is not played to give someone confidence; the game is played to win, and you never give away a chance to win when you've got your ace reliever ready to pitch in the ninth.

Berenguer is finally getting to the point where I think he might become a good pitcher. When he gets that forkball over, he can be awfully tough.

Kirk Gibson reached another couple of milestones tonight. He set a club record with his 15th game-winning RBI. But he did something even more amazing. He became the first player in Tiger history to hit 20 homers and steal 20 bases in the same season. Can you imagine that with the long history of the Tigers, he became the first player ever to do that?

Gibby is the only player on the club who has been steady right from the start. He's a king right now. When he walks through that clubhouse door, everyone knows he's there. There's just something about a player like Gibson. You always get players who want a two- or three-game rest here and there when you're fighting for a pennant. When they do that,

I automatically place them in another category. Gibson is different. He's a man. He comes to play and is ready to fight, down and dirty, day after day.

Tom Brookens pulled a hamstring; Lou Whitaker has a back problem; Chet Lemon's finger is hurting—I'm glad Alan Trammell is back. We could use the help.

**Juan Berenguer hits his stride.**    Photo by Doc Holcomb, courtesy of *The Detroit News*

# SUNDAY, AUGUST 19

## AT DETROIT

# GAME 125

## MARINERS 4, TIGERS, 1

### (81–44, 10 GAMES AHEAD)

| SEATTLE | ab | r | h | bi | DETROIT | ab | r | h | bi |
|---|---|---|---|---|---|---|---|---|---|
| Percont 2b | 5 | 0 | 0 | 0 | Kuntz cf | 4 | 0 | 1 | 0 |
| PBradly cf | 4 | 2 | 3 | 0 | Trammi ss | 4 | 0 | 1 | 0 |
| ADavis 1b | 4 | 1 | 2 | 0 | Garbey 1b | 4 | 0 | 1 | 0 |
| Phelps dh | 3 | 1 | 1 | 1 | LNPrsh dh | 4 | 0 | 0 | 0 |
| SHendsn lf | 4 | 0 | 3 | 2 | Herndon lf | 3 | 1 | 0 | 0 |
| Caldern lf | 0 | 0 | 0 | 0 | KGibson rf | 3 | 0 | 1 | 0 |
| Milborn 3b | 3 | 0 | 0 | 0 | HJhnsn 3b | 3 | 0 | 0 | 0 |
| Ramos 3b | 0 | 0 | 0 | 0 | MCastill c | 2 | 0 | 0 | 1 |
| Bonnell rf | 3 | 0 | 1 | 0 | Baker 2b | 2 | 0 | 0 | 0 |
| Cowens rf | 0 | 0 | 0 | 0 | DEvns ph | 1 | 0 | 0 | 0 |
| Kearney c | 3 | 0 | 0 | 1 | | | | | |
| Owen ss | 4 | 0 | 0 | 0 | | | | | |
| Totals | 33 | 4 | 10 | 4 | Totals | 30 | 1 | 4 | 1 |

PBradley reach first on catcher's interference.

```
Seattle ............................ 102  001  000— 4
Detroit ............................ 000  100  000— 1
```

Game Winning RBI — SHenderson (2).
E—Milbourne, MCastillo. DP—Seattle 1, Detroit 1. LOB—Seattle 8, Detroit 8. S—Milbourne. SF—Kearney.

| Seattle | IP | H | R | ER | BB | SO |
|---|---|---|---|---|---|---|
| Langstn W,12-9 | 8 1-3 | 4 | 1 | 1 | 4 | 11 |
| VandBerg S,7 | 2-3 | 0 | 0 | 0 | 1 | 1 |
| **Detroit** | | | | | | |
| Petry L,15-6 | 9 | 10 | 4 | 4 | 3 | 11 |

HBP—Baker by Langston. WP—Petry.
T—2:51. A—43,277.

There is no way we should get beaten by Seattle in our own park. But I guess we weren't going to score many runs with the lineup we were forced to use. This was the worst offensive batting order I've made up in my 15 years in the major leagues. Our righthanders just aren't hitting, and this kid we faced [Mark Langston] is one of the finest lefthanders I've seen come along in a long, long time. Facing a lefthander doesn't give us much of a chance. We really haven't had a righthanded DH [designated hitter] all year.

# MONDAY, AUGUST 20

## AT DETROIT

# GAME 126

## TIGERS 14, A'S 1

### (82-44, 10½ GAMES AHEAD)

| OAKLAND | ab | r | h | bi | DETROIT | ab | r | h | bi |
|---|---|---|---|---|---|---|---|---|---|
| Phillips 2b | 4 | 0 | 1 | 0 | Garbey dh | 4 | 2 | 1 | 1 |
| Lansfrd 3b | 2 | 1 | 1 | 0 | Tramml ss | 5 | 1 | 2 | 1 |
| Burrghs lf | 1 | 0 | 0 | 0 | Kuntz cf | 1 | 0 | 0 | 0 |
| Murphy cf | 3 | 0 | 0 | 0 | KGibson rf | 3 | 3 | 2 | 2 |
| Almon rf | 1 | 0 | 0 | 0 | MCastill c | 1 | 0 | 1 | 0 |
| Kngmn dh | 4 | 0 | 1 | 0 | LNParsh c | 4 | 1 | 1 | 2 |
| Bochte 1b | 4 | 0 | 0 | 0 | Grubb rf | 2 | 1 | 1 | 0 |
| Heath lf | 3 | 0 | 0 | 0 | Herndon lf | 5 | 1 | 3 | 1 |
| MDavis rf | 3 | 0 | 1 | 0 | Lemon cf | 5 | 1 | 2 | 3 |
| OHill ss | 3 | 0 | 0 | 0 | DaEvns 1b | 3 | 2 | 3 | 1 |
| Essian c | 3 | 0 | 1 | 0 | Bergmn 1b | 0 | 0 | 0 | 1 |
| | | | | | HJhnsn 3b | 5 | 1 | 1 | 0 |
| | | | | | Baker 2b | 4 | 1 | 3 | 1 |
| Totals | 31 | 1 | 5 | 0 | Totals | 42 | 14 | 20 | 13 |

```
Oakland ........................001 000 000— 1
Detroit ..........................114 051 20x—14
```
Game Winning RBI — KGibson (16).
E—MDavis, Lansford. DP—Oakland 3.
LOB—Oakland 6, Detroit 11. 2B—Kingman, KGibson, Baker, Lansford. 3B—Herndon, Trammell. HR—LNParrish (28), Lemon '(16), DaEvans (11) SF—Bergman.

| | IP | H | R | ER | BB | SO |
|---|---|---|---|---|---|---|
| **Oakland** | | | | | | |
| CYoung L,6-2 | 2 | 8 | 6 | 6 | 1 | 1 |
| Rainey | 4 1-3 | 10 | 8 | 7 | 3 | 1 |
| Wagner | 1 2-3 | 2 | 0 | 0 | 1 | 1 |
| **Detroit** | | | | | | |
| Morris W,16-8 | 7 | 3 | 1 | 1 | 3 | 6 |
| Rozema | 2 | 2 | 0 | 0 | 0 | 2 |

CYoung pitched to 5 batters in 3rd.
HBP—Garbey by CYoung. WP—Morris, Rainey. T—2:45. A—38,431.

We hammered. What else do you say? We had 20 hits, and everybody got his share. I hope this helps the guys who have been struggling.

Kirk Gibson got two more hits and two RBIs. He's up to 74 RBIs, and I'd love to see him get 100 this year. I'd also like to see him win the MVP award. He deserves it; he plays so hard.

Jack Morris had it easy tonight. That's good because everything has been going bad for him lately.

When you have a night like this, you feel there's no way anyone can stop you. If we win 18 of the last 36, it's a lock. No way can we lose it. And without any doubleheaders, we should do it.

# TUESDAY, AUGUST 21

## AT DETROIT

# GAME 127

## TIGERS 12, A'S 6

### (83–44, 11½ GAMES AHEAD)

| OAKLAND | ab | r | h | bi |
|---|---|---|---|---|
| R Hndsn lf | 4 | 3 | 2 | 1 |
| Lansfrd 3b | 3 | 0 | 1 | 0 |
| Wagner 3b | 2 | 1 | 1 | 1 |
| Murphy cf | 2 | 0 | 0 | 0 |
| Essian c | 2 | 1 | 2 | 2 |
| Kngmn dh | 4 | 1 | 2 | 0 |
| M Davis dh | 1 | 0 | 0 | 0 |
| Bochte 1b | 3 | 0 | 2 | 2 |
| Heath c | 3 | 0 | 0 | 0 |
| Almon rf | 4 | 0 | 0 | 0 |
| DHill ss | 3 | 0 | 1 | 0 |
| Burghs ph | 1 | 0 | 0 | 0 |
| Phillips 2b | 4 | 0 | 0 | 0 |
| Totals | 36 | 6 | 11 | 6 |

| DETROIT | ab | r | h | bi |
|---|---|---|---|---|
| H Jhnsn 3b | 5 | 1 | 0 | 1 |
| Tramml ss | 4 | 2 | 3 | 0 |
| Garbey 2b | 0 | 0 | 0 | 0 |
| K Gibson rf | 5 | 1 | 2 | 0 |
| M Castill c | 0 | 0 | 0 | 0 |
| L N Parsh c | 3 | 2 | 1 | 4 |
| Grubb rf | 1 | 0 | 0 | 0 |
| D Evns dh | 5 | 3 | 4 | 3 |
| R Jones rf | 1 | 0 | 1 | 0 |
| Herndon lf | 3 | 1 | 2 | 1 |
| Lemon cf | 4 | 1 | 1 | 0 |
| Kuntz cf | 1 | 0 | 0 | 0 |
| Bergmn 1b | 2 | 1 | 0 | 2 |
| Baker 2b | 4 | 0 | 0 | 0 |
| Totals | 38 | 12 | 14 | 11 |

```
Oakland .......................... 200  000  022— 6
Detroit .......................... 403  004  01x—12
```

Game Winning RBI — LNParrish (8).
E—DHill, Baker. DP—Detroit 1. LOB—Oakland 7, Detroit 10. 2B—Kingman, RJones, Trammell, Bochte, KGibson, Essian, RHenderson. HR—RHenderson (13), LNParrish (29), DaEvans (12), Herndon (4). SF—Bochte, Bergman.

| Oakland | IP | H | R | ER | BB | SO |
|---|---|---|---|---|---|---|
| Sorensen L,5-12 | 2 | 6 | 7 | 6 | 5 | 2 |
| Conroy | 3 1-3 | 2 | 1 | 1 | 0 | 4 |
| Atherton | 2 2-3 | 6 | 4 | 4 | 2 | 0 |
| **Detroit** | | | | | | |
| Wilcox W,14-7 | 6 | 4 | 2 | 2 | 0 | 7 |
| Bair | 1 | 2 | 0 | 0 | 0 | 0 |
| Lopez | 1 | 2 | 2 | 2 | 2 | 1 |
| Hernandz | 1 | 3 | 2 | 2 | 2 | 0 |

Sorensen pitched to 4 batters in 3rd.
HBP—Murphy by Wilcox. PB—Heath.
T—3:04. A—34,065.

Nothing's over, but Toronto had to make a big move during our doubleheaders, and they didn't make a dent. They've had to shoot everything at us the past two months, and we're still fresh as a daisy. I'm not really concerned. We're in great shape and once we get the magic number under 20, we can end it quick.

I'd like to get it over with as soon as possible, but I won't rush it by doing anything crazy. When we do clinch it, I'll keep two people out of the lineup everyday. I won't put up with any nonsense though, or we'll get out of the mood of playing. The last five days I'll play the regulars.

The way we're playing right now, I just don't see how we can help from winning. We're strong and healthy. By the time we get to California on Friday, Lou Whitaker will have had six days of rest, Alan Trammell will have had a five-week rest, and our pitching is in line. Milt Wilcox got his 14th victory—the most he's ever had in a season. Lance Parrish decided the game in the first inning with a grand slam. We picked up another 14 hits.

I'll have to admit, I'd like to win 100 games. It would be the first time any manager has done it with two different teams. I won't get many more shots like this.

# WEDNESDAY, AUGUST 22

## AT DETROIT

---

# GAME 128

## TIGERS 11, A'S 4

### (84–44, 12½ GAMES AHEAD)

| OAKLAND | ab | r | h | bi | | DETROIT | ab | r | h | bi |
|---|---|---|---|---|---|---|---|---|---|---|
| RHndsn lf | 4 | 0 | 1 | 0 | | Garbey 3b | 5 | 0 | 2 | 2 |
| Lansfrd 3b | 5 | 1 | 0 | 0 | | Tramml ss | 5 | 1 | 2 | 1 |
| Murphy cf | 5 | 1 | 2 | 1 | | KGibsn dh | 4 | 2 | 1 | 0 |
| Kngmn dh | 4 | 1 | 1 | 2 | | Herndon lf | 2 | 1 | 1 | 1 |
| Bochte 1b | 4 | 0 | 2 | 0 | | Lemon cf | 5 | 0 | 1 | 1 |
| Heath rf | 4 | 0 | 0 | 0 | | DaEvns 1b | 2 | 2 | 0 | 0 |
| Phillips 2b | 4 | 0 | 1 | 0 | | Bergmn 1b | 2 | 0 | 0 | 0 |
| Essian c | 3 | 1 | 1 | 0 | | Kuntz rf | 2 | 2 | 0 | 1 |
| DHill ss | 3 | 0 | 1 | 0 | | MCastill c | 3 | 2 | 2 | 3 |
| Burghs ph | 1 | 0 | 0 | 0 | | Baker 2b | 4 | 1 | 2 | 1 |
| Totals | 37 | 4 | 9 | 3 | | Totals | 34 | 11 | 11 | 10 |

```
Oakland........................ 000  001  021— 4
Detroit......................... 210  240  20x—11
```
Game Winning RBI — Herndon (4).
E—DHill, Phillips, Essian, Garbey.
DP—Oakland 1. LOB—Oakland 9, Detroit
8. 2B—Baker, DHill, Garbey. 3B— MCastillo. HR—Murphy (26), Kingman (31).
SB—Trammell (16), KGibson 2 (24), Kuntz
(2), Garbey (5), Herndon (5). SF— Herndon, Kuntz.

| | IP | H | R | ER | BB | SO |
|---|---|---|---|---|---|---|
| **Oakland** | | | | | | |
| Krueger L,8-10 | 4 1-3 | 5 | 8 | 5 | 5 | 1 |
| CYoung | 1 2-3 | ? | 1 | 1 | 0 | 0 |
| Atherton | 1 | 3 | 2 | 2 | 0 | 1 |
| Caudill | 1 | 0 | 0 | 0 | 0 | 2 |
| **Detroit** | | | | | | |
| Berengur W,7-8 | 7 | 5 | 1 | 1 | 2 | 1 |
| Bair | 1 | 2 | 2 | 1 | 0 | 0 |
| Monge | 1 | 2 | 1 | 1 | 1 | 1 |

HBP—Herndon by CYoung, Kuntz by
Atherton. T—2:54. A—35,335.

We butchered them again, for the third straight day. Lance Parrish's hand is bothering him a little, but other than that, everything is fine.

Juan Berenguer gave us another strong game. His fastball is averaging between 90 and 93 mph. We stole six bases and got another 11 hits. The only thing we need right now is to get our bullpen some work. That's a nice problem.

# THURSDAY, AUGUST 23

## AT ANAHEIM

## (84–44, 12 GAMES AHEAD)

Flying to Anaheim, California, is a lot of fun after winning 10 of your last 13. We are in the driver's seat now. Toronto is the only club who could possibly catch us, and they won't.

Right now I'm picking the San Diego Padres and the Chicago Cubs in the National League playoffs. I think Minnesota will win in the American League West. We beat the Twins nine of the twelve games we have played them, but when you're playing the best three out of five, a lot of luck is involved.

Bill Lajoie is trying to get another lefthander. We're watching rosters now and seeing how we can improve for next year. We have to show at least one new face. If you win and don't show a new face, you can become fat cats in a hurry.

**Big bat Darrell Evans makes contact.**   Photo courtesy of Detroit Tigers

# FRIDAY, AUGUST 24

## AT ANAHEIM

# GAME 129

## ANGELS 5, TIGERS 3

### (84–45, 11 GAMES AHEAD)

| DETROIT | ab | r | h | bi | CALIFORNIA | ab | r | h | bi |
|---|---|---|---|---|---|---|---|---|---|
| Whitakr 2b | 4 | 0 | 2 | 0 | Pettis cf | 4 | 1 | 1 | 0 |
| Trammi ss | 4 | 0 | 0 | 0 | Sconirs 1b | 4 | 0 | 0 | 0 |
| KGibson rf | 3 | 1 | 3 | 0 | Lynn rf | 4 | 1 | 2 | 1 |
| DEvns dh | 4 | 0 | 1 | 0 | DeCncs 3b | 3 | 1 | 0 | 0 |
| R Jones lf | 4 | 0 | 1 | 0 | Downing lf | 3 | 1 | 1 | 0 |
| Bergmn 1b | 3 | 0 | 0 | 1 | ReJksn dh | 4 | 1 | 1 | 2 |
| Lemon cf | 3 | 1 | 1 | 1 | Grich 2b | 2 | 0 | 1 | 1 |
| HJhnsn 3b | 4 | 0 | 0 | 0 | Boone c | 3 | 0 | 0 | 0 |
| MCastill c | 3 | 1 | 1 | 1 | Schofild ss | 3 | 0 | 0 | 0 |
| Grubb ph | 1 | 0 | 0 | 0 | | | | | |
| Totals | 33 | 3 | 9 | 3 | Totals | 30 | 5 | 6 | 4 |

```
Detroit .........................010  001  001— 3
California ...................400  010  00x— 5
```
Game Winning RBI — ReJackson (8).
E—KGibson, HJohnson. DP—California 1. LOB—Detroit 6, California 4. 2B—Whitaker. HR—Lemon (17), MCastillo (1). SB—Pettis (45). SF—Bergman.

| | IP | H | R | ER | BB | SO |
|---|---|---|---|---|---|---|
| **Detroit** | | | | | | |
| Petry L, 15-7 | 8 | 6 | 5 | 5 | 3 | 3 |
| **California** | | | | | | |
| Witt W, 12-10 | 8 | 8 | 3 | 3 | 1 | 6 |
| Aase S, 4 | 1 | 1 | 0 | 0 | 1 | 0 |

Witt pitched to 2 batters in 9th.
WP—Petry. T—2:33. A—41,459.

Right now we're playing at a .500 level. Once we clinch this thing, I think you're going to see all of our guys relax. Right now they are really tight. I can understand that. They've never been through anything like this before. Once they win, though, I think you're going to see them awful tough in the playoffs.

Tonight we didn't hit the ball at all when it counted. We had our chances, but we just didn't take advantage of them.

Howard Johnson hasn't been hitting a thing lately. He's been in as good a slump as you can be for a month. Dan Petry walked a couple in the first inning; we made a couple of bad plays and it was over.

The only good thing about today was that I was able to visit Mama this morning. She's working hard to learn how to live alone now. We'll make her life real good when we have her move in with us.

# SATURDAY, AUGUST 25

## AT ANAHEIM

# GAME 130

## TIGERS 5, ANGELS 1

### (84–45, 11 GAMES AHEAD)

| DETROIT | ab | r | h | bi | CALIFORNIA | ab | r | h | bi |
|---|---|---|---|---|---|---|---|---|---|
| Whitaker 2b | 5 | 0 | 3 | 1 | Pettis cf | 5 | 0 | 1 | 0 |
| Trammell ss | 4 | 0 | 1 | 0 | Sconiers 1b | 1 | 0 | 0 | 0 |
| Gibson rf | 4 | 1 | 1 | 0 | Wilfong 2b | 2 | 0 | 0 | 0 |
| Evans 3b | 4 | 1 | 1 | 1 | Lynn rf | 3 | 0 | 2 | 0 |
| Johnson 3b | 0 | 0 | 0 | 0 | DeCinces 3b | 2 | 0 | 1 | 0 |
| Grubb dh | 3 | 1 | 1 | 0 | Downing lf | 4 | 0 | 2 | 0 |
| Jones lf | 4 | 1 | 1 | 3 | Jackson dh | 4 | 0 | 1 | 0 |
| Bergman 1b | 3 | 0 | 0 | 0 | Grich 2b | 3 | 1 | 1 | 0 |
| Lemon cf | 4 | 1 | 2 | 0 | Boone c | 2 | 0 | 0 | 0 |
| Castillo c | 4 | 0 | 0 | 0 | Narron c | 2 | 0 | 1 | 0 |
| | | | | | Schofield ss | 2 | 0 | 0 | 0 |
| | | | | | Brown ph | 1 | 0 | 0 | 0 |
| | | | | | Picciolo ss | 0 | 0 | 0 | 0 |
| | | | | | Beniquez ph | 1 | 0 | 0 | 0 |
| Totals | 35 | 5 | 10 | 5 | Totals | 32 | 1 | 9 | 0 |

Detroit ................................. 000 103 001 — 5
California ............................. 000 000 001 — 1
Game-winning RBI—Evans (6). E—Gibson. DP—Detroit 4, California 2. LOB—Detroit 6, California 9. 2B—Lemon. HR—Evans (13), Jones (10). SB—Trammell (17).

| Detroit | IP | H | R | ER | BB | SO |
|---|---|---|---|---|---|---|
| Morris (W 17-8) | 8 | 9 | 1 | 1 | 5 | 4 |
| Hernandez | 1 | 0 | 0 | 0 | 0 | 1 |
| California | | | | | | |
| Kison (L 3-3) | 6 | 6 | 4 | 4 | 1 | 8 |
| Corbett | 3 | 4 | 1 | 1 | 0 | 1 |

Morris pitched to 2 batters in 9th. HBP—by Kison (Trammell, Bergman). PB—Castillo. T—2:40. A—51,203.

I had a good feeling before this game even started. Minnesota beat Toronto and it gave us the chance to move back to 12 games up.

Jack Morris gave up a lot of hits early. But he battled and it was great to see him come out on top after fighting so hard. I brought in Willie Hernandez to pitch the ninth, but Jack was in control and his slider was particularly effective.

We played very sharply. We turned four double plays. Darrell Evans hit a homer and Ruppert Jones added a three-run shot. Give Jack a four-run lead and that's generally a lock. A great finish to a great day after starting out having breakfast with all of my kids.

# SUNDAY, AUGUST 26

## AT ANAHEIM

# GAME 131

## TIGERS 12, ANGELS 6

### (86–45, 12 GAMES AHEAD)

| DETROIT | ab | r | h | bi | | CALIFORNIA | ab | r | h | bi |
|---|---|---|---|---|---|---|---|---|---|---|
| Whitaker 2b | 4 | 1 | 1 | 0 | | Pettis cf | 4 | 0 | 0 | 0 |
| Trammell ss | 5 | 1 | 1 | 0 | | Brown rf | 1 | 0 | 0 | 0 |
| Baker ss | 0 | 0 | 0 | 0 | | Wilfong 2b | 5 | 1 | 3 | 1 |
| Gibson dh | 4 | 4 | 3 | 2 | | Lynn rf | 5 | 1 | 1 | 0 |
| Parrish c | 3 | 1 | 1 | 2 | | DeCinces 3b | 4 | 1 | 1 | 1 |
| Herndon lf | 4 | 1 | 1 | 3 | | Downing lf | 4 | 1 | 1 | 1 |
| Garbey 1b | 3 | 0 | 0 | 0 | | Jackson dh | 3 | 0 | 0 | 0 |
| Bergman 1b | 1 | 0 | 0 | 0 | | Grich 1b | 4 | 1 | 2 | 1 |
| Lemon cf | 2 | 1 | 1 | 4 | | Narron c | 3 | 0 | 1 | 2 |
| Grubb rf | 1 | 0 | 0 | 0 | | Schofield ss | 3 | 1 | 0 | 0 |
| Kuntz rf | 5 | 0 | 0 | 0 | | Beniquez ph | 0 | 0 | 0 | 0 |
| Castillo 3b | 4 | 3 | 3 | 1 | | Picciolo ss | 0 | 0 | 0 | 0 |
| Totals | 36 | 12 | 11 | 12 | | Totals | 36 | 6 | 9 | 6 |

Detroit ........................... 006 311 001— 12
California ......................... 000 003 120— 6
Game-winning RBI—Parrish (9). E—Garbey, Baker. DP—California 1. LOB—Detroit 5, California 7. 2B—Herndon, Parrish, Wilfong, Lynn, DeCinces. 3B—Grich. HR—Lemon (18), Castillo (2), Gibson 2 (22). SB—Garbey (6). SF—Parrish, DeCinces Narron.

| | IP | H | R | ER | BB | SO |
|---|---|---|---|---|---|---|
| **Detroit** | | | | | | |
| Wilcox (W 15-7) | 6 | 5 | 3 | 0 | 0 | 5 |
| Bair | 1 2-3 | 4 | 3 | 2 | 2 | 1 |
| Lopez | 1 1-3 | 0 | 0 | 0 | 0 | 1 |
| **California** | | | | | | |
| John (L 7-12) | 2 1-3 | 2 | 5 | 5 | 6 | 0 |
| Kaufman | 3 2-3 | 7 | 6 | 6 | 0 | 4 |
| Curtis | 3 | 2 | 1 | 1 | 1 | 2 |

Balk—Wilcox. T—3:01. A—33,008.

Finally, it looked like we're playing a little looser—with some confidence. If we win 14 of our next 31 games, it's a lock. We might even get by with 12.

If we play the way we played tonight, we're going to win a whole lot more than 14. We were hotter than a firecracker and played just like we did when we were 35-5.

Kirk Gibson busted two home runs, Marty Castillo hit one, and Chet Lemon connected for his first grand slam ever. Better than that, we got a real break with Lemon. For a couple of scary minutes, I really thought Chester was in real trouble.

He got hit by a high fly ball, just above the eye. He went down, and by the time I got there, the blood was pouring out like a hose watering the lawn. It looked awful. Just another inch lower and the ball would have split his eye. Fortunately, he wound up with just 12 stitches and a headache like a W. C. Fields hangover. I hate to think how bad it could have been.

Milt Wilcox got his 15th win today. He's really shown me something this year. I'm really pulling for him to win 20.

# MONDAY, AUGUST 27

## AT ANAHEIM

## (86–45, 11½ GAMES AHEAD)

I can't remember the last time we had a full day off in California where I could spend the whole day at home in Thousand Oaks. It was perfect. I visited with all three kids. We had a cookout, and I worked in the garden. It was refreshing. It's really a rejuvenation to be away from the park and all the players and all the hoopla once in awhile.

Bill Lajoie called to say we picked up lefthanded pitcher Bill Scherrer today from Cincinnati. I know a little about him and I think he's going to be great for getting a tough lefthanded hitter out in certain spots. He'll be a big help next year, too. Lajoie's also trying to get Lee Lacy from Pittsburgh. That would give us another strong righthanded bat.

**Dave Bergman stretches for the catch.**  Photo by Doc Holcomb, courtesy of *The Detroit News*

# TUESDAY, AUGUST 28

## AT SEATTLE

# GAME 132

## TIGERS 5, MARINERS 4

### (87–45, 11½ GAMES AHEAD)

| DETROIT | ab | r | h | bi |
|---|---|---|---|---|
| Whitakr 2b | 2 | 0 | 0 | 1 |
| Tramml ss | 4 | 1 | 1 | 2 |
| K Gibson rf | 4 | 1 | 1 | 1 |
| LNParsh c | 4 | 0 | 0 | 0 |
| DEvns dh | 4 | 0 | 2 | 0 |
| Kuntz pr | 0 | 1 | 0 | 0 |
| Grubb lf | 4 | 0 | 0 | 0 |
| MCastil 3b | 0 | 0 | 0 | 0 |
| R Jones cf | 3 | 1 | 2 | 1 |
| Bergmn 1b | 4 | 1 | 1 | 0 |
| HJhnsn 3b | 2 | 0 | 1 | 0 |
| Garbey 3b | 1 | 0 | 0 | 0 |
| Totals | 32 | 5 | 8 | 5 |

| SEATTLE | ab | r | h | bi |
|---|---|---|---|---|
| Percont 2b | 4 | 1 | 1 | 0 |
| PBradly cf | 4 | 0 | 1 | 2 |
| ADavis 1b | 4 | 0 | 1 | 0 |
| Phelps dh | 2 | 0 | 0 | 0 |
| Presley ph | 1 | 0 | 0 | 0 |
| Cowens rf | 4 | 0 | 1 | 1 |
| SHendsn lf | 2 | 1 | 0 | 0 |
| Moses lf | 1 | 0 | 0 | 0 |
| Milborn 3b | 4 | 0 | 2 | 0 |
| Kearney c | 3 | 1 | 0 | 0 |
| Owen ss | 4 | 1 | 0 | 0 |
| Totals | 33 | 4 | 6 | 3 |

Detroit .......................... 000  100  031— 5
Seattle ......................... 100  000  300— 4
Game Winning RBI — R Jones (5).
E—HJohnson. LOB—Detroit 3, Seattle 6. 2B—Perconte, ADavis, R Jones 2. HR—KGibson (23), Trammell (12). SF—Whitaker.

| Detroit | IP | H | R | ER | BB | SO |
|---|---|---|---|---|---|---|
| Berengur | 6 2-3 | 5 | 4 | 1 | 4 | 5 |
| Scherrer | 1-3 | 0 | 0 | 0 | 0 | 0 |
| Hernandz W,8-2 | 2 | 1 | 0 | 0 | 0 | 1 |
| Seattle |  |  |  |  |  |  |
| MMoore | 7 | 5 | 3 | 3 | 2 | 2 |
| VandBerg | 1 | 1 | 1 | 1 | 0 | 0 |
| Stanton L,4-4 | 2-3 | 1 | 1 | 1 | 0 | 2 |
| Geisel | 1-3 | 1 | 0 | 0 | 0 | 1 |

MMoore pitched to 2 batters in 8th.
WP—Stanton. T—2:51. A—8,353.

Juan Berenguer took us into the seventh, and that was all we needed. The bullpen did the rest. I brought Bill Scherrer in to face Alan Davis, and he got him to ground out. That's what we got Bill for—to face that one lefty that might turn the game around. And then, of course, Willie Hernandez finished it.

I'll keep Chet Lemon out of the lineup the whole series. He's experiencing dizziness now. With the big lead, we don't have to rush him back. Ruppert Jones jumped up and helped us out when we needed him. He started our three-run eighth inning, and then doubled home the winner in the ninth—off of a lefthander.

It's amazing how everyone chips in to do his part. Ours is almost the ideal lineup. We've got .300 hitters in the first two spots, speed and power in the third spot, power in the fourth, and production down the line. The only thing we don't have is base-stealing speed from Lou Whitaker.

The magic number is 20 now. I'd like to cut it down in a hurry.

# WEDNESDAY, AUGUST 29

## AT SEATTLE

# GAME 133

## MARINERS 5, TIGERS 1

### (87–46, 11½ GAMES AHEAD)

| DETROIT | ab | r | h | bi | SEATTLE | ab | r | h | bi |
|---|---|---|---|---|---|---|---|---|---|
| Whitakr 2b | 4 | 0 | 0 | 0 | Percont 2b | 4 | 1 | 2 | 0 |
| Trammi ss | 4 | 0 | 1 | 0 | PBradly cf | 4 | 1 | 1 | 0 |
| KGibson rf | 4 | 0 | 0 | 0 | ADavis 1b | 4 | 1 | 1 | 1 |
| LNParsh c | 2 | 1 | 0 | 0 | Phelps dh | 4 | 1 | 1 | 3 |
| Herndon lf | 3 | 0 | 0 | 0 | Cowens rf | 4 | 1 | 2 | 0 |
| Garbey 1b | 3 | 0 | 0 | 0 | SHendsn lf | 4 | 0 | 1 | 0 |
| Kuntz cf | 2 | 0 | 1 | 1 | DHedsn cf | 0 | 0 | 0 | 0 |
| MCastll 3b | 3 | 0 | 0 | 0 | MilBorn 3b | 3 | 0 | 1 | 1 |
| HJhnsn dh | 3 | 0 | 0 | 0 | Ramos 3b | 1 | 0 | 0 | 0 |
| | | | | | Kearney c | 3 | 0 | 0 | 0 |
| | | | | | Owen ss | 3 | 0 | 2 | 0 |
| Totals | 28 | 1 | 2 | 1 | Totals | 34 | 5 | 11 | 5 |

Detroit............................ 010 000 000— 1
Seattle............................ 010 040 00x— 5
Game Winning RBI — ADavis (10).
E—Milbourne. LOB—Detroit 4, Seattle
5. 2B—SHenderson. HR—Phelps (22).

| Detroit | IP | H | R | ER | BB | SO |
|---|---|---|---|---|---|---|
| Petry L, 15-8 | 4 1-3 | 10 | 5 | 5 | 0 | 1 |
| Rozema | 2 2-3 | 1 | 0 | 0 | 0 | 1 |
| Lopez | 1 | 0 | 0 | 0 | 0 | 1 |
| **Seattle** | | | | | | |
| Langstn W, 13-9 | 9 | 2 | 1 | 1 | 4 | 12 |

T—2:11. A—10,863.

This one was simple—Mark Langston. You don't feel too bad when you get beat like we did tonight. This kid just flat-out took it to us and deserved everything he got. In my 15 years in the major leagues, he's the best young pitcher I've seen walk out there. If he doesn't get hurt, he'll be an outstanding pitcher for the next 10 years. Imagine what he'd do on a good team. He stopped us on two hits.

Dan Petry pitched for us, and I'm a little concerned about Danny. He hasn't pitched badly, but for the last month, he hasn't pitched with his normal confidence. I'm going to have a talk with him.

This morning I had an interesting walk around the city. Seattle is a good walking city because there are a lot of hills, and it's nice down by the wharves. But the walk left me a little confused. I was down because of all the winos and vagrants that I passed along the way. There they were . . . passed out on the street. Some with no shoes. Some as dirty as a garbage dump.

At the same time, I felt a little high. It made me thankful for all the good things that have happened to me in my life. I wish the players would take time to take a look around themselves. Maybe they'd quit complaining over all the little things.

# THURSDAY, AUGUST 30

## AT SEATTLE

# GAME 134

## MARINERS 2, TIGERS 1

### (87–47, 10½ GAMES AHEAD)

| DETROIT | ab | r | h | bi | SEATTLE | ab | r | h | bi |
|---|---|---|---|---|---|---|---|---|---|
| Whitakr 2b | 4 | 0 | 1 | 0 | Percont 2b | 4 | 1 | 1 | 0 |
| Tramml ss | 4 | 0 | 1 | 1 | PBradly rf | 4 | 0 | 0 | 0 |
| KGibson rf | 5 | 0 | 1 | 0 | ADavis 1b | 3 | 0 | 1 | 0 |
| LNParsh c | 4 | 0 | 0 | 0 | Phelps dh | 4 | 0 | 0 | 0 |
| DaEvns 1b | 3 | 0 | 0 | 0 | SHendsn lf | 3 | 0 | 0 | 0 |
| R Jones cf | 3 | 0 | 1 | 0 | Moses lf | 0 | 0 | 0 | 0 |
| Garbey ph | 0 | 1 | 0 | 0 | DHedsn cf | 3 | 0 | 2 | 0 |
| Grubb dh | 2 | 0 | 0 | 0 | Kearney c | 2 | 0 | 0 | 0 |
| Lemon ph | 1 | 0 | 0 | 0 | Presley 3b | 3 | 0 | 0 | 0 |
| Herndon lf | 3 | 0 | 1 | 0 | Owen ss | 2 | 1 | 0 | 0 |
| HJhnsn 3b | 4 | 0 | 2 | 0 | | | | | |
| Totals | 33 | 1 | 7 | 1 | Totals | 28 | 2 | 4 | 0 |

Detroit............................ 000 000 001— 1
Seattle............................ 000 000 02x— 2
    Game Winning RBI — None.
    E—Morris, KGibson. LOB—Detroit 11,
Seattle 5. 2B—ADavis. SB—Trammell
(18).

| | IP | H | R | ER | BB | SO |
|---|---|---|---|---|---|---|
| **Detroit** | | | | | | |
| Morris L, 17-9 | 8 | 4 | 2 | 1 | 3 | 8 |
| **Seattle** | | | | | | |
| Beattie W, 10-15 | 8 | 6 | 0 | 0 | 3 | 7 |
| VandBerg | 0 | 0 | 1 | 1 | 1 | 0 |
| Nunez S, 4 | 1 | 1 | 0 | 0 | 2 | 1 |
|   VandeBerg pitched to 1 batter in 9th. | | | | | | |
|   T—2:34. A—9,583. | | | | | | |

We gave this one away—wrapped it up and put a ribbon on it. It's terrible when you lose like we did today. If you get beat, you get beat. But you shouldn't give it away.

Jack Morris was pitching an outstanding game. Then he walked the leadoff hitter in the eighth. The next man bunted and Jack threw the ball into rightfield. Gibby picked it up and fired it into our dugout. Two runs scored on a walk and two errors. Morris was upset and showed his temper on the mound. It wasn't good, but we got what we deserved. We didn't hit. Jim Beattie was pitching, and we just don't get around on guys who throw the ball real hard.

Lance Parrish is really struggling. We're going to have a talk.

**Jack Morris delivers a sizzler.** Photo by Clifton Boutelle

# FRIDAY, AUGUST 31

## AT OAKLAND

# GAME 135

## A'S 7, TIGERS 6

### (13 INNINGS)
### (87–48, 9½ GAMES AHEAD)

| DETROIT | ab | r | h | bi |
|---|---|---|---|---|
| Whitakr 2b | 6 | 0 | 1 | 0 |
| Tramml ss | 6 | 2 | 2 | 1 |
| K Gibson rf | 4 | 1 | 0 | 0 |
| LNParsh c | 4 | 0 | 0 | 1 |
| DaEvns 1b | 5 | 0 | 1 | 2 |
| R Jones cf | 6 | 1 | 1 | 1 |
| Grubb dh | 6 | 1 | 2 | 0 |
| Herndon lf | 3 | 1 | 1 | 0 |
| Kuntz cf | 2 | 0 | 1 | 0 |
| H Jhnsn 3b | 5 | 0 | 2 | 1 |
| Totals | 47 | 6 | 11 | 6 |

| OAKLAND | ab | r | h | bi |
|---|---|---|---|---|
| RHndsn lf | 6 | 2 | 3 | 1 |
| Lansfrd 3b | 4 | 1 | 2 | 3 |
| Morgan 2b | 3 | 0 | 0 | 0 |
| Wagner ss | 1 | 0 | 1 | 0 |
| Kngmn dh | 5 | 0 | 1 | 0 |
| Murphy cf | 6 | 0 | 0 | 0 |
| Bochte 1b | 3 | 1 | 1 | 0 |
| Almon 1b | 2 | 0 | 0 | 0 |
| Essian c | 2 | 1 | 0 | 0 |
| Heath c | 3 | 0 | 0 | 0 |
| MDavis rf | 5 | 1 | 1 | 0 |
| Phillips ss | 6 | 1 | 0 | 1 |
| Totals | 46 | 7 | 9 | 5 |

Detroit ................ 200 210 001 000 0— 6
Oakland ............... 100 400 001 000 1— 7
Two outs when winning run scored.
Game Winning RBI — None.
E—Wilcox. DP—Oakland 1. LOB—Detroit 12, Oakland 10. 2B—Grubb, Lansford,

This one stunk. You talk about gifts. The Three Wise Men didn't come close to what we gave the A's tonight.

We went 13 innings, and then gave it away on a wild pitch by Dave Rozema. We had a 4-1 lead, and then Milt Wilcox got wild and walked six men. There's no reason in the world we should have lost this game, but it happened.

We're going through one of those spells. I knew we'd have another one. I've always said the hardest thing to do is to close the door. We're 9½ games ahead now, but it'll go down to the wire. This is the first time our guys have been through this, so I'm not surprised. We've just got to forget this one or it'll get us down.

# THE STOPPERS

I used to kid around with Pete Rose all the time.

"Peter Edward," I'd tell him. "After God made you, He threw away the mold. There'll never be another Peter Edward Rose. The world couldn't handle it."

I'll never compare Pete Rose to anyone or anything. But there'll never be another bullpen like that of the Tigers of 1984. Never. There couldn't be.

All year long I've heard writers from all over the country talk about our bullpen. I've read and heard every adjective Daniel Webster ever included in that thick old book of his. None of them do justice. None of them even come close. How can anyone possibly describe what nobody can really believe?

And I'll tell you something right now. I've been in baseball for 31 years, and there's no way I can believe what I saw in Willie Hernandez this year.

In 1984, Willie Hernandez was to the Tigers what Michael Jackson was to the music industry. But somewhere along the line, even Michael must hit a sour note once in awhile.

Willie never did. I mean never. Roger Craig and I used to stand in the corner of the dugout and look at each other. We kept wondering what the heck was going on. It was spooky. If you don't believe in magic, then there's no way you could come close to appreciating Willie this year. He truly was magic. Harry Houdini was never this good.

Don't ask me to explain Willie. How do you explain a miracle? Every time Willie had a chance for a save, Willie got it. Every time we desperately had to have a win, Willie was there.

Near the end of the year, Tony Kubek teased me that if I happen to win the Manager of the Year Award, they should have it inscribed in Spanish.

I say the Cy Young and Most Valuable Player Awards ought to be renamed in honor of Willie Hernandez.

People who didn't see Willie everyday can't really appreciate the kind of year he had, because nobody is supposed to be perfect. He was more

189

of a deadbolt lock every time he took the mound than Mr. Yale himself. Wells Fargo couldn't have protected a lead better than Willie protected ours.

During all those good years in Cincinnati I had a pretty reliable reliever in a guy named Clay Carroll. We used to call him "Hawk." He was flat-out mean on hitters. We had some outstanding hitters in Pete Rose, Joe Morgan, Johnny Bench, and Tony Perez, to name a few. But without the "Hawk," we would have been in trouble. Without Willie this year, we may not have been in the American League.

There's a couple of things about Willie that puts him in a class by himself. From a pitching standpoint, he throws strikes. That sounds so simple. But that's what pitching is all about. He gets the ball over the plate. He paints the black parts of the plate and works the knees like an orthopedic surgeon.

It doesn't matter if Willie is pitching against a righthander or a lefty. Sometimes I don't think Willie even knows. He's got that wicked screwball against righthanders and a vicious breaking pitch for lefties. He's not afraid to challenge a hitter in any situation.

Willie learned that screwball from Mike Cuellar. Mr. Cuellar never will have a more accomplished student as long as he lives. There are a lot of guys who can throw a screwball. There have been a lot of outstanding relief pitchers over the years. The thing that set Willie apart from the rest in 1984 can't be explained in pitching terms. It's an intangible, but as real as all the saves Willie put on the board all year long.

A lot of pitchers think they are good. Willie knows it. That's half the battle. I've seen a lot of guys go out on that mound and pretend like no one can touch them. Willie actually believes he's the best. Now who's going to doubt him?

Willie is a proud man. That's good. I've never seen a truly great player who isn't.

I love to watch Willie walk down to our bullpen from the dugout near the end of the game. He doesn't walk. He struts. He knows all those people are watching. They stare; they applaud; they idolize him. He loves it and he deserves it. Our players used to watch him and tease him about it. But it shows how much confidence he actually has in himself.

I've never seen a pitcher who can pitch as much as he can. He never gets tired. He set the all-time Tiger record for appearances. His stuff didn't vary from day to day. Willie's stuff was the same on the first day or the fourth day in a row that he worked.

When we got Willie, no one in his right mind could have predicted

**Aurelio Lopez.** Photo courtesy of Detroit Tigers

**Doug Bair.** Photo courtesy of Detroit Tigers

what he'd do. Only God knew what 1984 would be like. We got Willie on March 24 with Dave Bergman from Philadelphia for Glenn Wilson and John Wockenfuss. All winter long we had tried and tried and tried to get a lefthander. I honestly felt we would have to play 1984 without one. But General Manager Bill Lajoie worked like a dog and just didn't give up. He asked me at the end of spring training if I'd be willing to give up Wilson and Wockenfuss. I knew both were favorites with the fans, but I felt we had to make the move.

I told Lajoie that no matter how long he stays in the game as a general manager, he'll never make another deal that even comes close to this one. Not taking anything away from him, but even with all those RBIs, I wouldn't trade Willie for Eddie Murray right now. Willie is the heart and soul of our bullpen.

But there is a whole body. Beyond a doubt, this is the deepest bullpen I've ever had. More than our defense and our bench, which are critical to our success, our bullpen is our biggest strength. Look at our starting pitching. Not one pitcher finished with 250 innings. Everyone stayed fresh. That's a tribute to our bullpen.

Without Willie and Aurelio Lopez, we would have been so far back we would have solidified. Not only would we have lost the great pitching they did, we would have lost more by having to use our other pitchers so much more.

That's what people overlook in Aurelio Lopez. Lopey has one of those amazing God-given gifts for an arm that allows him to pitch long, short, or middle relief—one day a week or several days in a row. Everyday Lopey would give me a wink. "I can pitch today if you need me," he'd say. He never minded that Willie was the short man. Lopey did his job and saved a lot of arms in the process.

That's the difference between us and Toronto—Hernandez and Lopez. You give Bobby Cox (Toronto manager) those two guys coming out of the pen and I'd trail him even more than he trailed me.

I don't have to be very smart to call down to the bullpen and ask for guys like that. All it takes is an I.Q. of three. It's a lot more difficult when you call down and have to say "Give me . . . umm . . . ah . . . ah." It's pretty tough when everytime you call the bullpen you get a wrong number. I've made the right connection all year long. My bullpen has made me look like a genius.

Doug Bair threw as well for me this year as he did in Cincinnati. He got his fastball back and he's a much smarter pitcher. With Bair and Bill Scherrer, we'll be able to bring in one or the other next year when we need a certain batter out early in the game. Bair can work the right-handers and Scherrer the lefties.

We picked up Scherrer in August. He's got a live young arm and is another tribute to Lajoie's keen eye. We wanted another lefty just for this role and I think we've got him in Scherrer.

Over the last 20 years, relief pitching has changed this game as much as any one factor. No team nowadays wins without a bullpen. I'll put ours up against anyone's. We've got the stopper and we've got the horses to get to him.

Willie and the Boys.

**Willie Hernandez.** Photo courtesy of Detroit Tigers

# SEPTEMBER

"Tonight we . . . pass[ed] the two million mark in both home and road attendance. That's a tribute to the great baseball fans around the league. They know a good team when they see one."

September 11, 1984

# SATURDAY, SEPTEMBER 1

## AT OAKLAND

---

# GAME 136

## A'S 7, TIGERS 5

### (87–49, 8½ GAMES AHEAD)

| DETROIT | ab | r | h | bi | OAKLAND | ab | r | h | bi |
|---|---|---|---|---|---|---|---|---|---|
| Whitakr 2b | 5 | 0 | 1 | 2 | RHndsn lf | 3 | 1 | 0 | 0 |
| Trammi ss | 4 | 0 | 0 | 0 | Lansfrd 3b | 5 | 0 | 2 | 0 |
| KGibson rf | 4 | 0 | 1 | 0 | Murphy cf | 3 | 2 | 1 | 1 |
| LNParsh c | 4 | 0 | 0 | 0 | Kngmn dh | 4 | 1 | 1 | 1 |
| Herndon lf | 4 | 1 | 1 | 0 | Bochte 1b | 2 | 0 | 0 | 1 |
| Garbey dh | 4 | 2 | 1 | 0 | Almon 1b | 1 | 0 | 0 | 0 |
| DaEvns 1b | 3 | 0 | 0 | 0 | DHill ss | 4 | 1 | 2 | 1 |
| Kuntz cf | 3 | 1 | 2 | 2 | Essian c | 1 | 1 | 0 | 0 |
| RJones ph | 1 | 0 | 1 | 0 | MDavis rf | 4 | 1 | 2 | 3 |
| MCastil 3b | 2 | 0 | 1 | 1 | Phillips 2b | 4 | 0 | 1 | 0 |
| HJhnsn 3b | 2 | 0 | 0 | 0 | | | | | |
| Totals | 36 | 5 | 8 | 5 | Totals | 31 | 7 | 9 | 7 |

Detroit..........................030 002 000— 5
Oakland.......................600 001 00x— 7
  Game Winning RBI — Kingman (13).
  E—Phillips. LOB—Detroit 5, Oakland 8.
2B—Kingman, DHill, Kuntz. HR—MDavis
(7), Murphy (28). SB—RHenderson 2 (52),
Lansford (9). SF—Bochte.

| | IP | H | R | ER | BB | SO |
|---|---|---|---|---|---|---|
| **Detroit** | | | | | | |
| Berengur L,7-9 | 2-3 | 3 | 6 | 6 | 3 | 1 |
| Bair | 3 2-3 | 4 | 0 | 0 | 3 | 4 |
| Scherrer | 3 2-3 | 2 | 1 | 1 | 1 | 3 |
| **Oakland** | | | | | | |
| CYoung W,7-3 | 5 2-3 | 7 | 5 | 4 | 1 | 0 |
| Rainey S,1 | 3 1-3 | 1 | 0 | 0 | 0 | 1 |

  PB—LNParrish. T—2:37. A—25,021.

Right now I can see that our guys are getting concerned. They've lost four games in the standings in the last five days, and it's starting to bother them. They keep looking back at Toronto. To be honest, it's got me concerned too.

We've got some problems. Chet Lemon is still feeling dizzy and hasn't even been able to come to the park. Tom Brookens is still out. Dave Bergman is experiencing back problems and can't play. Now Milt Wilcox is going to miss a turn because his arm is bothering him. Juan Berenguer gave up six runs in the first inning, and I had to get him out before it even ended. Doug Bair and Bill Scherrer pitched well, but we were out of it by then.

I went to Joe Morgan's house after the game. It was a palace; it must have cost a million dollars. You can see the ocean and the Golden Gate Bridge. I think I would have enjoyed it a little more if we didn't have a four-game losing streak going.

# SUNDAY, SEPTEMBER 2

## AT OAKLAND

# GAME 137

## TIGERS 6, A'S 3

### (88–49, 8½ GAMES AHEAD)

| DETROIT | ab | r | h | bi | OAKLAND | ab | r | h | bi |
|---|---|---|---|---|---|---|---|---|---|
| Whitakr 2b | 5 | 1 | 1 | 1 | RHndsn lf | 5 | 1 | 2 | 1 |
| Tramml ss | 4 | 0 | 0 | 0 | Lansfrd 3b | 4 | 0 | 2 | 0 |
| KGibson rf | 4 | 2 | 1 | 0 | Morgan 2b | 4 | 0 | 0 | 0 |
| LNParsh c | 4 | 0 | 2 | 2 | Kngmn dh | 4 | 2 | 2 | 1 |
| Herndon lf | 3 | 0 | 0 | 0 | Murphy cf | 4 | 0 | 2 | 0 |
| R Jones lf | 1 | 0 | 1 | 1 | Bochte 1b | 2 | 0 | 1 | 1 |
| Garbey dh | 4 | 1 | 2 | 1 | Almon 1b | 1 | 0 | 0 | 0 |
| DaEvns 1b | 3 | 0 | 0 | 0 | Essian c | 2 | 0 | 0 | 0 |
| Kuntz cf | 4 | 1 | 2 | 0 | Meyer ph | 1 | 0 | 1 | 0 |
| MCastil 3b | 3 | 1 | 1 | 1 | Heath c | 1 | 0 | 0 | 0 |
| | | | | | MDavis rf | 3 | 0 | 2 | 0 |
| | | | | | Phillips ph | 1 | 0 | 0 | 0 |
| | | | | | DHill ss | 3 | 0 | 0 | 0 |
| | | | | | Burghs ph | 1 | 0 | 0 | 0 |
| Totals | 35 | 6 | 10 | 6 | Totals | 36 | 3 | 12 | 3 |

```
Detroit............................ 004 100 010— 6
Oakland............................ 001 101 000— 3
```
Game Winning RBI — MCastillo (1).
E—MDavis. DP—Detroit 1, Oakland 1.
LOB—Detroit 6, Oakland 7. 2B— MCastillo, LNParrish, Lansford, Kingman. HR—RHenderson (14), Garbey (5), Kingman (33). SF—Bochte.

| | IP | H | R | ER | BB | SO |
|---|---|---|---|---|---|---|
| **Detroit** | | | | | | |
| Petry W,16-8 | 5 1-3 | 11 | 3 | 3 | 0 | 0 |
| Lopez | 1 2-3 | 1 | 0 | 0 | 0 | 1 |
| Hernandz S,27 | 2 | 0 | 0 | 0 | 0 | 2 |
| **Oakland** | | | | | | |
| Conroy L,1-4 | 3 1-3 | 6 | 5 | 5 | 3 | 5 |
| Sorensen | 3 2-3 | 3 | 1 | 1 | 0 | 2 |
| Leiper | 0 | 1 | 0 | 0 | 0 | 0 |
| Atherton | 2 | 0 | 0 | 0 | 1 | 3 |

Sorensen pitched to 2 batter in 8th.
Leiper pitched to 1 batter in 8th.
WP—Conroy. PB—LNParrish. T—3:01.
A—20,393.

Thank God we're going home on a winner. We finished the West Coast trip at 4–5. It would have been a little tough starting two weeks against Baltimore and Toronto riding a five-game losing streak.

The next 12 games are with the Orioles and the Blue Jays. We can win it ourselves right now. We have got to dig in. We've led wire-to-wire and the pressure is on us. We've got to defend it. If we can't hold on, then we don't deserve the win.

Today we jumped to a four-run lead, and I felt pretty good with Dan Petry pitching. He gave up 11 hits in less than six innings, though, and I went to Aurelio Lopez and Willie Hernandez. Willie has gotten all the attention this season, and he certainly deserves it. But I think sometimes the writers overlook what Lopez has done. He's pitched the same number of innings as Willie and has saved some arms for us. Without Lopez and Hernandez this year, we'd have a good chance of being third or fourth.

# MONDAY, SEPTEMBER 3

## AT DETROIT

# GAME 138

## ORIOLES 7, TIGERS 4
### (88-50, 8½ GAMES AHEAD)

| BALTIMORE | ab | r | h | bi | DETROIT | ab | r | h | bi |
|---|---|---|---|---|---|---|---|---|---|
| Bumbry cf | 3 | 1 | 1 | 1 | Whitakr 2b | 5 | 0 | 0 | 1 |
| MK Yng rf | 4 | 1 | 1 | 4 | Tramml ss | 5 | 0 | 2 | 0 |
| Ripken ss | 5 | 0 | 2 | 0 | KGibson rf | 1 | 0 | 0 | 0 |
| EMurry 1b | 4 | 1 | 2 | 0 | Garbey dh | 3 | 0 | 0 | 0 |
| Lownstn lf | 4 | 0 | 1 | 1 | LNParsh c | 3 | 1 | 0 | 0 |
| GRonck lf | 1 | 0 | 1 | 0 | DaEvns 1b | 3 | 2 | 1 | 1 |
| Singltn dh | 3 | 1 | 1 | 0 | RJones cf | 4 | 0 | 1 | 1 |
| Swgrty pr | 0 | 1 | 0 | 0 | Grubb dh | 4 | 1 | 2 | 0 |
| Ayala ph | 1 | 0 | 1 | 0 | Herndon lf | 3 | 0 | 1 | 1 |
| Gross 3b | 4 | 0 | 0 | 0 | HJhnsn 3b | 4 | 0 | 2 | 0 |
| TCruz 3b | 1 | 0 | 0 | 0 | | | | | |
| Dauer 2b | 3 | 1 | 1 | 0 | | | | | |
| Nolan ph | 0 | 0 | 0 | 0 | | | | | |
| Sakata 2b | 1 | 1 | 0 | 0 | | | | | |
| Dempsy c | 3 | 0 | 2 | 0 | | | | | |
| Dwyer ph | 1 | 0 | 0 | 0 | | | | | |
| Rayford c | 1 | 0 | 0 | 0 | | | | | |
| Totals | 39 | 7 | 13 | 6 | Totals | 35 | 4 | 9 | 4 |

```
Baltimore ......................020 001 040— 7
Detroit ..........................000 201 001— 4
```
Game Winning RBI — MK Young (6).
E—Lowenstein, HJohnson. LOB—Baltimore 11, Detroit 7. 2B—Lowenstein, Dempsey, EMurray, Herndon. 3B—Singleton. HR—DaEvans (14), MKYoung (13). S— Bumbry, MKYoung.

| | IP | H | R | ER | BB | SO |
|---|---|---|---|---|---|---|
| **Baltimore** | | | | | | |
| GDavis | 6 | 5 | 3 | 3 | 3 | 5 |
| SStewart W,7-2 | 3 | 4 | 1 | 1 | 0 | 2 |
| **Detroit** | | | | | | |
| Morris L, 17-10 | 7 2-3 | 9 | 6 | 6 | 4 | 6 |
| Lopez | 0 | 2 | 1 | 1 | 0 | 0 |
| Scherrer | 2-3 | 2 | 0 | 0 | 0 | 1 |
| Bair | 2-3 | 0 | 0 | 0 | 0 | 0 |

Lopez pitched to 2 batters in the 8th.
WP—Morris. T—3:14. A—36,797.

What's the old saying about when it rains, it pours? Chet Lemon still is having dizzy spells. Dave Bergman's back still bothers him. Tom Brookens still can't play. Now Kirk Gibson was taken to the hospital with some kind of virus that had him throwing up all day. I'll give credit to Gibby. He batted once, but he was throwing up so hard in the dugout between innings, we had to get him out of there.

There's no such thing as a lock. Don't think Yogi Berra wasn't right when he said, "It's never over 'til it's over."

Always remember—when you have to win, it's awful tough. It's a lot easier when there's no pressure to win.

Jack Morris pitched a good game, but he ran out of gas. When he loaded the bases in the eighth, I brought in Aurelio Lopez, and Oriole Mike Young hit a grand slam on the second pitch.

The writers asked about Morris and if there was a temper tantrum after the game. I told them that this Morris thing has gotten out of proportion. I'm tired of all the attention they're giving it. The guy is being stripped every time he moves. I know this: I've been here for five years, and he's only missed three turns. If it's a crime to win, then he's guilty. But this other stuff about him being mad all the time has gotten out of hand. That's the last time I'll say anything about it.

At least Toronto lost.

# TUESDAY, SEPTEMBER 4

## AT DETROIT

# GAME 139

## ORIOLES 4, TIGERS 1

### (88–51, 7½ GAMES AHEAD)

| BALTIMORE | ab | r | h | bi | DETROIT | ab | r | h | bi |
|---|---|---|---|---|---|---|---|---|---|
| Bumbry cf | 5 | 1 | 2 | 0 | Whitakr 2b | 5 | 0 | 1 | 0 |
| Shelby cf | 0 | 0 | 0 | 0 | Tramml ss | 2 | 0 | 2 | 0 |
| MKYng rf | 5 | 1 | 2 | 0 | R Jones cf | 4 | 0 | 0 | 0 |
| Ripken ss | 4 | 0 | 1 | 1 | LNParsh c | 2 | 0 | 0 | 0 |
| EMurry 1b | 3 | 0 | 2 | 1 | DaEvns 1b | 4 | 0 | 1 | 0 |
| Lownstn lf | 0 | 0 | 0 | 0 | Grubb dh | 2 | 1 | 0 | 0 |
| GRonck lf | 4 | 0 | 0 | 0 | Herndon lf | 4 | 0 | 0 | 0 |
| Singltn dh | 4 | 0 | 0 | 0 | NSimns rf | 4 | 0 | 1 | 1 |
| Gross 3b | 2 | 0 | 0 | 0 | HJhnsn 3b | 4 | 0 | 2 | 0 |
| TCruz 3b | 0 | 0 | 0 | 0 | | | | | |
| Dauer 2b | 3 | 1 | 0 | 0 | | | | | |
| Dempsy c | 4 | 1 | 1 | 2 | | | | | |
| Totals | 34 | 4 | 8 | 4 | Totals | 31 | 1 | 7 | 1 |

```
Baltimore ...................... 200 020 000— 4
Detroit ............................000 100 000— 1
```

Game Winning RBI — Ripken (11).
E—Herndon. DP—Baltimore 2, Detroit
1. LOB—Baltimore 8, Detroit 9. 2B—
EMurray. HR—Dempsey (8). SF—Ripken.

| Baltimore | IP | H | R | ER | BB | SO |
|---|---|---|---|---|---|---|
| Boddickr W,17-9 | 7 | 6 | 1 | 1 | 6 | 6 |
| SStewart S,11 | 2 | 1 | 0 | 0 | 0 | 3 |
| Detroit | | | | | | |
| Rozema L,7-6 | 1-3 | 3 | 2 | 1 | 0 | 0 |
| Scherrer | 2-3 | 1 | 0 | 0 | 1 | 1 |
| RMason | 8 | 4 | 2 | 2 | 3 | 6 |

Scherrer pitched to 1 batter in 2nd.
PB—LNParrish. T—2:41. A—27,767.

I didn't sleep at all last night. I'm sure the results of this game will make it two in a row.

I know our kids are under a lot of pressure now. They are very uptight. If they can just win a game and forget about Toronto, everything will be all right. I've got to let them know that the whole rest of the league is still looking up to us—so what's the problem?

Mike Boddicker walked six tonight. But Dave Rozema was giving up ropes all over the park, and I had to get him out of there in the first inning.

Roger Mason—one of the kids we brought up from Evansville yesterday—showed a lot of guts. He took the ball for eight innings and held the Orioles to two runs in his major league debut.

One positive thing: Morris talked to the press again. To be honest, I asked him, as a personal favor to me, if he'd talk to the writers again. I think he's helping himself by breaking the silence.

He handled himself well and made me feel real proud when he said, "I can't believe a lot of the things that were said about me. I may have shown bad judgment, but I never have said anything bad about a teammate, coach, or manager. I learned that from Sparky."

That's one less battle to worry about in this war.

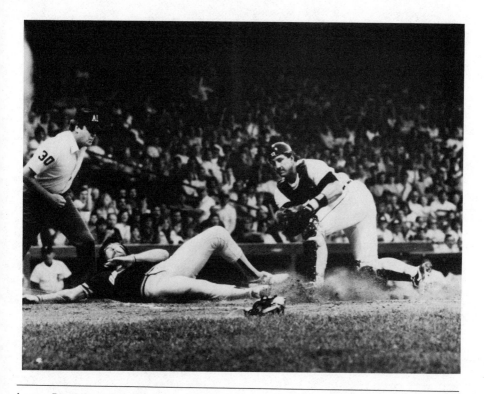

**Lance Parrish makes the tag.** Photo by Doc Holcomb, courtesy of *The Detroit News*

# WEDNESDAY, SEPTEMBER 5

## AT DETROIT

# GAME 140

## TIGERS 1, ORIOLES 0

### (89–51, 8½ GAMES AHEAD)

MAGIC NUMBER: 15

| BALTIMORE | ab | r | h | bi | DETROIT | ab | r | h | bi |
|---|---|---|---|---|---|---|---|---|---|
| Bumbry cf | 2 | 0 | 0 | 0 | Whitakr 2b | 4 | 0 | 1 | 0 |
| Ayala ph | 1 | 0 | 0 | 0 | Tramml ss | 3 | 1 | 2 | 0 |
| TCruz 3b | 0 | 0 | 0 | 0 | Garbey dh | 4 | 0 | 1 | 0 |
| MK Yng rf | 4 | 0 | 0 | 0 | LNParsh c | 2 | 0 | 0 | 0 |
| Ripken ss | 4 | 0 | 0 | 0 | Herndon lf | 3 | 0 | 1 | 0 |
| EMurry 1b | 3 | 0 | 1 | 0 | DaEvns 1b | 3 | 0 | 1 | 0 |
| Lownstn lf | 3 | 0 | 0 | 0 | Kuntz rf | 3 | 0 | 0 | 0 |
| Rayford c | 1 | 0 | 0 | 0 | R Jones cf | 3 | 0 | 0 | 0 |
| Singltn dh | 4 | 0 | 2 | 0 | MCastil 3b | 3 | 0 | 0 | 0 |
| VRdrgz pr | 0 | 0 | 0 | 0 | | | | | |
| Gross 3b | 3 | 0 | 0 | 0 | | | | | |
| Sakata 2b | 1 | 0 | 0 | 0 | | | | | |
| Dauer 2b | 1 | 0 | 0 | 0 | | | | | |
| Nolan ph | 0 | 0 | 0 | 0 | | | | | |
| Shelby cf | 0 | 0 | 0 | 0 | | | | | |
| Dempsy c | 2 | 0 | 0 | 0 | | | | | |
| Dwyer ph | 0 | 0 | 0 | 0 | | | | | |
| GRonck lf | 0 | 0 | 0 | 0 | | | | | |
| Totals | 29 | 0 | 3 | 0 | Totals | 28 | 1 | 6 | 0 |

```
Baltimore...................... 000  000  000— 0
Detroit........................ 100  000  00x— 1
```
Game Winning RBI — None.
E—Ripken 2. DP—Baltimore 2, Detroit 1. LOB—Baltimore 7, Detroit 5. 2B—Trammell, EMurray. S—Trammell.

| Baltimore | IP | H | R | ER | BB | SO |
|---|---|---|---|---|---|---|
| Flanagan L, 11-12 | 8 | 6 | 1 | 0 | 1 | 4 |
| **Detroit** | | | | | | |
| Berengur W, 8-9 | 7 1-3 | 2 | 0 | 0 | 3 | 7 |
| Hernandz S, 28 | 12-3 | 1 | 0 | 0 | 1 | 1 |

HBP—GRoenicke by Hernandez. WP—Hernandez. T—2:30. A—34,065.

I was right. I didn't sleep at all again last night. Tonight will be different. Juan Berenguer pitched perhaps the best single game of the season. He saved us from a deep skid, and you could sense a deep feeling of appreciation from all the guys in the clubhouse after the game. Juan took one run and won with it. He showed me something. He battled the heck out of them all the way. We won only because of him. He had all the pressure on his shoulders, and he answered the call.

We scored our run in the first inning on an error by Cal Ripken. How often do you see that?

Before the game, I made a point to get into the clubhouse and joke with the boys—tried to loosen them up without them knowing it. I had a long talk with Lance Parrish to try to relax him. He's putting too much pressure on himself. I told him to forget about his hitting and just handle the pitchers.

# THURSDAY, SEPTEMBER 6

## AT DETROIT

### (89–51, 8½ GAMES AHEAD)

**MAGIC NUMBER: 15**

We held a workout for our injured boys at Tiger Stadium before flying to Toronto at night. The news was great. I'm not saying I believe in miracles, but I honestly do believe that job by Juan Berenguer had some sort of psychological lift for everyone. Chet Lemon worked out hard and didn't experience any dizziness. Dave Bergman batted and said his back was OK. Gibson said he feels a lot better and wants to get back into the lineup in Toronto.

I'll tell you one thing—the Blue Jays better be ready because we're giving them our best.

We just caught some bad little injuries all at the same time. I honestly feel that without them we'd be up two or three more games. When you've never been through a pennant fight, it's really different. Only Willie Hernandez and Doug Bair have been there before.

The coaches and I are being very low key. We can't show concern. That would be the worst thing. I'll tell you another thing—Toronto had better be ready. I'm glad we're playing them now. Let's get down and dirty right now.

**Dave Bergman on a pick-off at first.**   Photo by Doc Holcomb, courtesy of *The Detroit News*

# FRIDAY, SEPTEMBER 7

## AT TORONTO

# GAME 141

## TIGERS 7, BLUE JAYS 4
## (10 INNINGS)

### (90–51, 9½ GAMES AHEAD)

MAGIC NUMBER: 13

| DETROIT | ab | r | h | bi | TORONTO | ab | r | h | bi |
|---|---|---|---|---|---|---|---|---|---|
| Whitaker 2b | 4 | 1 | 0 | 0 | Garcia 2b | 5 | 0 | 1 | 1 |
| Trammell ss | 6 | 0 | 1 | 0 | Collins lf | 2 | 0 | 0 | 0 |
| Gibson rf | 5 | 1 | 1 | 3 | Mullincks 3b | 3 | 0 | 0 | 0 |
| Parrish c | 4 | 1 | 0 | 0 | Iorg 3b | 2 | 0 | 0 | 0 |
| Evans dh | 3 | 0 | 0 | 0 | Upshaw 1b | 4 | 1 | 1 | 0 |
| Garbey dh | 2 | 0 | 1 | 0 | Bell rf | 4 | 0 | 1 | 0 |
| Jones lf | 3 | 0 | 1 | 0 | Aikens dh | 3 | 1 | 2 | 2 |
| Herndon ph | 0 | 0 | 0 | 0 | CJohnson ph | 1 | 0 | 1 | 0 |
| Castillo 3b | 0 | 0 | 0 | 0 | Shepherd pr | 0 | 0 | 0 | 0 |
| Laga ph | 1 | 0 | 1 | 0 | Whitt c | 3 | 0 | 0 | 0 |
| Brookens 3b | 0 | 1 | 0 | 0 | Webster ph | 1 | 0 | 0 | 0 |
| Lemon cf | 4 | 1 | 2 | 1 | Martinez c | 0 | 0 | 0 | 0 |
| Bergman 1b | 5 | 2 | 4 | 3 | Barfield cf | 4 | 1 | 1 | 0 |
| HJohnson 3b | 2 | 0 | 0 | 0 | Griffin ss | 2 | 1 | 0 | 0 |
| Grubb lf | 1 | 0 | 0 | 0 | Fernandz ph | 1 | 0 | 0 | 0 |
| Kuntz lf | 0 | 0 | 0 | 0 | | | | | |
| Totals | 40 | 7 | 11 | 7 | Totals | 35 | 4 | 7 | 3 |

Detroit ............................ 000 000 040 3– 7
Toronto ........................... 002 200 000 0– 4
Game-winning RBI—Bergman (5). E—
Parrish, Gibson. DP—Detroit 1. LOB—
Detroit 10, Toronto 5. 2B— Bergman.
HR—Aikens (9), Gibson (24), Bergman
(7). SB—Garcia (42). S— Griffin, Whit-
aker.

| | IP | H | R | ER | BB | SO |
|---|---|---|---|---|---|---|
| **Detroit** | | | | | | |
| Petry | 5 1-3 | 6 | 4 | 2 | 1 | 3 |
| Scherrer | 1-3 | 0 | 0 | 0 | 0 | 1 |
| Bair | 1 1-3 | 0 | 0 | 0 | 0 | 1 |
| Hernandez (W 9-2) | 3 | 1 | 0 | 0 | 1 | 2 |
| **Toronto** | | | | | | |
| Alexander | 7 2-3 | 6 | 4 | 4 | 2 | 5 |
| Key | 0 | 1 | 0 | 0 | 0 | 0 |
| Jackson | 0 | 0 | 0 | 0 | 2 | 0 |
| Gott | 2-3 | 1 | 0 | 0 | 1 | 0 |
| Clark | 1-3 | 0 | 0 | 0 | 0 | 0 |
| Msslmn (L 0-1) | 1 1-3 | 3 | 3 | 3 | 1 | 0 |

Key pitched to 1 batter in 8th; Jackson
pitched to 2 batters in 8th.
HBP—by Petry (Collins). T—3:28. A—
37,420.

I wouldn't say it to the writers after the game. But this one won it for us. This one put the nail in the coffin. It was the biggest game of the year for us. We did what we had to do—we stopped them in their home park. In my 15 years in the big leagues, this game ranks in my top 10.

It was a little unbelievable. Almost make-believe. We were losing 4–0 in the eighth when Kirk Gibson hit a three-run homer. A walk, a 75-foot bloop single by Barbaro Garbey, and two more walks later we had the game tied. Willie Hernandez came in to hold them long enough to let Dave Bergman win it with a three-run homer in the 10th.

Talk about storybook finishes; Cinderella doesn't even come close to this one. Bergman came back into the lineup and got four hits with the game-winning homer. Lemon was back and forced home the game-tying run with a walk in the eighth and also got two hits. Gibson came back and pounded that three-run shot. Tom Brookens came back and make an unbelievable defensive play in the 10th.

The game was in Toronto, but it seemed like we had more fans cheering for us than for the Jays. Somebody said 10,000 people came up from Detroit for the weekend. That's how big this game was for us.

# SATURDAY, SEPTEMBER 8

## AT TORONTO

# GAMES 142

## TIGERS 10, BLUE JAYS 4

### (91–51, 10½ GAMES AHEAD)

MAGIC NUMBER: 11

| DETROIT | ab | r | h | bi | TORONTO | ab | r | h | bi |
|---|---|---|---|---|---|---|---|---|---|
| Whitaker 2b | 3 | 2 | 1 | 0 | Garcia 2b | 4 | 1 | 1 | 0 |
| Trammell ss | 5 | 1 | 3 | 3 | Collins lf | 5 | 0 | 2 | 1 |
| Gibson rf | 5 | 0 | 1 | 2 | Mulliniks 3b | 4 | 0 | 1 | 0 |
| Parrish c | 5 | 1 | 1 | 0 | Upshaw 1b | 5 | 0 | 2 | 1 |
| Evans 3b | 3 | 1 | 1 | 1 | Bell rf | 4 | 2 | 2 | 1 |
| Castillo 3b | 1 | 0 | 0 | 0 | Aikens dh | 1 | 0 | 0 | 0 |
| Jones lf | 2 | 0 | 0 | 0 | Johnson dh | 2 | 0 | 0 | 0 |
| Herndon lf | 2 | 0 | 0 | 0 | Whitt c | 2 | 0 | 1 | 1 |
| Grubb dh | 4 | 3 | 2 | 2 | Webster ph | 1 | 0 | 0 | 0 |
| Lemon cf | 3 | 1 | 0 | 0 | Martinez c | 1 | 0 | 0 | 0 |
| Bergman 1b | 3 | 1 | 1 | 1 | Barfield cf | 4 | 0 | 0 | 0 |
| Laga 1b | 0 | 0 | 0 | 0 | Griffin ss | 4 | 1 | 1 | 0 |
| Totals | 36 | 10 | 10 | 9 | Totals | 37 | 4 | 10 | 4 |

Detroit .................................. 010 010 260—10
Toronto ................................. 010 100 002— 4

Game-winning RBI—Grubb (4). E—Griffin, Bell. LOB—Detroit 6, Toronto 10. 2B—Mulliniks, Bell, Upshaw. 3B—Bergman. HR—Evans (15), Bell (22), Grubb 2 (7). SB—Collins (52). S—Castillo.

| Detroit | IP | H | R | ER | BB | SO |
|---|---|---|---|---|---|---|
| Morris | 4 1-3 | 5 | 2 | 2 | 1 | 2 |
| Scherrer (W 1-0) | 1 2-3 | 0 | 0 | 0 | 1 | 3 |
| Lopez (S 13) | 3 | 5 | 2 | 2 | 1 | 1 |
| **Toronto** | | | | | | |
| Leal (L 13-6) | 6 2-3 | 7 | 4 | 4 | 3 | 9 |
| Clark | 2-3 | 1 | 1 | 1 | 0 | 0 |
| Lamp | 2-3 | 2 | 5 | 0 | 3 | 0 |
| Acker | 1 | 0 | 0 | 0 | 0 | 0 |

HBP—by Lopez (Garcia). WP—Leal. T — 3:06. A—41,059.

I've been here five years now and these last two games have been the biggest this team has played. You could sense before it started today; the boys were on.

Toronto stayed with us for seven innings. Then—pop—it was all over. John Grubb hit two home runs; Darrell Evans hit one. Alan Trammell came up with three RBIs, and Bill Scherrer got his first win for us.

Scherrer took over for Jack Morris in the fifth. Jack's shoulder tightened a little and there was no way I was going to take any chances with him now. He'll be ready to pitch next week. All we need to win are eight or nine more games and it's over. It was great to see 42,000 fans in the stands here. The Blue Jays have a great team. The only difference between them and us is our bullpen. It's got to be tough on Bobby Cox [the Blue Jays' manager]. Whenever he calls down to the bullpen, he gets a wrong number.

I made a switch before the game, and we'll stick with it the rest of the way. I moved Darrell Evans to third. He'll be there against right-handed pitching, and he'll be in the lineup somewhere against lefties, I just don't know where. Howard Johnson is really uptight and is having his problems. It'll be best for him to get rest now.

# SUNDAY, SEPTEMBER 9

## AT TORONTO

# GAME 143

## TIGERS 7, BLUE JAYS 2

### (92–51, 11½ GAMES AHEAD)

MAGIC NUMBER: 9

| DETROIT | ab | r | h | bi | TORONTO | ab | r | h | bi |
|---|---|---|---|---|---|---|---|---|---|
| Whitakr 2b | 5 | 1 | 1 | 0 | Garcia 2b | 4 | 0 | 1 | 0 |
| Trammll ss | 5 | 2 | 2 | 1 | Collins lf | 4 | 2 | 2 | 0 |
| KGibson rf | 5 | 1 | 3 | 3 | Mulinks 3b | 2 | 0 | 1 | 1 |
| LNParsh c | 5 | 0 | 2 | 2 | Glorg 3b | 1 | 0 | 0 | 0 |
| DaEvns 3b | 2 | 0 | 1 | 0 | Upshaw 1b | 4 | 0 | 2 | 1 |
| MCastil 3b | 1 | 0 | 0 | 0 | GBell rf | 4 | 0 | 0 | 0 |
| R Jones lf | 3 | 0 | 1 | 0 | Aikens dh | 3 | 0 | 0 | 0 |
| Herndon lf | 0 | 0 | 0 | 0 | Manrlq ph | 1 | 0 | 0 | 0 |
| Grubb dh | 3 | 1 | 1 | 1 | Whitt c | 2 | 0 | 0 | 0 |
| Lemon cf | 4 | 0 | 0 | 0 | BMartnz c | 1 | 0 | 0 | 0 |
| Bergmn 1b | 4 | 2 | 2 | 0 | Shphrd pr | 0 | 0 | 0 | 0 |
| | | | | | Barfield cf | 4 | 0 | 1 | 0 |
| | | | | | Fernndz ss | 3 | 0 | 1 | 0 |
| Totals | 37 | 7 | 13 | 7 | Totals | 33 | 2 | 8 | 2 |

```
Detroit..................... 002 001 400— 7
Toronto.................... 100 001 000— 2
```
Game Winning RBI — LNParrish (10).
E—Barfield, Trammell. DP—Detroit 1,
Toronto 1. LOB—Detroit 7, Toronto 6.
2B—Upshaw 2, Mulliniks, KGibson,
LNParrish. 3B—Collins. HR—Grubb (8),
KGibson (25). SB—KGibson (26). S—
Herndon. SF—Mulliniks.

| | IP | H | R | ER | BB | SO |
|---|---|---|---|---|---|---|
| **Detroit** | | | | | | |
| Wilcox W, 16-7 | 6 | 8 | 2 | 2 | 0 | 5 |
| Scherrer | 1 | 0 | 0 | 0 | 0 | 0 |
| Hernandz | 2 | 0 | 0 | 0 | 0 | 1 |
| **Toronto** | | | | | | |
| Clancy L, 11-14 | 6 | 11 | 6 | 5 | 2 | 2 |
| BClark | 0 | 2 | 1 | 1 | 1 | 0 |
| Gott | 3 | 0 | 0 | 0 | 0 | 1 |

Clancy pitched to 3 batters in 7th, Clark
pitched to 3 batters in 7th.
HBP—BMartinez by Hernandez. BK—
Wilcox. T—2:39. A—37,392.

This three-game series is the best this team has ever played. You could not have seen a more prepared team that executed more perfectly than the Tigers did in Toronto this weekend.

We came in here knowing we had a job to do. But no one in his right mind could have imagined we'd sweep. John Grubb hit another homer. So did Kirk Gibson. Gibby hit a three-run shot off the lefty (Bryan Clark) on the first pitch to him. Gibson is the man. Lance Parrish delivered the big two-run single in the third. If Lance breaks out of his slump now—look out. Milt Wilcox gave up a run in the first then settled down and showed how he's been all year.

I'll have to admit, this is an ego thing. Now that we're this close, I'd really like for us to win 100 games. No manager has ever done that with two different teams. I did it twice with the Reds. This would be a nice cap to the season.

It's hard to believe we came into Toronto with our magic number at fifteen and we're leaving at nine. I suppose Toronto finds it even harder to believe.

**John Grubb hits a homer.**   Photo by Clifton Boutelle

# MONDAY, SEPTEMBER 10

## AT BALTIMORE

# GAME 144

## ORIOLES 3, TIGERS 1

### (92–52, 11½ GAMES AHEAD)

MAGIC NUMBER: 8

| DETROIT | | | | | BALTIMORE | | | | |
|---|---|---|---|---|---|---|---|---|---|
| | ab | r | h | bi | | ab | r | h | bi |
| Garbey 1b | 4 | 0 | 0 | 0 | MKYng rf | 3 | 1 | 1 | 0 |
| Tramml ss | 4 | 0 | 0 | 0 | Shelby cf | 4 | 0 | 1 | 0 |
| K.Gibson rf | 4 | 1 | 2 | 1 | Rtpken ss | 2 | 0 | 0 | 0 |
| LNPrsh dh | 4 | 0 | 0 | 0 | EMurry 1b | 4 | 1 | 1 | 1 |
| Herndon lf | 4 | 0 | 1 | 0 | Lownstn lf | 2 | 0 | 0 | 0 |
| Lemon cf | 3 | 0 | 1 | 0 | GRonck lf | 0 | 0 | 0 | 0 |
| Brokns 2b | 4 | 0 | 1 | 0 | Singltn dh | 3 | 0 | 0 | 0 |
| MCastill c | 3 | 0 | 0 | 0 | Bmbry pr | 0 | 0 | 0 | 0 |
| HJhnsn 3b | 2 | 0 | 0 | 0 | Gross 3b | 3 | 1 | 1 | 1 |
| Kuntz ph | 0 | 0 | 0 | 0 | TCruz 3b | 1 | 0 | 0 | 0 |
| Earl 2b | 0 | 0 | 0 | 0 | Sakata 2b | 3 | 0 | 1 | 0 |
| | | | | | Dempsy c | 3 | 0 | 1 | 0 |
| Totals | 32 | 1 | 5 | 1 | Totals | 28 | 3 | 6 | 2 |

Detroit .........................000 100 000– 1
Baltimore .....................110 000 01x– 3
  Game Winning RBI.— None.
  E—Garbey, MCastillo. DP—Detroit 3.
LOB—Detroit 6, Baltimore 7. HR—Gross
(20), KGibson (26), EMurray (27). SB—
HJohnson (10), Bumbry (8).

| | IP | H | R | ER | BB | SO |
|---|---|---|---|---|---|---|
| **Detroit** | | | | | | |
| B..rnur L,8-10 | 7 | 5 | 2 | 2 | 4 | 3 |
| Lop. | 1 | 1 | 1 | 1 | 1 | 1 |
| **Baltimore** | | | | | | |
| Flanagn W,12-12 | 9 | 5 | 1 | 1 | 2 | 5 |

  HBP—Lowenstein by Berenguer  T—
2:38. A—27,440.

The writers asked me about a letdown. They wanted to know if I was worried. Sometimes I worry about the writers.

We're in an awfully good position. Something could happen, but, Lord, we'd have to do it all to ourselves, and that's not going to happen. I just feel sorry for Juan Berenguer. Nobody is pitching any better on this club than that man. He deserves far better than he's getting. Every year you find some pitcher on a club that is just jinxed. You get runs for everyone but him. After the game I walked right up to him and said "Sorry. . . . You couldn't have pitched any better than that."

Juan will be my long man in the playoffs. I've got to go with Jack Morris, Dan Petry, and Milt Wilcox because of the day off. Juan understands.

Baltimore's Mike Flanagan did it again to us. There always seems to be one pitcher who can't do anything but win against you. Flanagan is 12-12 overall. Against us, he went 3-1 with one earned run in 35 innings. And that run gave us a 1-0 win over him.

Kirk Gibson hit another homer and has a shot for 30 this year. I made a promise to him the other day: I will not talk about him to the press. I'll let him do his job and let the numbers tell the story. Those numbers will be talking long and hard.

# TUESDAY, SEPTEMBER 11

## AT BALTIMORE

# GAME 145

## TIGERS 9, ORIOLES 2

### (93–52, 11½ GAMES AHEAD)

MAGIC NUMBER: 7

| DETROIT | ab | r | h | bi | BALTIMORE | ab | r | h | bi |
|---------|----|----|----|----|-----------|----|----|----|----|
| Whitakr 2b | 6 | 0 | 0 | 0 | Bumbry cf | 4 | 0 | 1 | 0 |
| Earl 2b | 0 | 0 | 0 | 0 | GRnck ph | 1 | 0 | 0 | 0 |
| Tramml ss | 5 | 1 | 1 | 1 | MKYng rf | 3 | 0 | 1 | 0 |
| KGibson rf | 5 | 1 | 3 | 0 | Ripken ss | 3 | 0 | 0 | 0 |
| LNParsh c | 5 | 1 | 1 | 2 | EMurry 1b | 2 | 0 | 0 | 0 |
| Lowry c | 0 | 0 | 0 | 0 | Lownstn lf | 4 | 0 | 0 | 0 |
| DaEvns 3b | 4 | 2 | 4 | 1 | Singltn dh | 4 | 0 | 1 | 0 |
| Brokns 3b | 1 | 1 | 0 | 0 | Gross 3b | 4 | 0 | 0 | 0 |
| RJones lf | 1 | 0 | 0 | 0 | TCruz 3b | 0 | 0 | 0 | 0 |
| Herndon lf | 3 | 2 | 3 | 3 | Sakata 2b | 4 | 1 | 1 | 0 |
| Grubb dh | 4 | 0 | 2 | 0 | Dempsy c | 4 | 1 | 2 | 2 |
| Garbey ph | 1 | 0 | 1 | 1 | | | | | |
| Lemon cf | 4 | 1 | 1 | 0 | | | | | |
| Bergmn 1b | 4 | 0 | 0 | 0 | | | | | |
| Kuntz ph | 0 | 0 | 0 | 0 | | | | | |
| Laga 1b | 0 | 0 | 0 | 0 | | | | | |
| Totals | 43 | 9 | 16 | 8 | Totals | 33 | 2 | 6 | 2 |

```
Detroit ..........................000 050 202— 9
Baltimore ......................000 010 100— 2
```
Game Winning RBI — Trammell (5).
E—Ripken 2. DP—Baltimore 2. LOB—
Detroit 11, Baltimore 8. 2B—DaEvans,
Lemon, Dempsey. HR—Dempsey (10),
DaEvans (16), Herndon (5). SB—KGibson
(27).

| | IP | H | R | ER | BB | SO |
|---|----|----|----|----|----|----|
| **Detroit** | | | | | | |
| Petry W, 17-8 | 6 2-3 | 5 | 2 | 2 | 4 | 6 |
| Bair | 1 1-3 | 1 | 0 | 0 | 0 | 0 |
| Hernandz | 1 | 0 | 0 | 0 | 0 | 0 |
| **Baltimore** | | | | | | |
| Swaggerty L, 3-2 | 4 2-3 | 8 | 4 | 4 | 2 | 1 |
| Underwd | 0 | 3 | 1 | 1 | 0 | 0 |
| MrBrown | 2 1-3 | 3 | 2 | 2 | 0 | 0 |
| TMartnez | 2 | 2 | 2 | 0 | 1 | 1 |

TUnderwood pitched to 3 batters in 5th.
HBP—Lemon by MrBrown. WP—Pe-
try, TUnderwood. T—3:07. A—25,193.

Our bats are back. Lance Parrish had a big hit. He's a key if he can
get going. So is Darrell Evans. He had four hits, including a home run.
Larry Herndon followed Darrell's homer with one of his own. What a
bonus if Herndon picks it up right now! Kirk Gibson had three more
hits. If you're talking MVP, you talk two names—Willie Hernandez and
Kirk Gibson.

Dan Petry won his 17th game. It's amazing, but we may not have a
20-game winner this year. That's a tribute, though, to our bullpen. We'll
have three guys with more than 17 and a bullpen that's somewhere in
the stratosphere.

Tonight we became only the fifth club in American League history to
pass the two million mark in both home and road attendance. That's a
tribute to the great baseball fans around the league. They know a good
team when they see one.

# WEDNESDAY, SEPTEMBER 12

## AT BALTIMORE

# GAME 146

## ORIOLES 3, TIGERS 1

### (93–53, 10½ GAMES AHEAD)

MAGIC NUMBER: 7

| DETROIT | ab | r | h | bi | BALTIMORE | ab | r | h | bi |
|---------|----|----|----|----|-----------|----|----|----|----|
| Whitakr 2b | 4 | 0 | 1 | 0 | Bumbry lf | 4 | 0 | 1 | 0 |
| Tramml ss | 4 | 0 | 1 | 0 | Shelby cf | 4 | 1 | 1 | 0 |
| KGibson rf | 4 | 0 | 0 | 0 | Ripken ss | 4 | 0 | 2 | 0 |
| LNParsh c | 4 | 0 | 2 | 0 | EMurry 1b | 3 | 1 | 0 | 0 |
| DaEvns 3b | 3 | 0 | 0 | 0 | MKYng rf | 4 | 1 | 2 | 0 |
| R Jones lf | 3 | 0 | 1 | 0 | Singltn dh | 2 | 0 | 0 | 0 |
| Grubb dh | 3 | 0 | 0 | 0 | Gross 3b | 1 | 0 | 0 | 1 |
| Lemon cf | 3 | 1 | 1 | 0 | TCruz 3b | 1 | 0 | 0 | 0 |
| Bergmn 1b | 3 | 0 | 0 | 0 | Sakata 2b | 3 | 0 | 1 | 1 |
| | | | | | Dempsy c | 4 | 0 | 1 | 0 |
| Totals | 31 | 1 | 6 | 0 | Totals | 30 | 3 | 8 | 2 |

Detroit............................ 000 001 000— 1
Baltimore...................... 021 000 00x— 3
    Game Winning RBI — Gross (5).
    E—LNParrish. DP—Baltimore 2.
LOB— Detroit 3, Baltimore 9. 2B—
MK Young, Shelby, Ripken, R Jones, Lem-
on. SB— Shelby (12). S—Singleton. SF—
Gross.

| | IP | H | R | ER | BB | SO |
|---|----|----|----|----|----|----|
| **Detroit** | | | | | | |
| R Mason L,0-1 | 4 | 6 | 3 | 3 | 2 | 3 |
| ONeil | 3 | 1 | 0 | 0 | 1 | 2 |
| Scherrer | 1 | 1 | 0 | 0 | 1 | 2 |
| **Baltimore** | | | | | | |
| DMartnez W,6-7 | 9 | 6 | 1 | 1 | 0 | 6 |

WP—DMartinez. T—2:33. A—24,561.

It would have been nice to finish the trip with another win, but I'm not going to worry now. Our magic number is seven and I know we'll get it. It looks like we'll clinch at home. That'll be great for the fans.

We got a good look at new Tigers Roger Mason and Randy O'Neal tonight. These are two young pitchers who are going to help us next year. Mason throws hard. Roger Craig said that O'Neal has the best split-finger fastball on the staff. Baltimore may be out of it, but the Orioles are still a pretty good test for two young pitchers.

# THURSDAY, SEPTEMBER 13

## AT DETROIT

(93–53, 10½ GAMES AHEAD)

MAGIC NUMBER: 6

What a great way to spend an off day at home—40 games over .500 and a chance to put it all away in the next couple of days. Toronto is in town for three games starting tomorrow and you know they won't forget last weekend.

Carol came back from California and it was great just to relax quietly at home and reflect a little on all that's happened this year. There's still a long way to go. I won't stop until we've got everything won.

Photo by Doc Holcomb, courtesy of *The Detroit News*

Rusty Kuntz and Dave Bergman head back to the dugout.

# FRIDAY, SEPTEMBER 14

## AT DETROIT

# GAME 147

## BLUE JAYS 7, TIGERS 2

### (93–54, 10 GAMES AHEAD)

MAGIC NUMBER: 6

| TORONTO | ab | r | h | bi |
|---|---|---|---|---|
| Garcia 2b | 5 | 0 | 0 | 0 |
| Collins lf | 5 | 0 | 0 | 0 |
| Moseby cf | 3 | 1 | 1 | 0 |
| Upshaw 1b | 3 | 0 | 0 | 0 |
| Bell rf | 5 | 0 | 0 | 0 |
| Mulliniks 3b | 3 | 2 | 2 | 0 |
| Barfield ph | 0 | 1 | 0 | 0 |
| Iorg 3b | 0 | 0 | 0 | 0 |
| Aikens dh | 3 | 2 | 2 | 3 |
| C Johnson ph | 1 | 0 | 1 | 2 |
| Whitt c | 3 | 1 | 1 | 2 |
| Griffin ss | 4 | 0 | 1 | 0 |
| Totals | 35 | 7 | 8 | 7 |

| DETROIT | ab | r | h | bi |
|---|---|---|---|---|
| Whtker 2b | 4 | 1 | 2 | 1 |
| Trmmll ss | 4 | 0 | 1 | 0 |
| Gibson rf | 3 | 0 | 0 | 0 |
| Parrish c | 2 | 0 | 0 | 0 |
| Lowry c | 1 | 0 | 1 | 0 |
| Evans 3b | 4 | 0 | 0 | 0 |
| Jones lf | 1 | 1 | 0 | 0 |
| Herndon lf | 2 | 0 | 1 | 0 |
| Grubb dh | 2 | 0 | 0 | 0 |
| Kuntz dh | 2 | 0 | 1 | 0 |
| Lemon cf | 4 | 0 | 0 | 0 |
| Brgman 1b | 2 | 0 | 1 | 0 |
| Garbey 1b | 2 | 0 | 0 | 0 |
| Totals | 33 | 2 | 7 | 1 |

Toronto    010 103 200— 7
Detroit    100 010 000— 2
Game-winning RBI — Aikens (3).

E—Collins. DP—Toronto 1, Detroit 1. LOB—Toronto 7, Detroit 7. 2B—C. Johnson. HR—Aikens 2 (11), Whitt (13). SB—Moseby 2 (34), Mulliniks (2).

| | IP | H | R | ER | BB | SO |
|---|---|---|---|---|---|---|
| **Toronto** | | | | | | |
| Clancy (W 12-14) | 5 | 4 | 2 | 2 | 1 | 5 |
| Key (S 9) | 4 | 3 | 0 | 0 | 2 | 4 |
| **Detroit** | | | | | | |
| Morris (L 17-11) | 6 | 7 | 5 | 5 | 3 | 1 |
| Scherrer | 1 | 1 | 2 | 2 | 3 | 0 |
| Rozema | 2 | 0 | 0 | 0 | 0 | 1 |

T—2:51. A—46,040.

Everyone is thinking playoffs now, and I guess that's a normal reaction. But we've got to lock this thing up first, and the way we played tonight was no way to do it. We really just went through the motions, and I've got to kick us into gear. Jack Morris didn't pitch well, and we didn't hit a lick.

All the writers are talking about the playoffs. They want to know how it feels to lead all the way and then face the possibility of being knocked out of the playoffs because it's such a short series.

I went through that in 1973 with the Reds. We won 99 games, and then the Mets beat us. We were the odds on favorite, and they just barely finished above .500 for the year. But they had Tom Seaver, Jerry Koosman, and Tug McGraw.

The playoffs is pitching. Any time you cut down to three out of five, you need two good pitchers and a good bullpen. If you have that, you have a good shot. Three losses and you're out. You got to shoot everything, every game. You wake up on Tuesday and it starts; Sunday it's over. The regular season is a marathon. The playoffs are a 100-yard dash.

# SATURDAY, SEPTEMBER 15

## AT DETROIT

# GAME 148

## TIGERS 2, BLUE JAYS 1

### (94–54, 11 GAMES AHEAD)

MAGIC NUMBER: 4

| TORONTO | ab | r | h | bi | DETROIT | ab | r | h | bi |
|---|---|---|---|---|---|---|---|---|---|
| Garcia 2b | 4 | 0 | 1 | 0 | Whitakr 2b | 4 | 0 | 1 | 0 |
| Collins lf | 4 | 0 | 0 | 0 | Tramml ss | 3 | 1 | 1 | 0 |
| Moseby cf | 4 | 0 | 1 | 0 | KGibson rf | 4 | 0 | 1 | 0 |
| Upshaw 1b | 4 | 0 | 0 | 0 | DaEvns 3b | 3 | 0 | 1 | 1 |
| GBell rf | 3 | 1 | 1 | 1 | Brokns 3b | 0 | 0 | 0 | 0 |
| Mulinks 3b | 2 | 0 | 0 | 0 | RJones lf | 2 | 1 | 1 | 1 |
| Glorg 3b | 1 | 0 | 0 | 0 | Grubb dh | 3 | 0 | 1 | 0 |
| Aikens dh | 1 | 0 | 0 | 0 | Lemon cf | 4 | 0 | 1 | 0 |
| CJhnsn ph | 1 | 0 | 0 | 0 | Bergmn 1b | 4 | 0 | 0 | 0 |
| Whitt c | 2 | 0 | 0 | 0 | Lowry c | 3 | 0 | 0 | 0 |
| DMartnz c | 1 | 0 | 0 | 0 | | | | | |
| Griffin ss | 2 | 0 | 0 | 0 | | | | | |
| Barfild ph | 1 | 0 | 0 | 0 | | | | | |
| Totals | 30 | 1 | 3 | 1 | Totals | 30 | 2 | 7 | 2 |

```
Toronto          010 000 000— 1
Detroit          100 100 00x— 2
```

Game Winning RBI — RJones (6).
DP—Toronto 1. LOB—Toronto 3, Detroit 9. 2B—Trammell. HR—GBell (24), RJones (12). SB—KGibson (28), Garcia (45).

| | IP | H | R | ER | BB | SO |
|---|---|---|---|---|---|---|
| **Toronto** | | | | | | |
| Stieb L, 14-7 | 8 | 7 | 2 | 2 | 5 | 9 |
| **Detroit** | | | | | | |
| Wilcox W, 17-7 | 7 | 1 | 1 | 1 | 1 | 8 |
| Hernandz S, 29 | 2 | 2 | 0 | 0 | 0 | 2 |

WP—Stieb. T—2:33. A—44,349.

Toronto's Cliff Johnson walked over from the Toronto clubhouse into ours after the game. First he yelled at Ruppert Jones. "The score was Jones 2, Blue Jays 1. Don't ever let me catch you in a dark alley, man."

Then he looked over at me. "You dodged the bullet this time, George." He was kidding, but it was true. We dodged the bullet while Ruppert was busy pounding the nails into the Toronto coffin.

What a game Ruppert played. Two great catches . . . one a leaping grab over the leftfield screen to take a home run away from Johnson. The Rupe snapped a 1–1 tie with a home run. Milt Wilcox pitched a one-hitter for seven innings and I took him out when his shoulder tightened a little. Willie Hernandez got his 29th save.

Before the game John Hiller visited the clubhouse. Hiller is the man who held all the Tiger relief records until Hernandez came along. Maybe an old relief pitcher like that can really understand what Hernandez has done this season. I still have trouble believing what I'm seeing.

# SUNDAY, SEPTEMBER 16

## AT DETROIT

# GAME 149

## TIGERS 8, BLUE JAYS 3

### (95–54, 12 GAMES AHEAD)

MAGIC NUMBER: 2

| TORONTO | ab | r | h | bi | DETROIT | ab | r | h | bi |
|---|---|---|---|---|---|---|---|---|---|
| Garcia 2b | 5 | 1 | 2 | 0 | Whitakr 2b | 4 | 1 | 2 | 0 |
| Collins lf | 4 | 0 | 1 | 1 | Earl 2b | 0 | 0 | 0 | 0 |
| Moseby cf | 4 | 0 | 0 | 0 | Tramml ss | 4 | 1 | 1 | 0 |
| Upshaw 1b | 3 | 0 | 0 | 0 | Baker ss | 0 | 0 | 0 | 0 |
| Leach 1b | 0 | 0 | 0 | 0 | KGibson rf | 4 | 1 | 1 | 1 |
| GBell rf | 3 | 0 | 0 | 0 | LNPrsh dh | 5 | 0 | 0 | 0 |
| Mulnks 3b | 2 | 0 | 0 | 0 | Herndon lf | 4 | 2 | 2 | 1 |
| Gruber 3b | 2 | 0 | 0 | 0 | Garbey 1b | 3 | 1 | 1 | 2 |
| Aikens dh | 1 | 0 | 0 | 0 | Bergmn 1b | 1 | 0 | 0 | 0 |
| CJhnsn ph | 2 | 0 | 0 | 0 | Lemon cf | 4 | 0 | 1 | 1 |
| Whitt c | 2 | 1 | 1 | 1 | Brokns 3b | 4 | 1 | 2 | 2 |
| BMartnz c | 2 | 0 | 0 | 0 | MCastill c | 4 | 1 | 2 | 1 |
| Fernndz ss | 4 | 1 | 2 | 0 | | | | | |
| **Totals** | 34 | 3 | 6 | 2 | **Totals** | 37 | 8 | 12 | 8 |

Bell reached first on catcher's interference.

| Toronto | 000 110 001— 3 |
|---|---|
| Detroit | 412 001 00x— 8 |

Game Winning RBI — KGibson (17).
E—Whitaker, MCastillo 2, Mulliniks.
LOB—Toronto 9, Detroit 9. 2B—Whitaker,
KGibson, Lemon, Trammell. 3B— MCas-
tillo. HR—MCastillo (3), Brookens (4),
Whitt (14), Herndon (6). SB—Collins (54).

| Toronto | IP | H | R | ER | BB | SO |
|---|---|---|---|---|---|---|
| BClark L, 1-2 | 2-3 | 4 | 4 | 4 | 1 | 2 |
| Lamp | 2 1-3 | 3 | 3 | 3 | 0 | 2 |
| Mussiman | 2 | 2 | 0 | 0 | 3 | 0 |
| Acker | 2 | 2 | 1 | 1 | 0 | 1 |
| Gott | 1 | 1 | 0 | 0 | 0 | 1 |
| **Detroit** | | | | | | |
| Berengur W, 9-10 | 5 | 3 | 2 | 1 | 3 | 4 |
| Scherrer | 1 | 0 | 0 | 0 | 0 | 1 |
| Lopez | 2 | 1 | 0 | 0 | 1 | 2 |
| Hernandz | 1 | 2 | 1 | 1 | 0 | 0 |

WP—Lamp, Hernandez. PB—MCastillo. T—3:01. A—45,488.

In 1981 we lost the division title to the Brewers at Milwaukee on the next to last day of the season. I told all our players to sit down on the bench and watch the celebration because that was going to be us one day. That day is here. We actually won this thing a week ago Friday in Toronto when we rallied for four runs in the eighth inning and beat the Blue Jays in the 10th. That killed them. I didn't admit it to the press at the time, but it was over right then.

I know this is going to sound strange to some people, but winning in Milwaukee three years ago would have been the worst thing that could have happened to this team. We weren't ready for it. We wouldn't have done the things we had to do to create this team. And this is a good team.

Today was beautiful. Juan Berenguer pitched a super game and we came up with eight extra base hits. No one could have beaten us today. After the game Toronto's Ernie Whitt told the writers that we have an outstanding team and we should win it all. He may not know it, but he paid me what I consider the highest compliment when he said I did a good job of keeping all my players rested. I took a great deal of pain to make sure that happened this season.

# MONDAY, SEPTEMBER 17

## AT DETROIT

# GAME 150

## TIGERS 7, BREWERS 3

### (96–54, 12 GAMES AHEAD)

MAGIC NUMBER: 1

| MILWAUKEE | ab | r | h | bi | DETROIT | ab | r | h | bi |
|---|---|---|---|---|---|---|---|---|---|
| Yount dh | 4 | 1 | 1 | 1 | Whitakr 2b | 4 | 2 | 2 | 4 |
| Gantnr 2b | 5 | 0 | 0 | 0 | Bergmn 1b | 0 | 0 | 0 | 0 |
| Cooper 1b | 4 | 1 | 3 | 0 | Tramml ss | 4 | 0 | 1 | 0 |
| Loman lf | 3 | 0 | 1 | 1 | Earl 2b | 0 | 0 | 0 | 0 |
| RClark rf | 4 | 0 | 1 | 0 | KGibson rf | 4 | 0 | 0 | 0 |
| James cf | 4 | 1 | 2 | 0 | Kuntz rf | 0 | 0 | 0 | 0 |
| Sundbrg c | 4 | 0 | 0 | 0 | LNParsh c | 4 | 1 | 2 | 1 |
| Romero ss | 4 | 0 | 1 | 0 | Herndon lf | 4 | 1 | 2 | 0 |
| Lozado 3b | 4 | 0 | 1 | 1 | Lemon cf | 4 | 0 | 1 | 0 |
| | | | | | Garbey dh | 2 | 1 | 0 | 0 |
| | | | | | Laga dh | 1 | 0 | 1 | 0 |
| | | | | | DaEvns 1b | 3 | 1 | 0 | 0 |
| | | | | | Baker ss | 0 | 0 | 0 | 0 |
| | | | | | Brokns 3b | 2 | 0 | 1 | 0 |
| | | | | | Grubb ph | 0 | 1 | 0 | 1 |
| | | | | | MCastil 3b | 1 | 0 | 0 | 0 |
| Totals | 36 | 3 | 10 | 3 | Totals | 33 | 7 | 10 | 6 |

```
Milwaukee ....................010 010 001— 3
Detroit ...........................100 000 60x— 7
```

Game Winning RBI — Grubb (5).
E—Gantner 2. DP—Milwaukee 1. LOB— Milwaukee 8, Detroit 5. 2B—James, RClark. HR—LNParrish (30), Whitaker (11), Yount (14). SB—Trammell (19), Brookens (6), Cooper (7).

| | IP | H | R | ER | BB | SO |
|---|---|---|---|---|---|---|
| **Milwaukee** | | | | | | |
| Waits L,2-4 | 5 2-3 | 8 | 5 | 5 | 2 | 5 |
| Lazorko | 1-3 | 1 | 2 | 2 | 1 | 0 |
| Ladd | 2-3 | 0 | 0 | 0 | 0 | 0 |
| Cocanowr | 1 1-3 | 1 | 0 | 0 | 0 | 0 |
| **Detroit** | | | | | | |
| RMason W,1-1 | 6 | 6 | 2 | 2 | 2 | 4 |
| Lopez S,14 | 3 | 4 | 1 | 1 | 0 | 1 |

WP—RMason. T—2.40. A—34,091.

Now I know what a pregnant lady goes through with false labor pains. We kept watching that scoreboard and thought it was all over when Boston took a lead over Toronto in the ninth (Toronto had to lose and we had to win for us to clinch it today). Then the Blue Jays came back with two. We had four and a half cases of champagne on ice. The boys will have to wait.

I've won five division titles, four National League pennants, and two World Championships, but none of them compare to the feeling I have this year with this team. That's because I was in on this one from the beginning. I had something to do with putting it together. That's what makes it such a great feeling.

After the game, John Fetzer, Tom Monaghan, and Governor Blanchard were in the clubhouse. You can't work for better owners than Mr. Fetzer and Mr. Monaghan. I want them to taste that champagne.

What a job rookie pitcher Roger Mason did. The kid went out there for six innings and pitched like he had been in the league all year. Lance Parrish finally hit his 30th homer and Lou Whittaker gave us a grand slam.

# TUESDAY, SEPTEMBER 18

## AT DETROIT

# GAME 151

## TIGERS 3, BREWERS 0

### (97–54, 13 GAMES AHEAD)

WE CLINCHED IT!!!

| MILWAUKEE | ab | r | h | bi | DETROIT | ab | r | h | bi |
|---|---|---|---|---|---|---|---|---|---|
| Yount dh | 4 | 0 | 2 | 0 | Whitaker 2b | 3 | 1 | 0 | 0 |
| Ganiner 2b | 4 | 0 | 0 | 0 | Trammell ss | 4 | 1 | 2 | 0 |
| Cooper 1b | 3 | 0 | 1 | 0 | Gibson rf | 3 | 0 | 0 | 0 |
| Loman lf | 4 | 0 | 0 | 0 | Parrish c | 3 | 0 | 1 | 2 |
| Clark cf | 4 | 0 | 1 | 0 | Herndon lf | 4 | 0 | 1 | 0 |
| James cf | 4 | 0 | 1 | 0 | Garbey dh | 2 | 0 | 0 | 0 |
| Sundberg c | 4 | 0 | 0 | 0 | Grubb dh | 1 | 0 | 0 | 0 |
| Romero ss | 3 | 0 | 1 | 0 | Lemon cf | 3 | 0 | 0 | 0 |
| Lozado 3b | 3 | 0 | 0 | 0 | Evans 1b | 2 | 0 | 0 | 0 |
| | | | | | Brookens 3b | 3 | 1 | 1 | 1 |
| | | | | | Castillo 3b | 0 | 0 | 0 | 0 |
| Totals | 33 | 0 | 6 | 0 | Totals | 28 | 3 | 5 | 3 |

```
Milwaukee ............................ 000 000 000— 0
Detroit ................................ 100 001 10x— 3
```
Game-winning RBI—Parrish (11). DP—Milwaukee 1. LOB—Milwaukee 7, Detroit 6. 2B—Trammell 2. HR—Brookens (5).

| | IP | H | R | ER | BB | SO |
|---|---|---|---|---|---|---|
| **Milwaukee** | | | | | | |
| McClure (L 4-8) | 5 | 4 | 2 | 2 | 4 | 3 |
| Tellman | 2-3 | 0 | 0 | 0 | 1 | 1 |
| Caldwell | 1 1-3 | 1 | 1 | 1 | 0 | 1 |
| Kern | 1 | 0 | 0 | 0 | 0 | 2 |
| **Detroit** | | | | | | |
| O'Neal (W 1-0) | 7 | 4 | 0 | 0 | 1 | 6 |
| Hernandez (S 30) | 2 | 2 | 0 | 0 | 0 | 2 |

McClure pitched to 3 batters in 6th. WP—Tellman. T—2:26. A—48,810.

I thought I had seen some parties in Cincinnati, but they were nothing like this. It was crazy. I was so happy for these fans. They're the greatest in baseball.

I have to be honest. I've waited for this day since they fired me in Cincinnati. I think they made a big mistake when they did it. Now no one will ever question me again.

The clubhouse was packed after the game. Lance Parrish and Kirk Gibson came over to dump a bottle of champagne over me and accidentally cut my head. My uniform looked really good with a mix of blood and champagne all over it.

I'm not sure what time I got out of the clubhouse, but they were still partying out on the streets around the park. I've been very lucky in my life. I've been involved with a lot of baseball celebrations, but I can honestly say that none of them ever matched anything like this.

**Lance Parrish and Willie Hernandez show their jubilation after the Tigers clinch the American League East title.** AP laserphoto

# CELEBRATE!

First, I thanked God. I'm very fortunate to be in baseball and to have been blessed with good throughout my career.

Then, I thanked Hernandez . . . and Gibson . . . and Lemon . . . and Trammell . . . and each and every one of our players who really proved this year that it takes a whole team to win. Not just one or two guys.

The celebration was wild. That's the way it should be. I'm very glad we clinched this thing in Detroit because the fans deserved to see it. They're as much a part of this thing as anyone in uniform.

Hey, more than 2½ million showed up to see us at Tiger Stadium. Another 2 million showed up on the road. When you get support like that, you owe them something special. This city deserves something special. It died with us for a long time. Now it's time to celebrate. This is a blue-collar town with people who are real human beings. They work hard. They play hard. And they're loyal.

I've been accused of talking faster than I think. Words come out of my mouth faster than pizzas out of Domino's. But it's really hard to tell you all the thoughts that run through your head after you clinch a title.

You think about your family and how much it stuck by you through all the times you struggled. You think about all the good and bad things that happened throughout the year. You think about spring training and all the dreams you had but never really knew if they'd come true. You think about how you thought you'd never lose a game when you're winning and how you never thought you'd ever win again after dropping four in a row. You think about how hard the front office and your coaching staff sweat to make this all come about. And you think about how lucky you really are to be in baseball and to be able to share in this feeling of victory and camaraderie that only sports affords.

You think about a lot of things. Then you want to cry and laugh and love and share all those emotions with everyone, because deep down in your heart you know this happens only rarely in a lifetime.

I remembered the first day I came to Detroit after accepting the job. They had this big press conference for me out on the field, and I promised that before my five-year contract ran out in 1984 we'd have a championship here. I'll admit there were times when even I had my doubts. But it was all worth it. All the tears and heartaches and hard work.

I honestly don't think there's anyone in baseball who works harder than Jim Campbell [president and chief executive officer] and Bill Lajoie [vice-president and general manager]. These guys are workaholics. That's why we get along so well. A long time ago, I was told that if ever I got the chance to work for Jim Campbell, I shouldn't pass it up. Everyone in baseball shares that feeling. They're all right.

I can't say enough about the job Bill Lajoie did this year. I asked for a lefthanded pitcher, and he went out and got me Willie Hernandez. I asked for another hitter, and he went out and got me Ruppert Jones. I asked for another lefthanded pitcher near the end of the season, and he went out and got me Bill Scherrer. What else can anyone ask for?

My coaching staff contributed so much to this championship. Anything I ever asked them to do, they went one step further. Roger Craig absolutely is the best pitching coach in baseball. What a rapport he builds with his pitchers. I always said that I could have dropped dead in the middle of the season, and Roger could have taken over like nothing ever happened.

There are so many people to thank, there's no way to mention all of them. More important than anyone, though, are the fans themselves. Tiger fans are a special breed. They live and die for our team. From the time we take the field in spring training to the time we put away our spikes in the fall, these people celebrate our wins and cry over our losses.

These are the people who deserve this championship more than anyone else. They're the best, and we're going to give them the best. The championship of the world is the least we can offer.

**The Amazing Wave.** Photo by Doc Holcomb, courtesy of *The Detroit News*

# SPARKY:
## A TRIBUTE

The complexity of Sparky Anderson is created by the simplicity of his passions.

Sparky is a beautiful blend of a carload of characters—more colorful than a cast of Damon Runyan creations, yet more real than the old codger himself. A devilish imp with the sparkling smile of Father Flanagan's finest altar boy, Sparky is boyhood dreams bottled up in a 50-year-old body. A charmer who can pout; a leader who can cry. His compassion for life is more sincere than a monastery monk. His genuine feelings for human beings smacks you in the face faster than the glow of his white hair.

Sparky is a tireless talker. Yet he listens to anyone who has something to say. He's a philosopher with no formal education. And he's a warm hand to those who need a friend.

An old friend once described Sparky best. "He's a combination sandwich. A little bit of everything in the kitchen. And then a little more."

He's part businessman, part priest. Part con man, part poet.

"He's a street person," said former Anderson protégé Pete Rose—a sure bet for baseball's Hall of Fame. "That's the highest compliment I can give him. That's the highest compliment I can give anyone. He can deal with gamblers, pimps, priests, and bank presidents. He's never out of place with anyone he meets. That's why he's so successful. He's got great common sense. He's just like me. We never had no college. But we've got great street smarts.

"He knows how to handle all situations. He knows how to handle this guy and that guy. That's because he treats everybody the same. There are no exceptions. You better get used to that with Sparky. He looks at someone and sees a human being. Now what else can I say about someone?"

That's the kind of person Sparky Anderson is—a human being first and foremost. One of baseball's most successful managers second. One feeds off the other. Both make up the man.

Sparky proudly tells the story of how there are two distinct persons living inside of him. "There's Sparky Anderson," the snow-capped one says. "He's the guy who manages a baseball team. He talks to the nation and appears all over the country. Baseball is show business—that's the way it should be. And that's where Sparky belongs. I think he does a pretty good job there.

"Then there's George Anderson. He's the guy from Bridgewater. He's the guy who knows he's no smarter or better than the guy next door. He also appreciates everything his family and baseball have done for him. George Anderson is me.

"I'm lucky. I know both of those characters. If you're really my friend, you'll never call me Sparky."

George Lee Anderson was born in Bridgewater, South Dakota, on February 22, 1934. Sparky's parents, grandparents, and four other brothers and sisters moved to southern California in November, 1942. Sparky's father was a laborer who never made a lot of money, but willingly gave every ounce of love.

Living in the shadows of the University of Southern California, Sparky hung around the baseball field and eventually became batboy for the Trojan team under Coach Rod Dedeaux.

Sparky's intensity glued him to baseball and he wound up playing for the 1951 American Legion national championship team before signing a modest bonus with the old Brooklyn Dodgers. Ironically, that national championship game was played at Briggs Stadium in Detroit—which, 10 years later, was to be renamed Tiger Stadium.

Sparky's actual ability as a player was as extensive as the Bridgewater, South Dakota, yellow pages. There really wasn't much. Even Sparky realized that. "One of the best baseball decisions I ever made," Sparky jokes, "is the decision to admit that I would never be a major leaguer. I mean it didn't take a lot of brains to come up with that."

About the only thing his undistinguished minor league career accomplished was the establishment of a name that is recognizable even beyond baseball.

"There was a radio announcer in Fort Worth, Texas, my third year of baseball in 1955," Sparky recalls. "He used to take a snifter from time to time. I guess I spent a lot of time arguing with umpires then, and this guy would always say something like 'The sparks are really flying out there.' Finally, he'd just say, 'Here comes old Sparky again.' The writers picked up on it and the name stuck. I went to Montreal the next year and the name followed me there. I was embarrassed. It took me a while to get used to it. In fact, my first two years at Cincinnati I'd sign

**Sparky demonstrates batting technique.** Photo courtesy of Detroit Tigers

223

baseballs *George Anderson*. Finally the PR department got on me and said, 'People don't know who George Anderson is.' So I started signing *Sparky*.

"I'm used to that name now, but I'll be honest. As much as I enjoy being Sparky, I'm really George. That's who I see when I look in the mirror. In the summer, it's a lot of fun being Sparky Anderson. But in the winter I want to go home to Thousand Oaks and just be plain old George Anderson."

That's okay. Because George (or Sparky) makes the division between his two selves pleasant for the fans. Always sensitive to the needs of the fans, Sparky (or George) is the model of cooperation. There are never too many autographs to sign; there are never one too many kind words to say. Sparky graciously thanks every autograph seeker personally for asking his signature.

A devoted Sunday Mass goer who refuses ever to talk about religion, Sparky tries to exercise what many players simply try to preach. "Why should I go around telling people that I go to church or that they should go to church?" Sparky said. "If you really don't believe it, you won't do it anyway. If you're doing it and don't really believe in it, then it doesn't count anyway."

Sparky is married to Carol, the girl he met in grade school. She has been his bride for 31 years. "He never even went out with another girl," says childhood friend Billy Consolo, now a coach with the Tigers. "He met Carol in grade school and that was it. And, believe me, it's real. There's nothing phony baloney about their relationship. Both know what they want and they have it."

They have three kids who consume an enormous part of Sparky's life. They are George, Jr., 26; Shirlee, 23; and Albert, 22. All live within 15 minutes of each other in the Los Angeles area. Sparky endured the realization of possibly losing Albert during an auto accident in 1983. It changed both of their lives. It's something Sparky remembers each day.

Sparky also was faced with the death of his father in the spring of this year—another incident to hammer home the fragility of baseball success and the solidity of friendship and family ties.

The economic uncertainty of Sparky's past and the down-home feeling that was ingrained from an early age have surfaced throughout his managerial career and have, in their turn, contributed to his success. For instance, Sparky has a saying he carries from childhood. His father once taught him this and it's something he refuses to surrender: "There is one thing in this world that'll never cost you a dime, and that's being nice."

Sparky talks about how his father used to preach that lesson to his kids—certainly Sparky has never forgotten. While managing in Cincinnati, Sparky had a sign hanging over his office door. It said, "It doesn't cost anything to smile and say hello."

"I remember that sign real well," said Joe Morgan, another Hall of Fame sure-shot and one of Sparky's key players during the Cincinnati glory years. "He meant it. We used to have to go by and say hello to him. It wasn't a big thing. But it showed he cared more about you as a person than for what you did on the field. He cared about you, your family, and what was going on in your life. That's more than a manager."

It's only a small thing. But Sparky still maintains that intimate feeling with everyone he touches. He doesn't have that sign hanging above his office door in Detroit, but he makes it a point to visit every person in the front office before going down to work in the clubhouse every day. He calls everyone by name and never forgets the names of their family members.

"Let me put it this way," Morgan said. "After the second year I was there, I never thought of Sparky as a manager. I thought of him as part of my family. And you know I'll always do more for my family."

To put the record straight, nothing is more important to Sparky than winning. But he accomplishes that with warmth and feeling toward the players and their families.

What about Sparky's managing? What has pushed him to the ranks of the greatest in the game?

First you must determine how much a manager means to a team—nothing . . . a little . . . or that tiny edge that pushes everything over the top.

Sparky has been charged with the rap that anyone could have managed the Reds of the 1970s because they had more Hall of Fame candidates than Tom Monaghan has pizzas.

"We had a great team," Pete Rose said. "But Sparky wasn't the only manager in the 1970s to have great players. We had great players, but he knew how to handle them. He's a communicator and keeps his players happy. He's got great rapport. He's like a psychologist."

Rose once said he'd walk through a blazing fire wearing a gasoline suit for Sparky.

"He's no genius," Rose said. "He'll be the first to tell you that. He knew how to use his great players. He knew who he could scold and who he couldn't. He was a master. Even Hall of Famers need to be kicked in the butt once in a while, and he knew just when to do it."

Sparky talks about the way he'd ask Rose if he could use him for a

**Sparky watches the field intently.** Photo by Doc Holcomb, courtesy of *The Detroit News*

team meeting. If Sparky got on Rose, no one could question it. "To get the right effects," Sparky said, "you need props. I try to get things set up so that when I knock something over in a rage, it'll be there when I need it. I've had good luck with plastic trash cans in the past. All that trash knocked on the floor seems to attract a lot of attention. Getting Rose to be my target showed the other guys that no one was immune."

That's a last resort, but something he calls upon when the need arises. Ordinarily, Sparky breezes through his managerial musts and obligations of his position.

"Sparky has more human intangibles than anyone else I've ever played for," Joe Morgan said. "He's not the smartest strategist in the world. But he's the best in getting the most out of the players he has. The most overrated idea in baseball is that a manager wins and loses games with strategic moves on the field. Sparky is smart enough to know that if he can get the players to perform on the field the way they are capable, he doesn't have to make those strategic moves.

"He is able to get 25 players pointed in one direction—that's winning. It sounds so simple. But it's not. Players say they want to win and that nothing else counts. It sounds good, but most of them don't even know what they're saying.

"Winning hurts. I mean there's pain to winning after what you have to go through. You ask Sparky. He knows. That's what makes him so great. It hurts to win. And he's willing to pay any price.

"He's a little bit of a psychoanalyst," Rose said. "He knew everyone was a little different and treated players differently depending on their personalities. But he always treated everyone with respect.

"He'd never ask a player to do something he couldn't do. Sparky understands a player's limitations and works within them. He's very fair. But very demanding."

Morgan echoed those sentiments. "Rose and I are more like Sparky than anyone else," Morgan said. "None of us had a whole lot of natural talent. We had to scuffle from day one. That made us close. That's also why Sparky identifies with the average working man because he's had to sweat to get to where he's at. That's why Sparky never overlooks the little guy. He was concerned with everyone. When we took the field, number 5 was no different than number 10 or number 15. Everyone was the same. Everyone had to try to contribute toward winning."

Now the young mauling Tigers are reaping the benefits of this tireless baseball machine.

"When I first came up, I didn't understand him," said Dan Petry, who has blossomed into one of the deadliest righthanded starters in the game. "When you mature a little, then you begin to understand. He cares more about Dan Petry the person than he does about just Dan Petry the ballplayer. He wants you to have a long and successful career and won't take chances to mess up your arm. Sometimes you hear stories about managers only caring about what goes on on the field. That's not Sparky. He cares about you as a person.

"He's the closest thing to a Hall of Famer I've ever had the privilege of working with. He's something special. There's an aura about him. When I mess up, I feel bad. I feel like I let the team down and I also feel like I let Sparky down."

Kirk Gibson is a legitimate budding superstar. This year he became the first Tiger ever in the history of the franchise to hit more than 20 homers and steal more than 20 bases. Gibson was Sparky's special project. The confidence and patience Sparky demonstrated toward Gibson has paid tremendous dividends this season.

"Sparky taught me how to play," Gibson said. "He set me up with the right people and always took time to teach me the game. I don't really enjoy having to spend a lot of time talking to the media. I don't think most players do. This is where Sparky is great. He's able to keep the pressure off us by handling the media. That may sound like a little thing. But these days, it might be one of the most important parts of his job."

Sparky had a singular goal of winning for the Tigers since taking over the job on June 14, 1979. He originally signed a five-year contract which has been extended two extra seasons. At the press conference called to announce his appointment, Sparky predicted a pennant before the end of the 1984 season. He will make his promise good. But it wasn't easy along the way.

"I'll never forget the evening of June 23, 1979," Sparky said. "We dropped a doubleheader to the Orioles at Baltimore and were 2–9 since I took over as manager. I called Carol back in Thousand Oaks and will never forget how low I was feeling. I told her, 'Honey, we've made the gravest mistake of our lives. Here we had the pick of a half dozen teams and we picked absolutely the worst one. I've never seen a team so unprofessional. So satisfied just to come to the park and finish fifth or sixth every year. They actually like the fact that there's no pressure on them. Fans cheer them wherever they go in Michigan and they give nothing in return.' "

Finally that feeling ate away at Sparky. It came out in an explosion at a team meeting.

"You're a bunch of frauds," Sparky yelled at his players. "You walk through the clubhouse door and pretend you're major leaguers. You go to your locker and put on a major league uniform, but you're really a bunch of frauds. They wouldn't tolerate this in the places I've been. They wouldn't tolerate losing. I know God didn't put me on this earth to be a loser. Like every other major leaguer, I honestly feel I'm one of God's chosen people. I've been chosen to work hard and be on winning teams. I won't have it any other way. If we have to trade everyone, we'll do it. Why not? All you've done is give them fifth and sixth place anyway."

That was five years ago. Many of the same players are still with the ball club, but their attitudes under Sparky have gone through a complete metamorphosis.

That winning attitude translates into Detroit's first East Division championship since 1972. The Tigers did it in convincing fashion and they did it early by jumping off to a record-setting 35–5 start.

"I told everybody early in the season," Joe Morgan said, "that no one would catch the Tigers after the middle of May. I was giving 5-to-1 odds that no one could catch Sparky. He's impossible to catch once he gets in front.

"Look at the way he rested all of his players throughout the year. I knew that when the Tigers got down to the stretch, everyone would be rested and ready to play. That's a tribute to the manager."

Sparky used his entire roster all year long. Although a hunch player, Sparky believes strongly in a right and lefthanded attack. Lefthanded hitting John Grubb was part of Sparky's platoon system. The veteran is an accomplished role player.

"Whatever it takes to win, it seems that's what Sparky does," Grubb said. "Seems like all the guys on the team have taken that attitude. I come to the park every night. If my name is in the lineup, fine. If not, I try to keep ready. I respect Sparky. He puts out the lineup he thinks can win that night."

Sparky is the dean of American League managers. His 15-year record is unsurpassed by active managers and ranks 9th in major league history for those with at least 10 years of experience. Before joining the Tigers, Sparky managed the Reds for nine seasons. Under his guidance, the Reds won two world championships, four National League pennants, and five West Division titles. Twice Sparky was named Manager of the Year. But Sparky is the first to tell critics that a manager is only as good as his players on the field.

"Ain't it funny how the same managers always seem to be so lucky?" he asks. "Yeah, Casey Stengel sure was lucky. Some people can stand in front of trees and don't even know it's a forest. Other people know what they're looking at, but they're called lucky.

"I may not be the smartest guy in the world. But I do understand the Peter Principle and I never go beyond that. I couldn't be different if I tried."

Through the hearty times and the lean, one thing always remains a constant for Sparky—baseball rules his life.

"He's just like me," Pete Rose said. "Baseball is all Sparky knows. And it's all he wants out of life."

Sparky won't deny it. It's a passion over which he has no control.

"I need baseball," Sparky says. "It don't need me."

Yes it does, Sparky Anderson. It needs George, too.

Photo by Doc Holcomb, courtesy of *The Detroit News*

**Sparky congratulates Willie Hernandez after another fine save.**

**Sparky and some young friends.** Photo courtesy of Detroit Tigers

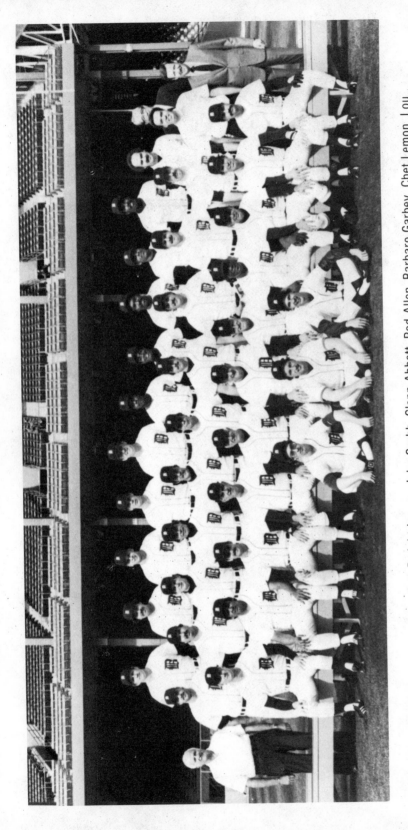

**TOP ROW:** Lance Parrish, Willie Hernandez, Dwight Lowry, John Grubb, Glenn Abbott, Rod Allen, Barbaro Garbey, Chet Lemon, Lou Whitaker, Larry Herndon, Trainer Pio DiSalvo, and Dr. Clarence Livingood.

**MIDDLE ROW:** Trainer Bill Behm, Kirk Gibson, Juan Berenguer, Rusty Kuntz, Darrell Evans, Dave Bergman, Marty Castillo, Milt Wilcox, Dave Rozema, Dan Petry, Jack Morris, Equipment Manager Jim Schmakel, and Traveling Secretary Bill Brown.

**FRONT ROW:** Doug Bair, Aurelio Lopez, Howard Johnson, Coach Billy Consolo, Coach Alex Grammas, Coach Roger Craig, Manager Sparky Anderson, Coach Gates Brown, Coach Dick Tracewski, Alan Trammell, and Tom Brookens.

**Seated:** Batboys Dom Nieto, Dave Cowart, and Dave Ruczko.